MANAGING
THE DYNAMICS
OF NEW
TECHNOLOGY

MANAGING THE DYNAMICS OF NEW TECHNOLOGY

Issues in Manufacturing Management

Hamid Noori
Wilfrid Laurier University

PRENTICE HALL, Englewood Cliffs, New Jersey 07632

Library of Congress Cataloging-in-Publication Data

Noori, Hamid.
  Managing the dynamics of new technology: issues in manufacturing management / Hamid Noori.
    p. cm.
  Includes bibliographies and index.
  ISBN 0-13-551763-X
  1. Technological innovations—Management. 2. Production management. I. Title.
  HD45.N63 1990
  658.5'14—dc 19   89-3860
                        CIP

Editorial/production supervision: Robert C. Walters
Interior design: Ann Lutz
Cover design: Ben Santora
Cover photo: Nubar Alexanian/Woodfin Camp & Associates
Manufacturing buyer: Ed O'Dougherty

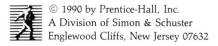 © 1990 by Prentice-Hall, Inc.
A Division of Simon & Schuster
Englewood Cliffs, New Jersey 07632

Printed in the United States of America

10 9 8 7 6 5 4 3 2 1

ISBN 0-13-069775-3

Prentice-Hall International (UK) Limited, *London*
Prentice-Hall of Australia Pty. Limited, *Sydney*
Prentice-Hall Canada Inc., *Toronto*
Prentice-Hall Hispanoamericana, S.A., *Mexico*
Prentice-Hall of India, Private Limited, *New Delhi*
Prentice-Hall of Japan, Inc., *Tokyo*
Prentice-Hall of Sutheast Asia Pte. Ltd., *Singapore*
Editora Prentice-Hall do Brasil, Ltda, *Rio de Janeiro*

To My Parents

CONTENTS

PART II
THE TACTICAL AND STRATEGIC EFFECTS

Chapter Five
THE STRATEGIC IMPLICATIONS OF NEW TECHNOLOGY 130

Chapter Thirteen
FUTURE PROSPECTS   363

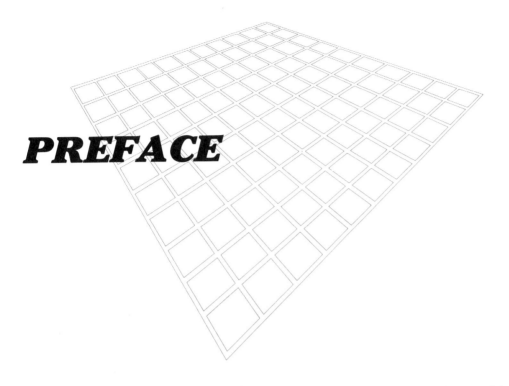

PREFACE

Throughout history, technological adoption in response to environmental forces has to a large degree determined the economic fate of nations, firms, and individuals. New technology exhibits some highly distinctive charateristics unique to its capabilities. Today, the key to survival for many firms is the ability to capitalize on the immense potential of advancing technology and channel it for economic and strategic well-being.

In spite of its promises, adopting any form of the new technology demands substantial changes in the ways a firm runs its operation. Whether or not the technology is successfully implemented, there are bound to be implications for employment. If it is not justified in the context of well-formulated business strategy, or if its implementation is poorly planned and executed, new technology adoption can, in fact, substantially erode a firm's competitive position. It is therefore imperative that any attempt to address the field of technology management include attention to many related issues and concerns.

Over the last several years, many scholars and practitioners have been focusing on different matters of importance related to technology doption. Most of these contributions, however, were scattered or too specific. My professional pursuit in the field of technology management convinced me of the need for a text which collectively and qualitatively looks at various aspects of technology acquisition and implementation. The book became a reality as soon as I began a course on management of new technology. That, and my involvement with the industry, through our Research Centre for Management of New Technology (REMAT), provided the opportunity to research the topic and investigate the problems and solutions based on the available materials. The book is based on the integration of several disciplines and is written for engineers and managers who are, or will inevitably be, involved with administering different forms of the new technology. An accompanying book entitled *Readings and Cases in Management of New Technology: An Operations Perspective,* also by Prentice Hall, provides up-to-date and related situation analyses and cases in this area. As well, a computer software named "NEWTECH Expert Choice" offers the decision makers an opportunity to consider and weigh a host of determinent factors affecting the technology adoption. The software is available through:

Expert Choice, Inc.
4922 Ellsworth Avenue
Pittsburgh, PA 15213
Tel: (412) 682–3844

Acknowledgments

I have had considerable help and support in making this book a reality. This work would have not been completed on time without the efforts of my two highly talented research associates, Mark Tonin and chris Schnarr, who have worked with me at different stages over the last two years. Many of the contentions and arguments presented in this text are based on research completed by many of my colleagues primarily in North America. Additionally, I have benefited from the suggestions and encouragement of Tony Bailetti, John Banks, Bruce Fournier, David Gillen, Jack Meredith, Richard Newman, Fred Raafat, Russell Radford, Howard Teal, and many of the reviewers who at different stages of preparation gave guidance on the topics covered in the book. My special thanks also to my students, who helped me to clarify my thinking in innumerable ways. For her invaluable assistance and willingness, and for her perseverance in word processing the manuscript, I am indebted to Carole Litwiller. Last, but certainly not least, I would like to thank my wife whose cheerful attitude and support made my work much easier.

I am fortunate to have been able to work with all of these people.

Hamid Noori

PROLOGUE

The real issue we face in the industry is not
Whether *we should automate, but* How. *Ironically,*
none of these are technology issues. *They are*
management issues!

The CAD/CAM Newsletter

INTRODUCTION

Advances in technology have meant radical changes in the world economy. Consider the following:

- Thirty years ago, it took several thousand operators to handle one million long-distance calls. Today, only a dozen or so are required.[1]
- The number of circuit components per microprocessor chip has approximately doubled every year since 1959.[2]
- A pound of glass fiber-optic cable, made mainly of sand, can carry as much information as a ton of copper.[3]

In addition, in the last decade we have witnessed a vast increase in international competition. The proliferation of diversified corporations has resulted in more companies competing in more markets and in more industries. Manufacturing has spread all over the globe, and Pacific Rim and some South American countries (the so-called newly industrialized countries) have gradually penetrated the traditional Western markets, particularly since the early 1970s.

With this growing competitiveness has come the need for productivity and quality improvement to improve the competitiveness of North American

---

[1]Cited from a manuscript published by the Economic Council of Canada [1986], pp. 2–3.
[2]Ibid., pp. 2–3.
[3]Ramo [1988], p. 126.

companies. Investing in new technology is seen by many as the most important means to improve (or maintain) a competitive market position. A number of studies, including a Delphi-type technological forecast of the future of production engineering, indicate that the trend in manufacturing between now and the year 2000 is toward the continued development and implementation of computer-integrated automatic factories.

While the benefits of adopting new technology are undeniable, a number of factors could either enhance or constrain its potential for productivity gains. In essence, the measure of productivity improvement itself needs to be reconsidered in order to capture all the conceivable contributions of the new technology, because new technology often encompasses major, discontinuous, structural change. It affects not only factory design, but also organizational relationships between R&D, engineering, marketing, and manufacturing.

The purpose of this chapter is to introduce the notion of management of the (new) technology and to provide an overview of the important topics discussed in the book. We present first a synopsis of the evolution of manufacturing and operations management, then describe the challenge of automation, and finally address important issues in managing the new technology.

THE INDUSTRIAL REVOLUTION AND BEYOND

Distinct Developments in Manufacturing

Some historians have described the Industrial Revolution as consisting of three fundamental and far-reaching structural changes, each of which resulted in a distinctive era of manufacturing:

1. *The Era of Power Engineering:* Started at the end of the 18th century, when human energy was replaced by machines (the steam engine).
2. *The Era of Mechanization:* Began at the end of the 19th century, when utilization of electricity resulted in the mechanization of operations.
3. *The Era of Automation:* Began around 1950 and was largely based on developments in information and microchip technology.

Of these three, the era of automation has brought about the most profound restructuring of our economy and social values, and of our factory and service organizations. There was a time when people were considered nothing but factors of production, and treated like other resources, such as machines or capital. This is no longer considered an acceptable way to manage people: "Today, when new technology is introduced, there is generally a counterbalancing human response."[4]

---

[4]Naisbitt [1984], p. 35.

The era of automation has resulted in a number of significant changes in the marketplace, including these:

- Market life cycles for products are getting shorter, so that new designs must follow one another more frequently.
- The marketplace is demanding a greater variety of products without increasing the volume desired. This means that a factory must produce smaller quantities of each product.
- The marketplace is time-sensitive; it wants its products on time. This time-based competition means that factories must produce in smaller batches on time-controlled schedules.
- The marketplace is cost-sensitive; it wishes to lower the breakeven point. Hence, highly efficient production capabilities are required, with high quality and reliability.

One consequence of these changes, in addition to increasing costs and shortages of qualified labor, as well as promoting more intense local, national and international competition, is pressure to automate and adopt new technology. Steele contends that ". . .new technology constantly chases the moving target of conventional technology, which is itself goaded to accelerated improvements by the threat."[5] Put differently, the pace at which a company adopts new technology is affected by the competitive environment of the industry. This environment, in turn, is determined by social and economic considerations and will include such factors as consumer values and average product life-cycles.

The insistence on automation has, of course, its own impact on work organizations, production processes, and manufacturing philosophies. Bullinger et al. [1985] use machine tool building to demonstrate the evolution and the trends that have influenced and will continue to influence the industry (see Exhibit 1.1). This propensity, it can be argued, is more or less generalizable to many other manufacturers of discrete parts.

Besides economic reasons, three major social forces have also contributed to the pressure for automation:

1. Shortage of skilled laborers. By 1968 the workforce employed in manufacturing in the United States dropped to 24.9 percent, down from 30 percent in 1947. (Some estimates suggest that by the year 2000, the total workforce in manufacturing will shrink to anywhere between 10 percent and 20 percent.)
2. A move by employers toward job satisfaction and job enrichment, which has resulted in removing employees from tedious and repetitive tasks.
3. The pressure from governments and unions to free workers from unhealthy and hazardous tasks.

[5]Steele [1983], p. 136.

Exhibit 1.1 Qualitative Changes in Machine Tool Industry: An Example of Trends in Manufacturing

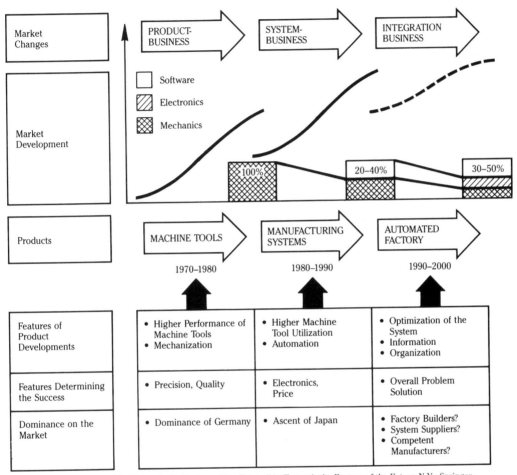

Source: Bullinger et al. [1985]. "Towards the Factory of the Future," in *Towards the Factory of the Future.* N.Y.: Springer-Verlag, p. XXX.

Corresponding Changes in Operations Management

Historically, the different eras of the Industrial Revolution have resulted in disparate types of management philosophy and control:

1. The Pre-Taylor Era. The era of transition when new working habits, new disciplines, and new incentives were created (see Skinner [1985]). Management tasks had to be transferred from a family-oriented operation to overseers who became responsible for worker assignments, discipline, and compensation.

2. The Mass Production Era. The era Chandler called "the end of technological constraints" [1977, p. 75]. The task of management began to involve "...plant design and system economies while continuing to delegate workforce management to powerful overseers or foremen..." (See Skinner [1985, p. 71]). This was the era in which, thanks to Taylor and his followers, a new profession—*industrial engineering*—was created. Industrial engineering resulted in the creation of the notion that factories should also be managed (Skinner [1985, p. 75]). This era witnessed the evolution of many scientific management methods, such as EOQ, MRP, and CPM/PERT, for the allocation of resources and for work scheduling and measurement. During this period, improvements in the control and coordination of manufacturing processes were also established (Skinner [1985, p. 82]).

3. The Flexible Production Era. The era of acceptance of technology's strategic importance and incorporation of flexibility into production systems. The task of management changed to that of involvement in making technological decisions (rather than leaving the decisions solely to technical staffs), and to creating organizations that are much flatter and more highly integrated. These efforts are benefiting immensely from advances in information technology which allow corporate managers to have access to vital data in a timely and cost-effective fashion.

The mass production era in particular, involved a unique mind-set that is best summarized by Skinner [1985, p. 64]). It includes:

1. Measuring the performance of the factory and its management by financial yardsticks (such as ROI, and cost reduction) that reflect a short-term rather than a long-term view.

2. Perceiving managers as custodians of fixed assets whose success is determined by controlling, coordinating, and stabilizing the existing system against external changes.

3. Directing and controlling the workforce, and considering workers as a constraint rather than a resource.

4. Engaging in mass production and mechanization processes whenever economically feasible without considering their strategic value.

The flexible production era, on the other hand, is a significant departure from that thinking. That is, it conceives of the management of technologically based organizations as requiring the involvement of different functional groups in a more coordinated fashion, and it views the factory not as a financial model, but as a strategic resource. Goldhar and Jelinek [1985] contrast the era of mechanization (conventional technology) with the era of automation (flexible technology), as illustrated in Exhibit 1.2.

Exhibit 1.2 Characteristics of Traditional Technology and Flexible Automation

Traditional Technology Described by	New Technology Described by
Economy of scale	Economy of scope
Learning curve	Truncated product life cycle
Task specialization	Multimission facilities
Work as a social activity	Unmanned systems
Separable variable costs	Joint costs
Standardization	Variety
Expensive flexibility and variety	Profitable flexibility and variety

Leading to Factories that Exhibit Characteristics of:	
Centralization	Decentralization
Large plants	Disaggregated capacity
Balanced lines	Flexibility
Smooth flows	Inexpensive surge and turnaround ability
Standard product design	Many custom products
Low rate of change and high stability	Innovation and responsiveness
Inventory used as a buffer	Production tied to demand
"Focused factory" as an organizing concept	Functional range for repeated reorganization
Job enrichment and enlargement	Responsibility tied to reward
Batch systems	Flow systems

Source: Goldhar and Jelinek [1985], p. 101.

To better comprehend the reasons for the move toward a more flexible operation and hence adoption of new technology, it is important to understand the changes that have been taking place in the global market.

TODAY'S CHALLENGES

Managing the New Technology

Today, microprocessor-based technology presents important new opportunities for manufacturing and service organizations. But if its potential is to be realized, companies must take a more holistic approach to managing resources. The different functional areas of the business must no longer be viewed as separate, but must be managed as an integrated whole. The challenge is not the expansion of frontiers, but understanding the dynamics of renewal (see Waterman [1987]). To remain competitive, it is necessary to change and to adapt to new developments on all fronts, not just manufacturing. This is where management of the new technologies becomes essential.

The impetus for change and the need to reorient manufacturing processes to create a more flexible and innovative operation makes the notion of management of technology of fundamental importance. As Skinner [1985] states: "The history of manufacturing leadership shows that basic changes in management focus and characteristics were brought about by major developments in technology and markets."[6]

There are signs that many companies have begun to realize that management and not technology alone will be critical in responding to the challenge. A recent survey of the automobile industry (see English [1987]) reveals that while in 1985 managers were putting their faith in "hard-side" elements, they now consider the "soft-side" factors to be of prime importance. Soft-side factors are described as the way a business is organized, how it is run, what is viewed as important, and how people are treated.

The field of management of the new technology is continuing to evolve. There is perhaps no clear-cut and widely accepted definition of the topic, and researchers are divided on how to conceputalize the idea and its characteristics. But despite the lack of consensus on what management of technology is, there is general agreement that: (a) technology advancement is inevitable; (b) the process is necessary for (manufacturing) survival; (c) technology carries considerable unknown risks; (d) the advent of new technology will create a greater need for cooperation among business, government, and labor; and (e) the costs, benefits, and values of technology will have to be continually reexamined by firms in particular and by society in general.

One prime reason for the difficulty in conceptualizing and comprehending the notion of technology management is that by nature, it is cross-functional and predominately problem-driven. It encompasses many disciplines and is based on an integrative style of management. According to the Task Force on Management of Technology sponsored by the National Research Council:

> Management of (new) technology links engineering, science, and management disciplines to address the planning, development, and implementation of technological capabilities to shape and accomplish the strategic and operational objectives of an organization.[7]

Management of the new technology is generally based on a systems approach which distinguishes between "...anticipating the need for future technological developments and the implementation of fully-fledged integrated systems of automation."[8] A systems approach allows a strategic decision outlook similar to the large-scale viewpoint taken by the Japanese with respect to automation. Further, a systems approach is inherently flexible, as it allows for the incremental alignment of new technology and infrastructure while taking into account future developments.

---

[6]Skinner [1985], pp. 65–66.
[7]Task Force on Management of Technology [1987], p. 2.
[8]Stanton and Challis [1983], p. 20.

The core of management of the new technology is technological change and management functions. That is, management of the new technology encompasses a wide range of issues concerning the development, acquisition, and implementation of technological skills. It bridges the existing gap between the field of management and the field of engineering and science (see Exhibit 1.3). It centers on the strategic importance of technology, and its basic thrust is to mesh technical and nontechnical resources of companies to enable them to compete, to survive, to grow, and to improve the quality of worklife. In short, management of new technology focuses primarily on the diffusion stage of the innovation cycles and as such is distinguishable from management of innovation. (This point will be discussed in detail later in this book.)

The challenge of establishing the link between engineering and management is indeed a live issue. It necessitates fundamental changes in traditional manufacturing wisdom, which is based on the application of conventional technology, to one which comprehends the manufacturing flexibility made possible by new technology. Exhibit 1.4 elaborates on some of the differences between traditional and contemporary manufacturing management philosophies.

Exhibit 1.3 The Issues and Responsibilities of Management of the New Technology

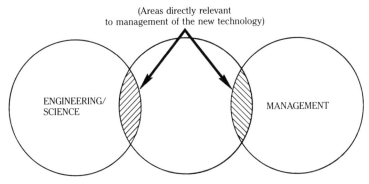

(Areas directly relevant to management of the new technology)

ENGINEERING/
SCIENCE

MANAGEMENT

- Discipline-based Knowledge
- Engineering Systems
- Computing Applications
- Manufacturing Technology
- Design for Automation or Assembly
- Risk Analysis
- Control Theory
- CAD/CAM
- Quality Assurance/Statistics
- Operations Research
- MIS/DSS
- Reverse Engineering
- Awareness of Available Technologies
- Strategic/Long-term Issues Relating to Technology
- Interfunctional Issues Relating to Technology

- Research, Development, Engineering and Manufacturing Current Operations Issues
- Technology Support Services and Issues
- Finance
- Marketing
- Business Policy/Strategy
- Control/Accounting
- Organizational Behavior
- Human Resource Management
- Production and Operations Management
- R&D Management
- Managerial Decision Theory/Statistics/ Operations Research
- Macroeconomics/International Trade
- Microeconomics
- MIS/DSS

Source: Task Force on Management of Technology [1987], p. 11.

Exhibit 1.4 Manufacturing Philosophy: From Traditional to Flexible Systems

Traditional (Conventional Technology)	Contemporary (Flexible Technology)
Division of Labor	

As Far As Possible
  Simple work with the lowest wage category
    possible
  Low implication of work
  Many interfacing points
	As Little As Possible
	  Qualified work with as qualified staff as
	    possible
	  High implication of work
	  Few interfacing points

Execution of Labor	
Batchwise One step after the other Bring-obligation/utilization-oriented	According to demand Overlapping Fetching-obligation/process-oriented
Time Required for Execution	
Minimum per operation Maximum output per minute	Minimum per order Maximum utilization per period
Material and Information Flow	
Separate consideration	Integration

Source: Bullinger et al. [1985]

Responding to the Challenge

To implement any form of automation, the right mix of people, equipment, and software systems is required. The challenge is to create an organization that is different from the old financial model. The new organization must be an institution that ". . . can tolerate and handle pluralistic values and measures for its success."[9] Firms must be conscious of the various stakeholders and measures of success that are prevalent and necessary in today's business environment in order to use the factory as the competitive weapon it has become (see Exhibit 1.5).

Research conducted by Frohman [1982] reveals that companies which use technology as a competitive weapon generally possess the following characteristics:

1. Management views the technology as a major competitive weapon but does not emphasize it at the expense of other areas.
2. The criteria used to support any project consist of:
   a. Whether the project supports the business goal
   b. Whether the project protects/establishes technological leadership
   c. Whether the project solves customer problems

[9]Skinner [1985], p. 98.

Exhibit 1.5   The Factory as a Competitive Resource

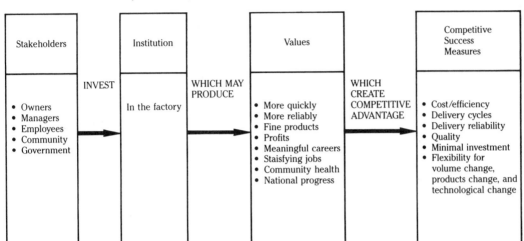

Source: Skinner [1985], p. 98.

    d. Whether the project develops a window of technology
    e. Whether the project pursues technological advancement
3. The organization is structured to provide a close connection between business and technological decisions in a consistent fashion.

ISSUES OF CONCERN IN MANAGEMENT OF THE NEW TECHNOLOGY

Both theoretical and applied management literature suggest that problems with the adoption of new technology could develop from a number of sources:

1. Technical factors such as the appropriateness of the particular new technology (for example, Group Technology versus CAD/CAM), debugging problems, synchronization with the total manufacturing system, and measurement of results.
2. Structural factors such as reporting relationships, information and control systems, reward systems, staffing, and differentiation and integration.
3. Behavioral-political processes such as decision-making systems, leadership styles, and conflict and power processes.
4. Strategic factors such as top management values, financial resources, the fit between the firm's strategy and structure, and the competitive environment.

The integration of new technology with the existing operation involves decision-making at the strategic level. A number of case studies cite senior management's lack of empathy with the impact of new technology on strategy as a major barrier to its effective use. The adoption of new technology procedures will affect not only manufacturing-related operations, but the other major functional areas of marketing, accounting and finance, and human resources (see Exhibit 1.6). For example, new technology could bring the ability to offer more products (marketing), challenge traditional capital justification methods to include intangible benefits (accounting and finance), and require retraining of the workforce and restructuring of the reward system (human resources).

In terms of technology adoption, managers should entertain a new set of strategic possibilities. What are these possibilities? Goldhar and Jelinek [1983] offer four process configurations which represent the range of technological options available to managers:

1. "Independent" of the design of the product and so can be used for many different products and designs (for example, simple manual tools, and stand-alone Numerically Controlled tools).

2. "Programmable" and so able to accommodate a range of different configurations, each reflecting a different product design.

3. "Flexible" enough to accommodate a range of product designs within a single configuration (for example, mass production lines for different automobile models).

4. "Dedicated" to a single product design (for example, transfer line in a chemical plant).

Exhibit 1.6   The Integrative Nature of Management of New Technology

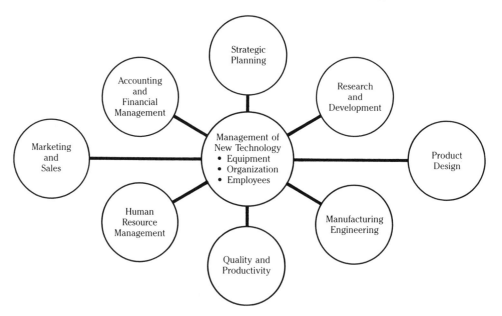

Specific to one process configuration will be a variety of new technology options that will affect an organization's strategic outlook. The organization's infrastructure must be rebuilt to fit the new technology and the organizational design. Such considerations as employment dislocation, changes in established practices and procedures (information systems), the impact of manufacturing decisions on other functional areas, and the need for tighter integration of product and process have to be accommodated.

Typically, product-specific factors such as production volume, variants, and product design will also affect the application of automation systems. The main areas of automation will be in batch manufacturing operations as opposed to continuous flow operations. Batch characteristics include the assembly of several products at low volume, with low standardization and no invariable sequencing. The competitive emphasis will increase the importance of product design, assembly line design, inventory maintenance, engineering input, and scheduling—operations that can be addressed through implementation of technology.

In this context, a number of interesting questions are worthy of consideration. Will the importance of the new technology push manufacturing personnel into a more prominent role in the organization? Is the nature of management really shifting back to a manufacturing orientation? Are Japanese companies ahead of North American firms because they have a more technical approach to management? Should North American firms concentrate on specific industries or functions when considering new technology? What is the role of government in facilitating technology adoption? Will new technology create more jobs or fewer jobs, and for whom? That is, will new technology simply eliminate unskilled jobs and leave managers and engineers working even harder? Finally, how will workers' attitudes toward leisure and their feeling of self-worth be affected?

WHAT LIES AHEAD?

We mentioned earlier that a number of motives can inspire the successful adoption of new technology, but there are really two major processes involved in adopting technology. One deals with the acquisition (selection and/or development) of new technology and the other with its implementation (operational issues and organizational interfaces). In this book, we address these two processes in detail.

It is a popular fallacy that new technology is necessarily the answer to manufacturing problems. We are perhaps too easily led to believe that a new machine here or a robot there will immediately boost productivity and competitiveness. This perception does a great injustice to the inherently complex process of new technology acquisition and implementation. In this book we will attempt to highlight some of the factors that enter into the decision. These include: the political environment (government policies); the social environment (consumer values, responsibility to labor); the economic environment (impetus to compete);

the corporate environment (strategy options expanded to include flexibility and economies of scope, basis of competition, infrastructure); the functional environment (impact on marketing, finance, human resources); and the manufacturing environment (machine and systems decisions, manufacturing strategy's role in corporate strategy). The studies conducted so far suggest that new technology will have the greatest impact on small and medium operations as the ability to compete on variety rather than on volume opens opportunities in global markets,

Exhibit 1.7   Addressing the Major Issues in the Management of New Technology

Chapter	Major Issue
2	• What is new technology? • How is new technology different from other forms of technology?
3	• Why do firms need new technology? • What is "flexibility" and why is it important? • Is new technology the only answer?
4	• What is innovation? • How can firms foster and manage innovation more successfully?
5	• How are technology and strategy related? • What is a technology strategy?
6	• How are new technology, productivity, and quality related? • How will new technology affect productivity and quality measurement and management?
7	• Will new technology force firms to change their cost management system? • How do firms measure the costs and benefits of new technology? • What are the most appropriate approaches to analyze the financial viability of adopting new technology?
8	• What organiational structure is best suited to a new technology environment?
9	• How can firms ensure that new technology is implemented successfully into their organization? • How and when should workers, customers, and suppliers be involved during the implementation of new technology?
10	• What social impacts will the adoption of new technology have?
11	• What role should the government have in the development, adoption, and implementation of new technology? • How do government policies regarding new technology differ from country to country?
12	• What is the decision process that a firm should go through from the moment it considers new technology until after it has been implemented?
13	• What are the challenges for the future?

and on job shop and batch operations (discrete parts manufacturing) as flexible capacity makes it as economical to run low volumes as to run continuous flow operations. However, a critical assessment of the total environment must be undertaken by any firm contemplating the acquisition of new technology. Different technology may be neither the only answer nor the best answer to a firm's particular problems.

This text is an attempt to look comprehensively at why new technology is important, what its potential is, and how it should be justified and implemented. It is an effort to look at macro (social and governmental) issues as well as micro (organizational and individual) matters. The book is divided into five parts and 13 chapters. Exhibit 1.7 presents some of the major issues that will be discussed. It is our hope that this text will provide readers with a thorough overview of the critical issues involved in managing the new technology.

RECOMMENDED READINGS

GAYNOR, G. H. [1988]. "Managing Technology—A Driving Force for the Future." In T. M. Khalil et al. (eds.), *Technology Management 1.* Proceedings of the First International Conference on Technology Management, Miami, Inderscience Enterprises Ltd., pp. 791–798.

SUMANTH, D. J. [1988]. "A Total System Approach to Technology Management for Inter-Organizational Competitiveness." In T. M. Khalil et al. [eds.], *Technology Management 1.* Proceedings of the First International Conference on Technology Management, Miami, Inderscience Enterprises Ltd., pp. 799–808.

REFERENCES AND BIBLIOGRAPHY

BULLINGER, J. J., H. WARNECK, and H. P. LENTES [1985]. "Towards the Factory of the Future." In H. Bullinger and H. Warnecke (eds.), *Towards the Factory of the Future.* Proceedings of the 8th International Conference on Production Research, Stuttgart, West Germany, Springer-Verlag, New York.

CHANDLER, A., JR. [1977]. *The Visible Hand.* Belknap Press of Harvard University Press, Cambridge, Mass.

Economic Council of Canada [1986]. *Workable Futures: Notes on Emerging Technologies.* Prepared by Words Associated and Keith Newton, Minister of Supply and Services Canada, Ottawa, Ontario.

FROHMAN, A. L. [1982]. "Technology as a Competitive Weapon." *Harvard Business Review,* January–February, pp. 97–104.

GOLDHAR, J., and M. JELINEK [1985]. "Computer Integrated Flexible Manufacturing: Organizational, Economic, and Strategic Implications." *Interfaces,* Volume 15, May–June, pp. 94–105.

GOLDHAR, J., and M. JELINEK [1983]. "Plan for Economies of Scope." *Harvard Business Review,* November–December, pp. 141–148.

HUNT, T., and G. STALK, JR. [1982]. "The Big Revolution." In "Manager's Journal," *Wall Street Journal,* 63, July 12, p. 18.

MEREDITH, J. [1986]. "Automation Strategy Must Give Careful Attention to the Firm's 'Infrastructure'." *Industrial Engineering,* Volume 18, No. 5, May, pp. 68–73.

NAISBITT, J. [1984]. *Megatrends.* Warner Books, New York.

RAMO, S. [1988]. "How to Revive U.S. High Tech." *Fortune,* May, pp. 124–133.

SKINNER, W. [1985]. "The Taming of Lions: How Manufacturing Leadership Evolved, 1780–1984." In K. B. Clark, R. H. Hayes, and C. Lorenz (eds.), *The Uneasy Alliance.* Harvard Business School Press, pp. 63–110.

STANTON, C., and H. CHALLIS [1983]. "Market Changes Make Automation Inevitable." *Material Handling,* July, pp. 19–22.

STEELE, L. [1983]. "Managers' Misconceptions about Technology." *Harvard Business Review,* November–December, pp. 133–140.

WADDELL, C. [1985]. "The Drive to Catch Japan." *Report on Business Magazine,* November, pp. 28–35.

WATTERMAN, R., JR. [1987]. *The Renewal Factor: How the Beat Get and Keep the Competitive Edge.* Bantom Books, New York.

Chapter Two

THE CHARACTERISTICS AND POTENTIAL OF NEW TECHNOLOGY

Technology is a tool that can multiply the effectiveness and hence the worth of time and work. Technology makes it possible to manufacture for our needs with less effort and less dissipation of valuable natural resources.

Simon Ramo

INTRODUCTION: OPERATIONALIZING THE NEW TECHNOLOGY

The word *technology* automatically brings the thought of machines to people's minds. However, machines are only a small part of technology. Ellul [1964] uses the word *technique* as an all-encompassing definition for (new) technology by explaining that technique is the most up-to-date and efficient method of attaining a predetermined result in any and every field of human activity. Although this definition is too wide in scope to be of practical use for managers, it does point out that technology embraces a lot more than just machines. Zeleny [1986] has highlighted this point by proposing that any technology consists of three interdependent, codeterminant, and equally important components:

1. Hardware. The physical structure and logical layout of the equipment or machinery that is to be used to carry out the required tasks.
2. Software. The knowledge of how to use the hardware in order to carry out the required tasks.
3. Brainware. The reasons for using the technology in a particular way.

Consider the role of these three components in defining a computer as a technology:

A computer is an identifiable *hardware* with its own physical structure and components which distinguish it from other objects. It has a set of rules for operating, maintaining, and repairing which represent its *software*. Its *brainware* consists of human knowledge and expertise which allows it to perform certain tasks. We refer to a computer as a *technology* only after all these three components are specified.

Zeleny further explains that every technology is ". . . embedded in a complex network of physical, informational, and socio-economic relationships which support the proper use and functioning of a given technology towards the stated goals and objectives."[1] This he calls the *technology support network* (or *net*):

> Technology support net consists of the requisite organizational, administrative, and cultural structures: work rules, task roles, requisite skills, work contents, formal and informal covenants of the workplace, systems standards and measures, management styles and culture, organizational patterns, and so on.[2]

He then defines *high technology* as any technology which affects the very nature of the support net: "It allows (and often requires) us to do things differently and to do different things."[3]

Our definition of the new technology corresponds directly to Zeleny's definition of high technology. The *new technology*, in general, is defined as any technology that has an explicit impact on the way a company produces its products or provides its services. Naturally, this broad definition embraces a wide range of technological alternatives. To give a sharper focus to our discussion, the term *new technology* is used in this book to represent *advanced* technologies, technologies characterized by their extraordinary flexibility and their rapid rate of change. In the past it may have taken 10 to 20 years for a technology to mature; today a new replacement might be developed in months. It is this degree of flexibility and rapidity of change that call for indispensable shifts in the way companies are managed. We also assert that the effective management of advanced technology requires a fundamentally different approach to the management of the firm's operations.

OPERATIONS TECHNOLOGY

Steed and Tiffin [1986] have identified 30 emerging technologies (see Exhibit 2.1) based on interviews with 215 university, industry, and government experts. *Emerging technologies* are defined as new technologies which are not yet commercialized but will become so within five years, or are currently in use but will evolve significantly. Although these technologies are recognized as different from one another, the distinctions between some of them are not, in practice, as clear-

---

[1]Zeleny [1986], p. 110.
[2]Ibid., p. 110.
[3]Ibid., p. 111.

Exhibit 2.1   Thirty Emerging Technologies and Sectoral Impact

Technology	Sector of Impact
1. Genetic engineering	Agriculture, Manufacturing (Pharmaceuticals), Services (Health), Forestry, Mining
2. Enhanced chips/gallium arsenide	Manufacturing (Electronic & Scientific Equipment), Communications, Defense
3. Artificial intelligence	Services, Manufaturing
4. Cell/tissue culture	Services (Health), Manufacturing (Pharmaceuticals, Food), Agriculture, Forestry
5. Microcomputers	Services, Manufacturing, Defense
6. CAD/CAM/CAP/CAE	Manufacturing, Services, Communications
7. Robotics	Manufacturing, Mining
8. Composite materials	Manufacturing (Automobile, Aircraft)
9. Remote sensing	Forestry, Agriculture, Mining, Services, Defense
10. Imaging	Manufacturing (Electronics), Services, Mining, Communications
11. Fibre optics	Communications, Manufacturing (Electronics)
12. Monoclonal antibodies	Agriculture, Manufacturing (Pharmaceuticals), Services (Health)
13. Computer software	Manufacturing, Services, Communications, Defense
14. Advanced polymers	Manufacturing
15. Lasers	Manufacturing (Electronics, Transportation, Medical Instruments), Services, Communications
16. Synthetic fuels	Manufacturing (Refining), Energy, Services (Transporation)
17. Coal technologies	Mining, Manufacturing
18. Food irradiation	Manufacturing (Food, Chemicals), Agriculture
19. Telecommunication	Communication, Services, Construction
20. Surface chemistry/plasma technologies	Manufaturing, Energy, Agriculture, Services
21. Biomass	Manufacturing (Chemicals), Agriculture, Energy, Forestry
22. Hydrogen energy technologies	Manufacturing, Utilities, Energy
23. Separation and membrane technologies	Manufacturing (Food, Chemical)
24. Fermentation	Manufacturing (Food), Agriculture
25. Structural Ceramics	Manufacturing (Metal, Transportation)
26. Optoelectronic/storage systems	Communications, Manufacturing (Electronics)
27. Construction technologies	Construction, Mining
28. Speech recognition	Manufacturing Services
29. Photovoltaics	Manufacturing (Electronics), Communications
30. New alloys	Mining, Manufacturing (Transportation)

Source: Steed and Tiffin [1986], with permission of the Science Council of Canada, pp. 23–24.

cut as Exhibit 2.1 might imply. For instance, ". . . robotics includes computers, imaging, artificial intelligence, computer software, and speech recognition. Some of the broader headings subsume a variety of other technologies."[4]

But as is clear from Exhibit 2.1, the range of advanced and emerging technologies is quite broad. However, in this chapter (and for that matter in

[4]Steed and Tiffin [1986], p. 25.

this book), we focus on advanced *operations technologies,* the new technologies actually used for production of goods and services. The rationale for focusing on the advanced operations technologies is twofold:

1. Operations technologies tend to be very similar across a wide range of industries. Therefore, our view of the new technology is an effective way of presenting the key issues involved in a fashion that appeals to a broad audience.
2. Many strategic gains can be made by firms through the effective use of operations technologies.

It is also important to note that our approach includes opearations technologies relevant to manufacturing and service sectors. For the purpose of this book, we consider only the *goods-embodied services.* That is, we shall assume a *service* to mean a product, the primary intention of which is to provide a service.

Advanced Manufacturing versus Information Technologies

We group operations technologies into two categories, namely, advanced manufacturing technologies and advanced information technologies. *Advanced manufacturing technologies (AMT)* refer to new technologies which are used directly by the firm in the production of a product (for example, a television set) or in the provision of a service (for example, a hospital operating room). *Advanced information technologies (AIT),* on the other hand, refer to those technologies which are used to generate and transmit information essential to support the production of goods and the provision of services (for example, banking operations).

This classification does not imply that manufacturing technologies apply to manufacturing firms, and that information technologies apply more to service organizations. On the contrary, we contend:

1. It is difficult, at least in some cases, to speak of advanced manufacturing technologies without talking about information technologies, and vice versa, as many of the specific new technologies involve a combination of these two categories.
2. Although manufacturing companies are engaged more directly with manufacturing technology and service firms more with information technology, this relationship is by no means exclusive. In other words, the information technologies employed in service should be regarded as instrumental in creating strategic advantages for a company.
3. A company can have the most sophisticated manufacturing equipment available and still fail if it does not receive timely and accurate information support. In the same way, a service firm will be limited in its ability to utilize information technologies if it does not have the necessary manufacturing support.

A recent internal study conducted by General Motors found that up to 50 percent of the costs for new automation projects were directly related to communication devices (Saul [1985]). In other words, new technology involves the automation of information systems as much as it involves the automation of production processes. Exhibit 2.2 illustrates our approach in focusing on a very specific form of the new technology—advanced operations technology. (In this book, we use *new technology* and *advanced operations technology* interchangeably.)

Exhibit 2.2   An Operational Definition of New Technology

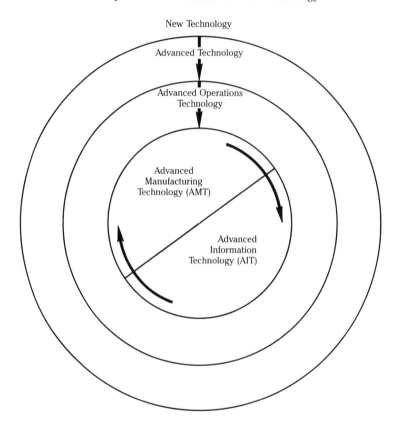

ADVANCED MANUFACTURING TECHNOLOGIES (AMT)

In terms of hardware, AMT makes substantial use of microchip technology. This results in a degree of automation never before experienced. Before discussing different forms of AMT, we need to separate the notion of *fixed* or *hard automation* (which is the automation devoted to most routine jobs in mass production or continuous operations) from *soft automation*. Soft (sometimes referred to as *super*) automation is the application of computer software and the ability to process software information.[5] There are essentially two types of soft automation: programmable and flexible. *Programmable* automation is not capable of providing instantaneous part changeovers, as time is lost due to program loading/unloading and changeover of the physical setup. In order to be truly flexible, a manufacturing system must be capable of producing a variety of parts with no significant time losses associated with part changeovers. That is, the system must be capable of automatically changing the operation programs and the physical equipment (fixtures, tooling) required to produce the part almost instantly. Generally, incremental advances in the technologies lead to a gradual shift from programmable automation toward flexible automation. Flexible automation lessens the need to utilize either independent machine tools to pursue product variety, or dedicated systems to produce high volumes economically. In other words, a firm may now use the same (flexible) manufacturing system to compete by producing either high volume or high variety (or both). This concept of achieving economies of scale (high volume) and economies of scope (high variety) simultaneously is referred to as *economies of integration*, and will be discussed further in Chapter 5.

To review the characteristics and potential of AMT, we first look at the new technologies used in the actual manufacturing process. These we call the *direct components*. We then examine the *manufacturing support facilities* and the *integrated systems*, which are a combination of direct components and manufacturing support facilities. Finally, we discuss two well-known management philosophies: *Just-In-Time* and *Group Technology*.

Direct Components

Computer-Aided Manufacturing (CAM).
Computer-aided manufacturing (CAM) refers to the use of computers to control or monitor manufacturing operations directly, including the use of NC, CNC, DNC, robotics, and other

---

[5]Lawrence [1984] has expanded the notion of (soft) automation even further by identifying the following four levels:

Level One: The application of control systems to directly control the operations of (production) machinery. A control system in effect tells the machine (e.g., a robot) what to do, and therefore involves only one-way communication.

Level Two: The application of supervisory systems to control, monitor, and adjust operations based on particular objectives (e.g. production specification tolerances). Supervisory systems involve two-way communication between the computer and the machinery.

Level Three: The application of integrated systems to blend and control various aspects of a firm's operations, such as production, design, and materials handling. These are combinations of level one and level two automation.

Level Four: The application of large-scale systems which link control and supervisory systems to corporate information systems.

Some of the advanced technologies that will be described fit precisely into one of these four levels of automation. However, the boundaries separating the levels are not absolute by any means, and many of the technologies that will be discussed cannot be clearly identified as belonging solely to one level.

process monitoring and control technologies. CAM is a generic term used to describe the complete range of computer applications in direct manufacturing activities.

Numerical Control (NC) Machines. Since the mid-1950s, trends in discrete parts manufacturing have been toward improving machine capability and internalizing more and more machine-control functions (see Ayren [1986]). NC machines in many respects represent the first departure by parts-making/ assembly industries from conventional technologies. They involve the use of software programs made up of numerical commands to operate a general-purpose machine tool such as a lathe, a grinder, or a drill press. The software programs essentially replace the skilled machinists who controlled the machine tool's operations with gears and cams.[6]

NC machines have a number of advantages over conventional machines:

1. Increased machine flexibility. NC adapts better to changes in jobs and production schedules.
2. Increased modification flexibility. NC makes it easier to accommodate engineering design changes—the tape as opposed to the hardware can be altered, which is especially beneficial for job shop operations.
3. Reduced labor requirements, setup times, lead times, cycle times, and inventory.
4. Improved quality through the elimination of human error during the machining process, as well as better conformity to specifications.

One drawback to NC machines is that programming mistakes are common, and often the only way to find the error is to run the part. The punched tapes also wear out with repeated use, and the tape reader is very susceptible to breakdowns. Finally, the hardwired nature of NC machinery means that the control features of the machine cannot be altered very easily.

In general, as the first generation of automated machines, NC machines provided better flexibility than the conventional machinery they replaced, but less than the more advanced CNC machines that were to follow them.

Computer Numerical Control (CNC) and Direct Numerical Control (DNC). The incorporation of the computer into numerical control systems has reduced (or eliminated) most of the operational problems associated with NC. Computer numerical control (CNC) refers to the control of a single machine tool by a dedicated minicomputer or microcomputer. Direct numerical control (DNC) exists when a number of different machine tools (generally CNC machines) are controlled by a central computer.

---

[6]NC programs are usually produced on a paper tape that is one inch wide. Holes are punched in the tape to indicate what machining operations are to be performed. The tape is then fed into a controller unit, and the tape reader component of the controller unit translates the instructions punched on the tape into mechanical actions to be performed by the machine tool.

In comparison with NC machines, CNC machines offer improved flexibility because they are softwired (that is, digital computer software is used in place of wired circuits), and as a result new options can be added easily, and hardware problems more easily serviced. With DNC, the problems associated with worn-out punched tapes and tape reader breakdowns are eliminated as part programs are transmitted directly from the central computer (as opposed to a punched tape) to the controller unit through telecommunication lines (as opposed to a tape reader). Some DNC systems replace the controller unit of NC systems with a special softwired machine control unit. This increases machine flexibility as improvements to the control functions of the system can be made relatively easily through programming changes as opposed to hardware changes. Finally, the computer allows some analysis of the accuracy of the parts program to be determined before any parts are run.

Although NC, CNC, and DNC machine tools are, on a stand-alone basis, more expensive than conventional machine tools,[7] the increased capacity they offer means that they are not necessarily more costly on a capacity basis (Meredith [1987]). There is additionally the possibility of retrofitting these machines with new tooling and/or controls (as opposed to purchasing new machines) when they become worn and inefficient due to extensive use. This enables them to retain their value longer than conventional dedicated machinery.

The advantages of numerical control systems can be expanded with the use of machining centers. A machining center is capable of performing more than one machining operation—for example, drilling, tapping, milling, reaming, and boring can all be performed at one machining center. Tool selection is made automatically, depending on the part program, and the part can be repositioned automatically so that it can be machined on different surfaces; CNC machines capable of operating on up to 15 axes are not uncommon today. Most machining centers have two machine tables so that one part can be loaded while another part is being machined. The capabilities of a machining center lead to increased machine utilization rates and therefore reduced manufacturing cycle times. And parts do not have to be routed to various individual machine tools, reducing parts handling and work-in-progress inventories.

Industrial Robots. An industrial robot is a general-purpose, multifunctional, programmable machine that can be used to perform a variety of tasks. In practice, robots have been used for parts and materials handling, machine loading and unloading, heat treating, welding, spray painting, testing and inspection, die casting, assembling, and finishing. Most applications of industrial robots today involve performing hazardous tasks, lifting or moving heavy parts, and performing dull, repetitive jobs. Depending on the nature of the application, some of the advantages robots can offer include increased flexibility, safer working conditions, improved quality, and reduced labor costs.

[7]In general, conventional machine tools cost anywhere from $10,000 to $30,000; NC machine tools cost from $80,000 to $150,000; and CNC machine tools cost from $250,000 to $1,000,000.

Industrial robots generally use servo technology and can have up to six degrees of freedom.[8] This ultimately gives the robot the ability to place a part in any position and orientation within its workspace.

Many industrial robots in use today should be classified as part of level one automation—that is, the robots are programmed to perform the same movements over and over again. However, external sensing devices such as vision systems, range and proximity sensors, and contact sensors are allowing robots to adjust their operations based on specific environmental factors. Furthermore, these sensors allow significant increases in accuracy. In fact, they are becoming so common that by 1990 a robot which does not have some sensing device (probably vision) will not be considered a robot (see Brody [1986]).

Robots are used in a number of industries, by many firms, to perform a variety of operations:

> Robots perform more than 98% of the spot welding on Ford's highly successful Taurus and Sable cars. At Doehler-Jarvis, a major Ohio metal fabricator, robots load and unload die-casting machines, trim parts and ladle molten metal. At IBM factories across the country, robots insert disk drives into personal computers and snap keys onto electronic typewriter keyboards. At a General Dynamics plant in Fort Worth, one robot drills 550 holes in the vertical tail fins of an F-16 fighter in three hours. It used to take three workers eight hours to do the same job.[9]

Although industrial robots are generally associated with manufacturing operations, they are also beginning to have a significant impact on the service industry. In fact, some experts predict that applications of robots in the service industry will eventually outnumber those in manufacturing (Bylinskey [1987]). Current applications of service robots include:

1. Performing hazardous underwater or outer space functions.
2. Caring for and assisting handicapped people.
3. Performing nursing activities in hospitals.
4. Performing security functions.
5. Performing a wide range of domestic activities such as cleaning and cooking.

Manufacturing Support Facilities

Computer Process Monitoring (CPM) and Computer Process Control (CPC). Computer process monitoring (CPM) refers to the use of a computer

---

[8]Degrees of freedom refers to an axis or vector of motion such as arm sweep, shoulder swivel, elbow extension, yaw, pitch and roll. In this context, servofeedback is important because without it, the robot could only move to the endpoints of its axes of motion—servotechnology enables it to stop anywhere along the axes.

[9]Bock [1987], p. 38.

to gather information about the manufacturing process. With CPM, information about the process flows only one way, from the process being monitored to the computer. In this case, process adjustments are made by human operators using the computer information. An enhancement over CPM is computer process control (CPC), which refers to a system where the process is monitored and controlled directly by the computer. For example, if the computer noticed that a machine tool was worn beyond a specified dimension, it would automatically shut the machine down, and perhaps even replace the tool automatically.

The main benefit of CPM and CPC is that they improve production scheduling and product quality. Machine malfunctioning, worn tooling, and variations in input materials may lead to a process difficult to schedule and that results in relatively poor quality products. Without CPM and CPC, many of these process problems may remain undetected or unidentified, delaying production and resulting in large volumes of products of an unacceptable quality. Furthermore, the advent of CPM and CPC has to some extent changed the methods used to measure and control quality. Instead of focusing on the quality of the finished product, more attention can be given to ensuring that the process is up to standard.

Computer-Aided Design (CAD) and Computer-Aided Engineering (CAE). The design of new products and tooling used to create new products has traditionally been done on drawing boards. A mechanical engineer would manually prepare the blueprint for the complete product and tooling design, and an electrical engineer would draw the circuit diagrams of the related electrical components. These would be preliminary drawings and throughout the process incremental improvements would be made to better both the esthetic appeal and the performance capabilities of the product. The problem is that this method is very time-consuming; a preliminary drawing usually requires many manual modifications before reaching its finished state.

Computer-aided design (CAD) and Computer-aided engineering (CAE) have significantly improved the design process. CAD refers to the use of a computer to create or modify an engineering design. CAE enables a design to be tested to ensure that it does not violate any mechanical, heat, stress, or other engineering properties. Many CAD software packaged include CAE capabilities.

CAD and CAE offer the potential for substantial gains over the traditional blueprint drafting method of design in the following areas:

1. Product Flexibility. New products can be designed and therefore introduced much more quickly.
2. Modification Flexibility. Existing product designs can easily be altered to meet particular customer needs.
3. Design Access. Designs can be stored and accessed far more easily on a computer than on paper.
4. Quality. Designs can be tested for performance before being run, and any

required changes to upgrade the quality of the product can be easily made. This also saves time and money because it removes the necessity to actually produce the product or a sample before realizing it is flawed.

5. Productivity. With the technology flexibility and information-storage capability, the productivity of design engineers is enhanced significantly. In fact, in many cases: "...increases of output per draughtsman range between 200 and 6,000 percent, depending on the specific application, with averages of between 200 and 500 percent."[10]

While installation of CAD (and CAE) was once considered a very expensive venture, the price for software packages are falling quickly, and some packages (excluding hardware) are now available for less than $2,000. This makes it possible for smaller companies to utilize this technology. Consider the following application:

> A CAD system utilized at the Automotive Group of Wickes Manufacturing Co. (Southfield, MI) is helping to reduce design time by 50% and testing time by 33%. What used to take three iterations now takes two. This saves the company and its customers hundreds of thousands of dollars annually. Today there are twice as many jobs as were available in 1983, with the same design staff. And today's work is faster and more accurate.[11]

Computer-Aided Process Planning (CAPP).   Manufacturing engineers usually determine the processing plans for the production of the parts. This involves documenting the routing path and the series of manufacturing operations required to manufacture a particular part. In many instances, however, these routings can be less than optimal due to machine breakdowns, equipment replacement, and selection of different routing paths for parts that have the same manufacturing requirements.

Computer-aided process planning (CAPP) involves the automatic generation of process plans for (new) parts. The most common way of doing this is called the *variant approach* (Wolfe [1985]). Parts are grouped into families based on similar manufacturing attributes (the sequence of steps required to make the part). Standard process plans are then generated for each part family. When a new part is developed, the processing requirements can be matched with the plans that have already been developed for the various families, and required operations and optimal routing paths can be more easily determined.

A newer and more advanced method of CAPP utilizes what is called the *generative approach* (Wolfe [1985]). This approach produces plans utilizing decision logic, algorithms, and geometric data. In this case, standard plans are required. Advances in expert systems (discussed later in this chapter) are making this approach to process planning much more viable.

---

[10]Ebel and Ulrich [1987], p. 353.
[11]Adapted for length—Doolittle [1987], p. 55.

CAPP can offer significant advantages to a firm in the following areas:

1. Process rationalization and standardization through the development of standard process plans. This leads to a more efficient utilization of production equipment, and possibly improved quality and increased capacity.
2. Reduced lead times for new products due to the ease of generating a process plan for a new part and introducing it into the manufacturing process.
3. Reduced labor requirements in developing the process plans for new parts.

While the benefits obtained through CAPP can be significant, even greater gains can be achieved by linking CAPP to CAD and CAM. (The integration of CAPP, CAD, and CAM is discussed on page 34.)

Machine Vision (MV).   At an approximate real annual growth rate of 55 percent, machine vision is expected to outperform the entire automated manufacturing sector through 1990 (Frost and Sullivan Inc. [1985]). Vision technology is especially in demand in the discrete parts manufacturing industry, where stringent quality regulations are virutally forcing companies to consider adoption. Vision is used, for example, in the semiconductor industry to check device alignment and solder connections; and in consumer goods industries to ensure quality of end products and minimize costly returns of damaged or defective products. The following example illustrates the potential benefits of machine vision:

> A manufacturer of communications equipment makes 2,000 printed circuit boards a day for an electronic switchboard. The board contains about 100 integrated circuits (ICs), loaded by automatic insertion equipment. About one percent of the time, IC pins don't fully project through the board. Human inspectors could find only about 75 percent of these defects. Therefore, about 500 errors a day went undetected until the circuit boards were tested electrically—a step that occurs after they've already been soldered. The rework cost for this manufacturer is about $1.00 per point after soldering and 10 cents if the defect is spotted before soldering. By using a machine vision system to inspect the boards, the company achieved a reduction of 90 cents per defect. In this case, a $45,000 vision system was justified in less than five months (100 working days).[12]

There are four basic MV applications:

1. Inspection. Determines whether the part being inspected is acceptable. This comprises well over half of the current machine vision installations, with sample uses such as PCB inspection to ensure that all components are present and inserted properly.

[12]Adapted for length—Lupidus [1986], p. 11.

2. Recognition. With virtually unlimited industrial applications, recognition addresses the question: What is it? Examples include use in sorting/packaging of parts, recognition of presence/absence of parts for machine loading, and automatic inventory control.

3. Gauging: In determining measurements and distances, gauging addresses the question: What size is it? It is used for such applications as measurement of drill hole depth, bottleneck width, or the separation between a door and its frame.

4. Robot Guidance and Position Control. While these applications constitute only a small percentage of current machine vision installations, they have great potential. Generally, the system is used to identify parts, determine their positions and orientations, and transmit this information to robots that will then grasp or handle the object. Basic applications include pick-and-place robots along moving production lines, and seam tracking for welding operations.

While the fundamental components of current machine vision systems probably will not change, the future holds some interesting applications in real-time robot path control and the development of automated guided vehicle systems with machine vision guidance. These applications also move into the area of machine intelligence, which we will discuss later in this chapter.

Automated Guided Vehicle Systems (AGVs). Automated guided vehicle systems (AGVs) are unmanned carriers/platforms controlled by central computers that dispatch carriers, track them, and govern their movements on various guidepath loops. AGVs fit into two broad manufacturing categories. First, in materials handling, they deliver inventory from holding to production areas or between workstations to replace conventional forklifts and rigid transfer lines. Second, in assembly systems, they act as production platforms supporting products (autombiles, engines) while the work is performed. In this sense, they do away with conventional industrial conveyor systems. There are several methods for guiding AGVs around the desired path: infrared, optical, inertial, embedded wire, and ultrasonic guidance (see Exhibit 2.3).

The enhancement of AGVS technology is comparable to the transportation revolution in which trucks largely replaced freight trains. A train passes each stop in sequence, and facilities served by trains must cluster near the rails. But a truck goes wherever there are roads. It does not have to pass every stop; it can bypass some and hit others in order of priority. AGVs also have this routing flexibility. The following example typifies the application of AGVs in GM's operation in Oshawa, Ontario, which houses about 1,100 separate carriers:

> In Oshawa's labor-intensive areas, AGVs permit workpieces to stop at each assembly station for an average of three and one-half minutes, allowing workers to perform more involved tasks than they can in the one minute permitted on a moving line.[13]

[13]Zygmont [1986], p. 16.

Exhibit 2.3 AGVs Guide Path Alternatives

Method	Description	Advantages	Disadvantages
1. Embedded Wire	Utilizes wire installed below floor level to guide vehicles and to handle communications	• Permanent • Does not have to be reapplied • Can handle dirty environments and heavy traffic • Interference free communications • Floor surfaces limited	• Can't be changed easily • Costly to repair wire breaks
2. Optical Path	Inch-wide ultraviolet paint strips are applied directly to floor surface	• Can be changed quickly and inexpensively • Can be applied to almost any floor surface (e.g.: clean room, carpet, wooden block)	• Must reapply every several months • Heavy traffic wears path • Can't be used in metal chip environment
3. Infrared	Reflectors are used throughout a facility for position triangulation	• Very accurate	• Needs line-of-sight reckoning (can't have obstructions in the way.
4. Inertial	Utilizes gyros and encoders much as aircraft currently do for navigation	• Most accurate of any guidance method	• Guidance system is very expensive; it requires high-precision components and on-board computer control
5. Ultrasonic	Transducers are utilized to measure relative differences in frequencies (similar to the principal of sonar)	• Can tolerate occasional interferences by people on the floor	• Can receive outside frequency interference from such items as garage door openers, etc. • Still a development technology

Source: Vester [1987], p. 38.

In addition, AGVs allow a single assembly line to split into several parallel lines where identical operations are performed. This approach could be used to increase manufacturing uptime significantly.

Automated Materials Handling (AMH).   Automated materials handling refers to the use of computers to direct the movement of raw materials, work-in-progress, and/or finished good inventories. These systems often make use of automatic bar coding to facilitate movements and handlings. Materials handling automation has three general applications:

1. It can be used to link various machines in the production process. This is done, for example, with Flexible Manufacturing Systems (FMS) (discussed later in this chapter).
2. It can be used to sort orders that consist of a large number of different items. Such systems make use of a network of conveyors and controls to sort orders automatically by store or shipping route.
3. It can be used to store and retrieve items from inventory automatically. Systems that do this are called Automatic Storage and Retrieval Systems (AS/RS).

Automated storage and retrieval systems (AS/RS) utilize a combination of cranes, conveyors, carousels, and AGVs. Materials handling is one of the two important functions of AGVs. In this case, they deliver inventory from holding to production areas, or between workstations; they replaced manually operated equipment like forklifts, or rigid equipment like transfer lines. AS/RS can lead to reduced storage space requirements, reduced product damage and improved product quality, reduced labor requirements, and more accurate inventory records. However, these systems can be very expensive to implement. Exhibit 2.4 illustrates one of many applications where AGVS are used in an AS/RS.

Exhibit 2.4   An Example of AS/RS Application

When Northrop Aircract Division installed its computerized storage system for small parts storage, productivity nearly tripled, storage space needs were reduced by 60 percent and inventory accuracy improved.

Northrop builds three planes at its El Segundo, CA, plant—the F/A–18, the F–5 and the T–38 trainer. Its Autocube automated storage and retrieval system has a capacity of 50,000 part numbers, which is enough to support four planes. The heart of the installation is three AS/RS aisles—each 100 ft long and 25 ft high—with storage space on either side. Inside each of the aisles is a computer-controlled crane which moves both vertically and horizontally to remove, then replace, some 7,000 containers.

Being able to consolidate what was once 45,000 sq. ft. of warehousing in two different buildings into a single, compact 19,000 sq. ft.—a space reduction of nearly 60 percent—gave additional economic benefits. The area was turned over to production, which badly needed the room;...if it had been necessary to lease that much square footage at current rates it would have cost Northrop Aircraft Division $300,000 or so a year.

In reducing manpower needs for order picking and by shortening the period during which production workers wait for parts, the company calculates savings of $312,000 a year.

Source: Adapted from Wenzel [1988], p. 48.

Manufacturing Resource Planning (MRP II). Manufacturing resource planning (MRP II) refers to the use of a computerized, comprehensive system to plan all the resource needs of a manufacturing company. MRP II is an extension of the materials requirement planning (MRP) concept. While MRP is concerned with production scheduling, materials ordering, and inventory control, MRP II extends beyond this to include purchasing, production control, receiving, distribution, subcontracting, product cost tracking, forecasting, order entry, engineering data, facilities planning, plant monitoring and control, maintenance, and other aspects of manufacturing. MRP II links the production function with the other functional areas of the company in order to make major planning decisions. Ideally, MRP II systems have two important characteristics:

1. They make use of a common database. Therefore, data must be entered only once into the system. This allows manufacturing data to be converted into financial data, meaning that one set of numbers can be used to run the company.
2. They enable "what if" simulations to be done to show the effects of implementing alternative plans and policies.

MRP II systems can reduce inventories, increase capacity, improve delivery reliability, reduce cycle times and lead times, and trim down labor requirements. Perhaps the most important aspect of MRP II systems, however, is their ability to aid the strategic decision-making process. For example:

> One firm, whose business objectives included level employment, used MRP II to convince marketing personnel that it was necessary to smooth the sales plan so that manufacturing could level its labor requirements. Another firm used the simulation capability to formulate contingency plans to minimize the adverse effects of strikes on the firm's operation. Using MRP II to identify strike-induced capacity shortages and to schedule vendors to make up projected capacity shortfalls, the firm was able to meet all its commitments during a 13-week strike. In a third firm, the use of MRP II enabled the lead times for new product development and introduction to be reduced. The system linked the materials-planning and product-engineering groups during the development process and was able to achieve better coordination.[14]

Although MRP II systems are being used by many firms, ". . . their success rate, in terms of completely operational systems, has not been very high."[15] This is due to some extent to the complexities involved in achieving two major requirements of MRP II:

1. Accurate, timely, and relevant information must be entered into the system to make it useful.

[14]Evans et al. [1987], pp. 482–483.
[15]Meredith [1987], p. 251.

2. The size and capabilities of the database required for an MRP II system are enormous. Database technology is discussed in greater detail later in this chapter.)

Integrated Systems

CAD/CAM.   CAD and CAM have done a great deal to improve the design and manufacturing functions, respectively. However, "...in many firms very little communication now exists between design engineering and manufacturing...engineering designs the product and then throws the drawing over the wall for manufacturing to make the product."[16] CAD/CAM refers to the integration of Computer-Aided Design and Computer-Aided Manufacturing. The synthesis of these two functions can lead to significant improvements in terms of reducing design-to-manufacture lead times for new and modified products, improving product quality, increasing production flexibility, and reducing labor requirements and inventory.

A CAD/CAM system enables the manufacturing requirements for parts to be generated automatically from design information. Computer-aided process planning (CAPP), discussed previously, can be used as a start to CAD/CAM integration, since CAPP enables the automatic generation of process plans from design information. In fact, the union of CAD, CAPP, and CAM is referred to as C^3 *integration.* However, CAD/CAM extends beyond CAP, as it allows automatic generation of parts programs in addition to process plans. Sarlin concluded: "With today's emphasis on decreasing the time required for transition of a product from design to manufacturing, improving quality and productivity, producibility and flexible automation, the ability to automatically generate machine control data is a necessity."[17]

Many firms have reported success stories in implementing CAD/CAM systems. The following is one of these notable applications:

> Within six months, Boart Canada had converted a labor-intensive design and CNC programming process to an automatic system for producing most of the firm's machined products. Immediate cost reduction benefits were visible. An annual cost of $25,000 for remote CNC program timesharing has been eliminated. A workload that would have previously required three staff members is now comfortably handled by two CAD/CAM operators at an annual saving of over $30,000. The lead time to produce CNC programs has been drastically reduced as well. A new product design can be created and plotted in minutes. Direct transfer of graphic data from designer to CNC programmer has eliminated errors in transcription...and finished programs are delivered to designated machines and loaded in minutes.[18]

[16]Wolfe [1985], p. 72.
[17]Sarlin [1985], p. 64.
[18]Van Bergen and Hobbs [1987], p. 101.

Flexible Manufacturing Systems (FMS). The term flexible manufacturing system (FMS) has been used to label a range of production systems with different capabilities. Generally, an FMS is a combination of workstations (such as CNC machines and/or machining centers) joined by an automated materials handling system and controlled by a central computer. There is little direct labor involved in parts production, except perhaps to load and unload parts from the system and/or input data to the computer.

An FMS is designed to produce a family of parts,[19] and is capable of producing different parts simultaneously and in random order. Note that: "...the number of different designs a firm can handle will become essentially infinite since the (FMS) system will automatically adjust to small variations in design."[20] This provides some of the flexibility associated with job-shop operations utilizing standalone machines, combined with some of the economies of scale characteristics (and therefore low production costs) associated with dedicated, continuous flow systems. Exhibit 2.5 compares FMS to dedicated systems and to independent machine tools in terms of the variety of parts to be produced by the system, and the batch quantity of each part (and thus determines the economies created by each).

As Exhibit 2.5 illustrates, flexible manufacturing systems are capable of responding to situations where there is a variety of parts and the demand for them varies. They act as a bridge between dedicated systems which produce high

Exhibit 2.5 A Comparison of the Capabilities of Different Production Systems

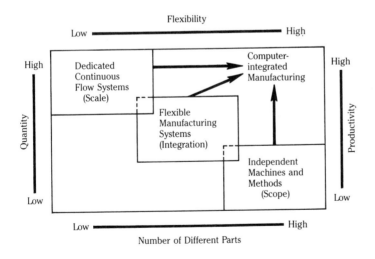

[19]An FMS can only produce different parts from a given part family. A *family of parts* refers to a number of parts which have similar characteristics with regard to shape, size, materials, machining precision required, etc. Thus, the same FMS cannot produce parts which have different attributes (such as one part made of steel and another made of titanium).

[20]Fraser [1985], p. 52.

volumes of low variety and general-purpose systems which manufacture a large variety of low volumes. This is defined as economies of integration, and will be discussed further in Chapter 5.

The potential operational benefits of an FMS include:

1. A reduction in the number of machine tools required to manufacture parts
2. A reduction in floor space requirements
3. A reduction in labor requirements
4. A reduction in nonproductive manufacturing time
5. An increase in machine utilization rates
6. A reduction in cycle time—the time it takes to transfer raw materials to finished goods
7. A reduction in work-in-progress and finished goods inventories

Exhibit 2.6 gives a good illustration of the potential magnitude of some of these benefits. Note, however, that the benefits are perhaps minor in significance relative to the strategic potential associated with the flexibility of FMS. (We will address the notion of flexibility and the concept of technology strategy in Chapters 3 and 5, respectively.)

The benefits of an FMS do not come cheaply; FMS units cost anywhere from $2 million to $50 million to install. However, this dollar figure is misleading for two reasons: (1) An FMS can be developed in stages, beginning with the acquisition of CNC machines or machining centers. (2) The cost of an FMS may in fact be less than the cost of achieving the same production capacity via conventional machinery. Although the characteristics and capabilities of an FMS differ from application to application, the example cited in Exhibit 2.7 will help to clarify the concept.

Exhibit 2.6   Benefits of Flexible Manufacturing Systems

	Prior Method	FMS	Improvement	Range of Improvements for Total Sample*
Machine tools	29	9	70%	60–90%
Direct labor	70	16	77%	50–88%
Machine efficiency	20%	70%	50%	15–90%
Processing time				
• Days	18.6	4.2	77%	30–90%
• Number of operations	15	8	47%	
Floor space	1,500m²	500m²	66%	30–80%
Product cost	$2,000	$1,000	50%	25–75%
Setups	13	5	50%	10–75%

*Based on a Frost and Sullivan, Inc. sample of 20 U.S. operating systems.

Source: Palframan [1987]. "FMS: Too Much, Too Soon," *Manufacturing Engineering,* p. 34.

Exhibit 2.7   An Example of an FMS Application

Cincinnati Milacron's Manufacturing Systems Division was given the responsibility for installing a flexible manufacturing system (FMS) in one of the company's most important corporate segments: Plastics Machinery Division (PMD).

PMD makes plastic injection molding machines in a variety of sizes with a sales price ranging from a few to many hundred thousand dollars.

The FMS consists of four machining centers, one automatic work changing station, a coordinate measuring machine, a wash station, four load/unload stations, one tooling station, three guided carts and a computer system for running the FMS.

In operation, work is prescheduled and prioritized for the computer and the computer directs the carts from the load/unload stations to the machining centers where the work is automatically unloaded to a shuttle.

When complete, the work is again automatically moved from the shuttle to a cart which may then take it to the wash station for cleaning and from there to the coordinate measuring machine or an unload station.

Source: Meredith, *Industrial Engineering* magazine, April 1988. Copyright Institute of Industrial Engineers.

A number of authors have described different forms of FMS according to the number of CNC machines installed and their arrangements (see for example, Kusiak [1985]). These classifications are essentially based on the recognition of "cell-type" progression as the cornerstone of FMS and consist of five groups:

1. Flexible manufacturing module (FMM)
2. Flexible manufacturing cell (FMC)
3. Flexible manufacturing group (FMG)
4. Flexible machining system (FMS)
5. Flexible manufacturing line (FML)

Exhibit 2.8 shows the relationship between these types of FMS, the variety of different parts, and the volume of production. As is clear from the exhibit, FML is the most comprehensive form of FMS systems. General Motors' well-publicized Saturn manufacturing facility is an example of an FML application (see Business Week [1985]). In contrast, FMM and FMC are the simplest dedicated to the production of a family of parts or products.

Computer Integrated Manufacturing (CIM). Standalone flexible manufacturing systems are often referred to as "islands of automation."[21] Ultimately, these cells will be linked with each other, with other manufacturing activities, and finally with other departments. This approach is known as computer integrated manufacturing (CIM). In a true sense, CIM is the ultimate

[21]Islands of automation occur where machines are grouped into cells, but where the cells are independent of each other.

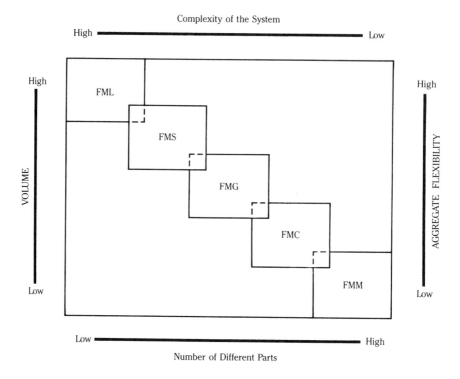

Exhibit 2.8   The Relationships Among Types of FMS, Volume, and Number of Different Parts
Source: Based on McDougall and Noori [1986]. From "Manfuacturing—Marketing Strategic Interface: The Impact of Flexible Manufacturing Systems," in Modeling and Design of Flexible Manufacturing Systems, N.Y.: Elsevier Science Publishers, p. 202.

version of the integrated system. It controls the factory through the use of a single master record that stores all important product and process information. CIM is the glue that holds everything together. Nazemetz et al. [1985] provides an excellent explanation of this concept:

> The ability to control all phases of the manufacturing system using computers from planning through design to shipping. CIM systems also imply the ability to take each system and subsystem that presently operates independently and create a single system which integrates all operations. This integration means that information could be shared by each area, thus making planning and control easier and more efficient. Rather than optimizing individual components, which often result in "islands of automation," the ultimate CIM system will optimize the operation as a whole.[22]

While most people consider CIM only in the technical sense, ". . .it is crucial to remember that CIM is not just another automated system, but a whole

[22]Nazemetz, Hamer, and Sadowski [1985], p. xi.

new way of looking at automation. Most importantly, CIM is not a technology. It is a way of using technology."[23] Exhibit 2.9 clarifies this point by illustrating the functional and managerial components of CIM. It shows the primary importance of complete functional integration, resource management, and communcation in fully realizing the technical capabilities of CIM.

CIM starts with the customer order, which becomes a master record for manufacturing. This record links the customer, research and engineering, manufacturing planning and plant operations into one complete system. In other words, CIM makes use of a computer network to integrate the new technologies

Exhibit 2.9 Functional and Managerial Components of CIM

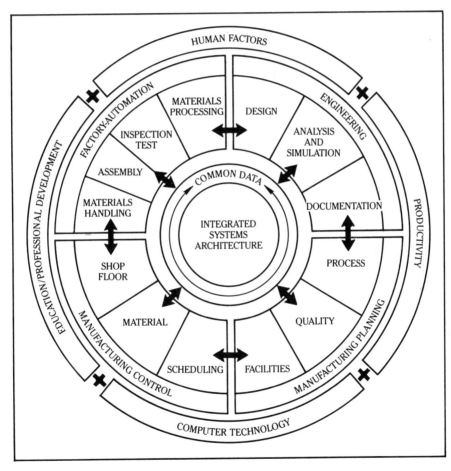

Source: Davis and Goedhart [1988]. From "Integrated Planning Functions," in *Intelligent Manufacturing*, edited by Michael Oliff, Copyright 1988 by The Benjamin/Cummings Publishing Company, Menlo Park, CA, p. 257

[23]Zygmont [1987], p. 33.

described previously to achieve optimal manufacturing efficiency. Exhibit 2.10 illustrates this concept.

It is difficult to separate the benefits of CIM from the advantages provided by the particular technologies that make up CIM. It is generally understood, however, that the integration of technologies to form a CIM results in vital synergistic benefits.[24] CIM applications are still at their early stages of development. As CIM develops further, manufacturing firms will gradually move towards the Factory of the Future concept. For example, planners at GM's Hamtramck facility in Michigan expect to cut the time involved in changing a manufacturing cell from one model to another from three days to 10 minutes. Exhibit 2.11 describes one of the first applications of CIM.

In short, CIM brings together complex manufacturing activities that have traditionally been isolated; it exemplifies how advanced operations technologies

Exhibit 2.10   Technical Components of CIM

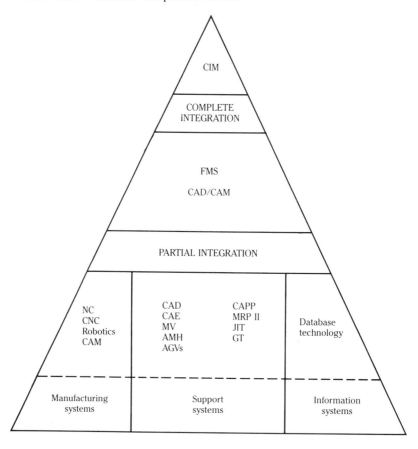

[24]Synergy refers to the phenomenon wherein the whole is greater than the sum of the parts.

Exhibit 2.11   CIM in Action

CIM is a reality at Tandem Austin. The Tandem computers are connected to and under the control of the Paperless Factory System, and direct the operation of the factory floor machines. Because the computer is always available, factory floor operations are never impacted because the computer is "down." As shown in the Exhibit below, Tandem is connected to several different types of equipment.

The connection to the AS/RS is direct from the Tandem to the DEC 11/44 controller on the Eaton-Kenway 8/8. The Paperless Factory system receives material at the back dock, updates the receiving system, determines the inspection quantity, assigns a storage location (with a hold) and routes the material to quality for inspection and to the AS/RS for put-away. After inspection, the inspected material is joined up at the AS/RS and the hold released by quality.

The Paperless Factory system maintains the inventory for a particular part in the entire stockroom (the AS/RS). When inventory levels fall below predetermined levels on the factory floor, the Paperless Factory system issues an electronic "pick" to the stockroom. The AS/RS operator simply indicates to the system that he is ready to begin picking. The Paperless Factory directs the Eaton-Kenway to deliver the correct bin to the operator and indicates the quantity to deliver and to what location. Packages are not broken. If 50 are required, and the package has 60, the package of 60 is issued and the system notified. Stock balances are corrected and the material is delivered to the floor. First-in/first-out is managed by the Paperless Factory system.

The entire material management system is operated without paper. Pick requests, miscellaneous issues, stock returns and over-issues are all performed electronically, without paper. The system maintains the inventory and stock level information for all material related activities, such as purchasing, inventory and quality data collection.

The result of the CIM implementation is that indirect labor normally associated with the operation of the material management function has remained flat while the growth of the operation has exceeded 60 percent every year for the last four years. Inventory accuracy in both the stockroom and four-wall inventory has exceeded 98 percent. The AS/RS unit is operating at peak efficiency because of the batching of picks and the issuing of material in bulk and the elimination of timely re-keying of material locations.

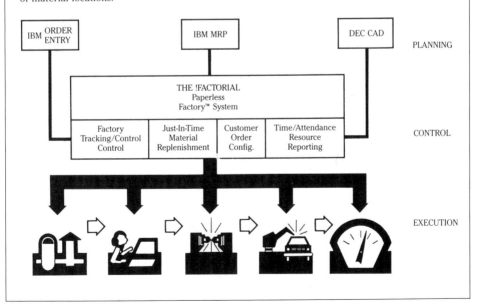

Source: Balcezak, *Industrial Engineering* magazine, September 1986. Copyright Institute of Industrial Engineers.

are in integration of manufacturing and information technologies (see Exhibit 2.12). Through CIM, the customer's objectives and the manufacturing process become one. This ensures optimum quality, flexibility, and efficiency.

Exhibit 2.12   Plant Information System Hierarchy

Level	System Hardware		Applications
5	Large mainframe computers	CORPO-RATE HOST	CIM MRP Payroll, CAD/CAM, Focus
4	Small mainframe computers Large minicomputers	PLANT HOST	Scheduling Receiving MRP
3	Minicomputers Data collection systems Machine monitoring Inventory control systems Process instrumentation systems Graphics systems	SUPERVISORY COMPUTER	Data Collection Time and attendance Order tracking Machine monitoring Inventory Activity reporting Graphics
2	Local area networks Dedicated networks Special interfaces	CONTROL AREA NETWORKS	Communiations Interface and networks Protocol software Menu-driven software
1	Programmable controllers Computer numerical controllers Microprocessors Relay panels	LOCAL CONTROL SYSTEMS	Real-time control programs Ladder logic Relay logic Micro programs
0	Machine data entry stations Limit switches Current transformers Pressure transducers Bar code readers	SENSORS	Basic inputs to all levels of control and information systems
	Interfaced to Process Equipment and Machinery		

Source: Ash, Gamble, and Shavit [1987], p. 57.

Management Philosophies

Just-In-Time (JIT).   JIT[25] is a management philosophy, and not a method or plan to achieve some end. The principle behind JIT is to eliminate the excess (waste) in all areas of the operation that does not add value to the final product.

[25]IBM calls it continuous flow manufacturing [CFM]; Harley Davidson, materials as needed [MAN]; and Motorola, inventory productivity process [IPP].

Ideally, this will create a pull system, which means that subassemblies, components, and raw materials are pulled forward as they are needed. For example, Electrolux can produce 300,000 vacuum cleaner bags per day; that's 3 per second. To produce bags at this rate, it uses JIT pull techniques to get materials from suppliers twice each day. However, getting the material to the back door is only one aspect (the manufacturing aspect) of JIT. The object is to synchronize all the activities of the firm to produce the right quality product at the lowest cost.

Although Myer's article [1980] is perhaps the first true paper to appear in North America on the application of JIT, the concept can be traced back to Henry Ford, who constructed his plant with the notion that materials were to flow into the assembly line as they were needed. This is the essence of JIT— having the right quantity, at the right time, in the right place, with perfect quality. Schonberger calls this "simplicity in all things" [1982]. Attaining these four objectives eliminates significant amounts of waste, such as setup time, machine breakdowns due to poor maintenance, rework time, waste material, and inventory storage. In fact, zero inventories and 100 percent quality are two of the basic principles in JIT. The following example illustrates the impressive results of one company utilizing this concept (for other examples, see Schonberger [1986, pp. 229–236]).

> In 1982, Xerox started out with 5,000 vendors; three years later it had about 300. . . .today Xerox claims a 66 percent improvement in outgoing product quality and about an 80 percent drop in parts rejected on the manufacturing line. More than half of all incoming materials now require no incoming inspection. And the company has achieved a 60 percent reduction in inventory (from three and a half months' supply to less than a month).[26]

As we noted, this way of thinking can be traced back over half a century. Nevertheless, the Japanese are credited with being the first to rediscover and benefit from JIT. North American companies are also beginning to recognize the contribution of JIT in their pursuit of manufacturing excellence. The change in philosophy needed to implement JIT successfully is similar to the change in attitude required to adopt any other form of new technology. However, JIT represents the softer side of management, and this makes its application even more difficult. For example, studies have shown that 75 percent of the reutrn from JIT comes from the people, while only 25 percent is generated by the technological components.

Burker [1988] suggests 10 specific principles which are crucial to successful JIT implementation. These are outlined in Exhibit 2.13. Many of the new manufacturing technologies described previously can be used by firms to reinforce a JIT approach. For example, the reduced setup times and increased flexibility associated with CAM and FMS lead to reduced work-in-process inventories and the ability to produce finished goods upon demand.

[26]Gould [1987], p. 60.

Exhibit 2.13   10 Principles to JIT Advancement

1. Management Education and Leadership for top management, operating management and the critical mass to understand the changes that need to be made.

2. Worker Involvement Programs that include small group activities and employee suggestion programs, using the power of problem-solving throughout an organization and communicating from the bottom up as well as from the top down.

3. Total Quality Control that begins with designing a product and process to produce a quality product that doesn't rely on inspection after it is produced.

4. Simplify Product Design so that it incorporates producibility, simplicity, standardization, modularity, flexibility, quality and cost effectiveness for total productivity.

5. Reduce Inventory Levels to approach zero because excess inventory is a waste and a coverup for problems and poor planning.

6. Produce in Small Lots, reducing setups and using a "pull" production system rather than a "push" system.

7. Improve Plant Layout by designing for flow rather than function, cutting manufacturing cycle times and emphasizing flexibility and responsiveness.

8. JIT Purchashing requires the vendors to be partners in a production process. Schedule materials so they flow from vendors on the appropriate monthly, weekly, daily or hourly basis with source inspection and validation required before delivery.

9. Total Preventive Maintenance means scheduling regular machine maintenance to eliminate breakdowns and protect the work flow.

10. Philosophy of solving and preventing problems, eliminating waste and striving for continuous improvement.

Source: Buker [1988], p. 55.

Group Technology (GT).   Group technology (GT) refers to the manufacturing practice of clustering similar parts into part families. This implies organizing the plant into cells of machines, with each cell being responsible for the complete production of one part family.

Parts can be grouped together based on similarities in design attributes or manufacturing characteristics. Parts grouped by design would generally have similar shapes and sizes, whereas parts grouped by manufacturing attributes would require the same processing steps during production (for example, drilling, grinding, coating, and assembly).

The plant layout of a firm utilizing GT would be significantly different from the layout of a firm following a more traditional process. For example, in a GT configuration, one cell might contain a lathe, a mill, and a grinder, and dedicated to producing 40 different parts that make up one part family. Another cell might contain two lathes, two mills, two drills and a grinder in order to produce 60 different parts that compose another part family. In contrast, the process layout concept has all the lathes located together, all the mills located together, and so on. In other words, with GT, cells of machines would be grouped together depending on the manufacturing requirements of a particular part family. Exhibit 2.14 illustrates the GT concept.

Traditional Process Layout

MACHINES	Parts				
	1	2	3	4	5
1	*	*	*	*	*
2		*		*	
3	*		*		
4		*		*	*

Group Technology Concept

Cell One

MACHINES	Parts	
	1	3
1	*	*
3	*	*

Cell Two

MACHINES	Parts		
	2	4	5
1	*	*	*
2	*	*	
4	*	*	*

Exhibit 2.14   Illustrating the Concept of Group Technology

Implemented successfully, GT can bring substantial benefits to a firm. Consider the following example:

> At the General Dynamics plant in Pomona, Calif., group technology has reduced production time by 55 percent. In some instances jobs that previously traveled a total of two and a half miles from machine to machine now travel less than 200 feet.[27]

In general, the benefits of GT may be roughly classified into eight areas:

1. Product Design. The grouping and classification of parts into families makes it easier for a design engineer to determine whether any existing (or slightly modified) products will serve a particular function before a completely new part is designed. That is, design standardization is promoted.
2. Tooling and Setup. The grouping of machines required to produce particular part families leads to increased standardization of tooling and decreased changeover times.
3. Materials Handling. The materials handling and movement of parts is reduced relative to traditional process layout plants.
4. Production Scheduling and Process Planning. Production scheduling is simplified, as scheduling must now accommodate only those parts in the part family associated with a particular production cell.

[27]Warner [1988], pp. 22–24.

5. Lead Times. Lead times are reduced through decreased design-to-production time requirements, and through reduced cycle times (a reduction in the actual production time required to produce a part).

6. Capacity. The reduction of lead times leads to an increase in manufacturing capacity.

7. Inventory. The reduction of lead times also leads to a reduction in inventory requirements, especially for work-in-process inventory.

8. Employees. Greater employee satisfaction is possible because a small group of employees are now responsible for the production of a part from raw materials to finished product. Along with this, product quality may improve because it will be easier to trace problems back to the source.

Schonberger [1987] advocates the principles of GT through a concept that he calls *frugal manufacturing*. By focusing a factory according to product family, emphasis can be placed on the production of a high-volume, quality product without unnecessary design attributes, as opposed to spending significant time and money on the logistical requirements inherent in a large process-type operation.

The following example describes a successful GT application:

Westinghouse's Asheville, North Carolina, plant has shortened machine setup times, eliminated many computer transactions, and cut inventories and direct labor costs by two-thirds, all by employing the concept of GT. The interior of the plant is arranged into clusters of machines and operators, or mini-factories, each making a finished product and organized according to flow of work. This eliminates the department-to-department distances usually spanned by conveyors. Machines are arranged by product type—you do not see shears all lined up together, but a shear next to a turret punch press next to a press brake.[28]

Although GT can provide significant advantages, many firms have been slow to adopt the concept for a number of reasons, including these:

1. The problems and costs of identifying, classifying, and coding part families.

2. The cost of rearranging the production system into machine cells.

3. The general resistance (of both workers and management) associated with any type of change.

Group technology is a natural (and in most cases necessary) philosophy to follow if the firm wishes to adopt a flexible manufacturing system or computer-aided process planning. With FMS, as with GT, machines are grouped in order to produce a family of parts. With CAPP, as with GT, parts are classified into families. However, as Schonberger [1987] also stresses, automation is not a necessary condition for the application of the GT concept. In other words, com-

---

[28]Schonberger [1987], p. 95.

panies do not have to spend enormous amounts of money automating in order to benefit from group technology.

We have discussed a number of advanced manufacturing technologies, including both hardware and management philosophies which have a fundamental impact on the ways goods are produced. Exhibit 2.15 presents a synopsis of the relevant technologies.

Exhibit 2.15 A Short Description of Some of the Advanced Manufacturing Technologies

Technology	Description
Numerical Control (NC) Machines	A tape-driven machine tool.
Computer Numerical Control (CNC)	A single machine tool controlled by a dedicated computer.
Direct Numerical Control (DNC)	A number of machine tools controlled by a central computer.
Industrial Robots	A general purpose, multifunctional, controllable machine.
Computer Process Monitoring (CPM)	The use of a computer to gather information about the manufacturing process.
Computer Process Control (CPC)	The use of a computer to monitor and adjust the manufacturing process.
Computer-Aided Manufacturing (CAM)	The complete range of computer applications in direct manufacturing activities.
Computer-Aided Design (CAD)	The use of a computer to create or modify engineering designs.
Computer-Aided Engineering (CAE)	Computerized testing of designs.
Computer-Aided Process Planning (CAPP)	Computer-generated process plans.
Machine Vision	Computerized vision systems used in manufacturing to inspect, recognize, gauge, guide, and control parts.
Automated Materials Handling	The use of computers to direct the movement of inventories.
Manufacturing Resource Planning (MRP II)	A computerized system used to plan the resources of a manufacturing company.
CAD/CAM	The integration of computer-aided design and computer-aided manufacturing.
Flexible Manufacturing Systems (FMS)	A group of machines joined by an automated materials handling system and controlled by a computer.
Computer-Integrated Manufacturing (CIM)	The computerized integration and control of all of the functions of the manufacturing system.
Just-In-Time (JIT)	A philosophy which advocates the elimination of excess (waste) in all areas of the operation that does not add value to the final product.
Group Technology (GT)	The organization of machines into cells, with each cell being used to produce a different family of parts.

ADVANCED INFORMATION TECHNOLOGIES

Advanced Information Technologies (AIT) not only contribute to the provision of services; they are also fundamental to effective utilization of AMT. In fact, one of the basic tenets of CIM is that it effectively integrates advanced manufacturing technologies with advanced information technologies. The following example verifies this point:

> CIM has been introduced at Ford Electronics Manufacturing Corp. of Markham, Ontario, one of the most automated electronics plants in Canada. The CIM project at Ford encompasses robots, numerical-control machines, engineering, design, the shop floor, management information, quality control, and just-in-time materials handling, all tied to a common database.[29]

We will look now at different forms of AIT, including computerized database systems and artificial intelligence.

Computerized Database Systems

A database is simply a collection of data maintained in some organized way.[30] When computers first became affordable, one of their primary uses was for the collection and manipulation of data. The original approach was to design the specific data files required for each job with the underlying logic of the program(s) to use that data.

An improvement on this initial approach led to the development of a common centralized database containing all the relevant information and accessible by all programs. Centralization helps eliminate redundant data entry and ensures that data used by various departments are consistent.

Common Database Systems.   The first aggregated systems were *hierarchical* systems which stored information in organizational chart form. However, these systems are limited to certain types of information relationships. The next database systems were the *network* models, which addressed the problems associated with the hierarchical systems. Nevertheless, they also have problems, the greatest of which is inflexibility. Every program that uses a network database has to state explicitly where all the information is stored and how to access the information. Consequently, if a new program requires that the underlying network design change, every program using the database could potentially be affected. This causes major problems in large installations, when several teams are working on several projects at once, and each team has its own list of changes to the database which would affect each of the other teams.

Relational Databases.   *Relational* databases offer the most significant potential for achieving a fully integrated system. Although the concept behind relational databases has been around since at least 1970 (Codd [1970], it is only

---

[29]Romain [1988], p. C24.

[30]Throughout this section, the term *database* will be used to refer to such collections stored on computers, although any organized data such as those found in a filing cabinet or even a shoebox can also be considered a database.

recently that their applications, particularly in manufacturing environments, have become apparent.

The best quality of relational databases is their simplicity and ease of use.[31] In principle, these systems are based on data independence. That is, with relational systems tables can be modified at any time, and only the programs that use the modified tables are affected. This enables relational databases to offer more flexibility than network systems because the connections among data which are fully specified in the network model are not defined in relational databases. Any two tables can be related to each other in any way, even if that relationship was not considered by the database designers. For example, an effort to form car pools might look for people with common postal codes, even though that was not the original intention of the postal code information in the database.

One of the primary complaints concerning relational databases is their performance time. That is, with these systems, relationships are determined at execution time rather than when the program is written. Therefore, requests for data are produced more slowly. To improve the speed, the database system keeps an internal index which allows it to look up the attributes more quickly. Recent reports (Weinburg [1987]), suggest that new relational database products perform as fast or faster than network databases in retrieving information. As more and more intelligence is applied to relational database design, it appears it will be possible to have the database management system create and manipulate efficient data structures internally, while maintaining the user view of the database as just a group of tables.

There are at least four major barriers to the widespread application of relational databases in manufacturing operations, especially with reference to CIM. These are:

1. The performance speed of relational databases
2. The complexity involved in achieving transactional integration—that is, the complexity involved in using only one transaction to update the information system
3. The size of the database needed to support CIM
4. The incompatibility of existing functional database systems

Research and development in various fields is geared toward alleviating the problems in these four areas. In particular, advances in artificial intelligence and expert systems will improve the performance speed and transactional integration capabilities of relational databases.

Distributed Databases.   A perceived problem with centralized databases, particularly when CIM is applied, is that the system needs to communicate with

---

[31]A relational database is simply a collection of tables, with each table consisting of a rectangular grid of rows and columns. Each column has an attribute name, such as Name or Address, and each row contains data for each of the columns. For example, the first row might contain information about employee Smith, the second Jones, and so forth.

multiple users (sometimes thousands) simultaneously, necessitating powerful computer hardware to hold the centralized data. This is even more evident given the varied nature of the data required by different users. For example, designers require complex graphics capabilities; engineers must perform complex numerical calculations; and manufacturing requires high performance speeds. *Distributed databases* can be used to allocate data in the database among many computers. In other words, designers might have their own computer with CAD information, engineering might have a computer capable of performing the numerical calculations it requires, and manufacturing would have another computer with CAM information. Information would be shared among these distributed systems only when requested or required.

Distributed database theory is still largely a research topic. In the future, these systems will be able to access data from anywhere in the network of computers. Further, these accesses will be efficient, so that information which is frequently requested will automatically be copied to the requested computer. For example, if a particular PC user frequently accesses current work-in-progress information stored on the manufacturing mainframe computer, the database management system would copy the information to his PC and automatically update the file whenever the information on the mainframe changed.

Manufacturing Automation Protocol (MAP).   Many firms utilize computer support for various manufacturing activities. However, in many cases this has resulted in the development and acquisition of numerous hardware and software packages that perform like islands of automation. So long as these island solutions (CNC machines, robotics, or CAD/CAM systems) are judged independently and there is no requirement to share information among them, there is no need to be concerned with communications between devices. In an integrated manufacturing environment, however, such connections are essential.

Recognizing this drawback, an international standard known as the *OSI (open systems interconnections)* format has begun to receive industrial acceptance. Conceptually, this format allows various computers and electronic devices to communicate. In North America, GM, in conjunction with Boeing Computer Services and IBM, have applied the OSI concept and together are completing the development of what is known as manufacturing automation protocol (MAP). Briefly stated, MAP is a communications standard that will enable component technologies such as computers, CNC machines, and robots to be interconnected. MAP standards are recognized by many suppliers and users of technology, and eventually the ability to connect different equipment may no longer be an issue. Presently, however, the ability to integrate various technologies presents a significant problem that must be resolved:

> In the last eight years, General Motors has spent over $40 billion on new manufacturing equipment in an effort to turn itself into the cheapest carmaker in America. But GM knows that time is running out; that without MAP many of the benefits of factory automation will be squandered. All its clever high-

tech tools will remain deaf and dumb—capable of doing an honest day's work, but unable to use their time intelligently. In 1986, GM started wiring up its first factory, a truck assembly plant in Pontiac, Michigan, containing 21 types of machines from 13 different suppliers. Since then, it has connected up machines in several more factories to its computers, and has set a deadline of 1990 for having all its new flexible manufacturing plants communicating via MAP to the corporate-planning and marketing departments.[32]

While many see MAP as the solution to the factory communications problem, others suggest that MAP's software requirements may be inordinately complex and its hardware too expensive. This has led to the development of simpler, cheaper systems such as Ethernet, DECnet, and Allen-Bradley's Vistanet. In short, it appears that manufacturing companies planning for any degree of integration would have to use either MAP or some other standard protocol to connect their islands of automation in order to benefit fully from the potential of advanced technologies.

Artificial Intelligence (AI)

AI was once considered theoretical technology; however, great advances have been made in this area to make it practical, feasible, and eventually, essential. It is thought that AI will account for over 20 percent of the computer market by the year 2000 (see Barnes [1986]). To draw an appropriate comparison, AI may do to intellectual donkey work what the robot did to manual labor. Two classifications of AI which we will discuss in this part are (1) machine intelligence, and (2) expert systems.

Machine Intelligence.   Many applications of robots today utilize what is referrerd to as machine intelligence. *Machine intelligence* occurs when robots become capable of applying knowledge in order to respond to various environmental situations. This typically involves the application of vision systems, range and proximity sensors, and contact sensors. A machine may not be creative, but it has total recall, and its mind does not wander. It never tires, and it certainly will never go on strike! The following example illustrates the potential of intelligent robots:

A vision system was used at the Chevrolet Motor Division of General Motors in Flint, Michigan to determine if valve covers for engines were properly assembled. Four cameras were mounted overhead in protective enclosures with transparent windows. The first task performed by the vision system was to determine whether a left- or right-side cover was being inspected. The second task was to determine the presence or absence of all necessary characteristics, such as clinch nuts, metal brackets, baffles, and holes. This step also deter-

---

[32]Adapted from Valery [1987], p. 10.

mined whether any extra parts had been added. This information was analyzed, and an accept or reject decision was made. This decision information was then given to the robot controller, which also had information available from other tests. The robot controller then determined whether the part should be put into an accept chute, a visual reject chute, or a leak test reject chute. The robot then put the part in the appropriate location. The system increased productivity from 300 to 1,200 parts per hour—a 400 percent productivity increase with 100 percent inspection.[33]

An interesting advance in machine intelligence is the use of voice to control robots. With voice control, robots respond to various commands through speech recognition equipment. Research in this area promises a simple way to utilize robots and takes us a step closer to the factory of the future. To date, a number of different speech recognition systems have been developed worldwide. Recognition capabilities presently are limited to about 32 to 260 words.

Expert Systems (ES). To introduce the topic of expert systems (ES), let us consider the following definition:

> Computer programs that use specialized symbolic reasoning to solve difficult problems well. (They)...(1) use specialized knowledge about a particular problem area (such as geological analysis or computer configuration) rather than just generate purpose knowledge that would apply to all problems, (2) use symbolic (and often qualitative) reasoning rather than just numerical calculations, and (3) perform at a level of competence that is better than that of nonexpert humans.[34]

Expert systems apply heuristic reasoning (rules of thumb) rather than algorithms (precise rules) to general good but not necessarily optimal answers. Expert systems can be used to solve problems that have previously been unsolvable using the conventional "if...then" programming technique. The following is a typical example of ES contributions:

> Digital Equipment Corporation claims to save $25 million a year in labor costs using an expert system that converts product orders into detailed engineering parts specifications. The system, called XCON, replaces a team of engineers that had to develop a special configuration for each computer system ordered. Designing XCON without expert system technology would have been impossible because conventional programs are too rigid.[35]

According to Kumara et al.[36], an expert system is comprised of:

[33]Hall and Hall [1985], p. 126.
[34]Luconi, Malone, and Morton [1986], p. 4.
[35]Adapted from Guterl [1986], p. 31.
[36]Kumara, et al. [1986], p. 1108.

1. Knowledge consisting of domain-related facts
2. Knowledge consisting of domain-related rules for drawing inferences
3. An interpreter that applies the rules
4. An ordering mechanism that orders the application of rules
5. An enforcer that ensures consistency when new knowledge is created or deleted from the knowledge base
6. A justifier that explains the system's reasoning

Exhibit 2.16 shows the basic structure of an expert system.

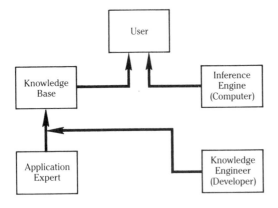

Exhibit 2.16   The Basic Structure of an Expert System

The role of a knowledge engineer, or the developer of the system, is to extract knowledge from the application expert and input it into the system. The purpose of this is to get the application expert to articulate the rules of thumb used in practicing the trade, so that this expertise can be exercised by others when using the system. For example:

> At American Express Co., they call the new computer "Laurel's brain." It is actually an expert system based on the decision-making talents of Laurel Miller, a credit authorization manager. With Laurel's expertise fed into its memory, the system weeds out bad risks among the company's 23 million cardholders. Amex expects big productivity and financial gains from its investment in "Laurel's brain." About 60 percent of the savings will come from a reduction in losses from authorizing fradulent charges; the system also cuts the time it takes to make decisions by 25 percent. As a result, Amex hopes to keep up with an anticipated 25 percent increase in credit-card volume without having to hire more authorizers.[37]

One of the major problems with heuristic reasoning is that the expert is unlikely to be fully aware of the process he/she actually uses to solve the

[37]Guterl [1986], p. 32.

problem(s). Put another way: Experts often do not know what they know! Still, there is no doubt that expert systems are beginning to have a major impact on both manufacturing and service industries. They are currently being used in medicine, oil field research, complex engine repair, computer configuration, financial and tax planning in banks and insurance companies, and brokerage houses. They have also been adopted by manufacturing companies as diverse as General Electric, Proctor and Gamble, General Motors, Ford, and Campbell Soup (Guterl [1986], Kumara et al. [1986] and Kupfer [1987]).[38]

In this section we have used a great deal of terminology and acronyms to define the various forms of advanced information technologies. Exhibit 2.17 provides a summary of these for an easy reference.

Exhibit 2.17   A Short Description of Some Advanced Information Technologies

Technology	Description
Computerized Database System	A collection of data stored on a computer
Common Database System	A centralized database containing all the data used by an organization
Relational Database	A common database that is easy to understand and flexible to use
Distributed Databases	The distribution of common data among many computers
Manufacturing Automation Protocol (MAP)	A communications standard which enables component technologies to be interconnected
Artificial Intelligence (AI)	The ability to apply reasoning to solve a problem
Machine Intelligence	Computer programs that use "if-then" logic to respond to various environmental stimuli
Expert Systems (ES)	Computer programs that apply heuristic reasoning to solve problems that do not have a discernible optimal answer

CONCLUDING OBSERVATIONS

The primary objectives of this chapter were to define the new technology as the term is used in this book, and to provide a general understanding of different forms of the technologies of interest. In general, the new technology is defined as any technology that has an explicit impact on the way a company produces its products or provides its services. Advanced technology is a subset of new technology characterized by high flexibility and rapid rate of change. The notion of new technology used in this book is based on advanced operations technology. It is the dynamics of this form of technology which requires a fundamentally different approach to the management of the firm's operations.

Advanced operation technologies were further divided into advanced manufacturing technologies (AMT) and advanced information technologies

---

[38]For further reading on the development and the structuring of expert systems, see Keller [1987].

(AIT). Cognizance of the potential of these technologies is essential in understanding and assessing the benefits and the difficulties of acquiring and implementing them. The aim of this book is to provide managers (or future managers) with information that will enable them to understand the issues involved in acquiring, implementing, and managing the new technology.

RECOMMENDED READINGS

VALERY, N. [1987].   "Factory of the Future." *The Economist,* May 30, pp. 3–18.

DISCUSSION QUESTIONS

1. A firm's capacity to expand and remain competitive depends on its endowment of resources, its stock of technical and managerial knowledge, its structure, and its political and economic organization. The resource base serves as a source of factors of production, or inputs, from which various goods and services are generated. As the system of production becomes complex, managing these resources becomes more difficult. Do you think automation would necessarily add to the already existing set of (complex) problems confronting managers today? Comment.
2. Explain what you believe to be the characteristics and capabilities of a factory of the future.
3. Given our definition of the new technology and the focus of this book, is the management of technology more important now than it has been in the past? Explain.

REFERENCES AND BIBLIOGRAPHY

ASH, R. H., R. L. GAMBLE, and G. SHAVIT [1987].   "Integrating Plant and Facility Management Systems." *Plant Engineering,* February, pp. 56–59.

AYREN, R. U. [1986].   "Computer-Integrated Manufacturing and the Next Industrial Revolution." In J. Dermer (ed.), *Competitiveness Through Technology.* Lexington Books, Lexington, Mass., pp. 11–24.

BARNES, J. [1986].   "Artificial Intelligence." *Computers in Industry,* Spring.

BOCK, G. [1987].   "Limping Along in Robot Land." *Time,* July 13, pp. 38–39.

BRODY, H. [1986].   "The Robot: Just Another Machine?" *High Technology,* October, pp. 31, 35.

BUKER, D. W. [1988].   "10 Principles to JIT Advancement." *Journal of Manufacturing Systems,* p. 55.

Business Week [1985].   "How GM's Saturn Could Run Rings Around Old-Style Carmakers." January 28, pp. 126–128.

BYLINSKY, G. [1987].   "Invasion of the Service Robots." *Fortune,* September 14, pp. 81–88.

CODD, E. F. [1970].   "A Relational Model of Shared Data for Large Shared Data Banks." *Communications of the ACM,* Volume 13, pp. 377–397.

DAVIS, E. W., and J. L. GOEDHART [1988].   "Integrated Planning Frontiers." In M. D. Oliff (ed.), *Intelligent Manufacturing.* Proceedings from the First International Conference on Expert Systems and Leading Edge in Production Planning and Control. The Benjamin/Cummings Publishing Company, Menlo Park, California, pp. 249–276.

DOOLITTLE, M. G. [1987].   "CAD System Slashes Design Time." *Manufacturing Engineering,* February, pp. 55–56.

EBEL, K. H., and E. ULRICH [1987].   "Some Workplace Effects of CAD and CAM." *International Labour Review,* Volume 126, No. 3, May–June, pp. 351–370.

ELLUL, J. [1964].   *The Technological Society.* Alfred A. Knopf, New York.

EVANS, J. R., D. R. ANDERSON, D. J. SWEENEY, and T. A. WILLIAMS [1987].   *Applied Production and Operations Management,* 2nd ed. West, Boulder, Colorado.

FRASER, J. M. [1985]. "Justification of Flexible Manufacturing Systems," *Decision Science.* Volume 18, No. 3, pp. 51–55.

Frost and Sullivan Inc. [1985]. "Industrial Vision Systems Market in the U.S." A Company Report, Summer.

GOULD, L. [1987]. "Xerox Strikes Success." *Managing Automation,* July, pp. 60–63.

GUNN, T. G. [1985]. "CIM Must Start at the Top." *Production,* March, pp. 43–49.

GUTERL, F. V. [1986]. "Computers Think for Business." *Dun's Business Month,* October, pp. 30–37.

HALL, E. L., and B. C., HALL [1985]. *Robotics: A User Friendly Introduction.* Holt, Rinehart and Winston, New York.

HESS, G. J. [1984]. "Computer Integrated Flexible Manufacturing—Ingersoll Milling Maching Company. *Conference Proceedings: Synergy '84,* pp. 37–40.

Industrial Engineering [1886]. "CIM in Action." September, p. 71.

KAPLAN, R. S. [1986]. "Must CIM Be Justified by Faith Alone?" *Harvard Business Review,* March–April, pp. 87–95.

KELLER, R. [1987]. *Expert Systems Technology.* Prentice Hall, Englewood Cliffs, N.J.

KUMARA, S.R.T., S. JOSHI, R. L. KASHYAP, C. L. MOODIE, and T. C. CHANG [1986]. "Expert System in Industrial Engineering." *International Journal of Production Research,* Volume 24, No. 5, pp. 1107–1125.

KUSIAK, A. [1985]. "Flexible Manufacturing Systems: A Structural Approach." *International Journal of Production Research,* Volume 23, No. 6, pp. 1057–1073.

KUPFER, A. [1987]. "Now, Live Experts on a Floppy Disk." *Fortune,* October 12, pp. 69–82.

LAWRENCE, J. [1984]. "Levels of Automation." *Systems International,* March.

LUCONI, F. L., T. W. MALONE, and M.S.S. MORTON [1986]. "Expert Systems: The Next Challenge for Managers." *Sloan Management Review,* Summer, pp. 3–13.

LUPIDUS, S. N. [1986]. "Cost-Justifying Vision." *Quality,* June, pp. 10–12.

MYERS, C. R. [1980]. "Japan Vs. United States—How Materials Management Differ." Satellite Inventory Management and Material Planning Seminar Proceeding, Atlanta, Ga., APICS, pp. 9, 14.

McDOUGALL, G., and H. NOORI [1986]. "Manufcaturing–Marketing Strategic Interface: The Impact of Flexible Manufacturing Systems." In A. Kusiak (ed.), *Modelling and Design of Flexible Manufacturing Systems.* Elsevier, New York, pp. 189–205.

MELKANOFF, M. A. [1984]. "The CIMS Database: Goals, Problems, Case Studies, and Proposed Approaches Outlined." *Industrial Engineering,* November, pp. 78–93.

MEREDITH, J. [1988]. "Installation of Flexible Manufacturing System Teaches Management Lessons in Integration, Labor, Cost, Benefits." *Industrial Engineering,* April, pp. 18–27.

MEREDITH, J. [1987]. "The Strategic Advantages of New Manufacturing Technologies for Small Firms." *Strategic Management Journal,* Volume 8, pp. 249–258.

NAZEMETZ, J., W. HAMMER, and R. SADOWSKI [1985]. "Computer Integrated Manufacturing Systems: Selected Readings." *Industrial Engineering and Management Press.*

PALFRAMAN, D. [1987]. "FMS: Too Much, Too Soon." *Manufacturing Engineering,* March, p. 34.

RAMO, S. [1988]. "How to Revive U.S. High Tech." *Fortune,* May, pp. 124–133.

ROMAIN, K. [1988]. "Auto Industry Moves to Forefront as Automation Continues Advance." *Globe and Mail,* Monday, March 7, p. C24.

SARLIN, R. A. [1985]. "CIMS Methodology is Applied to CAD/CAM Integration in Factory of Future." *Industrial Engineering,* September, pp. 58–64.

SAUL, G. [1985]. "Flexible Manufacturing System Is CIM Implemented at the Shop Floor Level." *Industrial Engineering,* pp. 35–39.

SCHONBERGER, R. J. [1987]. "Frugal Manufacturing." *Harvard Business Review,* September–October, pp. 95–100.

SCHONBERGER, R. J. [1986]. *World Class Manufacturing.* The Free Press, New York.

SCHONBERGER, R. J. [1982]. *Japanese Manufacturing Techniques: Nine Hidden Lessons in Simplicity.* The Free Press, New York.

STEED, G., and S., TIFFIN [1986]. "Discussion Paper: A National Consultation on Emerging Technology." Science Council of Canada, May.

SKINNER, W. [1969]. "Manufacturing—Missing Link in Corporate Strategy." *Harvard Business Review,* May–June, pp. 136–145.

VALERY, N. [1987]. "Factory of the Future." *The Economist,* May 30, pp. 3–18.

VAN BERGEN, J., and G. HOBBS. "Automated Part Manufacturing at Boart Canada." *CAD/CAM & Robotics,* June, pp. 100–101.

VESTER, J. [1987]. "The Increasing Importance of AGV's in Inventory Control." *P&IM Review,* November, pp. 36–39.

WARNER, T. [1988]. "Computers as a Competitive Burden." *Technology Review*, February–March, pp. 22–24.

WEINBURG, B. [1987]. Speech given in Toronto, March. Ms. Weinburg is the president of Codd and Date Associates, one of the foremost consulting companies in the database field.

WENZEL, C. D. [1988]. "Computerized Storage System Speeds Parts Delivery, Increases Inventory Accuracy, Saves Money." *Industrial Engineering*, Volume 20, No. 3, March, pp. 48–54.

WOLFE, P. M. [1985]. "Computer Aided Process Planning Is Link Between CAD and CAM." *Industrial Engineering*, August, pp. 72–77.

ZELENY, M. [1986]. "High Technology Management." *Human Systems Management*, Volume 6, pp. 109–120.

ZYGMONT, J. [1987]. "Manufacturers Move Toward Computer Integration." *High Technology*, February, p. 33.

ZYGMONT, J. [1986]. "Guided Vehicles Set Manufacturing in Motion." *High Technology*, December, pp. 16–21.

From Inception to Reality:
A Visual Process of Design
to the Final Assembly of a Car
(Photos 1–19)

Photo #1 *Source: Manufacturing Systems,* March 1988, "Graphics Terminals: A Critical Link in Shop Floor Automation," by Gary Conner, p. 56.

A flexible machining cell can take advantage of a graphics terminal for shop-floor information.

Photo #2 *Source: Managing Automation,* June 1987, p. 58.

Autocarrier assembly, essential for moving parts and subassembly components.

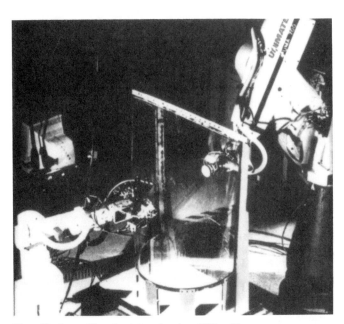

Photo #3 *Source: Managing Automation,* June 1987, p. 58.

Sensor robots are used to select the right parts.

Photographs 4 through 19
Display the Use of Conveyors,
Carriers, and AGVS
for Moving Semi-Finished Parts
to Different Production Cells.

Photo #4 *Source: Manufacturing Systems,* May 1988, "Three Approaches to Automated Material Handling," by Daniel Sullivan, p. 35.

Photo #5 *Source: Managing Automation,* June 1987, p. 58.

Photo #6 *Source: Managing Automation,* June 1987, p. 58.

Photo #7 *Source: Managing Automation,* June 1987, p. 58.

Photo #8   *Source: Managing Automation,* June 1987, p. 58.

Photo #9   *Source: Managing Automation,* June 1987, p. 58.

Photo #10 *Source: Materials Handling Engineering,* May 1988, "Automated Factory: It Takes More Than Machinery," by Clyde E. Witt, p. 48.

Photo #11 *Source: Managing Automation,* June 1987, p. 58.

Photo #12 *Source: Managing Automation*, June 1987, "European Autos:
Quality Endurance," by Robert Malone, p. 63.

Photo #13 *Source: Managing Automation*, June 1987, p. 58.

Photo #14   *Source: Managing Automation,* June 1987, p. 58.

Photo #15   *Source: Managing Automation,* June 1987, p. 58.

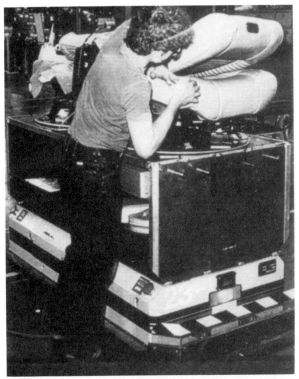

Photo #16   *Source: Managing Automation,* June 1987, "European Autos: Quality Endurance," by Robert Malone, p. 63.

Photo #17   *Source: Managing Automation,* June 1987, p. 58.

Photo #18 *Source: Managing Automation,* June 1987, p. 58.

Photo #19 *Source: Managing Automation,* June 1987, p. 58.

Chapter Three

THE IMPETUS FOR TECHNOLOGY ADOPTION

Technology is not the first, second, or third wave.
It is the permanent wave. But it is now of tidal
proportions, and rising. Everything is carried by it.
                                                    Derm Barrett

INTRODUCTION

The world revolves around change. Throughout history, technological adoption in response to environmental forces has to a large degree determined the economic fate of nations, firms, and individuals. Today, the key to survival for many firms is the ability to capitalize effectively on the immense potential of advancing technology and channel it for the economic and strategic well-being of the comany. To do this, firms must be able to understand the changes that are unfolding in their surroundings. The purpose of this chapter is to discuss the transformation that is taking place in today's business environment and explain how the new technology can be used effectively to respond to these challenges. Exhibit 3.1 provides a brief overview of the thrust of the chapter.

FACTORS PROMOTING TECHNOLOGY ACQUISITION

Responding to the challenges of the marketplace compels firms to employ new production methods to improve product quality and delivery reliability, to reduce costs, and above all, to achieve greater flexibility. Put simply, utilization of the growth potential of product and process innovation is required to compete successfully in today's dynamic environment. Companies that fail to recognize the potential of advanced technologies will not be able to respond to the changes in the marketplace and are doomed to failure. Hence the popular saying,

Exhibit 3.1   The Impetus for Technology Adoption

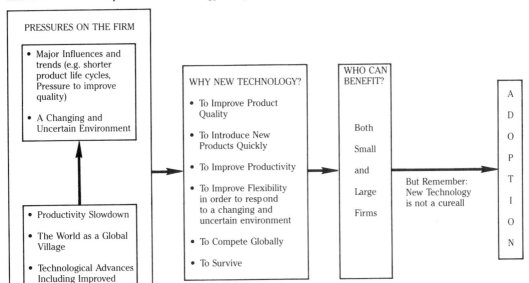

"Automate, Emigrate, or Evaporate!" A look at the declines in the watch and clock making industry in Germany and the steel industry in the 1970s and early 1980s in the United States illustrates this point.

Generally, the need for new technology stems from three factors:

1. A slowdown in productivity growth
2. Increased international competition
3. Advances in technologies

The Productivity Slowdown

From an operations perspective, productivity is considered a very effective measure of the economic performance of a firm. Stagnant productivity levels of the late 1970s, along with the recession of the early 1980s and increased international competition, practically forced many North American firms to consider ways to improve productivity.

Investment in new technology has been an important factor in the recent productivity improvements of some North American firms; productivity levels have once again reached the 3 to 4 percent growth rate of the late 1960s and early 1970s. Nevertheless, this recent resurgence has by no means won the competitive battle for North American firms! Increasing international competition has been intensifying the pressure on these firms to improve even further. The rapid pace of technological advancement in other countries (see Nasar [1988]) and the ability of foreign firms to respond quickly to maket needs raise questions about the merit of focusing on productivity improvement.

Skinner [1985] has effectively argued that one important reason for the decline in the competitiveness of North American firms has been management's preoccupation with improving productivity. Skinner further suggests that improving productivity (maximizing production per labor hour and per machine hour) is not the only rule for success in today's environment. Firms must also be concerned with improving quality, flexibility, and reliability. Yet it is possible that managers shy away from these objectives as they tend to worsen traditional productivity measures. Productivity levels, while an important measure of a firm's operations are by no means the only objective that should be considered; productivity must be evaluated in the context of other important factors. (These issues and the impact of technology on productivity will be discussed further in Chapter 6).

International Competition

The growth of international competition is arguably the most significant factor that has stimulated the reassessment of North American business practices in general, and the need for new technology in particular. Increased global competition has shaken the manufacturing sector and changed the rules of the competitive game. It has caused North American firms to lose customers, to suffer shrinking profit margins, and in some cases, to fail. Consider the following example:

> Up until recently, developments in the U.S. auto industry were determined mostly by government policies and economic forces particular to North America. The sheer extent of the U.S. market and its productive base had long guaranteed the industry a largely self-contained posture. Over the past 15 years, however, the competitive boundaries have expanded drastically until now they are virtually worldwide in scope.[1]

The automobile industry is by no means an isolated example. Others, including the television, textile, machine tool, household appliance, steel, computer, aerospace, and telecommunications industries, have been affected significantly as well. The changes encompass both consumer and industrial goods. As international competition becomes even more prevalent in the future, firms will be forced to reorient their objectives and strategies from a national to an international focus. Yet in spite of this realization, North American firms have been unusually slow in adopting new technology as a response strategy, especially when compared to Japan. Consider the following two points:

[1]Abernathy et al. [1981], p. 71.

- It is estimated that Japan, with half the population of the U.S., has 50 percent more flexible manufacturing systems, and 40 percent more than the UK, Germany, France, and Italy combined.[2]
- (Approximately) 40 percent of the computerized numerically controlled machine tools installed throughout the world have been in Japan, twice the U.S. number. Moreover, not only are there 2.5 times more CNC machines, there are five times as many engineers and four times as many skilled workers trained to use them.[3]

There are a number of identifiable reasons for the acceleration of international competition in recent years, including the following:

1. Improved transportation and communication networks—for example, Texas Instruments' global network for its semiconductor designs (see Kirkland [1988])
2. A reduction of trade barriers
3. Universal access to both basic and advanced industrial knowhow and technology
4. A colossal increase in manufacturing output by countries outside North America
5. New types of international technology agreements
6. The ability of small firms to compete with larger multinationals by focusing on niche markets

The first two points are relatively straightforward; the last four will be discussed further.

Universal Access to Technology.   The Industrial Revolution and its powerful descendant, the micro-electronics revolution, have ceased to be the exclusive property of Western countries. Take integrated circuit (IC) manufacturing, for example. At one point not too long ago, this was the exclusive domain of Western countries and primarily the United States. While the United States continues to have a technical lead in certain sophisticated IC products, Japan has all but taken over the high-volume, dynamic random-access memory market, and South Korean companies today have enough manufacturing capacity in place to supply half the world demand for these products.

Scientists and technically trained personnel have also become more available throughout the world. Consider India:

> Since 1950 the number of Indians with degrees in science or engineering has blossomed from 190,000 to 2.6 million—a talent pool exceeded only by the U.S. and the Soviet Union.[4]

---

[2]McMillan [1987], p. 65.
[3]McMillan [1987], p. 66.
[4]Kirkland [1988], p. 42.

In short, the knowledge and technology required to compete in the global economy are now available to many more nations.

Increase in Manufacturing Output.   There has been a proliferation of goods produced throughout the world. For example, Japan's aggregate manufacturing output jumped by a total of 65.2 percent between 1977 and 1984, as compared to an increase of 17.9 percent in the United States, and 10.1 percent in Canada (CAD/CAM Newsletter [1987]). Newly industrialized countries such as Brazil, South Korea, and Singapore are becoming serious contenders by taking advantage of their cheap labor and mass producing goods for export. This increase in the total number of products manufactured worldwide is one of the prime factors pushing companies to become more cost effective, competitive, and customer focused.

International Technology Agreements.   Various forms of technology accords are making the transfer of technology across international boundaries more widespread than ever before; these types of agreements are one of the main reasons for the universal access to technological knowhow. Roman and Puett [1983] have identified a number of such agreements, including:

1. Licensing. Purchasing the rights to utilize someone else's invention.
2. Agency Agreements. The use of locally based agents to represent the company in a foreign country.
3. Franchise. A hybrid form of licensing in which the franchiser usually provides some form of support (for example, marketing, training, capital).
4. Coproduction. A domestic and a foreign firm combine componentry and technology to produce a finished product; final assembly of the product is accomplished in the foreign country by the foreign firm.
5. Joint Ventures. Two or more firms combine their interestes in a particular business enterprise and agree to share the profits or losses jointly or in proportion to their contribution. "For example, Motorola and Toshiba have a joint venture based on the former's lead in microprocessor technology and the latter's lead in memory chips."[5]
6. Technological Consortiums. Ventures between two or more nations and/or between two or more companies where extensive resources are required to accomplish a technological objective. For example, a newly formed Canadian consortium, including Hydro-Quebec, Atomic Energy of Canada Ltd. and Canada Wire and Cable Ltd., is planning a $5 million laboratory project to produce a practical high-temperature superconductor.[6]

Modular manufacturing policies and multinational manufacturers are also increasing the scope of international operations. An example of the former

[5]Dallmeyer [1987], p. 52
[6]Globe and Mail [1988], p. B7.

is Ford Motor Company, which produces a number of different components for its Escort model in several countries, and then ships them to the United States for assembly. This is also prevalent in the semiconductor industry, where international competitors have plans in each other's countries, and team up on major research, development, and production projects (see Dallmeyer [1987]).

Competition from Smaller Firms.   Although the rise in international competition is primarily attributed to the growing operations of multinationals, smaller firms have also contributed to increased competition. As we will see later in this chapter, new technology eliminates some of the advantages traditionally enjoyed by large firms employing a capital-intensive, economies-of-scale strategy and enables smaller firms to compete head-to-head with larger firms.

Technological Advances

The rate of technological advance is increasing rapidly. Close to 90 percent of all scientific discoveries have been generated in the past 30 years. Equally dynamic is the forecast that this pool of knowledge is expected to double in the next 10 to 15 years. Consider the following:

> The various types of technologies used to improve productivity and quality in the early 1960s had an average life cycle of about 10 years. . . . In 1986, most technology life cycles have been shortened to about two years and are projected to be six months by the year 2000. The continued shortened technology life cycle poses a real challenge for all organizations that desire to use the technology as a mechanism for productivity and quality improvement.[7]

Firms that continue to ignore the strategic and organizational implications of the new technology will eventually find themselves hopelessly behind in their efforts to remain competitive. Furthermore, given the rapid rate of technological advance, it is apparent that firms do not have that big a window of time in which to defer adoption.

A word of caution is perhaps appropriate at this point. That is, while it is important for firms to keep up with the latest advances in technology, at the same time, it is essential not to regard the technology as a savior. If it is not justified in the context of a well-formulated business strategy, or if its implementation is poorly planned and executed, adopting new technology can in fact substantially erode a firm's competitive position. Put simply, new technology acquisition should not be thought of as a guaranteed solution to the competitive challenge. Honda's Marysville plant in the United States, for example, uses fewer robots than any other car manufacturer in North America, and yet its employees turn out cars almost twice as fast as those at GM (see Waddell [1985]). The last equipment installed in the TVA Gallutin Steam Plant in Tennessee was in 1959.

[7]Edosomwan [1986], p. 263.

There is no computer control equipment in place, and yet the plant is one of the most efficient of its kind in the United States!

MAJOR INFLUENCES AND TRENDS

Lower productivity levels, international competition, and technological advances have jointly escalated the competitive pressures facing North American firms. It is becoming increasingly difficult for firms to identify and maintain a long-term competitive advantage. In this section, we look at two sets of trends: those influencing the market, and those affecting manufacturing. Understanding these environmental trends can help firms to respond effectively to the challenges in today's comnpetitive business environment.

Trends in the Marketplace

Shorter Product Life Cycles.   Research has shown that the average life cycle for new products has declined over time. For example, Qualls et al. [1981] have shown that the product life cycle of 37 household appliances over 50 years (ending 1979) declined by as much as 85 percent for the introductory stage and by about 80 percent during the growth stage. New technology will accelerate the trend toward even shorter product life cycles as it provides firms with the capacity to develop and produce timely new products very quickly. For example, it has taken Compaq Computer less than two years to develop and produce its new 386 base microcomputer system. In comparison, Compaq's 286 series took several years to find its way to the market. The impact of new technology on the product life cycle is illustrated graphically in Exhibit 3.2.

In response to the trend to shorter product life cycles, firms must be able to:

- Introduce new products into the marketplace quickly
- Modify existing products to meet changing demands
- Produce a wide enough range of products so that manufacturing processes do not become obsolete quickly

Increased New Product/Process Introductions.   New product/process innovation has risen dramatically in the past few years, and this trend is likely to continue, as it is becoming evident that much of the growth potential for companies will come from new products (McDougall and Munro [1984]). For example, a survey of 700 United States companies revealed that: (a) they expected nearly one-third of their profits in the 1980s to come from new products (compared with slightly over one-fifth in the late 1970s), and (b) that the median number of new product introductions forecasted by these companies for 1981–1986 was double the number of new product introductions that occurred during the previous

Exhibit 3.2 The Product Life Cycle Reduction Due to New Technology

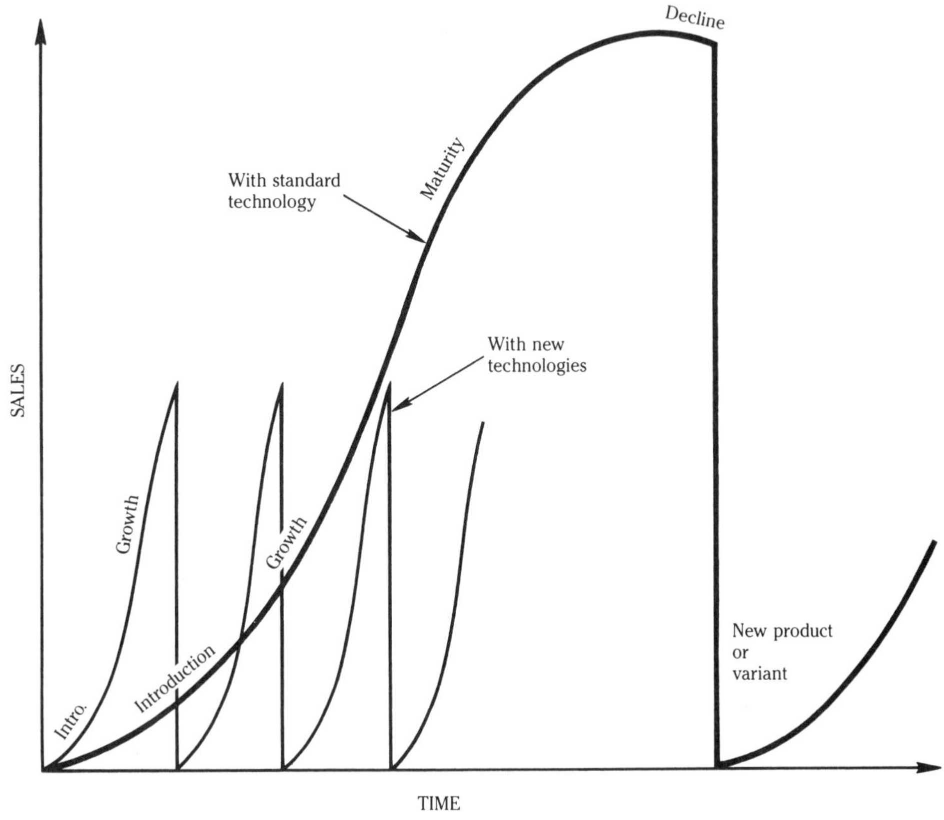

Source: Meredith, J. [1987]. "The Strategic Advantages of New Manufacturing Technologies for Small Firms," *Strategic Management Journal*, Vol. 8, p. 253. Reprinted by permission of John Wiley and Sons, Limited.

Note: This graph implies that as a new product is introduced into the marketplace, the older version becomes obsolete. One can think of examples (microchips) or CAM-CORD where this does in fact occur, especially when the capabilities of the new product are significantly higher than those of the older version.

However, in other cases, the new product introduced is not a replacement for the older version, but rather a modified product with different features but roughly the same performance capabilities. In these situations, there might be no abrupt breakdown of the life cycle.

five years (Fraker [1984]). Consider the case of Siemens of Germany: Half of its turnover is currently being generated from the sale of products developed in the last five years (Bullinger et al. [1985]). This growing tendency toward faster product development makes it essential that firms assess their capabilities in the area of product and process innovation and determine potential areas of improvement. Exhibit 3.3 uses three examples (mainframe computers, calculators, and microprocessors) to illustrate the rapid pace of new product introductions that is occurring in many industries.

Increased buying sophistication, particularly in purchasing departments

Exhibit 3.3 The Pace of New Product Introductions

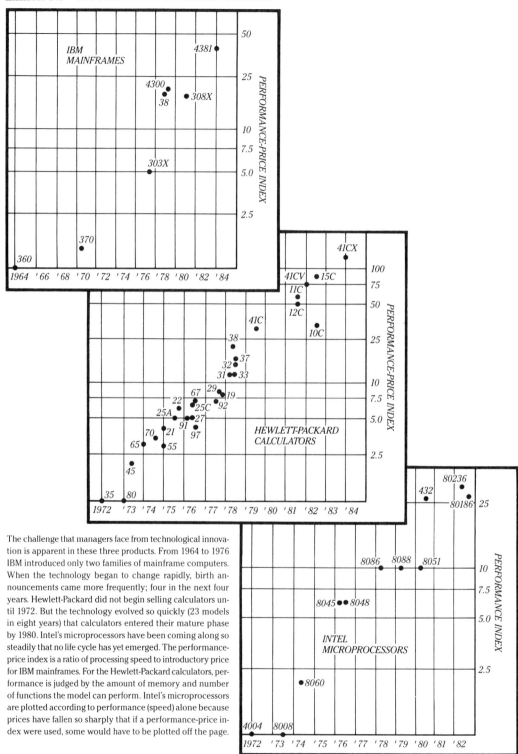

The challenge that managers face from technological innovation is apparent in these three products. From 1964 to 1976 IBM introduced only two families of mainframe computers. When the technology began to change rapidly, birth announcements came more frequently; four in the next four years. Hewlett-Packard did not begin selling calculators until 1972. But the technology evolved so quickly (23 models in eight years) that calculators entered their mature phase by 1980. Intel's microprocessors have been coming along so steadily that no life cycle has yet emerged. The performance-price index is a ratio of processing speed to introductory price for IBM mainframes. For the Hewlett-Packard calculators, performance is judged by the amount of memory and number of functions the model can perform. Intel's microprocessors are plotted according to performance (speed) alone because prices have fallen so sharply that if a performance-price index were used, some would have to be plotted off the page.

Source: Courtesy of *FORTUNE* Magazine; 1984.

replenishing industrial goods, is a major factor contributing to the faster rate of new product introduction. Purchasers now demand new products more quickly and also expect a high-quality, high-value product "package" based on performance, reliability, service, and price. The embedded characteristics of the new technology make it a logical response to such market demands.

Fragmented Markets.   The trend towards highly segmented markets is more pronounced than ever. The once large middle-class consumer market which purchased the majority of goods and services is now shrinking in both numbers and purchasing power. At the same time, several new segmented markets are emerging from this change (see Steinberg [1983]).

Several factors lead to market segmentation, including the use of product proliferation and market niche strategies, and increased competition for smaller markets. With this comes market segment instability, which occurs because increasing fragmentation of markets lead to: (a) less distinct boundaries between segments, (b) an increase in customer expectations for customized products, and (c) an increase in the ability of customers to switch from one product/segment to another. Firms competing in fragmented markets will find that they need the flexibility of a manufaturing system capable of producing a variety of products in various volumes and in random orders.

Unexpected Competitors.   With more design and production flexibility, a firm can easily switch its resources from producing products geared to one market to manufacturing others intended for another. The market fragmentation noted above, as well as new entries and blurred industry boundaries, make it difficult for firms to anticipate sources of competition. Consequently, more contingency planning and greater flexibility are required. Consider the following:

> With the introduction of new information technologies, both established and new firms will increasingly compete for the same markets. So, for example, the telephone, telegraph, computer, software, service bureau, semiconductor, satellite, motion picture, and business equipment firms are focusing on the same customers, wherever they may be: in the office, home, factory, retail store, or bank. Traditional boundaries of industry are blurring and shifting, and it is becoming increasingly difficult to know to which industry a firm belongs.[8]

Demand Uncertainty.   Forecasting the demand for products has always been far from an exact science. However, shorter product life cycles, more new product introductions, fragmented markets, and unexpected competitors have all contributed to the trend toward increasing demand uncertainty. This makes it riskier for firms to follow a high-volume, low-cost strategy (mass production), because products may become obsolete before costs can be recovered. Firms today can benefit greatly from the ability to adapt (rather than scrap) their operations if the forecasted demand for a particular product does not materialize.

---

[8]Cordell [1985], pp. 64–65.

Trends in Manufacturing

Product and Process Simplification.   Many firms are finding that they can achieve tremendous gains in efficiency and effectiveness by designing products which have fewer parts and are thus simpler to manufacture and assemble. Consider the following:

> Northern Telecom has responded to the challenge of low-cost telephones made in Pacific Rim countries by redesigning its telephone so that it has 156 parts, down from 325. Both IBM and Ford have improved the quality and manufacturability of their products through design simplifications. IBM's Proprinter is made up of only 60 parts, compared with a competitor's 150, and Ford has reduced the number of pieces in the sidepanel of its Taurus automobile from 15 to 2.[9]

This trend is very much in line with the creed followed by Japanese companies, which emphasizes simplification.[10] In practice, Japanese companies score the product design to justify its manufacturability. If the score is low, some redesigning (simplification) must be done before actual assembly.

Process simplification is also being pursued in an attempt to provide firms with the capability to produce a wider range of high-quality, low-cost products. Traditional mass production technology is dependent on specialized and dedicated machinery and equipment. This inflexibility makes it prohibitively difficult to introduce new products frequently, a requirement of today's marketplace. Given the growing trend toward more customized and complex products, pressure will continue to mount for ". . . simplification of the production process and minimization of decision-making opportunities for workers so as to minimize problems associated with human error."[11]

Need to Reduce Inventories.   It is now a well-known reality that maintaining inventories results in significant expenditures not only in terms of carrying costs, but also in terms of hidden manufacturing problems. Shorter product life cycles and increased new product introductions have increased the risk that inventories will become obsolete. Because of these costs and risks, manufacturers are rushing to reduce inventories. For example:

> NCR was forced to write off $140 million in inventory and lay off 20,000 workers when it realized the quality of electromechanical cash registers was eclipsed by electronic machines.[12]

---

[9]Adapted from Warner [1988], p. 22.

[10]It is generally believed that in the manufacturing and assembly process, the number of coordinations required is proportional to the number of part interfaces in the product. The key point is that if there are N parts, the number of decisions is greater than N (but probably somewhat less than N^2). Thus the amount of information that must be processed in manufacturing is at least proportional to product complexity (N) (See Ayres [1986], p. 17).

[11]Ayres [1986], p. 15.

[12]O'Guin [1987], p. 37.

The implementation of more scientific inventory control systems and applications of the JIT principle also exemplify the desire of manufacturers to cut inventory levels. As programs are implemented by large manufacturers in an effort to reduce their inventories, smaller suppliers are forced to bear more of the cost of carrying inventories. Firms in this situation may find the costs prohibitive. Naturally, the capability to alter production schedules quickly and easily, and thus reduce the need to hold inventories to meet due dates, is of great interest.

Pressures to Improve Quality. The pressure on manufacturers to improve product quality without increasing costs is certainly very real. The following provides a good example of this situation:

> Foreign manufacturers are building more and more Transplants in North America. However, they are reluctant to use North American produced component parts, stating that these parts do not meet the quality standards that they require. As well, North American manufacturers are requiring that suppliers achieve a certain quality rating before they are awarded business.[13]

Companies that consistently achieve high quality standards are in a much better position to receive future contracts from large manufacturers. With inherent high precision and consistency, the new technology provides an important means of producing high-quality products.

Changing OEM/Supplier Relationships. Increasingly, original equipment manufacturers (OEMs) are outsourcing their manufacturing parts rather than producing them in-house, preferring simply to assemble the finished product. For example, at Chrysler's ultramodern plant in Bramalea, Ontario, many major components, such as stampings, instrument panels, and seats, are delivered from a network of satellite suppliers operating within a 40-mile radius of the plant.

The consequence of this is, of course, a reduced incidence of vertical (especially backward) integration strategies. This is an interesting development, given that the flexibility provided by new technology enhances the feasibility of such a strategy from an operations point of view. Apparently, firms do not value operations flexibility over the strategic and organizational complexity and rigidity often associated with integration. Firms appear to be realizing that "...long-term contracts and long-term relationships with suppliers can achieve many of the same benefits as backward integration without calling into question a company's ability to innovate or respond to innovation."[14]

Therefore, as an alternative to backward integration, and in an attempt to improve the quality and delivery reliability of their purchased materials, firms are shifting to single sourcing methods by awarding contracts to a small number of reliable suppliers. For example, Northern Telecom is endeavoring to reduce its

---

[13]Blenkhorn and Noori, [1988].
[14]Kumpe and Bolwijn [1988], pp. 75–76.

total number of suppliers from a 1985 level of 12,000 to a target of a few thousand (Campbell [1987]); Chrysler is attempting to cut its parts and material suppliers from the 1985 level of 2,700 to fewer than 1,500 by 1991 (Taylor III [1987]).

Outsourcing implies that more business will be available to component manufacturers. Single sourcing implies that fewer companies will benefit from this increased business. In other words, there will be winners and losers. The winners will probably be well-managed companies which can consistently produce a range of high-quality products on schedule. General Motors, for instance, has changed its Spear Program to what it calls Targets of Excellence. Through this new program, GM assesses suppliers not only on quality, but also on technologies, production methods, and labor relations. In this highly competitive environment, suppliers can utilize the new technology to strengthen their position vis-à-vis other suppliers.

> A superb example of using new technology to work "shoulder-to-shoulder" with customers is provided by Peerless Saw Co. which took a substantial risk and developed a computer-driven laser-cutting system. As Peerless cut their lead time from 14 weeks down to three and began supplying their customers with laser-cut saw blades (and noting them as such), customers began to change also. First, the word went around that these blades were being produced on a laser cutter, improving Peerless's image and attracting new customers.
>
> But more important, with three-week lead times, orders started coming in with the phrasing: "The same as last time except...." Peerless soon realized that customers were using the facilities to "experiment" with their saw blade designs, eking out one percent improvements in productivity, or two percent improvements in quality.
>
> Taking advantage of this new market, Peerless started encouraging sales people to work more closely with customers to produce specialized blades that would fit their unique needs. The simplicity of their menu-driven computerized system allows their sales people to even take the terminal with them when they visit cusotmers, tie into Peerless's computer over a phone line, pull their customers' last order up on the screen, and, together with the customer, modify it. Once the customer is happy with the new design, the salesman punches a button and the laser goes to work back in the Peerless plant cutting the blade.[15]

Single sourcing methods are usually accompanied by closer supplier-customer relationships. In many respects, Japanese companies have demonstrated the extent of this cooperation. The basis for this is the existence of the business relationships that have dominated Japanese culture for centuries. Japanese suppliers have a secure link with their OEM customers, who often have partial ownership and significant control of their suppliers. This alliance, which is based on long-term commitment and trust, provides a climate whereby both suppliers

---

[15]Meredith [1987], pp. 28–29.

and their customers can share the information and resources needed to pursue joint innovation projects.

For example, as Blenkhorn and Noori [1988] explain, Japanese OEMs in the auto industry often work closely with their suppliers to come up with new and improved products and processes; this includes the exchange of information, research facilities, and engineering technical staff. Furthermore, suppliers are often awarded business on the basis of how capable and compatible their manufacturing equipment is with their customers'. Suppliers therefore have an added incentive to work closely with the OEM on new technology development. In fact, many of them are capable of producing machine tools and robots in-house to facilitate the synchronization of their production processes with those of major customers. This is in direct contrast to North American suppliers, who typically do not design and manufacture their own equipment, desire to retain a high degree of autonomy from their OEM customers, and are awarded contracts primarily on the basis of price. It is argued that the differences in supplier-customer relationships is a primary factor in the competitive success of many Japanese industries. A summary of these differences is provided in Exhibit 3.4.

Smaller Plants. There is growing evidence to indicate that plant sizes are shrinking (Schumacher [1984] and Starr [1984]), and that more companies will choose to build smaller plants in the future. There are at least four reasons for this. First, new manufacturing technologies have reduced the cost advantages of pursuing economies of scale (which advocated high-volume, standard products). Second, Just-in-Time production has made it all but necessary for many firms to locate a number of smaller plants close to their various customers rather than operating out of one large centralized plant. Third, management-worker relationships appear to be more productive in a smaller environment. Finally, building small plants may reduce the risk involved in pursuing markets with uncertain demand:

> If a plant is going to become obsolete sooner than expected, the lower the investment, the better. . . . The new emphasis on specialized products in industries ranging from telecommunications to steel will require that companies be able to change their capacity very quickly.[16]

Smaller Production Lot Sizes. Some experts estimate that in coming years most manufactured parts will be in small lot sizes (50 or fewer). Presently, ". . . batch manufacturing is estimated to be the most common form of production in the United States, constituting perhaps 50 percent or more of the total manufacturing activity."[17] Many factors, including increased market segmentation, just-in-time delivery requirements, and new technology capabilities have contributed to the growing trend toward production in small batch sizes. This

---

[16]Adopted from Gold [1984], p. 153.
[17]Groover [1987], p. 433.

Exhibit 3.4   A Comparison of Japanese and North American Suppliers

Criterion	Attribute	
	Japan	North America
1. Quality	• Part of the process	• Monitored after production
2. JIT delivery	• Not a new phenomena; part of the total supply-delivery system	• Imposed by external forces—customers or threat of competition from the Japanese
3. Process—equipment	• Synchronized with their major customer(s) and suppliers	• Firm specific centered rather entire system centered
4. Culture/people/attitude	• Team playing, job enlargement, attempts to play down rank or hierarchy on job	• Union centered them-us attitude
5. Innovative thinking	• Mandatory to survive as auto assemblers demand innovative, cost saving solutions	• Encouraged but historically not mandatory to survive as parts maker
6. Efficiency	• Efficiency enhanced through our manufacture of robots or modifications of purchased equipment	• Often look to external sources to increase efficiency
7. Competitiveness—price	• Other Japanese firms seen as major competitors and inhouse capability of auto assemblers	• Offshore parts makers viewed as major competitors
8. User/producer interface	• On ongoing R&D thrust with regular exchange of personnel	• Often limited to the order at hand
9. Degree of computer linkage— sophistication	• The supplier-assembler interface perhaps is very similar in both Japan & North America • Extensive use of CAD/CAM in design engineering	• Much less use of CAD/CAM
10. JIT—necessity	• Pressure to adopt came from the auto assemblers • Much more commonly utilized and understood	• Being adopted by those suppliers which wish to remain suppliers
11. Design to cost criteria	• Historically a common occurrence in the Japanese auto industry, but the rise in the yen has has intensified its use	• No data re N/A
12. Outsourcing	• More outsourcing often offshore caused principally by increased value of the yen • More for both groups but for different reasons	• More outsourcing precipitated by OEM's desire to reduce fixed costs

Source: Blenkhorn and Noori [1988], p. 17.

in turn makes improved production flexibility a necessity for many firms, as the following example illustrates:

> Batch production, which accounts for about 40 percent of value-added in U.S. manufacturing (about 60 percent in European countries) involves small lot production and is very labor intensive. Given the extreme diversity of parts in a batch production system, there is a great need for flexibility in the operating environment. This is the major reason why costs remain high and productivity is relatively low.[18]

This section has described some of the major influences and trends that have resulted from an increasingly competitive business environment. These are summarized in Exhibit 3.5. Firms must cope effectively with these environmental trends to remain competitive. The following section will describe different forms of flexibility and their uses in dealing with the changing competitive environment.

Exhibit 3.5 Major Influences and Trends in Today's Environment

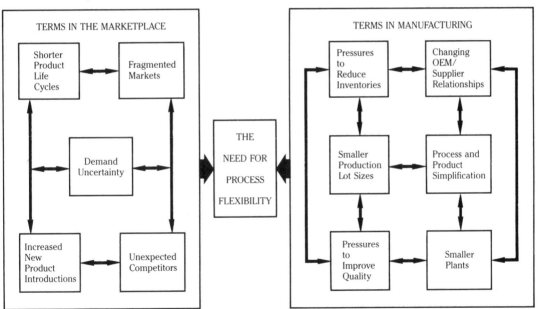

FLEXIBILITY: THE FUTURE OF MANUFACTURING

Flexibility has always been regarded as an important strategic tool. Companies operate in uncertain environments, and flexibility provides them with the ability

---

[18]McMillan [1987], p. 64.

to respond effectively to unexpected changes. The potential consequences of building a less flexible and more dedicated operation can be severe:

> Ford Motor Company offers a graphic illustration of the problems inherent in using a highly dedicated system. Every major piece of equipment in its most automated factory was specifically designed and tooled to accommodate a narrow range of processing operations. When market conditions led Ford to opt for the smaller engines, the company reluctantly closed the plant because it could not convert its specialized equipment to a different set of tasks.[19]

A productive unit can have various types of flexibility, each of which can be useful in competing through manufacturing. Cohen and Zysman [1987] have distinguished between static flexibility (the ability of a company to adjust at any moment to changing conditions in the market), and dynamic flexibility (the aptitude of the company to increase productivity through improvements in production processes and industrial innovation). Gerwin [1985] has examined several types of flexibility and has related each of them to a primary strategic objective. Browne et al. [1984], and Kumar and Kumar [1987] have looked at the various uncertainties present in a firm's environment and have elaborated on different types of flexibility relevant to these environmental uncertainties. Based on their contributions, and given the environmental uncertainties and trends described previously, we will look at how differnt types of flexibility can be strategically applied to enhance a firm's competitive stance.

Mix flexibility is measured by the number of different parts that can be produced at any one time. With this type of flexibility, a company can respond to competitive pressures which have increased market segmentation and offer customers a diverse product line. For example:

> Komatsu in Japan has adopted a straight line flow system whereby it produces 35 different models, all intermixed, of bulldozers, dozer shovels, hydraulic excavators, wheel-leaders and crawler dump trucks ranging from two tons to 10 tons on a single 490 foot long progressive assembly line.[20]

Closely related to mix flexibility is *product-range flexibility*, which refers to the range of products a system can produce. The diversity of the product line offered to customers is limited by the range flexibility of a firm's operations. For example, a firm capable of producing shovels, rakes, pitchforks, and axes would have greater range flexibility than a firm that could produce only shovels.

Machine flexibility reflects the ease of changing the production process to produce a different set of parts. With machine flexibility, companies can reduce inventories and still compete through short lead times, mainly for special or rush orders. For example:

[19]Gold [1982], p. 89.
[20]Sessions [1985], p. 70.

In Japan's motor industry, production engineers have taken advantage of the programmability of robots to develop "mix-model" assembly lines that can produce several hundred variations on a few basic models. As a result, Japanese carmakers can not only change the production mix quickly in response to market demands but also accommodate year-to-year model changes without extensive plant shutdowns and retooling.[21]

Machine flexibility can also be used to a firm's advantage if suppliers are late in delivering the material inputs required to produce particular parts. With machine flexibility, a firm can easily switch its operations over to produce a different set of parts, and it can switch them back to produce the originally planned parts once the necessary materials have arrived.

Machine flexibility (along with mix and range flexibility) can also enable firms to provide a full range of replacement parts to customers at lower cost. That is, companies are potentially capable of producing the replacement parts required on demand, through the flexibility of their machines.

Modification flexibility is the ability of a process to implement design changes on a given product. It enables standard products to be modified to meet various customer specifications. This type of flexibility is an important attribute if customer preference for a particular product option changes frequently. For example:

> The body shop of one automobile assembly plant quickly adjusted its flexible, programmed spot-welding robots to a shift in consumer preference from the two-door to the four-door version of a certain car model. Had the line been equipped with nonprogrammable welding equipment, the adjustment would have been far more costly.[22]

With *routing flexibility*, a manufacturing system becomes capable of altering the sequence of machines through which a given part passes. In other words, if a certain machine breaks down or if it is busy performing another operation, a part can be rerouted to another machine and/or the order of operations performed on the part can be altered so that the finished part is still completed on time. Routing flexibility enables a company to follow a strategy which focuses on meeting customer due dates (delivery dependability). For example:

> GM's newly built AUTOPLEX in Oshawa, Ontario assembles a new generation of mix-size models. By combining the Volvo's team approach concept with AGVs, GM is replacing the assembly line principle with a new ystem called "Tracking Signal," whereby certain cars can get all the proper options, colors, and specified parts ordered by customers.

---

[21]Bairstow [1986], p. 28.
[22]Kaplan [1986], Page 92.

Expansion flexibility refers to the capability of redesigning and expanding the system's size as needed, easily and modularly. This enables a company to react quickly to large increases in aggregate product volume demands and avoid lost sales. Expansion flexibility is a potentially strong competitive tool when sales forecasts are difficult or uncertain. For example, an automated materials handling system utilizing automated guided vehicles has expansion flexibility, because new vehicles can be added to the system easily if materials handling requirements increase.

Innovation flexibility reflects the ease and speed of introducing new products into the production process. With innovation flexibility, a company can compete in an industry with short or uncertain product life cycles through continuous product innovation. The capabilities of innovation flexibility combined with mix flexibility can enable a firm to significantly alter the way it competes in an industry. For example:

> Illinois Tool Works (ITW) produces keyboards and other computer entry devices. By employing new technology, ITW has reduced product life cycles and expanded product variety. What took three years to develop, test and sell now goes through the same cycle in six months. They have intentionally fractured their original market into smaller mini-markets to provide more options, models, sizes, colors, and customizing.[23]

Volume flexibility refers to the ability to operate the system profitably at different volume levels for different parts. For example, GM plants in Delaware and North Jersey, which produce the Chevy Corsica and Beretta, are equipped "...with flexible automation that permits switching production from, say, 70 percent coupes and 30 percent sedans to a 50-50 mix with a simple change in computer programming."[24] This type of flexibility can potentially provide a significant advantage in industries where products have seasonal or varying sales patterns.

Material flexibility is the ability of a manufacturing process to handle variations in the raw materials (or tooling) inputed to the process. This results in reduced defect levels and high and consistent product quality. Material flexibility is often obtained through process control and sensor technologies. An example occurs in auto body framing, since operators can locate bent metal and straighten it or position it so that welding can be done properly (Gerwin [1985]).

The types of flexibility explained thus far can be grouped, with some overlaps, into two broader categories, *process flexibility* (which includes mix, product-range, machine, modification, routing, volume, and expansion flexibilities) and *product flexibility* (which consists of design, material, and innovation flexibility). Added to this is what Swamidass [1985] calls *infrastructure flexibility*. This deals with brain technology (discussed in Chapter 2), and denotes the ability

---

[23]Meredith [1987], page 255.
[24]Hampton [1987], p. 139.

of the organization itself to adapt to changes. As we will discuss in Chapters 8 through 10, infrastructure flexibility is an important requisite for successful new technology implementation.

Product, process, and infrastructure flexibilities together define *aggregate production flexibility*, which represents the set of flexibilities available to the firm that enable it to respond to environmental changes. A summary illustration of each of the types of flexibility discussed, as well as their potential strategic advantages and how they interrelate to produce aggregate production flexibility, is provided in Exhibit 3.6.

Exhibit 3.6 Defining the Notion and Potential of Flexibility

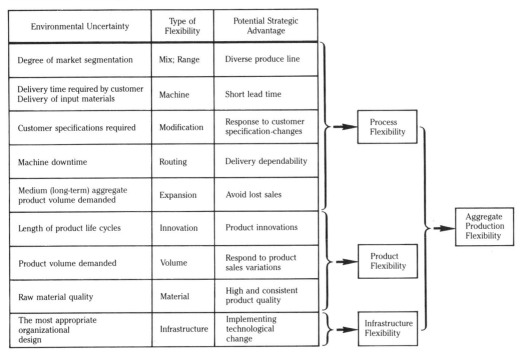

Environmental Uncertainty	Type of Flexibility	Potential Strategic Advantage
Degree of market segmentation	Mix; Range	Diverse produce line
Delivery time required by customer Delivery of input materials	Machine	Short lead time
Customer specifications required	Modification	Response to customer specification-changes
Machine downtime	Routing	Delivery dependability
Medium (long-term) aggregate product volume demanded	Expansion	Avoid lost sales
Length of product life cycles	Innovation	Product innovations
Product volume demanded	Volume	Respond to product sales variations
Raw material quality	Material	High and consistent product quality
The most appropriate organizational design	Infrastructure	Implementing technological change

Three important issues arise from the concept of aggregate production flexibility. First, new technologies can provide firms with various types and degrees of individual flexibilities, and hence various levels of production flexibility. However, a company must consider which type(s) of flexibility are most important to competitive success before deciding which technologies will be acquired. Second, the definitions presented above did not address the relationships between various types of flexibility. From a practical point of view, there are potential overlaps among these forms of flexibility. Depending on the form and configuration of the technology, a firm can simultaneously capture many of the flexibilities outlined. Finally, any discussion of flexibility must consider the potential connection between the level of technology (or automation) and the inherent degree of flexibility. Exhibit 3.7 graphically depicts this relationship.

Exhibit 3.7   A Typical Technology-Level and Flexibility Relationship

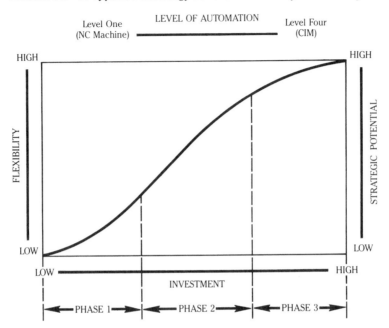

The exhibit presents what we believe to be the most appropriate representation of the alliance between flexibility and levels of automation. The trajectory in the graph can be divided into three phases:

Phase 1:   With early investments in automation, before experience with the technology is gained, the flexibility returns to investment are relatively low. This holds because true flexibility is difficult to achieve. It depends not just on programmable robots and machine tools, but on the coordination and control of a host of other factors we have discussed.

Phase 2:   As the company becomes more familiar with new technology applications, the flexibility improvements for a given amount of investment increase rapidly.

Phase 3:   With a high level of investment and automation, the law of diminishing returns takes hold, and it becomes increasingly difficult to continue getting large flexibility increases with further investment.

Nevertheless, depending on the form of flexibility, if implementation is managed correctly firms can achieve many of the flexibility benefits of the new technology with a relatively small investment. This, as we will discuss further on, implies that even smaller firms can benefit from the strategic capabilities of new technology.

WHO BENEFITS MOST: THE MATTER OF SIZE

"Is our company large enough to consider the new technology?" In business circles, this is a common question. Apparently, some believe that only large manufacturing companies can benefit from the new technologies available today. However, substantial evidence has been gathered to suggest that the new technology can benefit small manufacturing firms as much or more than large ones (see, for example, Meredith [1987]).

Small and large manufacturers differ in their ability to capitalize on the strategic potential of the technology. Large firms have traditionally pursued economies of scale in order to minimize costs and capture a large market share. Smaller firms, on the other hand, have generally sought economies of scope which are geared toward competing for a particular market niche by concentrating on quality, customized products, localized facilities, and production flexibility.

Although the new technology can benefit both large and small manufacturing firms, there are a number of differences in the desire and ability of these companies to capitalize fully on its potential. These differences arise at both the acquisition and implemention phases. Exhibit 3.8 outlines the various positive and negative forces which allow or prohibit small and large manufacturing firms from realizing the advantages of the new technology.

Acquisition Considerations

Despite its enormous potential for small manufacturers, research has shown that small firms lag behind larger firms in their plans to adopt technology (Craig and Noori [1985]). Consider that ". . .65 percent of the dollars spent on CIM come from the top 2 percent of manufacturers."[25] There are at least three possible reasons for this. First, smaller firms lack the financial resources to acquire the new technology. Although some of the technologies available today are relatively inexpensive, a number of the more advanced technologies (like FMS and CIM) would require the management of smaller firms to gamble the company. Business cycles and trends add to the risk involved, and in general, larger firms have a greater pool of resources to cushion them against an unsuccessful new technology venture.

Second, smaller firms may lack the management time required to investigate the potential of new technology. Managers in smaller companies tend to rely on the media (trade, technical magzines, newspapers, newsletters) and on discussions with colleagues for new technology information, whereas managers in larger organizations obtain more first-hand information through visits to other automated organizations and specific feasibility studies on automation, as well as through the media (Craig and Noori [1985]).

[25]Krouse [1987], p. 32.

Exhibit 3.8 A Comparison of the Ability of Small versus Large Manufacturers to Capitalize on the Benefits of New Technology

		Small Firm	Large Firm
A C Q U I S I T I O N	C O N S	Financial Barriers to Acquisition ("bet of company"; financial justification methods) Lack of resources to fully investigate the potential of new technology Lack of in-house technical expertise	Upper management unaware of the potential strategic benefits of new technology Financial barriers to acquisition (financial justification methods)
	P R O S	Owner/operator more aware of the potential strategic benefits of new technology	Unsuccessful attempt at utilizing doesn't necessarily bankrupt the company (a large resource base to fall back on) More resources to thoroughly investigate the potential of new technology Greater in-house expertise to evaluate potential new technology
I M P L E M E N T A T I O N	C O N S	Lack of in-house technical expertise Production slowdown/shutdown during implementation	Bureaucracy and interdepartmental conflict make implementation difficult Union resistance and negative employee attitudes Lack of top management support Difficult to get away from traditional economies of scale philosophy
	P R O S	Greater risk promotes greater desire to successfully implement Guaranteed top management support Easier to implement in a smaller environment Less worker resistance due to smaller environment and nonunionized employees Benefits of new technology fit the strategies of many small firms	Greater in-house technical expertise Greater volume flexibility during implementation

Third, the need for in-house technical expertise also appears to be a concern of the managers of smaller firms (Craig and Noori [1985]). This usually results in confusion, as managers do not know who to believe (Gunn [1985])— vendors want to sell their own equipment, and even many consultants sell some of their own software and hardware or specialize in only one area of technology.

Naturally, problems are not limited to smaller firms. There are also significant barriers preventing large manufacturers from adopting new technology.

One very important barrier is the apparent inability of top management to realize the enormous competitive potential of the new technology, and in some cases, the necessity of investing in it. In fact, consultants at Canadian CAD/CAM centers consistently report difficulty in reaching the senior corporate managers to whom their message is directed, particularly with regard to CIM (CAD/CAM Newsletter [1987]). Here are some reasons:

1. Many executives perceive manufacturing to have a supportive role and hence technology decisions are not considered part of the strategic planning process. In other words, discussions on the new technology often focus on the technical features rather than on the potential strategic benefits.

2. Many executives do not have a good grasp of their competitors' manufacturing capabilities, and this leads to a lack of the sense of urgency required to get a new technology project off the ground.

3. Managers lack an understanding of how the new technology will change corporate organizational requirements.

4. Top managers do not realize the serious implications of not investing in the new technology—the longer a company waits, the further behind it is versus the competition (Skinner [1969], Gunn [1985]).

5. Top managers fail to recognize that a capital market orientation which results in shareholder pressure for short-term performance improvements makes strategic investments in the new technology difficult to justify.

Finally, an important barrier preventing the acquisition of the new technology by all manufacturers is the inability of traditional capital justification techniques to consider fully all the benefits of the technology. (This topic will be discussed in detail in Chapter 7.)

Implementation Considerations

The implementation of the new technology at larger firms is often impeded by bureaucracy and interdepartmental conflict. Union resistance and negative worker attitudes can also make the implementation process more difficult. Furthermore, these problems can be compounded by lack of top management support.

Smaller firms do not face most of these hurdles. However, they meet other limitations in their ability to implement the new technology successfully. For example, lack of in-house technical expertise can potentially create difficulties during implementation, especially if supplier relations break down. Smaller firms may have to reduce or completely shut down their operations during the implementaion process, forcing them to hold large amounts of finished goods inventory or miss customer orders. Large firms with multiline, multiplant operations have the capability to shift some production to other lines or facilities during the implementation period.

IS THE NEW TECHNOLOGY A CUREALL?

With all the discussion that has focused on the need for and the capabilties of the new technology, one might get the impression that it is the solution to all the problems firms currently face. This is, of course, a fallacy. Consider the following example:

> GM spent $500 million on its Hamtramck factory which was built on a 77 acre bulldozed site on Detroit's east side. The plant contains the largest standing army of robots to be seen anywhere—some 260 articulated contraptions for welding, painting and assembling motor cars, 50 mobile robots for fetching parts from stores, and everywhere computers reaching in and checking the quality of the workmanship. Hamtramck is a technological tour de force, a "factory-for-the-day-after-tomorrow."
>
> Hamtramck's only problem is that it barely matches the quality and productivity of an aging GM plant at Fremont in California, where the world's largest motor manufacturer has a joint venture with Toyota stamping out copies of compact Japanese cars for the American market. Fremont does it all without fancy automation, just a lot of painstaking Toyota-style management.[26]

Firms should always explore less expensive alternatives for improving their operations. As Schonberger [1987] advocates, firms do not have to make massive investments in technology and automation in order to substantially improve their manufacturing operations. In fact, the philosophy of group technology can be implemented with very limited capital investment, and in many cases does not require any additional technology, just a different and more productive way of utilizing the firm's existing technology. The following example illustrates this point:

> An electronic equipment company had planned to build a factory of the future by replacing three old production lines with five automated lines. When management realized that the new process wouldn't necessarily insure the same level of quality, it decided to think the whole project through again. In the end, it decided upon a more conservative course—selectively upgrading and rearranging its existing machines and adding material-handling devices. By making these relatively minor changes in its existing plants, the company improved both throughput and quality to the point where the three renovated lines could handle the anticipated increase in volume. Customers gained through lower prices for higher quality goods.[27]

Japanese firms have also demonstrated that it is not solely the adoption of the latest technology that makes a firm competitive. It is equally important

---

[26]Valery [1987], pp. 13–14.
[27]Haas [1987], p. 77.

to understand the capabilities of the technology and utilize it to its fullest potential. Managers must take a more long-term, holistic view emphasizing the link between the new technology and the company's competitive advantage and business strategy. Apparently many North American managers are not cognizant of this:

> With few exceptions, the flexible manufacturing systems installed in the United States show an astonishing lack of flexibility. In many cases, they perform worse than the conventional technology they replace. The technology itself is not to blame; it is management that makes the difference. . . . The average number of parts made by an FMS in the United States was 10; in Japan the average was 93. . . . The U.S. companies used FMSs the wrong way—for high volume production of many parts at low cost per unit. . . . Nor have the U.S. installations exploited opportunities to introduce new products. For every new part introduced into a U.S. system, 22 parts were introduced in Japan.[28]

The recent trend suggests that while many North American firms are more interested in developing and/or adopting the most sophisticated technology possible, they are rather reluctant to evaluate the benefits that less advanced technology can provide. Japanese firms actually lag behind their American counterparts in their adoption of CIM (see Valery [1987]). Although they are in general much farther ahead in automating their plants, they have done so by implementing CNC machines, automated materials handling, robotics, and flexible manufacturing systems rather than by attempting to create factories of the future through the implementation of computer-integrated manufacturing systems.

CONCLUDING OBSERVATIONS

We began by suggesting that sluggish productivity growth, slow technology adoption, and intense international competition have all combined to lead to increased competitive pressures on North American firms. Major influences and trends in the market and manufacturing have resulted in increasing environmental uncertainties which exert pressure on firms to adopt new technology.

Firms competing in a dynamic environment must find effective ways of coping with changes in the marketplace. New technology, particularly through its inherent flexibility, has the potential to provide firms with such capabilities. In this chapter we expanded the notion of flexibility by defining eight types of flexibility and by explaining how each of these can be used by firms to respond to various environmental uncertainties.

There are also many barriers to acquiring and implementing the new technology that may inhibit full realization of the potential benefits. The chapter

---

[28]Jaikumar [1986], p. 69.

elaborated on this point by comparing the ability of small and large firms to capitalize on the benefits of the new technology.

Although many firms can conceivably benefit from the new technology, it does not provide a guaranteed solution or even the only possible solution to the problems facing North American firms. Managers must realize that there are alternatives to adopting the new technology that may be just as (or even more) appropriate in some cases.

Finally, this chapter has raised a number of issues that will be dealt with in much more detail later in the book. Chapter 4 will discuss how firms can foster technological innovation in order to keep up with the latest advances in technology; Chapter 5 will explain how technology and business strategy are related, and Chapters 7 and 9 will discuss ways to overcome the barriers preventing firms from acquiring and successfully implementing the new technology.

RECOMMENDED READINGS

CAPON, N., and R. GLAZER [1987]. "Marketing and Technology: A Strategic Coalignment." *Journal of Marketing*, Volume 51, July, pp. 1–14.
GROOVER, M. P., and J. C. WIGINTON [1986].   "CIM and the Flexible Automated Factory of the Future." *Industrial Engineering*, January, pp. 75–85.
MEREDITH, J. [1987].   "The Strategic Advantages of New Manufacturing Technologies for Small Firms." *Strategic Management Journal*, Volume 8, pp. 249–258.

DISCUSSION QUESTIONS

1. Will the new technology have the same impact on all types of industries? Pick three industries and discuss the relative significance of the new technology in each of these industries.
2. In Chapter 2, a number of advanced manufacturing technologies were defined. In this chapter, a number of different flexibilities have been described. Match each new technology with the types(s) of flexibility it provides.
3. A firm is deciding which three possible technologies to purchase. Each provides a different level of each type of flexibility described in this chapter. Develop a model that would help management choose the right technology.
4. Why have North American firms been so slow to adopt the new technology? What can or should be done to accelerate the pace of adoption?
5. Do you think that the new technology can help to save North America's economy? Even if they successfully adopt the new technology, can North American firms hope to compete with the firms from newly industrialized countries who have lower labor costs, fewer social constraints, and a strong desire to upgrade their standard of living?
6. Some people argue that the enormous financial and human resources needed to adopt new technology successfully prohibit small firms from doing so, and as a result these firms will become uncompetitive and eventually extinct. Do you agree or disagree? Explain.
7. What implications do the trends in the marketplace described in this chapter have for traditional marketing practice? Similarly, how will trends in manufacturing affect traditional marketing practices?
8. Given the trends in the marketplace and the trends in manufacturing described in this chapter, which functional area (manufacturing or marketing) do you feel will become more important to a firm's future competitive success?

9. In the past 30 years, close to 90 percent of all scientific discoveries have been generated. Forecasts suggest that the pool of scientific knowledge is expected to double in the next 10 to 15 years. What implications does this rapid acceleration of technological advancement have for North American firms?

REFERENCES AND BIBLIOGRAPHY

ABERNATHY, W. J., K. B. CLARK, and A. M. KANTROW [1981]. "The New Industrial Competition." *Harvard Business Review*, September–October, pp. 68–81.

AYRES, R. V. [1986]. "Computer Integrated Manufacturing and the Next Industrial Revolution." In J. Dermer (ed.), *Competitiveness Through Technology*. Lexington Books, Lexington, Mass., pp. 11–24.

BAIRSTOW, J. [1986]. "Automated Automaking." *High Technology*, August, pp. 25–28.

BARRETT, D. [1985]. "Technology: The Permanent Wave." *Business Quarterly*, Spring, pp. 43–52.

BLENKHORN, D., and H. NOORI [1988]. "Responding to Challenge: A Blueprint for North American Suppliers." *Sloan Management Review* (under review).

BROWNE, J., K. RATHMILL, S. P. SETHI, and K. E. STECKE [1984]. "Classification of Flexible Manufacturing Systems." *The FMS Magazine*, Volume 2, No. 2, pp. 114–117.

BULLINGER, H., H. WARNECKE, and H. LENTES [1985]. "Toward the Factory of the Future." In H. Bullinger, H. Warnecke and H. Lentes (eds.), *Towards the Factory of the Future*. Springer-Verlag, New York, pp. xxix–liv.

CAD/CAM Newsletter [1987]. Canadian CAD/CAM Council, June.

CAMPBELL, A. [1987]. "Improving Productivity Is Becoming Vital for Survival on World Scene." *The Globe and Mail*, November 9, p. B9.

CAPON, N., and R. GLAZER [1987]. "Marketing and Technology: A Strategic Coalignment." *Journal of Marketing*, Volume 51, July, pp. 1–14.

COHEN, S., and J. ZYSMAN [1987]. *Manufacturing Matters: The Myth of the Post-Industrial Economy.* Basic Books, New York.

CRAIG, R., and H. NOORI [1985]. "Recognition and Use of Automation: A Comparison of Small and Large Manufacturers." *Journal of Small Business and Entrepreneurship*, Volume 3, No. 1, pp. 37–44.

DALLMEYER, D. G. [1987]. "National Security and the Semiconductor Industry." *Technology Review*, November–December, pp. 47–55.

EDOSOMWAN, J. A. [1986] "Productivity and Quality Management—A Challenge in the Year 2000." *1986 Fall Industrial Engineering Conference Proceedings*, December 7–10, Boston, pp. 263–267.

FRAKER, S. [1984]. "High-Speed Management for the High-Tech Age." *Fortune*, March 5, pp. 62–68.

GERWIN, D. [1985]. "Organizational Implications of CAM." *International Journal of Management Science*, Volume 13, No. 5., pp. 443–451.

Globe and Mail [1988]. "Superconductor Project Seeks $5 Million." Friday, February 19, p. B7.

GOLD, A. [1984]. "Small Is Beautiful Now in Manufacturing." *Business Week*, October 22, pp. 152–156.

GOLD, B. [1982]. "CAM Sets New Rules for Production." *Harvard Business Review*, November–December, pp. 88–94.

GOLDHAR, J. D. [1984]. "What Flexible Automation Means to Your Business." *Modern Materials Handling*, Volume 39, No. 12, pp. 63–65.

GROOVER, M. P., and J. C. WIGINTON [1986]. "CIM and the Flexible Automated Factory of the Future." *Industrial Engineering*, January, pp. 75–85.

GROOVER, M. P. [1987]. *Automation, Production Systems, and Computer-Integrated Manufacturing.* Prentice-Hall, Englewood Cliffs, N.J.

HAAS, E. A. [1987]. "Breakthrough Manufacturing." *Harvard Busines Review*, March–April, pp. 75–81.

HAMPTON, W. J. [1987]. "Why Image Counts: A Tale of Two Industries." *Business Week*, June 8, pp. 138–139.

HAYES, R. H., and S. C. WHEELWRIGHT [1984]. *Restoring Our Competitive Edge: Competing Through Manufacturing.* Wiley, New York.

HEPPENHEIMER, T. [1988]. "1988's Hottest Superconductor Companies." *High Technology Business*, January, pp. 18–27.

KAPLAN, R. S. [1986]. "Must CIM Be Justified by Faith Alone?" *Harvard Business Review*, March–April, pp. 87–95.

KIRKLAND, R. I. [1988]. "Entering a New Age of Boundless Competition." *Fortune*, March 14, pp. 40–48.

KROUSE, J. [1987]. "The Segmented CIM Market." *High Technology*, February, p. 32.

KUMAR, V., and U. KUMAR [1987]. "Manufacturing Flexibility: A New Approach to Its Measurement." *Proceedings: World Productivity Forum*, IIE, Washington, May 17–20.

KUMPE, T., and P. T. BOLWIJN [1988]. "Manufacturing: The New Case for Vertical Integration." *Harvard Business Review*, March–April, pp. 75–81.

McDOUGALL, G.H.G., and H. MUNRO [1984]. "The New Product Process: A Study of Small Industrial Firms." *Journal of Small Business: Canada*, Fall Edition, pp. 24–29.

McDOUGALL, G.H.G., and H. NOORI [1986]. "Manufacturing–Marketing Strategic Interface: The Impact of Flexible Manufacturing Systems." In A. Kusiak (ed.), *Modelling and Design of Flexible Manufacturing Systems*. Elsevier, New York, pp. 189–198.

McMILLAN, C. J. [1987]. "The Automation Triangle: New Paths to Productivity Performance." *Business Quarterly*, Volume 52, No. 2, pp. 61–67.

MEREDITH, J. [1987a]. "The Strategic Advantages of New Manufacturing Technologies for Small Firms." *Strategic Management Journal*, Volume 8, pp. 249–258.

MEREDITH, J. [1987b]. "The Strategic Advantages of the Factory of the Future." *California Management Review*, Volume XXIX, No. 3, Spring, pp. 27–39.

NASAR, S. [1988]. "America's Competitive Revival." *Fortune*, January 4, pp. 44–52.

O'GUIN, M. C. [1987]. "Information Age Calls for New Methods of Financial Analysis in Implementing Manufacturing Technologies." *Industrial Engineering*, Volume 19, No. 11, November, pp. 36–40.

QUALLS, W., R. W. OLSHAVSKY, and R. E. MICHAELS [1981]. "Shortening of the PLC—An Empirical Test." *Journal of Marketing*, Fall, pp. 76–80.

ROMAN, D. D., and J. F. PUETT, JR. [1988]. *International Business and Technological Innovation*. Elsevier, New York.

SCHONBERGER, R. J. [1987]. "Frugal Manufacturing." *Harvard Business Review*, September–October, pp. 95–100.

SESSIONS, R. E. [1985]. "IEs Must Be Key Players in Manufacturing Strategy to Combat Global Competition." *Industrial Engineering*, Volume 17, No. 12, December, pp. 69–75.

SKINNER, W. [1969]. "Manufacturing—Missing Link in Corporate Stratregy." *Harvard Business Review*, May–June, pp. 136–145.

SKINNER, W. [1985]. "The Taming of Lions: How Manufacturing Leadership Evolved, 1780–1984." In K. B. Clark, R. H. Hayes, and C. Lorenz (eds.), *The Uneasy Alliance*. Harvard Business School Press.

STARR, M. [1984]. "The Effects of New Technology on Optional Size for Productivity." Research Working Paper No. 439A, Graduate School of Business, Columbia University.

STEINBERG, B. [1983]. "The Mass Market Is Splitting Apart." *Future*, November 28, pp. 76–82.

SWAMIDASS, P. [1985]. "Manufacturing Flexibility: Strategic Issues." *Discussion Paper No. 305*, Graduate School of Business, Indiana University.

TAYLOR III, A. [1987]. "Lee Iacocca's Production Whiz." *Fortune*, June 22, pp. 36–44.

VALERY, N. [1987]. "Factory of the Future." *The Economist*, May 30, pp. 3–18.

WADDELL, C. [1985]. "The Drive to Catch Japan." *Report On Business Magazine*, November, pp. 28–35.

WARNER, T. [1988]. "Computers as a Competitive Burden." *Technology Review*, February–March, pp. 22–24.

TECHNOLOGICAL INNOVATION

Countless innovations fail because no one wants or needs them. But too often good ideas are lost to poor management.

Myers and Sweezy

INTRODUCTION: MANAGEMENT OF TECHNOLOGY AND OF INNOVATION

The field of technology management is still evolving and its boundaries are somewhat undefined. In a manufacturing context, *technology* can be defined as "knowhow" or information required to produce a product (see Capon and Glaxer [1987], p. 2]). As such, it is an exogenous variable at least conceptually separable from "innovation." While the boundary between the management of innovation and the management of technology is at best fuzzy, it is nevertheless wrong to assume that they refer to the same thing.

We propose that the management of innovation is predominantly concerned with the creation and development of new ideas, whereas the management of technology focuses on the acquisition and application of existing innovations (the diffusion process). As is illustrated in Exhibit 4.1, these two disciplines do overlap to some extent, so it is useful to include a discussion on the management of innovation. However, in future chapters, the focus will be on the acquisition and implementation (rather than on the development) of new technology.

In Chapter 3, we mentioned a number of reasons for the decline in North American companies, including their reluctance to stay abreast of new technological developments. One reason frequently cited for this unwillingness is a misperception of the innovation cycle. Technological innovation is a complex process of several distinct stages, each of which requires a different focus of time and a different corporate strategy. Typical questions of great importance include: (a) Should the firm start up with the inception of an idea (invention)? (b) Is it

Exhibit 4.1   Management of Innovation versus Management of (New) Technology: An Illustration

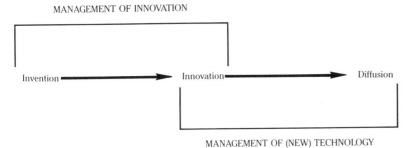

more beneficial to take up a well-developed concept and focus on commercialization? or (c) Should the firm spotlight an existing technology and aim at perfecting or modifying it? We will start with a discussion of the issues involved in technological innovation and how they relate to advanced manufacturing and information technology.

INVENTION VERSUS INNOVATION

In an often-cited paper, Utterback [1971] describes the process of innovation within the firm as consisting of three overlapping phases: (1) idea generation, (2) problem-solving, and (3) implementation, possibly followed by diffusion. The first two phases, which usually take place at the research and development level, result in an invention: implementing the invention for the first time precipitates innovation. Diffusion occurs if the innovation spreads and has an economic impact outside the firm. Utterback's model showing the process of innovation within the firm is shown in Exhibit 4.2.

The distinction between invention and innovation is an important one to make. Martin [1984] explains one of the reasons why:

> Laypersons, probably because of the mystique that surrounds science, generally view invention as a relatively rare event and assume that once it has occurred, the process of innovation can be completed in a straightforward manner. In actuality, the converse situation pertains here. All who have worked in R&D will agree that . . . the R&D community is quite prolific in generating inventions, and companies can rarely afford to fund all promising R&D projects. It is the subsequent path to technological innovation that is typically fraught with numerous obstacles to be overcome, if the R&D invention is to be commercially successful.[1]

The transformation of an invention into a commercially successful innovation occurs relatively infrequently. One study, for example, revealed ". . . an

---

[1]Martin [1984], pp. 2–3.

Exhibit 4.2 The Process of Technological Innovation within the Firm

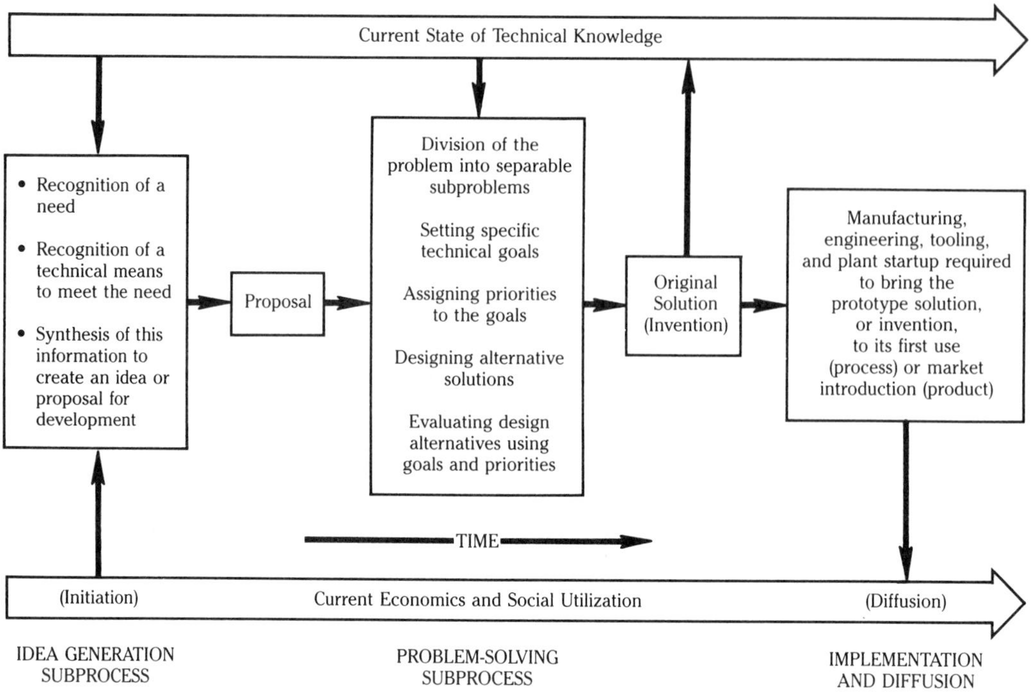

Source: Utterback [1971], p. 78.

average probability of only 12 percent that an R&D project would result in a commercially successful product or process...and another study...showed a slightly higher probability of success—about 20 percent."[2] It is based on this judgment that many people argue that one way to generate successful innovations is to have many potential innovations.[3] The following analogy brings home this point:

> If you had the best geologists, the latest in geophysical techniques, the most sophisticated equipment, and so on, the success rate in wildcat drilling in established fields would be about 15 percent. Without all of these pluses, the success ratio dips to about 13 percent. That finding suggests that the denominator—the number of tries—counts for a great deal.[4]

Aside from the validity of the multiple choices approach, we also contend that effective innovation management can contribute to, and indeed enhance,

[2]Mansfield [1981], p. 100.
[3]Peters and Waterman [1982] describe this as "a bias for action." and Quinn [1985] speaks of "multiple approaches."
[4]Peters and Waterman [1982], p. 141.

the potential success of any innovations generated. By the same token, poor management can just as easily result in the market failure of an otherwise potentially successful innovation. Consider the following example:

> One firm spent a good deal of money to develop a special welding torch for use in repairing automobiles. Not one was sold. Puzzled, management representatives visited potential customers to find out why. Only then did they learn the torch couldn't be used on the auto body with the upholstery already in place. The torch would have been a fire hazard. Obviously, management could have avoided this failure had it checked with its potential customers before developing such a product.[5]

In many instances the cost of bringing innovations to market is prohibitive. As a result, maximizing potential success through effective innovation management is necessary for the long-term profitability of a firm.

It is also important to understand that there is often a natural time lag between the time a technical discovery is made and the time it is used in an innovation. In other words, research and development often leads to major scientific advances and inventions; however, these discoveries and inventions do not necessarily have an immediate impact. There is generally a period of diffusion, or adjustment, before the economic impact of the innovation becomes apparent, as nuclear energy and computers illustrate.

Revolutionary versus Evolutionary Innovation

Innovations are commonly classified into two categories, revolutionary and evolutionary. *Revolutionary* innovations represent major product or process breakthroughs that create a new industry (examples include the transistor and the electronics industries) or significantly change a mature industry (the change from discrete transistors to integrated circuits in the electronics industry). There is another category as well—those that result in the "creative symbiosis of previously unrelated technologies."[6] Computer-integrated manufacturing fits into this category of innovation.

Revolutionary innovations typically originate outside the firms within an industry and are often generated by small, entrepreneurial individuals or organizations. The innovations enable them to establish a niche within an industry. There are, of course, excpeitonal cases in which a dominant firm is involved in a revolutionary innovation. Among some examples are IBM's innovation of the sytem 360, RCA's innovation of color television, and Texas Instrument's innovation of the integrated circuit.

Evolutionary innovations, on the other hand, are relatively common incremental product or process improvements that occur within the firm and are

[5]Myers and Sweezy [1978], p. 42.
[6]Martin [1984], p. 30.

necessary for its survival. Utterback's model, shown in Exhibit 4.2, was structured to explain the process involved in fostering evolutionary innovations. Exhibit 4.3 summarizes the differences between revolutiuonary and evolutionary innovations.

There is a marked difference in innovation habits between North American and Japanese firms. The Japanese tend to innovate incrementally; that is, the process is more evolutionary. They master one technology before they attempt to apply the next. While this appears to be the slower method, it is consistent with their strategic, long-term approach to manufacturing, and it has been effective. North American firms, with their characteristic short-term outlook, attempt to develop and adopt more revolutionary innovations. This is exemplified by the actions of companies that attempt to introduce CIM without performing the necessary intervening, evolutionary technological steps, and without first establishing the appropriate infrastructure. Unfortunately, this often results in unsuccessful adoption attempts, like the GM Hamtramck example described in Chapter 3.

The traditional relationship between revolutionary and evolutionary innovations creates somewhat of a paradox for firms. Firms must incrementally innovate in order to improve their operations and remain competitive, yet these improvements often lead to the standardization (and inflexibility) of products and processes. As firms standardize their operations, they become more exposed to the possibility of a revolutionary innovation making their existing products and processes obsolete.

Exhibit 4.3 A Comparison of Revolutionary versus Evolutionary Innovations

Revolutionary	Evolutionary
• Major product/process breakthrough	• Incremental product/process improvement
• Create or change an industry	• Maintain competitive position within an industry
• Typically, originate outside of the firms in an industry	• Typically, originate within the firms in an industry
• Relatively rare	• Relatively common
• Generated by and create opportunities for small entrepreneurial firms to enter an industry	• Improve operations of established firms

Product versus Process Innovation

Innovation at the firm level involves both the creation of new products (product innovation) and the adoption of new manufacturing processes (process innovation). Although our definition of the new technology warrants an emphasis on process innovation, firms should be cognizant of the fact that these two forms of innovation are interrelated, as Exhibit 4.4 demonstrates. There is a time lag

Exhibit 4.4   The Relationship between Product and Process Innovation Over Time

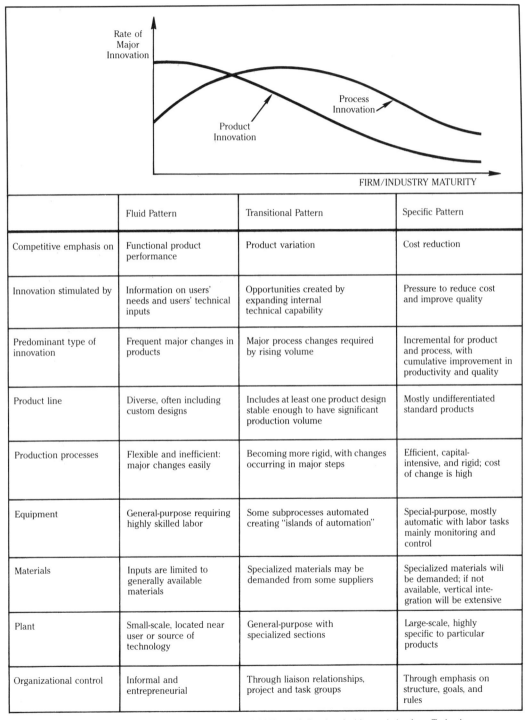

	Fluid Pattern	Transitional Pattern	Specific Pattern
Competitive emphasis on	Functional product performance	Product variation	Cost reduction
Innovation stimulated by	Information on users' needs and users' technical inputs	Opportunities created by expanding internal technical capability	Pressure to reduce cost and improve quality
Predominant type of innovation	Frequent major changes in products	Major process changes required by rising volume	Incremental for product and process, with cumulative improvement in productivity and quality
Product line	Diverse, often including custom designs	Includes at least one product design stable enough to have significant production volume	Mostly undifferentiated standard products
Production processes	Flexible and inefficient: major changes easily	Becoming more rigid, with changes occurring in major steps	Efficient, capital-intensive, and rigid; cost of change is high
Equipment	General-purpose requiring highly skilled labor	Some subprocesses automated creating "islands of automation"	Special-purpose, mostly automatic with labor tasks mainly monitoring and control
Materials	Inputs are limited to generally available materials	Specialized materials may be demanded from some suppliers	Specialized materials will be demanded; if not available, vertical integration will be extensive
Plant	Small-scale, located near user or source of technology	General-purpose with specialized sections	Large-scale, highly specific to particular products
Organizational control	Informal and entrepreneurial	Through liaison relationships, project and task groups	Through emphasis on structure, goals, and rules

Source: Abernathy and Utterback, in Burgelman and Maidique [1988], p. 142. Reprinted with permission from *Technology Review,* copyright 1978.

between the product and process life cycle. During the early stages of the product's life cycle, the level of prototype innovation is high. This is because firms modify, change, and update the product in an effort to establish a dominant design that best fits the needs of potential users. This stage is called the *fluid pattern.*

Once a dominant design is established, emphasis shifts to process innovations in order to provide the capability to mass produce the product. This typically requires a shift from general-purpose to specialized equipment. This period, during which the level of product innovation falls dramatically, is referred to as the *transitional pattern.*

Finally, the product enters the *specific pattern* of its life cycle. This stage involves incremental process innovations that further specialize the production process in an effort to reduce costs, enhance quality, and perhaps make further improvements. This leaves a firm highly inflexible, and it may find it very difficult to adapt to environmental changes with a rigid process and an aging product.

Here is a classic example of the transition from the fluid pattern to the specific pattern:

> During a four-year period before Henry Ford produced the renowned Model T, his company developed, produced, and sold five different engines, ranging from two to six cylinders. These were made in a factory that was flexibly organized much as a job shop, relying on trade craftsmen working with general purpose machine tools not nearly so advanced as the best then available. Each engine tested a new concept. Out of this experience came a dominant design, the Model T; and within 15 years 2 million engines of this single basic design were being produced each year (about 15 million all told) in a facility then recognized as the most efficient and highly integrated in the world. During that 15-year period there were incremental—but no fundamental—innovations in the Ford product.[7]

As firms enter the final stage, or the specific pattern, of a product life cycle, they become vulnerable to the possibility of a revolutionary new product introduction that makes their existing product and specialized production process obsolete. Henry Ford and his black Model T eventually met this fate when General Motors introduced its high-performance, closed body cars. Ford experienced this problem again in the late 1970s when the Japanese introduced small cars to the American market. This left some of Ford's plants economically undesirable, since they were specialized to produce large automobiles.

The Effect of the New Technology on Product and Process Innovation. There is ample evidence to support the notion that technological changes have positive effects on the rate of innovation (see, for example, Kim and Hayes [1985], and Utterback and Kim [1985]). It has been shown that productivity and innovation are linked to technological evolution as well as competitive pressures and

---

[7]Abernathy and Utterback [1978], p. 145.

managerial policy. In addition, radical innovation due to an invading technology often results in the production of a much better product with dramatically better performance, or significantly lower production costs, or both. At the same time, we contend that innovations that result in significant changes in both performance and costs will result in the highest degree of uncertainty and will be the most compelling and yet the most disruptive of all, and the most likely to be introduced by a company outside the current set of competitors.

The following four separate patterns of discontinuous change in product and process innovations due to changes in organization and technology are based on this line of reasoning:[8]

- If both product and process are changed, as in the case of functional competition of one product with another, not only will performance of the old technology be surpassed, but cost will usually be as well.
- If a product alone is changed, the performance of an existing technology will certainly be surpassed in some way.
- If process alone is changed, production cost will almost certainly be improved dramatically.
- If a process discontinuity results in a great change in product quality or availability, its performance and usefulness may be greatly increased as well.

The relationship between product and process innovation will most certainly be affected by the new technology. With traditional dedicated production systems, product and process innovations occur together; new systems are needed to produce new products. In this situation, the *technology life cycle* of a firm's production process corresponds directly to the life cycle of the firm's product(s). With the new technology, on the other hand, firms can achieve both the flexibility required to fabricate various products and the efficiency that is needed to produce high volumes economically. This, in turn, implies that firms will not have to match every one of their product innovations with a corresponding process modernization, because the flexibility of the production process will enable it to adapt to product modifications. By cutting down the process obsolescence factor in this way, companies can better justify expensive capital equipment investment decisions. With the new technology, the life cycle of a firm's products and that of its processes will deviate; companies may go through several product innovation cycles before they start a new process innovation cycle. Exhibit 4.5 (particularly if compared to Exhibit 4.4) illustrates this point clearly.

The new technology may have another positive impact on the relationship between product and process innovation. Generally, product design and manufacturing are considered two separate entities in most firms. This often creates operational difficulties, because new or modified (product) designs require substantial adjustments to the manufacturing process before they can be manufactured. In other words, process innovations might be needed to accommodate

[8]Utterback and Kim [1985], p. 118.

Exhibit 4.5   A Relationship between Product and Process Innovation
Over Time—The Impact of New Technology

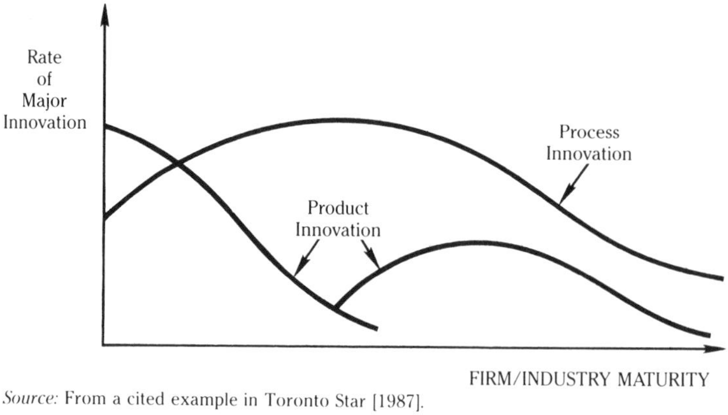

Source: From a cited example in Toronto Star [1987].

desired product innovations. The integrative effects of the new technology (for
example, CAD/CAM) can allow firms to better manage the dynamic interface
between product and process innovation. In other words, the idea is not to concentrate on product innovation alone and then move to process innovation. A
more proactive and responsive approach is to focus on a simultaneous, integrative
approach to product and process innovation. From a practical standpoint, what
makes this integration feasible is unification of R&D, design, engineering, manufacturing, and marketing. This integration may well be a primary factor in the
success of North America's top manufacturers. Exhibit 4.6 provides an example.

Research versus Development

Although research and development are commonly linked, it is useful to
distinguish between them here. Ansoff and Stewart [1967] make this distinction
by describing the characteristics associated with research oriented (R-intensive)
versus development oriented (D-intensive) organizations. R-intensive companies
are those that attempt to generate original inventions that have the strong
possibility of being used within the firm. D-intensive companies focus their efforts on modifying inventions and existing innovations to meet their specific
needs. Companies that attempt to pioneer technological advances in their industry (technological leaders) tend to be R-intensive, whereas companies that
adopt already proved technologies (technological followers) are inclined to be
D-intensive.

Basic versus Applied Research.   The concept of research can also be
divided into two categories, basic (or fundamental) and applied (or directed).
Basic research, being nondirective, involves generating new knowledge or truths.
Many firms, particularly those competing to remain at the leading edge of
technological advances, have been successful at basic research, although in North

Exhibit 4.6   Integrating Product and Process Innovation: A GM Example

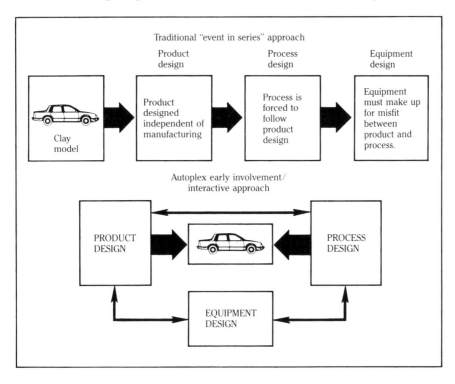

America, the bulk of basic research is still being funded by the government.[9] For example, in 1987 Dupont spent 7 percent of its $1.2 billion R&D budget on basic research.[10] One view among researchers is that it is only through basic research that potential opportunities for exploiting technical knowledge and inventions can be spotted and acted upon quickly. *Applied research,* on the other hand, is geared towards solving practical problems within the firm. It is more directed than basic research and is used to generate inventions that have a high probability of being adopted. Advocates of applied research argue that there is a sufficient inventory of scientific knowledge for most firms to draw upon without having to perform their own basic research.

Despite the differences between basic and applied research, their boundaries often overlap, and firms can utilize elements of both approaches to improve their competitive position. For example:

[9]In 1987 basic research spending in the United States amounted to about $15 billion: $10 billion was contributed by the federal government; $3 billion was spent by private corporations; and the remaining $2 billion came from individual states and nonprofit institutions (see Gannes [1988]).

[10]Other companies that invest heavily in basic research include AT&T Bell Laboratories, IBM, and GE (see Bylinsky [1988]).

At Bell Laboratories (the research arm of AT&T), AT&T's corporate budget pays for basic research (about $200 million last year). Bell Labs is striving to help AT&T's businesses by tailoring this research more closely to company needs without sacrificing the scope and sweep of investigations. Bell Labs executives scrutinize research activities for their contribution to the parent company's business, defined as "management and movement of information."[11]

So far we have discussed three separate notions: basic research, applied research, and development. Exhibit 4.7 summarizes their characteristics. While the distinctions between them are useful, they are not in fact as discrete as the exhibit might imply. Most R&D projects are neither purely basic nor applied, but rather a hybrid of the two. Strategically, companies must make a conscious decision on the form(s) of R&D on which they will concentrate. This decision is of primary importance in formulating an overall business and technology strategy, and will be a topic of further discussion later in this chapter and in Chapter 5.

Exhibit 4.7   A Comparison of the Primary Characteristics of Basic Research, Applied Research, and Development

Characteristics	Type of Research		
	Basic	*Applied*	*Development*
Primary objective	To generate new knowledge and scientific truths	To generate inventions that can be used within the firm	To modify inventions and innovations to meet the specific needs of the firm
Focus	Nondirected (low focus)	Directed toward solving general problems (medium focus)	Directed toward solving specific problems (high focus)
Source	Government and university labs; some technological leaders	Technological leaders	Technological followers
Philosophy	To discover something that will change the way things are done; to expand the the frontier of knowledge	To be at the leading edge of technological advances within the industry	To implement already proven technologies and perfect them

MODELING THE INNOVATION PROCESS

Generating successful innovations is a complex process. A number of models have been discussed in the literature to help clarify this process. In this section, we will discuss three simple models explaining the ways and means of innovation, as well as some related issues.

[11]Adapted from Bylinsky [1988], p. 61.

Matching Technical Abilities and Market Needs

The basic philosophy behind innovation is that it brings together technical abilities and market needs. In other words, for an innovation to be successful, there must be a recognition of market needs and a technical means of meeting those needs. Utterback's model, shown in Exhibit 4.1, addresses this issue by explaining that the process of innovation is influenced to a large extent by two environmental factors: (a) the current state of technical knowledge, and (b) the current use of products and processes as well as the needs and wants for new products and processes. The following models explain how this matching of technical abilities and market needs can happen.

Technology Push.   Early models explaining innovation are based on the view that research and development is the primary source of innovation ideas. This view, called the technology-push or discovery-push model of innovation, argues that a new discovery will trigger a linear sequence of events which will eventually result in an application of the invention. The technology-push model of innovation is illustrated below.

The technology-push approach can be given credit for major revolutionary innovations such as radio and the computer. However, in many instances it appears that relying solely on R&D to come up with innovations may result in products that have no market potential. For example:

> NABU Network Corp. of Ottawa was at the leading edge of satellite technology that uses cable-television networks to deliver software to subscribers' home computers. However, while the company had been admitting that the service may be "ahead of its time," it was defending its continuation only on the grounds that "if NABU hadn't done it, somebody else would have utilized this type of distribution." Apparently, the market for this technology was not sufficient to make it economically successful; NABU began operations as a separate company in 1983, in the first half of 1984 it suffered losses of $10 million, and by 1986 it no longer existed.[12]

Market Pull.   To cope with the possibility that innovations may have no market potential, others have proposed a market-pull approach. This process is illustrated as follows:

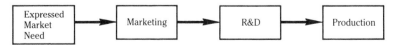

[12]Adapted from Lilley [1984], p. 39.

With a market-pull approach, expressed market needs create new product opportunities which in turn stimulate R&D to determine if a solution is possible. In theory, this approach would ensure that the innovations would be suited to a particular market need. Here is an example:

> In the steel industry, intense competition for business has meant that customers now demand higher and more consistent product quality than ever before. One example of this is for cold rolled products that are used in the production of pop cans, where specification tolerance limits are one half to one quarter of what they used to be. Dofasco (one of the largest steel companies in Canada) realized that in order for the company to maintain its competitive edge, a new system for thickness measurement and control had to be developed to replace what was currently available in the marketplace. Less than one year later, Dofasco had developed, tested, and implemented a product into its production process which could not be purchased on the outside. The product, called Non-Contact Thickness Gauge, allows Dofasco to produce coils of accurate and consistent thickness. For the customer, this means that more cans can be cut from the same coil, thus increasing the already greater cost efficiency of steel cans.[13]

Naturally, investing all of a firm's resources in projects that are solely the result of expressed market needs rather than potential technical opportunities is not wise.

Tauber [1979] suggests that the measurement of consumer needs is not valid for innovations that are unusual or discontinuous.[14] Discontinuous innovations require major changes in attitudes and behavior by consumers (one example is microcomputers), and these changes do not happen immediately. Therefore, test marketing and other marketing research experiments will not provide an accurate indication of what the consumer wants. Test marketing is done for a relatively short period of time, before consumer attitudes and behaviors have had a chance to adjust.

Finally, there is the issue of the quality of an innovation. Although research in this area is very limited, it is posisble that while market demands lead to a large number of innovations, they may not necessarily lead to innovations that have as great an impact as those that stem from technical opportunities. That is, continuous (evolutionary) innovations tend to come through market-pull, while discontinuous (revolutionary) innovations originate more often through technology-push.

The Integrative Approach.   Much research has been done in an attempt to support the presence of both the technology-push and market-pull models of innovation. For example, research indicates that the majority of innovation ideas (anywhere from 60 percent to 90 percent) come from market demands or

---

[13]Adapted from *Financial Times of Canada* [1987], p. A5.

[14]*Discontinuous innovations* are defined as being innovations which are considered as completely new products. *Continuous innovations* are simply new brands in an existing category that are the result of product differentiation.

production needs, rather than from the recognition of a technical opportunity.[15] This supports our contention that failure to integrate marketing into the innovation process early often seriously jeopardizes the fate of a new product by introducing one which the market may or may not respond positively to. Both technical and market factors must therefore be considered together.

Recently, an integrative approach to innovation has been proposed. It involves the consolidation of marketing and technical tasks that reinforce both the technology-push and the market-pull innovation models. Additionally, it is based on the notion that management engages in a matching process between market needs and new technology capabilities. In this case, feedback between marketing and R&D is essential.

Preliminary findings offer some support for the notion that innovativeness is greater when an integration of push and pull forces is driving the decision (see Munro and Noori [1988]). In general, the integration of push and pull factors leads to a greater commitment to new ideas (such as the acquisition of new manufacturing technology) than does just a market-pull, and to a lesser extent, a technology-push approach. A model illustrating the integrative approach to innovation is shown in Exhibit 4.8.

In short, it is believed that an integrative approach to innovation can best ensure that management remains aware of (but not blinded by) and capable of responding to technological advances such as those characterized by new manufacturing and information technologies. The model shown in the exhibit

Exhibit 4.8   A Framework for an Integrative Approach to Technology Push and Marketing Pull

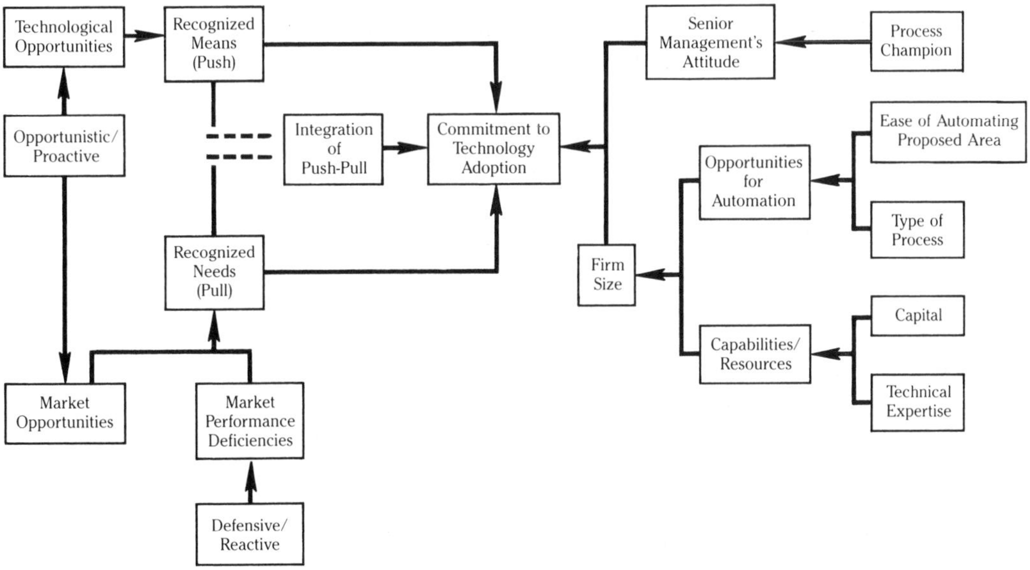

Source: Munro and Noori [1988], p. 64.

[15]For example, see Marquis [1969], Utterback [1974].

displays various forces that affect a firm's commitment to innovation, and to technology adoption.

Factors Affecting Innovation

As explained previously, successful innovation requires that technical capabilities and market needs be matched. The models presented in the previous section are useful in describing some of the primary issues involved in fostering successful innovations. They do not, however, take into account the many other external and internal factors that may affect the innovation process. The purpose of this section is to describe some of the underlying variables that facilitate or inhibit innovation.

External Variables.   A number of external variables influence the degree and type of innovation undertaken by firms. These variables include:

- The prevailing economic environment
- Market and supply factors
- Industry characteristics
- Government policies

An economy characterized by steady growth and low interest rates typically creates an environment conducive to innovation. Poor growth, high cost of capital, and overcapacity, among others, lead to a situation that inhibits innovation and technology adoption. Market and supply factors also influence innovation. That is, "... the frequency of innovation may be expected to increase when the market for a particular product is expanding. Similarly, when the cost of a particular input rises, innovations may be expected to be aimed at reducing the use of that factor in producing an end product."[16] The oil embargo of the 1970s was the primary catalyst behind the move to smaller cars, just as rising labor costs contributed to the push for automated production processes.

Industry characteristics can influence the degree and type of innovation undertaken by firms. For example, young industries are commonly characterized by many products but few process innovations, whereas firms in mature industries traditionally implement only a small number of incremental product and process innovations. Government policies too can have a major impact on the degree and type of innovation done by firms. Such policies include R&D incentives and tax breaks. Public policies and the role of government in facilitating innovations are important matters that will be dealt with explicitly in Chapter 11.

Internal Variables.   A number of firm-specific variables influence the innovation process within a company. These internal factors include both people characteristics and organizational structure.

[16]Utterback [1971], p. 80.

The process of innovation within an organization is facilitated by entrepreneurs who desire and create change. Stevenson and Gumpert [1985, pp. 86–87] have used the following set of questions to contrast entrepreneurs with managers who are more concerned with stability:

QUESTIONS ENTREPRENEURS ASK	QUESTIONS MANAGERS SEEKING STABILITY ASK
• Where is the opportunity?	• What resources do I control?
• How do I capitalize on it?	• What structure determines our organization's relationship to its market?
• What resources do I need?	
• How do I gain control over them?	• How can I minimize the impact of others on my ability to perform?
• What strucutre is best?	• What opportunity is appropriate?

The size of the given firm also appears to have an impact on the level of innovation and entrepreneurship. Large firms may be more able to pursue potential innovations because of their sizable resources base, both in terms of capital and expertise. Small firms, on the other hand, seem to have strong, informal communication networks, minimal bureaucracy, and a bias for action that is necessary for innovation. This suggests that big companies can stay innovative if they behave like small entrepreneurial ventures. In fact, the term *intrapreneurship* " . . . was coined to emphasize the problems of fostering entrepreneurship in large organizations."[17] Quinn [1985] discusses this by describing seven "bureaucratic barriers to innovation" which often restrict the process in large firms.[18]

Internal and external information and communication systems are also important variables influencing the innovation process. Peters and Waterman [1982] have identified five effective attributes of internal communication systems that help to foster innovation:

1. Communication systems are informal.
2. Communication intensity is extraordinary.

[17] Betz [1987], p. 20.

[18] These seven barriers are:
   a. Top Management Isolation–Top managers have minimal contact with customers and with plant personnel, therefore they cannot accurately weigh the risks and benefits of potential innovations.
   b. Intolerance of Fanatics–Entrepreneurial fanatics are often viewed as embarassments or troublemakers.
   c. Short Time Horizons–Short-term profit reporting and evaluation conflicts with the long time spans that many innovations require.
   d. Accounting Practices–The strict allocation of costs makes development expenses much higher, and therefore, net present values much lower.
   e. Unreasonable Rationalism–Excessive planning at the early stages of the innovation process drives out the flexibility that is required to create successful innovations.
   f. Excessive Bureaucracy–Bureaucratic structures and approval systems cause many delays and can dampen the interactive feedback that fosters innovation.
   g. Inappropriate Incentives–Reward and control systems usually are not designed to take into account the risks and uncertainties involved in generating innovations.

3. The intense informal communication system acts as a remarkably tight control system.

4. Communication is given physical supports (for example, people are located close to each other, with minimal barriers).

5. "Forcing devices" ensure that innovation is virtually institutionalized. For example, Technology Centers are established by some companies to guarantee that some time is devoted explicitly to innovation.

Aside from the requisite attention to internal communication systems, it is important that the organization be structured to promote communication flows between the firm and its external environment.

MANAGING AND FOSTERING INNOVATION

Invention—Innovation—Diffusion Time Lags

There are often significant time lags between a scientific discovery, its use in an invention, and the time the invention is applied as an innovation. Similarly, there is generally a time delay between an innovation and its commercialization and/or utilization by firms (a diffusion time lag). This is shown in Exhibit 4.9. The length of the time lags noted in the exhibit can have a significant impact on the effectiveness of the technological strategy employed by firms. If we draw a hypothetical line in the exhibit separating diffusion from innovation, we can more clearly observe that: (a) the innovation process is in reality a continuous cycle, and (b) there are two viable strategic and technological alternatives open to firms.

Exhibit 4.9 Invention–Innovation–Diffusion Time Lags: The Total Manufacturing Chain

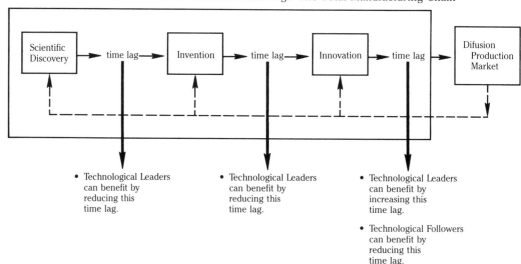

Technological leaders can increase the effectiveness of their strategy by reducing the time lag between scientific discovery and invention, and/or by lessening the time lag between invention and innovation. By reducing either one (or both) time lags, firms can effectively increase the rate at which they generate technological innovations. This in turn will effectively give the technological followers less time to adopt and exploit the new ideas.

Similarly, technological leaders can increase the effectiveness of their strategy if they are able to lengthen the diffusion time lag for competitors. If these firms can keep their original innovations from spreading quickly to other companies, they will be able to exploit the advantages of the innovations for a longer period of time. Clearly, and on the contrary, technological followers could benefit by reducing the diffusion time lag.

Many technologies, once diffused, would directly or indirectly result in the conception of the next generation of technology (for example, circuit boards). After a given time lapse, this cycle then repeats itself. Furthermore, depending on their focus and market strengths, firms might find it convenient to spend time and effort commercializing an existing concept and tailoring it to create their own market niche. This approach provides a potential stepping stone to market supremacy. Japanese firms have clearly followed this approach; for many years, their strategy has been to take the ideas from other countries and use them to advantage to produce consumer products of high quality (they refer to this as the *kaizen* concept[19]). Consider the following:

> The video recorder is a classic example of how production knowhow can yield important technical advances. Sony, along with Matsushita Electric and its partner, Japan Victor Corp. (JVC), redesigned a professional-use product from the United States that cost $20,000 or more and turned it into a $1,500 home product with a relatively small market.[20]

The strategy the Japanese pursue on an international scale can also be followed successfully by individual firms within an industry, especially if they share trade secrets.

Trading Trade Secrets. Evidence has recently shown that "...direct competitors generally secure detailed information about a new product or process within a year."[21] Apparently, managers have been unable to prevent technological innovations from diffusing quickly to competitors. However, Von Hippel [1988] explains that a large part of this diffusion of R&D information is done purposely by engineers, who often volunteer proprietary information to competitors in return for future favors.

There are two suggested scenarios, one where information trading is

---

[19]*Kaizen* means ongoing improvements in the product (see Imai [1986].

[20]Wood [1987], p. 17.

[21]Von Hippel [1988], p. 58.

beneficial to the firm, and another where it is not. Apparently, most engineers implicitly understand both the benefits and risks of trading R&D knowledge. However, in some cases engineers may not be acting in the best interests of the company (knowingly or not) by trading proprietary information. Von Hippel argues that management should not restrict the trading of information, because restricting it will simply drive the trade underground. Instead, management should consider formally supporting this practice and attempt instead to reduce the risks and gain the benefits available through knowhow trading. Peters [1988] calls this "creative swiping" and suggests that it can, and indeed should, be institutionalized by the firm to gain competitive advantage.

Cooperative Interfirm Agreements

There has recently been an increased awareness of the potential benefits of sharing resources and knowledge when developing and applying innovations and new technology. North American firms seem more willing than ever before to combine forces with their competitors and/or with producers of the new technology, perhaps because they have seen the Japanese success at doing so.

Competitor Cooperation.   The magnitude of many new technology projects all but necessitates cooperative efforts. The following example exemplifies this point:

> Baxter Travenol Laboratories Inc. recently joined with AT&T and IBM to bid on a Department of Defense hospital automation contract. This $1.1 billion project to install a state-of-the-art computer-information system for 700 military health-care facilities throughout the world could eventually result in $3 billion worth of government business. Baxter brings its expertise as a health-care provider to the team; AT&T handles the telecommunciations and IBM contributes the computer hardware.[22]

Producer/User Relationships.   Traditionally, North American producers (of technology) have been relatively independent in their efforts to generate innovations. In other words, innovations have typically occurred in either of two ways:

1. The user builds and employs an innovation before a producer builds and sells a commercial version.
2. The producer builds and sells a commercial version of an innovation before a user builds and uses a home-made version.

More [1986] explains that the development of many new CAD systems often follows a "developer-driven serial process" whereby the:

[22]McCoy [1988], p. 17.

CAD system supplier goes through the development process unilaterally to the point of producing a particular system configuration with a particular data input mode, screen resolution, display monitor characteristics, screen size, price, accessories, and other characteristics. . . . In this example the developing organization would also produce this system to inventory (unit commitment), and at that point enter the market and commence actual relationships with potential adopting organizations.[23]

The complexities inherent in the development and adoption of the new technology make it all but necessary for both producers and users to participate in joint innovation projects and in the development and implementation of the technology. This is especially true for integrated systems technologies such as CAD/CAM, FMS, and CIM. Consider the following example:

The oil equipment division of a multinational steel company generated $100 million and was growing. Management wanted to accelerate the introduction of new products to increase market share. Recently, the division installed a computerized business system and felt that CAD/CAM technology was the next step in automation.

Management . . . would select two vendors, one with design expertise and the other with manufacturing expertise. The division would install the systems separately and link them later when a drawing database suitable for manufacturing could be established. Once the two-vendor approach was decided upon, vendors were screened based on their commitment to integrating the two systems.[24]

There are also a number of implications for both producers and users of the new technology who are considering a cooperative approach to the development and implementation of the new technology. These are listed in Exhibit 4.10.

In the development and application of any new technology, there are a number of requisite stages. Where the cooperative approach is employed, both developer and user of the technology must go through these stages. Exhibit 4.11 illustrates the stages, and the different actions and goals of each stage, for both users and developers. The most important requirement for successful co-development is that user and developer move through these stages more or less together. Through negotiation, and exchanges of information and resources, user and developer work in tandem from problem recognition to implementation along the optimal path shown in Exhibit 4.12. Ideally, the result of this will be the design and implementation of a technological innovation that is beneficial and profitable for both parties. Note that a nonintegrative approach will result in uncoordinated progress by the two parties, causing one or both to move off the diagonal away from the other. Given the necessarily interactive nature of the

[23]More [1986], p. 11.
[24]Adapted from Schaefer [1985], p. 104.

Exhibit 4.10   Implications for Producers and Users of New Technology: A Co-Development Approach to Innovation

Implications for Producers	Implications for Users
• Investment needs and cash flow requirements may be significantly reduced as development costs and resource expenditures can be spread over a longer period of time. • The supplier may be able to identify at a much earlier stage what product concept(s) would be desired by other users. • The supplier will have a "longer" relationship with the user. This can reduce the uncertainty of the project, enable more people from the supplier organization to get involved in the process, and as a result, increase the effectiveness of the project. • The experience gained from this project will enable the supplier to better plan and estimate the financial and human resources needed for future projects. • The new technology developed may be too user-specific to be marketable to other organizations.	• Rather than being constrained by the characteristics of systems that have already been developed, users will be able to approach the problems and needs of their organization from an unconstrained point of view. • The user will be able to evaluate the system over a longer period of time, which allows the user to assemble the financial and human resources needed to indepthly consider the system characteristics needed by the firm. • The user can have a greater influence on the system configuration developed by the supplier.

Source: Based on More [1986].

Exhibit 4.11   Stages in the Development and Adoption Subprocesses

Stage	Developing Organization	User Organization
Problem recognition	Analysis and definition of the users and rationale for automating	Analysis and definition of the internal need and rationale for automating
Need analysis	Analysis and definition of needs, payoffs and risks of developing the controls	Analysis and definition of needs, payoffs and risks of automation
	Estimation of final product costs	Acceptance/rejection of preliminary cost
Product/process specifications	Analysis and definition of the choices between alternative product performance dimensions and required process specs	Analysis and detailed definition of the required performance dimensions and process specifications
Technology choice	Analysis definition choice, linkage of available technologies to meet the product/process specs	Analysis, definition choice linkage of physical technologies-in-use for the product specs
Product design	Analysis, definition, and translation of specs and technologies into a product design and/or prototype	Analysis of product design and product specifications
Financial analysis	Detailed proposal of the financial requirements to build the product and analysis of the method of payment alternatives	Analysis of the proposal and method of payment

Exhibit 4.11   (Continued)

Stage	Developing Organization	User Organization
Production testing	Sourcing of suppliers and production and testing of product	Analysis of any product alterations during production
Implementation	Integration of automation controls into user's facility	Process implementation and integration of new controls, analysis and evaluation of effectiveness and satisfaction
Post implementation	Required product modifications and additions	Analysis of further automation opportunities and repurchases

Exhibit 4.12   Subsequent Developer/User Relationships

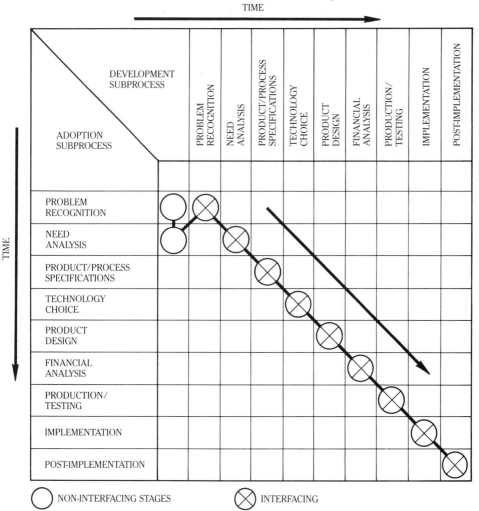

Source: The Exhibit is based on More's research [1986].

innovation process, and the fact that the unit of measurement on both axes is time, a nonintegrative method will take longer (and thus cost more) than the integrative approach to produce a particular innovation.

The value of the integrative approach (as well as the difficulty of managing it) is particularly clear when we consider that on a given innovation project, not one but many suppliers may be involved. Consider, for example, a firm developing specialized automated machinery for its production process. It may conceivably require input from a machine builder, a PLC (Programmable Logic Control) supplier, a materials handling expert, and an engineering house specializing in systems integration to pull the others together. Undoubtedly, the complexity of coordinating and integrating the efforts of several participants is vast. However, the necessity of pursuing this coordination and integration is also essential, since with more suppliers, the innovation process is more likely to become uncoordinated and lead to time delays and cost overruns.

Technology Transfer

Generally, the transfer of technology can be viewed in four different contexts:

- International technology transfer
- Transfers from government (and universities) to industry
- Interfirm technology transfer (between different firms)
- Intrafirm technology transfer (within the same firm)

In this section, we will focus exclusively on intrafirm technology transfer: the other types will be covered in Chapter 11.

There are two types of intrafirm technology transfers: (a) horizontal transfers, transfers of technology across different divisions of the same firm, and (b) vertical transfers, transfers that occur during the innovation process, such as from research to development to application. Naturally, companies can benefit economically and can save time by ensuring that innovations and technological capabilities generated within one division are transferred to other divisions. Horizontal technology transfer is popular among companies such as Litton and TRW which often translate military innovations into commercial ones (see Senia [1987]). In general, however, many North American firms lack the ability to transfer technology between their divisions, because management has traditionally pitted one division against another in an effort to improve productivity. This does not promote the tightly coupled organization and exchange of ideas needed to foster transfer. Companies that benefit from horizontal technology transfer generally promote cross-fertilization in two ways (Senia [1987]):

1. Set up a corporate culture that encourages open communication among divisions.
2. Establish networks that provide a formal way for divisions to exchange technology.

Vertical technology transfers can be impeded by a number of barriers. Many of these occur at technology transfer points; that is, at the boundaries separating basic research from applied research, applied research from development, development from design, design from production, and eventually production from marketing. These barriers can include both technical constraints (the invention generated by R&D is too complicated to be reproduced in volume by manufacturing), and nontechnical considerations (basic researchers may be more interested in understanding the theory behind how an invention works rather than in actually commercializing the invention). The same two requirements needed to promote horizontal technology transfer also appear to hold for vertical transfers. Specifically:

1. Set up a corporate culture that encourages open communication among functional groups.
2. Establish networks that provide a formal way for functional groups to exchange technology.

How to Make New Things Happen: The Five Critical Components

Martin [1984] has developed a chain equation to explain the innovation process. The chain is a chemical analogy which states that a commercially successful innovation ". . . requires the synthesis of scientific, engineering, entrepreneurial and management skills, combined with a social need and a supportive sociopolitical environment."[25] Roberts [1977] explains that any project team working on an innovation must be able to perform five critical functions: idea generation, technological and market gatekeeping, project championing, project managing, and coaching. It is crucial that these five key staff roles are filled if innovative ideas are to be generated, developed, and implemented on a large scale in the organization and its environment.

Martin's innovation chain link and its relationship to these five critical functions is illustrated in Exhibit 4.13. Ideally, each of these critical functions should be performed by an individual with recognized and well-defined responsibility. This will minimize the probability of overlooking an important variable in the innovation process and expand the level of commitment of project team members. We will now describe each of the five critical components that are necessary to generate successful new innovations.

Ideas Generator. The generation of ideas is the first step. The ideas generator is the person (or persons) responsible for this task. He/she is usually a creative problem-solver with the ability to view obstacles in different ways. The following example illustrates:

[25]Martin [1984], p. 20.

Exhibit 4.13 The Critical Functions That Are Required to Produce Successful Innovations

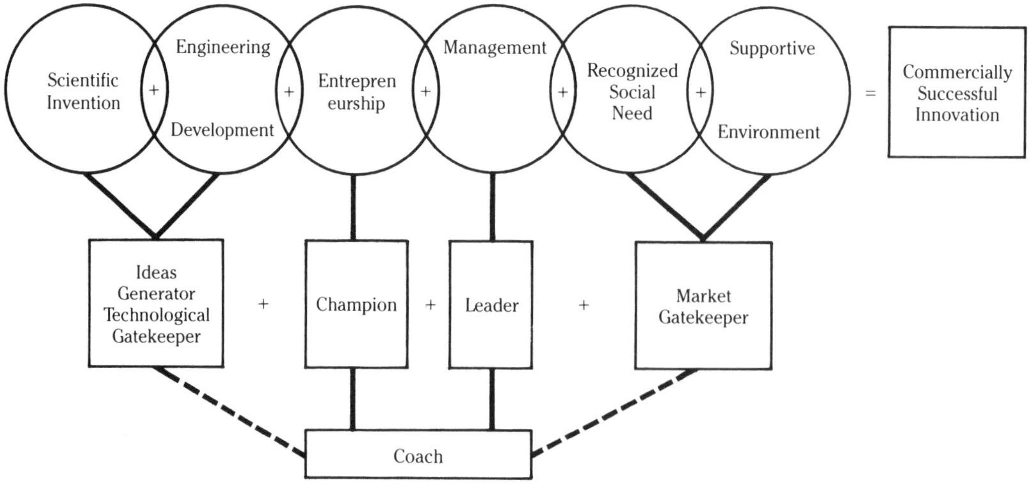

Source: Martin [1984], p. 223

I often ask beginning robotics students to design a robot to wash a stack of dishes. Usually the students conceive an expensive machine with two hands that lift up each dish in turn, inspects it visually for dirt, picks up a brush, dips it in soap, scrubs the dish, and so on. After the discussion has gone on for a while, I remind the class that local department stores sell automatic dishwashers for about $250.[26]

Technological and Market Gatekeepers. The technological gatekeeper is an individual with highly developed technical skills who keeps up with the latest technical developments. He/she supports the ideas generator by providing him/her with information on technical developments, opportunities, and limitations. At Texas Instruments, for example, ". . . each division has a technical coordinator, who serves as a gateway through which outside developments may enter."[27] The market gatekeeper is responsible for gathering information on potential market opportunities and ensuring that innovation efforts are geared toward an identifiable market.

The value of both gatekeeping roles should not be underestimated. It is the technological and market gatekeepers who ensure that the technical abilities and the market need information are brought into the firm to foster successful innovations. It is they who together facilitate the successful application of the integrative approach to innovation discussed earlier.

Project Champion. The project champion (or entrepreneur) is the engine that keeps the project moving forward until it is completed. It is this person who

[26]Whitney [1986], p. 112.
[27]Senia [1987], p. 38.

often has the fanatical tendencies frowned upon by the managers of many large companies. The following example illustrates the importance of this role:

> A senior officer in a successful consumer goods company says that product winners are always championed by a brand manager who has ventured far beyond the rules. He has worked with R&D on an intense, personal basis (most of his less successful cohorts worked only formally with researchers); as a result, he garners an "unfair" share of R&D time and attention. Similarly, straying beyond his official charter, he gets involved in a hands-on way with pilot manufacturing. All in all, his intensity leads him to try more things, learn faster, get lots more time and attention from other functions—and eventually to succeed.[28]

Innovations can be divided into two categories, (a) those which are unplanned and result from spontaneous ideas, and (b) those which are created to solve a specific problem. With the first type of innovation, it is probable that in many cases the idea generator and the project champion are the same person. With the second type, however, it is likely that some sort of project team has been set up by management to solve the specific problem. In these cases, a different person may assume responsibility for the ideas generation and project champion roles. In either case, the need for a committed project champion is clear. Gerwin [1982] exemplifies this with regard to advanced manufacturing technology by explaining that many companies require a project champion who is willing to take risks and provide tenacius commitment to new projects before a decision to adopt new technology will even be seriously considered. This commitment is also needed to ensure that the technology is implemented successfully. The need for a project champion during the implementation of new technology will be discussed further in Chapter 9.

Project Manager and Leader. The project manager is a general administrator who is responsible for planning, organizing, and coordinating the project. This person must be sensitive and responsive to the needs and characteristics of the individuals making up the project team to ensure that their efforts are coordinated. The project manager must also ensure that various parts of the project are completed on time, that expenses are controlled, and that needed resources are available when required.

Coach. The coach (or sponsor) is often a senior executive who serves as an advisor to the project team and ensures that the project gets top management support. This role is critical because the attitude of senior management is usually a primary force in the decision whether or not to adopt a new manufacturing technology. Furthermore, studies of industrial research and development suggest that "...many projects would not have been successful were it not for

---

[28]Peters and Waterman, Jr. [1982], p. 207.

the subtle and often unrecognized assistance of such senior people acting in the role of sponsors."[29] In other words, the support provided by the coach is not just token, figurehead support.

The project teams assembled to generate innovations are sometimes referred to as *skunkworks*. Typically, skunkworks refer specifically to project teams assembled to work solely on a particular project, with no organizational distractions. Although this type of arrangement can be used to generate innovations relatively quickly, the nature of a skunkwork means that other everyday functional activities performed by the members of the team will be disrupted. Some would argue that this arrangement should be used infrequently and only when absolutely necessary (Riggs [1983]).

CONCLUDING OBSERVATIONS

In the first section of this chapter we discussed some key innovation issues:

1. The difference between invention and innovation. Innovation involves the implementation of inventions. In other words, innovation carries invention one step further, and it is this step that is most difficult to manage.

2. The concepts of evolutionary (or incremental) innovation and revolutionary (or major) innovation, and how they affect the firm.

3. The relationship between product and process innovation and how new technology may change this relationship.

4. The differences between basic research, applied research, and development. Firms must make a conscious decision as to how much of each of these R&D functions to perform, and ensure that innovation within the firm is not adversely affected by lack of support for R&D functions.

5. The time lags that occur between scientific discovery, invention, innovation, and diffusion may influence the effectiveness of the innovation strategy a firm follows.

6. Firms may in some cases be forced to "innovate or evaporate"—in other words, in order to be competitive, they may have to develop innovations rather than purchase them from outside sources.

In the second section, we stressed that innovation involves the matching of technical abilities and market needs. Three models explain how this matching may occur. We concluded that an integrative approach to technological innovation is the best route for a firm to follow. Integrative innovation requires constant feedback between marketing, R&D, and manufacturing to ensure that potential technical capabilities are matched with market needs and that the product can, in fact, be produced. Other factors, both internal and external to the firm, also affect the firm's ability to innovate effectively.

[29]Roberts [1977], p. 28.

Finally we discussed six critical functions that are necessary to foster successful innovation:

1. Ideas generator—source of ideas
2. Technological gatekeeper—source of technical information
3. Market gatekeeper—source of market need information
4. Project champion—person who moves the project forward.
5. Project manager and leader—those who administer and coordinate the project
6. Coach—provider of top management support

Firms should assign clear and explicit responsibility for each of these six functions with any innovation project that is being pursued. They must also realize that different stages of the innovation process require different types of people who should be managed and motivated in unique ways.

RECOMMENDED READINGS

BURGEL, R. A., and M. A. MAIDIQUE [1988]. *Strategic Management of Technology and Innovation.* Richard D. Irwin, Homewood, Ill.
BYLINSKY, G. [1988]. "The New Look At America's Top Lab." *Fortune,* February 1, pp. 60–65.
FREEMAN, C. [1982],. *The Economics of Industrial Innovation,* 2nd ed. The MIT Press, Cambridge. Mass.
QUINN, J. B. [1985]. "Managing Innovation: Controlled Chaos." *Harvard Business Review,* May–June, pp. 73–84.
VON HIPPEL, E. [1988]. "Trading Trade Secrets." *Technology Review,* February–March, pp. 58–64.

DISCUSSION QUESTIONS

1. It is often argued that many innovations fail because they are not market oriented and the sales forecasts for these fail to materialize. This implies that more money should be spent researching the market potential of innovation possibilities.
   a. Considering the fact that a company has limited resources, do you feel that companies would enjoy more success if they allocated more of their resources to determine market needs and less of their resources to research and development?
   b. Does the market always know what it needs or wants?
2. Is it "idealistic" to pursue an integrative approach to innovation, given the fact that many companies will be marketing or research focused based on the background of management? What steps could be taken to promote an integrative approach to innovation?
3. Firms that innovate incrementally in order to improve the efficiency of their operations often reduce the flexibility of their operations. These incremental innovations expose the firm to the possibility of a revolutionary innovation making their standardized and inflexible operations obsolete. Can a firm guard against this? How?
4. How will the new technology affect the relationship between product and process innovation?
5. Discuss methods that you feel could be used to increase the probability of innovation within a firm.
6. In Japan, suppliers and customers tend to share information and resources (including technological developments) more than in North America. Japanese competitors within an industry share information and technical knowledge, whereas North American firms traditionally do not (and in some cases are prevented by law from doing so). On one hand, one

can argue that if a firm shares its knowledge with others, it is giving up the competitive advantage it could exploit with that knowledge. On the other hand, the sharing of information within an industry should enable the industry as a whole to progress more quickly and become more competitive. Which of these two approaches should be pursued by North American firms? Could the Japanese approach work in North America? Explain.

7. Management is considering the adoption of a policy that would strictly forbid the trading of R&D information with competitors. Would you support such a policy? Explain.

REFERENCES AND BIBLIOGRAPHY

ABERNATHY, W. J., and P. L. TOWNSEND [1975]. "Technology, Productivity, and Process Change." *Technological Forecasting and Social Change*, Volume 7, pp. 379–396.

ABERNATHY, W. J., and J. M. UTTERBACK [1978]. "Patterns of Industrial Innovation." *Technology Review*. In Burgelman and Maidique [1988], pp. 141–148.

ABERNATHY, W. J., and K. WAYNE [1974]. "Limits of the Learning Curve." *Harvard Business Review*, September–October, pp. 109–119.

ANSOFF, H. I., and STEWART, J. M. [1986]. "Strategies for a Technology-Based Business." *Harvard Business Review*, November–December, pp. 71–83.

BARRETT, F. D. [1980]. "Tools and Tricks for Innovators." *Business Quarterly*, pp. 57–62.

BETZ, F. [1987]. *Managing Technology: Competing Through New Ventures, Innovation, and Corporate Research*. Prentice-Hall, Englewood Cliffs, N.J.

BLENKHORN, D., and H. NOORI [1988]. "Responding to Challenge: A Blueprint for North American Supplier Survival." Working Paper, *REMAT*, Wilfrid Laurier University, Waterloo, Ontario, January.

BURGELMAN, R. A., and M. A. MAIDIQUE [1988]. *Strategic Management of Technology and Innovation*. Richard D. Irwin, Homewood, Ill.

BYLINKSY, G. [1988]. "The New Look at America's Top Lab." *Fortune*, February 1, pp. 60–65.

BYLINSKY, G. [1984]. "America's Best Managed Factories." *Fortune*, May 28, pp. 16–24.

CAPON, N., and R. GLAZER [1987]. "Marketing and Technology: A Strategic Coalignment." *Journal of Marketing*, Volume 51, July, pp. 1–14.

CLARK, K., and H. HAYES [1985]. "Exploring Factors Affecting Innovation and Productivity Growth Within the Business Unit." In D. Clark, R. Hayes, and C. Lorenz (eds.), *The Uneasy Alliance: Managing The Productivity—Technology Dilemma*. Harvard Business School Press, pp. 425–458.

DRUCKER, P. F. [1985]. "The Discipline of Innovation." *Harvard Business Review*, May–June, pp. 67–72.

FALCONER, T. [1986]. "WRSM: Cutting the Cost of CAD." *Canadian Business*, May, pp. 82–89.

Financial Times of Canada [1987]. "Dofasco: The New Age of Steel." Special Advertising Feature, November 23, pp. A1–A24.

FREEMAN, C. [1982]. *The Economics of Industrial Innovation*, 2nd ed. The MIT Press, Cambridge, Mass.

GANNES, S. [1988]. "The Good News About U.S. R&D." *Fortune*, February 1, pp. 48–56.

GERWIN, D. [1982]. "Do's and Don'ts of Computerized Manufacturing." *Harvard Business Review*, March–April, pp. 107–116.

GOLDHAR, J. D. [1987]. "Evolution in Manufacturing—The Inevitability of Strategic Impacts of CIM." In *Computer Applications in Production Engineering*. Elsevier, North-Holland, pp. 3–14.

GROSSMAN, L. [1984]. "Economic Transformation: Technological Innovation and Diffusion in Ontario." Ministry of Treasury and Economics, March.

GUPTA, A. K., S. P. RAJ, and D. WILEMON [1985]. "The R&D-Marketing Interface in High-Technology Firms." *Journal of Productivity and Innovation Management*, Volume 2, pp. 12–24.

HAYES, R. H., and S. C. WHEELWRIGHT [1984]. *Restoring Our Competitive Edge: Competing Through Manufacturing*. Wiley, New York.

IMAI, M. [1986]. *KAIZEN: The Key to Japan's Success*. Random House Business Division, New York.

LAPP, PHILIP A. [1985]. "Technology Transfer in Ontario: Awareness and Program Mechanisms." Prepared for Ministry of Industry, Trade and Technology, September.

LILLEY, W. [1984]. "Leading-edge Disasters." *Canadian Business*, December.

MAIDIQUE, M. A. [1980]. "Entrepreneurs, Champions, and Technological Innovation." *Sloan Management Review*, Winter, pp. 59–76.

Management Review [1984]. "What's Ahead in Technology . . . Blind Spot in Strategic Planning." October, pp. 26–28, 49–52.

MANSFIELD, E. [1981]. "How Economists See R&D." *Harvard Business Review*, November–December, pp. 98–106.

MARQUIS, D. G. [1969]. "The Anatomy of Successful Innovations." *Innovation*. In Tushman and Moore [1982], pp. 42–50.

MARTIN, M.J.C. [1984]. *Managing Technological Innovation & Entrepreneurship*. Reston Publishing Company, Reston, Va.

McCOY, C. W. JR. [1988]. "Competitors Team Up: Joint Efforts Reduce Project Risks." *High Technology Business*, January, p. 17.

McGINNIS, M. A., and M. R. ACKELSBERG [1983]. "Effective Innovation Management: Missing Link in Strategic Planning." *The Journal of Business Strategy*, Volume 4, No. 1, pp. 59–66.

MORE, R. A. [1986]. "Developer/Adopter Relationships in the Adoption of CAD/CAM Systems: Implications for Operations Management." *National Center for Management Research and Development*, Working Paper Series No. NC 86–02, July.

MUNRO, H., and H. NOORI [1988]. "Measuring Commitment to New Manufacturing Technology: Integrating Push and Pull Concepts." *IEEE Transactions on Engineering Management*, Volume 35, No. 2, pp. 63–70.

MYERS, S., and E. E. SWEEZY [1978]. "Why Innovations Fail." *Technology Review*, March–April, pp. 40–46.

PETERS, T. [1988]. *Thriving on Chaos*. Alfred A. Knopf, New York.

PETERS, T. J., and R. H. WATERMAN, JR. [1982]. *In Search of Excellence*. Warner Books, New York, pp. 200–234.

QUINN, J. B. [1985]. "Managing Innovation: Controlled Chaos." *Harvard Business Review*, May–June, pp. 73–84.

RIGGS, H. E. [1983]. "Communication Between Engineering and Production: A Critical Factor." *Managing High-Technology Companies*. Van Nostrand Reinhold. In Burgelman and Maidique [1988], pp. 279–288.

ROBERTS, E. B. [1977]. "Generating Effective Corporate Innovation." *Technology Review*, October–November, pp. 26–33.

SCHAEFER, T. J. [1985]. "Modular Approach to CIM: Integrate Your Factory in Pieces." *Production Engineering*, April, pp. 102–104.

SENIA, A. [1987]. "Companies Turn Old Ideas into Profits." *High Technology Business*, December, pp. 36–39.

STEELE, L. [1983]. "Managers Misconceptions about Technology." *Harvard Business Review*, November–December, pp. 134–140.

STEVENSON, H. H., and D. E. GUMPERT [1985]. "The Heart of Entrepreneurship." *Harvard Business Review*, March–April, pp. 85–94.

TUSHMAN, M. L., and W. L. MOORE [1982]. *Readings in the Management of Innovation*. Pitman.

UTTERBACK, J. M. [1974]. "Innovation in Industry and the Diffusion of Technology." *Science*, Volume 183, February 15, pp. 658–662.

UTTERBACK, J. M. [1971]. "The Process of Technological Innovation within the Firm." *Academy of Management Journal*, March, pp. 75–88.

UTTERBACK, J. M., and L. KIM [1985]. "Invasion of a Small Business by Radical Inovation." In P. R. Kleindorfer (ed.), *The Management of Productivity and Technology in Manufacturing*. Plenum Press, New York.

VON HIPPEL, E. [1982]. "Appropriability of Innovation Benefit as a Predictor of the Source of Innovation." *Research Policy*, Volume 11, No. 2, April, pp. 95–115.

VON HIPPEL, E. [1988]. "Trading Trade Secrets." *Technology Review*, February–March, pp. 58–64.

WHITNEY, D. E. [1986]. "Real Robots Do Need Jigs." *Harvard Business Review*, May–June, pp. 110–116.

WOOD, R. C. [1987]. "Assembly Lines Build Ideas: Manufacturing Excellence Aids Creativity." *High Technology Business*, p. 17.

Chapter Five

THE STRATEGIC IMPLICATIONS OF NEW TECHNOLOGY

A critical link between technology and strategy exists; the only real choice is whether managers want to see it.

Alan M. Kantrow

INTRODUCTION

Until recently, few North American companies carefully considered the strategic implications of technology. The following quote exemplifies this point:

> Senior managers at a major U.S. corporation recently decided to count the number of lines devoted to technology in their strategic business units' strategic plans. They found four. An unusual discovery? Not in the least, the fact that the corporation operates in a high tech industry notwithstanding. A growing number of high level managers are finally waking up to the dismaying realization that they have failed to do any strategic technological planninig.[1]

Although many firms are beginning to realize the need for strategy and technology alliance, there are still many who do not. Furthermore, even those who are aware of the need may not fully appreciate all the issues involved. This is so because the concept of technology strategy is still relatively new and undeveloped. The discussion in this chapter attempts to foster a better understanding of the need for and concept of integrating technology with strategy.

Specifically, this chapter will discuss the role of manufacturing as a function and technology as a resource in the strategic planninig process, the potential strategic benefits of the new technology, and the primary components of a technology strategy. However, before these topics are addressed, we will briefly review the strategic planning process.

[1]Management Review [1984], p. 26

131

STRATEGIC PLANNING—A BRIEF REVIEW

What Is Strategic Planning?

Generally, strategy deals with objective(s) of a company, its product/market focus and scope, and its competitive emphasis. Strategic planning (or strategy formulation) is a process through which the firm develops a strategy that is consistent with its environment (for example, industry and competitive environments), resources, managerial values, and organizations.

Hax and Majluf [1984], and Hamermesh [1987] have identified various levels of strategy that should be explicitly formulated in many organizations. From their analysis, four strategy levels can be identified: (1) institutional strategy, (2) corporate strategy, (3) business unit strategy, and (4) functional strategy.

Institutional strategy refers to the development of the basic character and purpose of an organization; it is also called the corporate mission. It involves a visionary outlook in order to answer questions such as: Who are we? Where are we going? *Corporate strategy* refers to the practice of corporate-level portfolio planning. Strategy at this level involves determining which businesses within the corporation should be divested, which businesses could be acquired to strengthen the organization, and how the individual business units will interact in terms of shared resources, market focus, and so forth.

Business unit strategy consists of developing a clear and detailed plan outlining an individual business unit's goals and objectives (growth, market share, new product introductions), and the means by which the unit will compete to achieve these objectives (low cost, market niche). This strategy is developed by looking at the organizational capabilities), the preferences, values, and culture of the organization (both within the individual business unit and the corporation), and the environment (industry, political, technological) the firm operates in.

Functional strategies (manufacturing, marketing) are formulated to ensure that the business strategy is implemented successfully throughout the organization. Discussion in this chapter will focus primarily on the business unit and functional strategies of an organization, and on the relationship between them. We begin with a brief discussion of the interface between manufacturing strategy and business (unit) strategy.

Strategic Planinng and Manufacturing Considerations

The manufacturing function of an organization is primarily concerned with internal activities (the production process), whereas another like marketing is involved primarily in external operations (customer contact). Furthermore, the (internal) manufacturing capabilities of an organization determine how effectively the (external) marketing function can satisfy the customers. Many authors[2]

---

[2]For example, see Skinner [1969], Wheelwright and Hayes [1985], Hill [1985], and Haas [1987].

have demonstrated how manufacturing decisions can be instrumental in restricting, reinforcing, or determining the company's overall business strategy. We will also contend and later demonstrate that an effective business strategy can only be developed by fully integrating manufacturing decisions into the strategic planning process. This is the best way to ensure that manufacturing and other functional objectives are harmoniously geared to enhancing the competitive strengths of the firm.

Manufacturing's role in the strategic planning process should include two general stages of involvement: (1) assessing manufacturing capabilities and restrictions, and (2) formulating and implementing a manufacturing strategy. Manufacturing must adopt both a strategic role (to enhance the competitive advantage of the firm) and a supportive role (to serve the market and to produce the right product) during each of these stages. This is to ensure that the company is not missing any strategic opportunities available through manufacturing, and to ensure that the manufacturing function is supporting the company's business strategy. Exhibit 5.1 compares the two roles of manufacturing in the strategy formulation process.

Exhibit 5.1   Manufacturing's Roles in the Strategic Planning Process

		Stage of Involvement	
		Assess Manufacturing Capabilities and Restrictions	*Formulate and Implement a Manufacturing Strategy*
N A T U R E O F	S t r a t e g i c	Can manufacturing provide a distinctive competence?	Are manufacturing decisions being made strategically?
P A R T I C I P A T I O N	S u p p o r t i v e	Can manufacturing perform the requirements inherent in business strategy proposals?	Do manufacturing decisions reinforce our business strategy?

Assessing Manufacturing Capabilities and Restrictions

The capabilities and restrictions of a firm's manufacturing facilities must be considered during the strategy formulation process. A particular manufacturing capability or policy may be the key to generating a distinctive competence (certain potencies vis-à-vis its competitors), allowing the firm to compete more effectively. The following example illustrates how a proper manufacturing decision can enhance the company's competitive advantage:

> In the highly cyclical electronics industry, manufacturers have habitually ordered from their suppliers on a very short-term basis. Hewlett-Packard took a different tack. It committed itself to firm orders six months ahead. This change enabled Hewlett-Parkard's silicon suppliers to exploit economies of scale and improve their quality. In turn, Hewlett-Packard could rely on component quality and delivery even in times of industry shortage, thereby better serving its own customers and reaching a strategic breakpoint.[3]

Manufacturing must also be capable of meeting the requirements of a particular business strategy. Yet it cannot be all things to all people. Typically, manufacturing decisions involve tradeoffs (cost, quality, flexibility, and dependability) that limit its capabilities. For example, a decision to locate the company's manufacturing facilities near sources of raw materials as opposed to near customer markets may make it difficult (or impossible) to pursue a strategy based on just-in-time delivery.

Conflict often exists between manufacturing and other functional areas such as marketing as they find themselves striving toward different objectives. This conflict occurs because of a lack of understanding of the tradeoffs inherent in manufacturing decisions. Exhibit 5.2 describes the areas of conflict between manufacturing and, in this example, marketing (Shapiro [1977]). The incorporation of manufacturing decisions into the strategic planning process should reduce these conflicts, since the relevant tradeoffs in manufacturing would be discussed and consolidated into the plan.

FORMULATING AND IMPLEMENTING
A MANUFACTURING STRATEGY

The formulation of a responsive manufacturing strategy has been a hot research topic over the last two decades. Hayes and Wheelwright's investigation [1984] into strategic management of the manufacturing function, for example, resulted in the unfolding of a simple and yet an important two-dimensional grid: the product-process matrix (see Exhibit 5.3). The matrix is intended to allow managers to ascertain the strategic positioning of their business units and focus on a single

[3]Haas [1987], p. 79.

Exhibit 5.2 Potential Areas of Manufacturing-Marketing Conflict

Problem Area	Typical Marketing Comment	Typical Manufacturing Comment
1. Capacity planning and long-range sales forecasting	"Why don't we have enough capacity?"	"Why didn't we have accurate sales forecasts?"
2. Production scheduling and short-range sales forecasting	"We need faster response. Our lead times are ridiculous."	"We need realistic customer commitments and sales forecasts that don't change like wind direction."
3. Delivery and physical distribution	"Why don't we ever have the right merchandise in inventory?"	"We can't keep everything in inventory."
4. Quality assurance	"Why can't we have reasonable quality at reasonable cost?"	"Why must we always offer options that are too hard to manufacture and that offer little cusotmer utility?"
5. Breadth of product line	"Our customers demand variety."	"The product line is too broad—all we get are short uneconomical runs."
6. Cost control	"Our costs are so high that we are not competitive in the marketplace."	"We can't provide fast delivery, broad variety, rapid response to change, and high quality at low cost."
7. New product introduction	"New products are our life blood."	"Unnecessary design changes are prohibitively expensive."
8. Adjunct services such as spare parts inventory support, installation, and repair	"Field service costs are too high."	"Products are being used in ways for which they weren't designed."

Source: Reprinted by permission of the *Harvard Business Review.* An exhibit from "Can Marketing and Manufacturing Coexist?" by Benson P. Shapiro (September–October 1977). Copyright © 1977 by the President and Fellows of Harvard College; all rights reserved.

Exhibit 5.3   The Hayes and Wheelwright Product-Process Life-Cycle Matrix

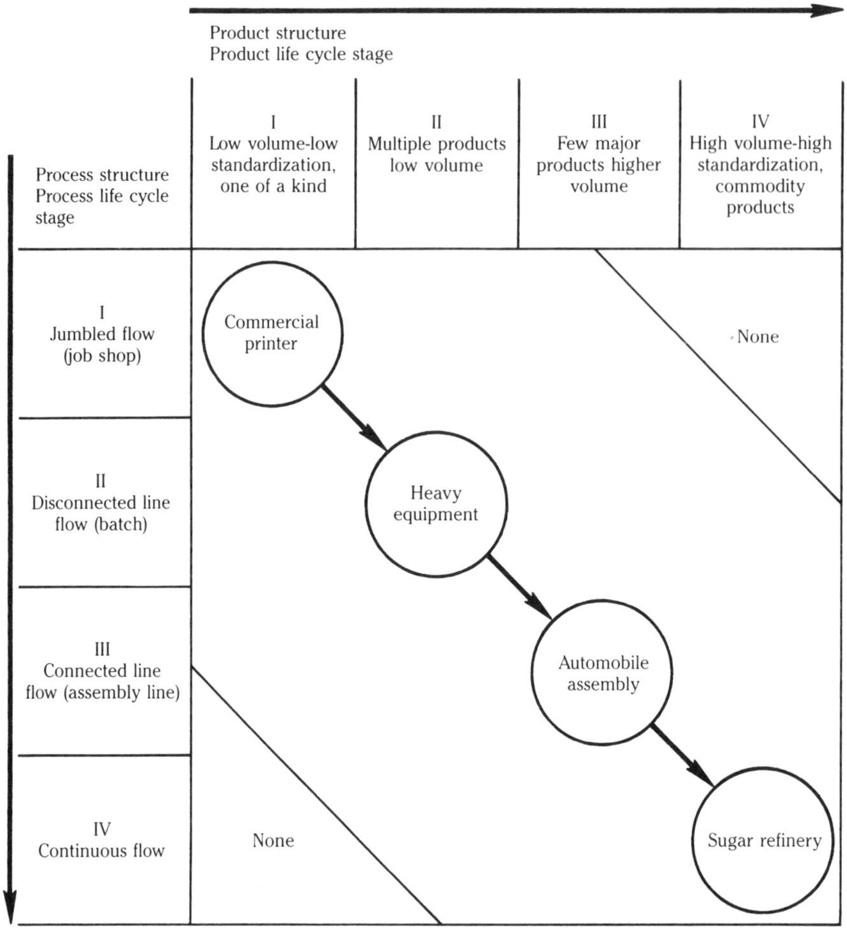

	Product structure Product life cycle stage			
Process structure Process life cycle stage	I Low volume-low standardization, one of a kind	II Multiple products low volume	III Few major products higher volume	IV High volume-high standardization, commodity products
I Jumbled flow (job shop)	Commercial printer			None
II Disconnected line flow (batch)		Heavy equipment		
III Connected line flow (assembly line)			Automobile assembly	
IV Continuous flow	None			Sugar refinery

Source: Hayes and Wheelwright [1984], from *Restoring our Competitive Edge: Competing through Manufacturing.* Copyright © 1984, John Wiley & Sons, Inc.

patch in the matrix which determines a specific process-product combination. Subsequently, appropriate processes and technologies can be pursued.

Any manufacturing system must produce and provide specific products. A successful manufacturing strategy, however, should ensure that manufacturing rulings are in line with corporate goals and objectives. In other words, decisions such as choice of equipment and technology must be made from a strategic rather than from an operational perspective. The following is a list of manufacturing decisions that should be dealt with from an overall strategic point of view. These decisions are directed at operationalizing the manufacturing strategy of the firm:

1. The number, size, capacity and location of plants
2. The choice of equipment and process technology
3. The degree of vertical integration
4. The number of and relationship with vendors
5. The choice of making or buying component parts
6. The new products to be developed and introduced
7. The selection and training of human resources
8. The quality control system to be used
9. The production scheduling system to be used
10. The amount of inventory to carry

A company that adopts a purely operational approach to manufaturing decisions may be overlooking the potential strategic benefits of these decisions. Consider the following:

> An appliance maker found that it could extend the life of its product and save $1.75 per unit in warranty costs by substituting a newly designed part. Against expectation, it turned out that the new part would add more than $2 to the cost of each unit—hardly an attractive proposition, operationally speaking. But on strategic grounds the move still made exellent sense. By sparing the end user cost and inconvenience over the product's lifetime, it would strengthen the company's sales message and increase the product's value in the customer's eye. Management's decision to go ahead has since been rewarded by a hefty gain in market share.[4]

Manufacturing decisions which do not appear operationally sound may make sense strategically. Similarly, manufacturing decisions of operational importance may have no strategic value. Ideally, a manufacturing strategy should ensure that operational decisions reinforce the company's business strategy. The next example shows the potential consequences if this does not occur:

> Company ABC produced plastic molding resins. A new plant under construction was to come on stream in eight months, doubling production. In the meantime, the company had a much higher volume of orders than it could meet. In a strategic sense, manufacturing's task was to maximize output to satisfy large, key customers. Yet the plant's production control system was set up as it had been for years—to minimize costs. As a result, long runs were emphasized. While costs were low, many customers had to wait, and many key buyers were lost. Consequently, when the new plant came on stream, it was forced to operate at a low volume.[5]

[4]Haas [1987], p. 75.
[5]Skinner [1969], p. 137.

Finally, a manufacturing strategy must be well-defined and include specific statements of goals and objectives, plus time frames for each. That is, it must be more than just a generalized statement. In practice, it seems that many companies lack a well-defined manufacturing strategy. Without one, however, managers cannot consistently make enlightened operational decisions. For example:

> A large automotive supplier was in the process of developing a production monitoring system. As part of the design process a statement of their manufacturing strategy was reviewed. The formal strategy called for the lowest industry cost position and at the same time the highest industry quality level. Given that six other companies had larger market shares, it was very unlikely that the company would obtain its ambiguous objectives. Thus, the strategy statement was of little use in designing a monitoring system that would reinforce a defendable strategic position.[6]

In the following sections we look at different perspectives concerning the role of manufacturing in the strategy formulation process and present a conciliatory view that incorporates the intrinsic potential of the new technology.

Applying the Conventional Wisdom

At present, there are two basic schools of thought on business strategy formulation. We call them the convergent cycle and the divergent cycle.

The Convergent Cycle.   This approach is based on the conventional idea that strategy dictates organizational structure (Chandler [1962]). This method, exercised fully, leads to what Skinner [1969] called top-down strategic management of the manufacturing function. Hayes [1985] calls this the "ends-ways-means" model. The argument, in this case, is that firms should define their competitive advantage first, and then determine manufacturing capabilities (and other functional needs). This process focuses on product/market strategy.

The Divergent Cycle.   This approach relies on a more recent premise that strategy follows structure (Hall and Saias [1980]). This view argues that an awareness of the dynamics and characteristics of the organization (the flexibility of manufacturing) will result in the development and execution of a more responsive business strategy. This framework is based on a process/manufacturing focus rather than the product/market focus of the convergent approach.

The Myopia of the Conventional Approaches

Clearly, when it comes to formulating a responsive business strategy which consolidates the strategic benefits of the new technology, neither of the two

[6]Orne and Hanifin [1984].

approaches is fully satisfactory. Following the convergent approach, for example, might result in missing product/market opportunities that manufacturing can potentially open up for the firm. The following example highlights this point:

> Company ABC adopted CAM technology to manufacture a new part without understanding the equipment's potential for machining several parts. When demand for the new part fell off, management was unprepared and had to rush to come up with new tooling fixtures and parts programs while idle time mounted. Had management identified the possibility of utilizing CAM to manufacture a range of different parts, the problem would have been far less serious, as new markets could have been entered quickly.[7]

Furthermore, as will be discussed in detail in Chapter 7, technology acquisition might not be justified if the convergent (product) approach is pursued, because many of the potential benefits of the new technology may not be recognized or acknowledge.

At the same time, the divergent (process) approach may lead the firm into areas where it lacks knowledge (industry structure, competitive threats, and government regulations). This could expose the firm to additional environmental risks for which it is unprepared. Consider the following scenario:

> Company XYZ initially began its operation as a manufacturer of sales promotion items for industrial marketers. The president, while attending a trade show, decided to acquire state-of-the-art machinery capable of welding plastic parts together using ultrasound technology. The company originally used the technology for the existing product line but later on, realizing its flexibility and speed, began to diversify to other products. Over a period of three years, the product line expanded to include a diverse number of houseware and hardware items, and eventually manufaturing parts for subassemblies. Consequently, the product line became so varied that the control of the marketing and production activities of the company became an impossible task. The newly hired marketing manager had no way to defining the business except as anything which could be made on the company's machines!

Due to the deficiencies inherent in these approaches, we suggest a third view that integrates their strengths, while avoiding their limitations. We shall call this the balanced approach.

The Balanced Approach

Rather than being based solely on product/market focus or process/manufacturing focus, the balanced approach encompasses the vitality of both. It not only ties the acquisition of technology to the firm's competitive emphasis, but also

---

[7]Adopted from Gerwin [1982], p. 114.

allows for an exploration of the capabilities of the new technology in enhancing the firm's competitive advantage. Consider the following example:

> Echlin Canada is a major producer of slack adjusters, a brake system device. For approximately 20 years, the assembly of this product was done in a very conventional, manual way. In 1984, Echlin decided to supplement one of its production lines with highly sophisticated robots. This resulted in Echlin cutting prices and eventually becoming one of the largest producers of slack adjusters in the world. Moreover, the company has since been able to advantageously deploy the acquired new technology to expand its initial product mandate into other autopart components, further strengthening its competitive position.

The balanced approach involves an ongoing iterative process consisting of five phases:

Phase I: The Assessment Phase. Decide on the competitive advantage of the firm which then determines, among other things, its manufacturing strategy.

Phase II: The Implementation Phase. Ascertain whether the appropriate and supportive components of the business strategy are in place (for example, proper manufacturing technology is obtained).

Phase III: The Awareness Phase. Recognize and explore the full capability of the available resources—for example, the potential of producing other products with the flexible technology.

Phase IV: The Integration Phase. Search for new opportunities to apply the recognized potential and to integrate them with the existing (business) strategy.

Phase V: The Alteration Phase. Review and redefine the current competitive advantage to take account of the present and future potential of available resources. This phase determines the imminent direction of the company based on the full capabilities of existing resources.

Exhibit 5.4 shows the three approaches to formulating a manufacturing strategy.

THE STRATEGIC POTENTIAL OF THE NEW TECHNOLOGY

Economies of Scale versus Economies of Scope

Traditionally, many firms have pursued an economies of scale strategy which advocates that large volumes of few products must be produced on specialized (but inflexible) equipment in order to minimize long-run average costs and reduce throughput times. The major reasons for exercising this approach have been these:

- To take advantage of learning curve effects
- To minimize changeover times
- To maintain a manufacturing focus

Exhibit 5.4   Progression to the Balanced Approach of Formulating a Manufacturing Strategy

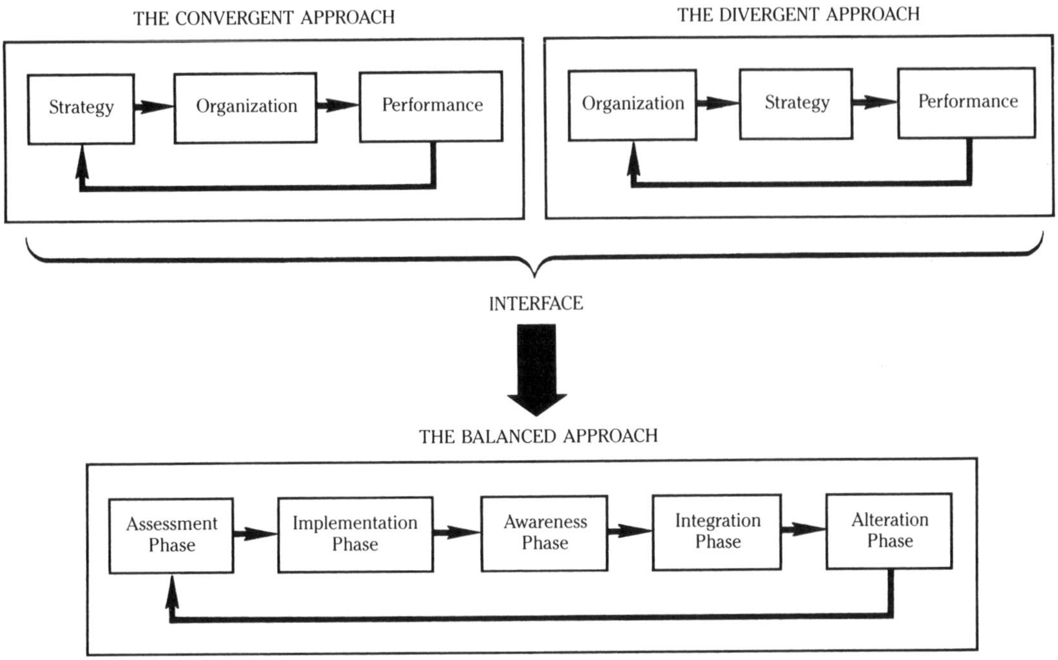

THE CONVERGENT APPROACH   THE DIVERGENT APPROACH

| Strategy | ➤ | Organization | ➤ | Performance |

| Organization | ➤ | Strategy | ➤ | Performance |

INTERFACE

⬇

THE BALANCED APPROACH

| Assessment Phase | ➤ | Implementation Phase | ➤ | Awareness Phase | ➤ | Integration Phase | ➤ | Alteration Phase |

The inflexibility inherent in technologies exhibiting economies of scale can be contrasted with the concept of economies of scope. Economies of scope are realized where it is less or equally costly to produce two or more products in combination than separately (Goldhar and Jelinek [1983]). The savings arising from economies of scope are derived from spreading the fixed costs of the machinery across several products. Firms pursuing this strategy depend on using general-purpose equipment to gain the flexibility required to produce small volumes of customized products.

Economies of Integration

The specialization that was previously incorporated into a machine's hardware can now be achieved through software capabilities. This enables flexible machinery to act and perform as efficiently as specialized machinery with instructions being changed instantaneously, ensuring that the process is not delayed by lengthy setup times.[8] The new technology has paved the way for the simultaneous presence of economies of scope and economies of scale. It is now possible for a plant to have the capability associated with the two economies concurrently. This we will call *economies of integration*. Integration economies

[8]It is recognized that setup times for fixtures or tooling can be quite high, for example on an FMS, as a *new* batch of parts is introduced. However, within the current batch, multiple tooling can be effectively utilized without lengthy setup times.

stem from these characteristics of scale and scope which possess the greatest flexibility. For example, economies of integration provide a high degree of production, process, and infrastructure flexibility and the ability to produce a variety of customized products (characteristic of scope economies), as well as the ability to produce a large aggregate volume of low-cost products (characteristic of scale economies). Conceptually, we expect that economies of integration will encourage firms to maintain medium-sized plants.

The notion of integration economies favors a product focused and not plant focused (as characterized by Skinner [1974]) organization. At GM's recently completed AUTOPLEX in Oshawa, Ontario, the conventional assembly line principle has been replaced by a new sytem called tracking signal,[9] whereby custom-made cars are assembled with all the various options (colors, and the other accessories) without interruption in the production flow. In this context, economies of integration reflect the highest degree of aggregate flexibility because the technology makes it possible to switch the production process at no significant cost, allowing variations in output at lower unit cost.

Economies of integration are made possible through the application of technologies such as computer integrated manufacturing. In practice, CIM has all but eliminated the factors that have kept scale and scope economies apart by:

1. Allowing the specialization that has normally been embedded into the production hardware to be built into the computer software—this significantly reduces the inflexibility of a dedicated production process because general-purpose machines with specialized software can be used in the place of specialized hardware.

2. Eliminating learning curve effects (or direct labor) through software that can perform the required operations perfectly every time.

3. Eliminating the confusion of an unfocused factory through the computer direction of scheduling, machinery, materials flow, and tooling.

4. Allowing setup changes that can be accomplished with no significant time loss—this along with point 2, effectively reduces the economic batch quantity (EBQ) to one.

In other words, economies of integration connote a progression toward a more flexible and dynamic operational system. Exhibit 5.5 further contrasts the characteristics of economies of integration with those of scale and scope.

Economies of integration offer the potential for a new and revitalized manufacturing strategy. Its adoption increases machine utilization and scheduling flexibility and decreases direct and indirect labor, manufacturing lead time, and in-process inventory. In this way, it has a fundamental impact on Hayes and Wheelwright's [1984] product-process life-cycle matrix (shown in Exhibit 5.3),

[9]In tracking signal, the Volvo's team approach concept and the Automated Guided Vehicle Systems (AGVS) are combined to give a much broader flexibility to the employees and the production system.

Exhibit 5.5   Principal Characteristics of the Three Economies of Scale, Scope, and Integration

Characteristics	Scale (Volume)	Scope (Variety)	Integration (Variety & Volume)
Process	Continuous flow	Jumbled flow batch	Continuous flow
	Special purpose machinery	General purpose machinery	Specialized software, computer integrated multipurpose machinery
Product	Standardized—commodity	Customized—multiproducts	Customized—commodity
Facility	Centralized	Decentralized	Moderately decentralized
	Large (in size)	Small (in size)	Medium (in size)
Level of automation	Low (hard to programmable automation)	High	Highest (flexible automation)
Total added flexibility	Low	High	Highest
Relative unit costs:			
• Fixed	Low	High	Highest
• Variable	High	Low	Lowest
Experience curve	Not too flat	Flat	Flatter and lower
Organization	Process focus	Product focus	Product focus
Managerial characteristics	Technical	Entrepreneurial	Entrepreneurial—technical
Marketing	Low cost, dependability	Flexibility, product innovation	Low cost, dependable product innovation, flexibility

which assumes long life cycles for products. Exhibit 5.6 presents a revised product-process matrix which demonstrates the strategic positioning of economies of integration in comparison with those of economies of scale and scope.[10]

The existence of multipurpose machinery allows the excess capacity of one product's production run to be made available for another product's production run—an effective way to address capacity problems and fluctuating demand for different products. It is no longer necessary to focus the manufacturing strategy on one or two competitive areas. Attempting to be competitive on all four conventional manufacturing tradeoffs—cost, dependability, flexibility and quality—is not at all inconsistent with the concept of economies of integra-

---

[10]In spite of its potential, realizing the benefits of integration economies requires substantial financial commitment from management. In order to justify the acquisition of technologies which allow for economies of integration, management must determine whether or not the volume of products that can be sold will be large enough to cover the enormous capital costs of acquiring the technology. Chapter 7 will address in greater detail the methods of financially evaluating new technology and the potential sources of capital available to fund a technology acquisition.

Exhibit 5.6 A Revised Product-Process Matrix

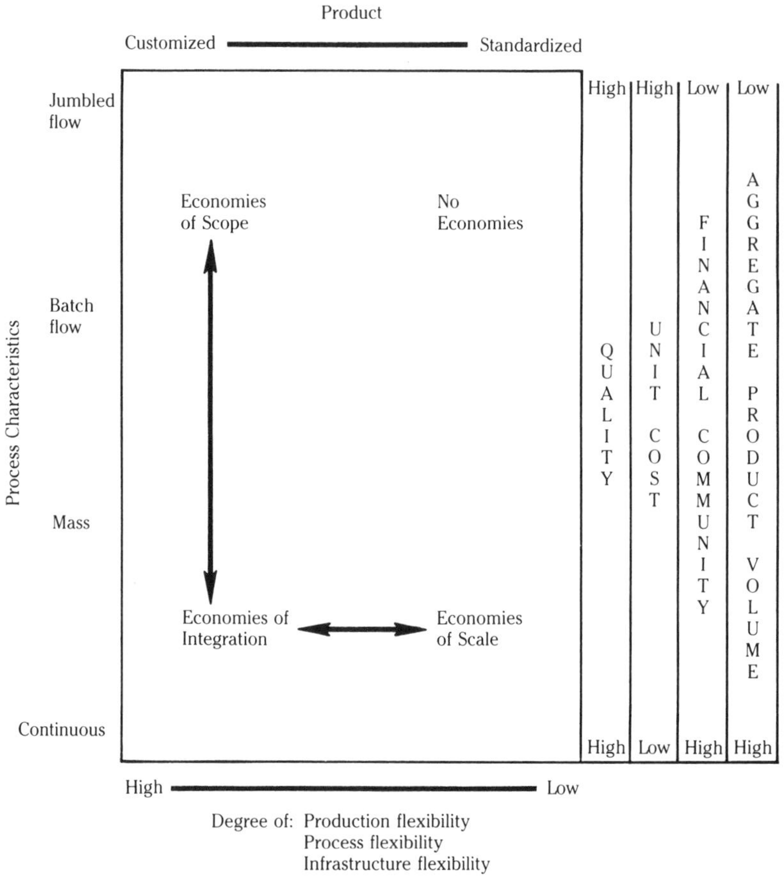

Source: Noori [1988]

tion. By eliminating these tradeoffs, imagination and strategic foresight become the new constraining factors.

The Strategy-Technology Alliance

We mentioned that manufacturing decisions can be instrumental in restricting, reinforcing, or determining a company's strategy. The same holds true for technology-choice decisions. In practice, however, it appears that technology selections have suffered from a general lack of strategic awareness, causing them to commonly appear ". . . in a fragmented, piecemeal fashion as part of other functional strategies such as marketing."[11]

[11]Burgelman, and Maidique, [1988], p. 12.

The new technology, with its inherent flexibility and potential, has highlighted the importance of a technology strategy. It is becoming essential for companies to view technology as a central part of their business thinking. This implies a need for consolidation of technology decisions with manufacturing strategy and subsequently with overall strategic planning. Several distinctive characteristics of the new technology inspire this thinking. First, technology helps to define the range of strategic opportunities available to the firm. Second, technology is one of the important means through which business strategies can be implemented. Third and last, technology can shift the structure of an entire industry.

In short, the concept of technology strategy highlights three important points:

1. Technology strategy must be developed collectively with manufaturing, marketing, and other functional strategies, because technology decisions can have a major impact on each of these areas, and vice versa.
2. Technology strategy must be formed in conjunction with the firm's business strategy because a right choice of technology provides key competencies.
3. Technology strategy must support any future revision of the firm's business strategy and its competitive advantage.

THE PRIMARY COMPONENTS OF FORMULATING A TECHNOLOGY STRATEGY

A technology strategy is essentially a cross-functional, integrated framework for consideration and assessment of technologies available to the firm within the current (and future) scope of its business. This section will discuss some of the technological concerns that should be addressed during the formulation of the company's business strategy. Considering and comprehending these issues, as outlined in Exhibit 5.7, will help to ensure a balanced approach to strategy formulation.

Exhibit 5.7 A Framework Identifying the Primary Commponents of Formulating a Technology Strategy

Technology Assessment	Assess internal resources in terms of flexibility.
	Assess environmental trends through technology forecasting.
Technology choice	What technologies should the firm pursue in the future?
Technological leadership or followership	Should the firm be the first in its industry to adopt new technology, or should it wait until the technology is proved by others?
Technology acquisition	How should the firm acquire the technologies that it wishes to pursue (develop or purchase)?

Technology Assessment

An understanding of the firm's organizational resources and environment is crucial to the development of an effective business strategy. In part, this understanding requires an analysis of the firm's technological resources and environment, in order to:

1. Determine what technological resources can be used to create a strategic advantage for the firm, and what resources are required to support the firm's chosen business strategy. These resource capabilities and requirements should be addressed in terms of flexibility.
2. Determine what future technological trends may have a significant impact on the firm's ability to pursue its competitive strategy. These trends can be assessed through technology forecasting.

Flexibility Requirement.   Prior to deciding on the form of new technology that should be acquired, a company must consider which types of flexibility are most important to its competitive success. This, once again, reflects the importance of using the balanced approach in developing business, manufacturing, and technology strategies.

The inherent flexibilities of the new technology (as described in Chapter 3) can now be used advantageously to eliminate some of the implicit operational tradeoffs in manufacturing decisions. For example, machine flexibility can provide a firm with the capability to switch over its production process very quickly to produce a different set of parts. This enables a firm to reduce its finished goods inventory significantly while still offering short lead times to customers, thus reducing manufacturing/marketing conflicts over delivery and physical distribution policies. Exhibit 5.8 extends the points characterized in Exhibit 5.2 and describes how different manufacturing flexibilities available through the new technology will minimize the conflict in particular manufacturing and marketing problem areas.

Technology Forecasting.   Technology forecasting involves predicting the evolution of individual technologies, and determining how these technologies will affect the industry. Its purpose is to provide management with a better understanding of future trends so that decisions can be made in the light of potentially available technologies. Exhibit 5.9 lists some of the ways in which technology forecasting can assist business decision-making.

Given that technology forecasting is important, the question now becomes: How much forecasting should be done, and what methods and techniques should be used? The frequency of forecasting depends on a number of factors, including:

1. The size of the firm (the resources that can be devoted to forecasting)
2. The impact of technology on the industry (high or low)

Exhibit 5.8 Using New Technology Flexibilities to Eliminate Manufacturing-Marketing Conflict

Problem Area	Typical Marketing Comment	Typical Manufacturing Comment	Possible Flexibility Solution
Capacity planning and long-range sales forecasting	"Why don't we have enough capacity?"	"Why didn't we have accurate sales forecasts?"	Expansion flexibility, volume flexibility
Production scheduling and short-range sales forecasting	"We need faster response. Our lead times are ridiculous."	"We need realistic customer commitments sales forecasts that change like wind direction"	Volume flexibility, machine flexibility, routing flexibility
Delivery and physical distribution	"Why don't we ever have the right merchandise in inventory."	"We can't keep everything in inventory."	Machine flexibility
Quality assurance	"Why can't we have reasonable quality at reasonable cost?"	"Why must we always offer options that are too hard to manufacture and that offer little customer utility?"	Material flexibility, commodity of parts
Breadth of product line	"Our customers demand variety."	"The product line is too broad—all we get are short, uneconomical runs."	Mix flexibility
Cost control	"Our costs are so high that we are not competitive in the marketplace."	"We can't provide fast delivery, broad variety, rapid response to change and high quality at low cost."	Economies of integration
New product introduction	"New products are our life blood."	"Unnecessary design changes are prohibitively expensive."	Innovation flexibility, modification flexibility
Adjunct services such as spare parts inventory support, installation, and repair	"Field service costs are high."	"Products are being used in ways for which they weren't designed."	Machiine flexibility, mix flexibility, range flexibility

Exhibit 5.9   How Technology Forecasting Assists Business Decision-Making

1. Wide-ranging surveillance of the total environment to identify developments, both within and outside the business's normal sphere of activity, which could influence the industry's future and, in particular, the company's own products and markets.
2. Estimating the time scale for important events in relation to the company's decision-making and planning horizons. This gives an indication of the urgency for action.
3. The provision of more refined information following a detailed forecast in cases where an initial analysis finds evidence of the possibility of a major threat or opportunity in the near future, but where this evidence is insufficient to justify action,

   OR

   continued monitoring of trends which, while not expected to lead to the necessity for immediate action, are, nevertheless, likely to become important at some time in the future and must consequently be kept under review.
4. Major reorientation of company policy to avoid situations which appear to pose a threat or to seek new opportunities by:
   a. Redefinition of the industry or the company's business objectives in the light of new technological competition.
   b. Modification of the corporate strategy.
   c. Modification of the R&D strategy.
5. Improving operational decision-making, particularly in relation to:
   a. The R&D portfolio.
   b. R&D project selection.
   c. Resource allocation between technologies.
   d. Investment in plant and equipment, including laboratory equipment.
   e. Recruitment policy.

Source: Twiss, in Burgelman and Maidique [1988], p. 60.

3. The choice as to how close the firm wants to be to the leading edge of technology adoption
4. The time period over which a firm must strategically plan

There are two common classifications of technology forecasting methods: exploratory and normative. Exploratory forecasting involves extending past and present trends into the future. It can be very useful in projecting the advancement of continuous innovations (product/process improvements). Normative methods, on the other hand, are generally used to project the technology advances that will be involved in discontinuous or breakthrough innovations (like the United States STAR WARS defense plan).

Many specific techniques can be used to do technology forecasting. A brief description of some of these techniques is provided below.[12]

> *Intuitive forecasting.* An educated guess approach that can vary from a very naive pronostication to a forecast based on extensive contact with experts in the field.

[12]For a detailed description of forecasting techniques, see Jones and Twiss [1978]).

Trend extrapolation. The use of mathematical curve fitting to project past performance trends into the future.

Purcursor trends. Identifying a relationship between the time an intervention is first applied and the time it is commercialized (for example, the trend line for the speed of transport aircraft has lagged behind the speed of combat aircraft for a period which has slowly extended from nine years in 1930 to 11 years in 1970) (Twiss [1980]).

Relevance trees. The use of a decision tree to show the possible paths that could be followed in order to realize a normative objective.

Scenarios. A method of forecasting which assumes that certain event(s) will occur in the future and logically extends the possible developments that may result from those event(s).

Technology maps. Determining the major technological advances which are pushing and the major market needs which are pulling advances in various technologies forward. (See Betz [1987], pp. 96–100, for further reading.)

It is interesting to note that a great deal of technological progress follows an S-shaped curve similar to the path generated by the product life cycle (Twiss [1980]). In other words, initially minimal improvements are made on some performance parameters. Then, following this slow introductory phase, exponential improvements are often made during a relatively short period of time. Finally, this growth slows to only minimal performance improvements as the natural limits to performance are reached.[13] Exhibit 5.10 illustrates this process.

From a practical point of view, an understanding of the S curve can improve the technology forecasting process. Without this, there is a strong possibility of either (1) seriously underestimating the potential of a new technology in forecasts made during the slow initial growth stage, or (2) overestimating the future potential of a new technology once the exponential growth of performance improvement is almost completed.

Technology Choice

Following the assessment phase, management must decide on the appropriate form of technology the company should pursue. This is a very difficult process, and perhaps the most important aspect of it is to ensure that the technologies selected provide the means for effectively supporting the firm's business strategy. For example:

> General Electric influences the project selection process by ranking technologies in terms of interest or urgency to the corporation. Before a project even gets

---

[13]For example, the performance potential of silicon chips may eventually be restricted because of a physical limit to the number of transistors that can be put on one chip (see Betz [1987], pp. 66–68).

Exhibit 5.10 The S-Curve

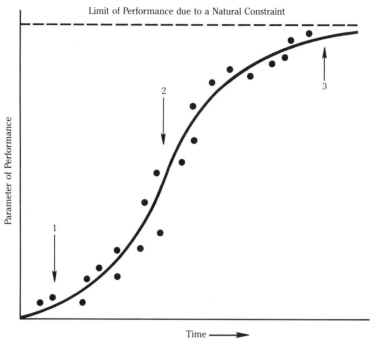

LEGEND
1. Period of slow initial growth
2. Rapid exponential growth
3. Growth slows as performance approaches a natural physical
   limit asymptotically.

Source: Twiss, in Burgelman and Maidique (1988), p. 68.

proposed, the researcher knows that the likelihood of getting funded is tied to how well he supports the corporate strategy.[14]

The choice of which form of new technology to select must naturally come before other relevant decisions. For example, the choice of installing an FMS may have been made so that a firm could follow a competitive strategy based on reliable deliveries; it is only after this choice is made that management can address the areas of justification and implementation.

White and Graham [1978] suggest that any new technology has four major dimensions that must be considered when evaluating its potential for success. These are:

Inventive Merit. A concept that lifts a constraint (or adds additional constraints) to the old technology. For example, the new technology may enable economic runs of one part, but it may also require a more skilled workforce.

[14]*Management Review* [1984], p. 52.

Embodiment Merit. Additions to the basic invention that result in enhancement (or dilution) of the core product. For example, the new technology may become even more effective when combined with better scheduling methods.

Operational Merit. The effect (either positive or negative) on a company's existing business practices. For example, computerized statistical process control technologies may lead to the elimination of rework departments; new process technologies will require a different means of allocating overhead.

Market Merit. How strongly the customer will want the new innovation over what is currently available. For example, questions like "How much will my customers pay for a two-week reduction in lead time?" must be answered.

The first two dimensions, in combination, deliver *technological potency,* or the power of the core technology in terms of what it can do. The last two dimensions provide *marketing advantage,* or the implications for business practice and whether or not the technology offers a distinct business advantage. Exhibit 5.11 indicates how this framework can be used to evaluate the potential success of a new technology acquisition.

It is important to identify the significance of each of the individual impacts in the four dimensions described in Exhibit 5.11. For example, two (or more) pluses could be used to identify the positive factors of most importance which are available through the technology. Although the decision will ultimately be somewhat subjective in nature, engaging in this process will enable management to better comprehend: (1) whether the new technology can be of strategic benefit to the company, and (2) what organizational changes will have to be made to accommodate the technology if it is adopted. The decision support system presented in Chapter 12 illustrates some of these issues.

Naturally, it is conceivable that the choice of technology involves a number of tradeoff decisions. Two important ones to consider are: (1) the choice between developing or acquiring the technology, and (2) how much should be spent on developing and adopting low-risk versus high-risk technologies. While we will address these two points in the following sections, it is important to stress once again that these decisions must be made with the business strategy of the company in mind.

Technological Leadership or Followership

Technological leadership refers to cases where firms attempt to be the first to introduce product, process, or management technologies. Technological followership, on the other hand, applies to companies who adopt already proved technologies or who make a conscious choice not to adopt particular new technologies at all. The decision as to which is appropriate for a given firm depends directly upon many of the issues discussed in Chapter 4.

Porter [1985] describes three factors that must be considered when deciding whether or not to pursue a technological leadership strategy:

5.11 A Framework to Evaluate the Feasibility of New Technology Acquisition

Inventive Merit	Embodiment Merit	Operational Merit	Market Merit
(+) more retooling but less time between changeover	(+) point of sale order can go direct to manufacturing to be built	(+) easier to schedule lines, no need to balance line	(+) expansion of the market base, better quality and variety
(+) ability to respond, i.e. put a product right into the line, design change	(+) increased forecasting ability	(+) elimination of warranty costs, field service, glitches in the system	
	(+) automatic reordering, better scheduling		(−) unit cost sensitive consumers lost
(+) shorter runs, EOQ of 1		(+) eliminate rework, defects	
	(+) ability to move inventory on AGV's		(−) perhaps new technology will not produce 100% of your line and focusing will have to take place
(+) 100% quality potential, less inventory costs reduced scrap		(−) change to strategic focus	
(−) ripple effect, need to make sure inventory is available	(−) less innovative thinking due to smaller workforce	(−) closer marketing and production link	
	(−) possibility of having to design the products to fit the system	(−) different shipping and distribution systems	
(−) high initial costs, i.e. technology, economic, people, etc.		(−) changing perspective	
(−) need to develop new skills, job displacement		(−) can't look only at capital budgeting	
(−) software availability is a problem		(−) allocation of overhead changes	

Technology Potency

Marketing Advantage

NEW TECHNOLOGY—IS IT A WINNER?

(+) = Advantage gained.
(−) = Need for change.

1. The degree to which a firm can sustain its technological lead over the competition
2. The advantages of being the first to adopt a new technology
3. The disadvantages of being the first

Exhibit 5.12 outlines the variables that affect these three factors.

Whether a firm can successfully follow a technological leadership strategy depends on the status of these variables. Once a firm does decide to pursue a

Exhibit 5.12 A Framework for Identifying the Feasibility of a Technological Leadership Strategy

	Variables Which Favor Technological Leadership
1. Sustainability of technological lead	1. Technology is developed within as opposed to outside of the firm.
	2. High R&D costs prevent competitors from following a leadership strategy.
	3. High technological skills relative to competitors.
	4. A low rate of technology diffusion within the industry.
	Variables Which Favor Technological Leadership
2. First-mover advantages	1. Reputation as pioneer or leader.
	2. Opportunity to preempt an attractive marketing position, forcing competitors to adopt less attractive ones.
	3. Customer switching costs.
	4. Choice of prime channel access.
	5. Proprietary learning curve.
	6. Favorable access to facilities, inputs, and other scarce resources.
	7. Chance to define the standards of the technology.
	8. Institutional barriers such as patent protection.
	9. Ability to earn temporarily high profits by following a high pricing strategy until competitors enter the market.
	Variables Which Inhibit Technological Leadership
3. First-mover disadvantages	1. High pioneering costs.
	2. Demand Uncertainty.
	3. Changes in buyer needs that render the technology useless.
	4. Inability to or cost of updating technology.
	5. The possibility of low-cost imitations.

Source: Based on Porter [1985], pp. 182–191.

particular strategy, it must keep these variables in mind and manage its operations accordingly. For example, if a firm chooses to follow a leadership strategy, it should attempt to obtain the maximum patent protection available for any technology that it develops.

Technology Acquisition

Technology acquisition is the next step following the technology choice process. Two basic alternatives are available to a firm; develop the technology internally, or purchase it from an external source. Exhibit 5.13 highlights some reasons for internally developing or externally acquiring technology. Many of these reasons

Exhibit 5.13   Reasons for Internal Development or External Acquisition of Technology

Internal Development
Expense: internal R&D is cheaper than external acquisition
Technological distance: R&D area is close to current corporate skills
Learning: firm wishes to gain expertise in a particular technology
Secrecy: firm wishes to keep its technological thrust confidential
"Not invented here" (NIH) syndrome: firm culture fosters belief that the only good technology is developed internally
External Acquisition
Avoid reinventing the wheel: technology already developed saves time and effort
Achieve faster growth: cannot reach growth objectives from internal development
Complex technology needs: firm does not have all the skills to develop its future desired portfolio
Aggressive posture: firm has an aggressive self-image to protect
Risk reduction: firm lets others take big risks before participating
Competitive threat: need to keep up with competitor whose new technology threatens
Increase returns to manufacturing investment: obtain technology for products that can be made on present equipment
Increase returns to marketing investment: obtain technology for products that can use present brand names, distributor channels, and so forth.

Source: Capon and Glaser [1987]. Reprinted from *Journal of Marketing,* published by the American Marketing Association, p. 6.

are closely related to the advantages and disadvantages of following a technological leadership strategy.

In general, a firm that is following a leadership strategy would tend to spend more on R&D because the company's ability to produce innovations is closely related to (although not entirely determined by) the amount it spends on R&D. In other words, a leadership strategy tends to be based on a proactive approach to R&D, whereas a followership strategy involves a reactive approach. While this may be the case, it does not mean that leaders ignore the option of purchasing technologies externally. In fact, it may be necessary for leaders to explore other means of obtaining technologies in order to maintain their leadership position. For example:

> Dupont is considered a technological leader in the chemicals industry. An analysis of Dupont's 25 major product and process innovations over the period 1920–1950 indicates that licensing technology made an important contribution to Dupont's success. Of the 25 innovations, only 10 were invented by Dupont's own R&D staff.[15]

[15]Maidique and Patch [1978], p. 281.

Furthermore, acceleration of the rate of technological change implies that firms will find it more expensive to remain at the leading edge of technologies relevant to their business, because (1) there is a larger number of projects that firms could potentially consider and hence more R&D funds are needed, and (2) each project is advancing more quickly, meaning more R&D resources are needed to stay abreast of the latest developments. High costs of conducting internal reserach and development have resulted in a growing trend toward acquiring new technologies by some other means (Chisnall [1985], and Friar and Horwitch [1985]). These alternative methods include:

1. Contracting out research and development
2. Taking over a firm with a proven record for producing innovations
3. Licensing another firm's technology
4. Entering joint ventures to develop technology
5. Taking an equity position in a firm in order to acquire or monitor technology

From a practical point of view, firms can pursue a combination of alternatives when it comes to acquiring new technology. For example, a firm may purchase component technologies (CNC machines, or a materials handling system) from vendors, and then internally develop the expertise needed to integrate the components into an FMS. Similarly, firms can choose various methods of acquisition for different new technologies they wish to utilize. For all practical purposes, companies can classify their technologies as: (a) generic, (b) basic, or (c) key. *Generic technology* is essentially used across an industry and is fairly common (conveyors that keep assembly line moving). *Basic technologies*, on the other hand, are those which provide some degree of strategic maneuvering and flexibility (use of optical readers on the auto assembly line for quality control). *Key technology* is proprietary and indigenous to the firm, and for that matter, to the industry as well. It involves continually regarding technology as a strategic weapon that will provide a competitive edge.

The decision as to what combination of technologies is needed is very complex. To address this, we propose a matrix similar to Exhibit 5.14. Such a matrix would allow companies to evaluate the options available for procuring and/or developing different technologies. To illustrate the use of the exhibit, consider a company in an industry where automated materials handling systems like conveyors are fairly standard. The company may choose to evaluate different vendors, purchase a system, and have the vendor install it. A little more flexibility is gained through the use of machine vision inspection units along the conveyor lines. The company may choose to purchase the hardware, but then do the integration work internally. With standalone CNC machinery, the company may again want to evaluate what is available and then have an appropriate vendor do the installation and software. Finally, to enhance its competitive advantage, and having gained some experience with the new technologies, the

Exhibit 5.14   A Proposed Matrix to Determine the Dynamic Mix of Technologies

Composition of Technology		Options				
		Scanning	*Buying*	*Leasing*	*Merging*	*Internal Development*
GENERIC	Materials Handling Systems	X	X			
BASE	Machine Vision	X	X			
	CNC	X	X			X
KEY	FMC				X	X

Note: "X" represents the decision made.

company may choose to integrate the CNC machinery with the vision and materials handling systems in-house into a flexible manufacturing cell (FMC).

By considering the method of adoption for each of its technologies together, the company can minimize problems and maximize the chances of future successful installations. Since different amounts and types of resources are required in each case, total resource allocations may be addressed in the context of the company's overall technology strategy, and help facilitate the assessment and justification process to be discussed in Chapter 7.

CONCLUDING OBSERVATIONS

This chapter addressed the strategic implications of the new technology. The roles that both manufacturing and technology should have in a firm's strategic planning process and the primary components of a technology strategy were outlined. Here are some of the key concepts presented in this chapter:

- Manufacturing decisions can restrict, reinforce, or determine a company's strategy. Therefore, manufacturing must play a key role in strategy formulation and implementation.
- A balanced approach to formulating and implementing a manufacturing strategy will ensure that firms do not miss opportunities available to them through flexible technologies. It will also ensure that firms do not encounter avoidable environmental threats they are unable or unprepared to deal with.
- The technology can greatly enhance the manufacturing capabilities of an organization. Therefore, the technology has created an even greater head for a balanced approach to manufacturing strategy.

- The increased capabilities offered by the new technology culminate in the potential for economies of integration. Firms achieving economies of integration can achieve high flexibility (characteristic of economies of scope) and high productivity (characteristic of economies of scale) simultaneously.

- A firm's technology strategy should include the following major components: (1) an assessment of the firm's existing technologies, (2) an assessment of the firm's technological environment (which includes technology forecasting, (3) a determination of the degree and type(s) of flexibility required by the firm, (4) a choice of which technologies the firm will pursue, (5) a decision whether to be a technological leader or follower, and (6) a decision as to how to acquire the desired technology.

RECOMMENDED READINGS

HAAS, E. A. [1987]. "Breakthrough Manufacturing." *Harvard Business Review,* March–April, pp. 75–81.
NOORI, H. [1987]. "Economies of Integration: A New Manufacturing Focus." National Center for Management Research and Development, Working Paper Series No. NC 86-06.

DISCUSSION QUESTIONS

1. Manufacturing has traditionally assumed only a supportive role in a company's strategic planning process. It appears that this limited role may prevent firms from capitalizing fully on the benefits of the new technology. How could corporate attitudes be altered to bring manufacturing more fully into the strategic planning process? Assume the role of a concerned VP of operations.
2. Where do some of the new technologies of today fit the S curve shown in Exhibit 5.10? Is there currently a problem in North American industry with managers underestimating or overestimating the potential of the new technology?
3. Given the framework for identifying the feasibility of a technological leadership strategy shown in Exhibit 5.12, devise a strategy based on technological followership.
4. Identify some of the functional requirement differences of following a technological leadership versus a technological followership strategy. For example, marketing's principal role in a leadership strategy might be to stimulate primary demand and provide excellent after-sales service, whereas marketing's role in a followership strategy might be to find a way to differentiate the company's products.
5. Suppose you had the option of producing three different products in one of two ways: (a) Three separate dedicated systems, each one used to produce one of the three products, or (b) an FMS which could produce all three products. What factors would you consider when evaluating which method of production to utilize?
6. Develop a framework which illustrates the role that both manufacturing and technology should have in the strategic planning process.
7. Why do you think many firms do not have any sort of formal technology strategy? How should it be formed? What should it consist of?
8. Do you feel that the potential for economies of integration will encourage firms to maintain a medium-sized plant? Why or why not?
9. In this chapter, a balanced approach to formulating and implementing manufacturing strategy was proposed as the best approach that could be used by firms to realize the full potential

of the new technology. Are there any drawbacks to pursuing a balanced approach? Is the balanced approach a viable option for all firms? Has the new technology made it more necessary than ever before to pursue a balanced approach to manufacturing strategy? Explain.

10. Take the role of VP Operations of a well-known firm. Using Exhibit 5.14, and given the considerations outlined in this chapter and in Chapter 4, determine what your generic, base, and key technologies would be, and what route you would pursue to acquire/develop them. Repeat the process for three different firms in three different industries.

REFERENCES AND BIBLIOGRAPHY

BAETZ, M. C., and P. W. BEAMISH [1987]. *Strategic Management: Canadian Cases.* Richard D. Irwin, Homewood, Ill.

BETZ, F. [1987]. *Managing Technology: Competing Through New Ventures, Innovation, and Corporate Research.* Prentice-Hall, Englewood Cliffs, N.J.

BURGELMAN, R. A., and M. A. MAIDIQUE [1988]. *Strategic Management of Technology and Innovation.* Richard D. Irwin, Homewood, Ill.

CAPON, N., and R. GLAZER [1987]. "Marketing and Technology: A Strategic Coalignment." *Journal of Marketing,* Volume 51, July, pp. 1–14.

CHANDLER, A. F. [1962]. *Strategy and Structure.* MIT Press, Cambridge, Mass.

CHISNALL, P. M. [1985]. *Strategic Industrial Marketing.* Prentice-Hall, Englewood Cliffs, N.J., Chapter 7.

FORD, D., and C. RYAN [1981]. "Taking Technology to Market. *Harvard Business Review,* March–April.

FRIAR, J., and M. HORITCH [1985]. "The Emergence of Technology Strategy." *Technology in Society,* Volume 7, pp. 143–178.

GERWIN, D. [1982]. "Do's and Don'ts of Computerized Manufacturing." *Harvard Business Review,* March–April, pp. 107–116.

GOLDHAR, J. E., and M. JELINEK [1983]. "Plan for Economies of Scope." *Harvard Business Review,* November–December, pp. 141–152.

GUNN, T. G. [1985]. "CIM Must Start at the Top." *Production,* March, pp. 43–49.

HAAS, E. A. [1987]. "Breakthrough Manufacturing." *Harvard Business Review,* March–April, pp. 75–81.

HALL, D. J., and M. A. SAIAS [1980]. "Strategy Follows Structure." Strategic *Management Journal,* Volume 1, pp. 149–163.

HAMERMESH, R. G. [1986]. "Making Planning Strategic." *Harvard Business Review,* July–August, pp. 115–120.

HAX, A. C., and N. S. MAJLUF [1984]. "The Corporate Strategic Planning Process." *Interfaces,* Volume 14, No. 1, January–February, pp. 47–60.

HAYES, R. H. [1985]. "Strategic Planning—Forward in Reverse?" *Harvard Business Review,* November–December, pp. 111–119.

HAYES, R. H., and S. C. WHEELWRIGHT [1984]. *Restroing Our Competitive Edge: Competing Through Manufacturing.* Wiley, New York.

HILL, T. [1985]. *Manufacturing Strategy.* Macmillan, London.

JONES, H., and B. C. TWISS [1978]. *Forecasting Technology for Planning Decisions.* Macmillan, New York.

KANTROW, A. [1980]. "The Strategy-Technology Connection." *Harvard Business Review,* July–August, pp. 1–7.

KAPLAN, R. S. [1986]. "Must CIM Be Justified by Faith Alone?" *Harvard Business Review,* March–April, pp. 87–95.

MAIDIQUE, M. A., and P. PATCH [1978]. "Corporate Strategy and Technological Policy." *Readings in the Management of Innovation,* M. L. Tushman and W. L. Moore. Pitman.

Management Review [1984]. "What's Ahead in Technology . . . Blind Spot in Strategic Planning?" October, pp. 26–52.

MANSFIELD, E. [1981]. "How Economists See R&D." *Harvard Business Review,* November–December, pp. 98–106.

MEREDITH, J. [1987a]. "The Strategic Advantages of New Manufacturing Technologies from Small Firms." *Strategic Management Journal,* Volume 8, pp. 249–258.

MEREDITH, J. [1987b]. "Acquiring New Manufacturing Technologies for Competitive Advantage." *Operations Management Review,* Winter, pp. 9–13.

NOORI, H. [1987].   "Economies of Integration: A New Manufacturing Focus." National Center for Management Research and Development, Working Paper Series No. NC 86–06.

ORNE, D. L., and L. E. HANIFIN [1984].   "The Interfacing Role of International Manufacturing Strategy and CIM." Rensselaer Polytechnic Institute, Conference Proceedings, Synergy '84.

PORTER, M. E. [1985].   *Competitive Advantage.* The Free Press, New York.

SCHONBERGER, R. J. [1987].   "Frugal Manufacturing." *Harvard Business Review,* September–October, pp. 95–100.

SHAPIRO, B. P. [1977].   "Can Marketing and Manufacturing Coexist?" *Harvard Business Review,* September–October, pp. 104–114.

SKINNER, W. [1974].   "The Focused Factory." *Harvard Business Review,* May–June, pp. 113–121.

SKINNER, W. [1969].   "Manufaturing—Missing Link in Corporate Strategy." *Harvard Business Review,* May–June, pp. 136–145.

STOBAUGH, R., and P. TELESIO [1983]."Match Manufacturing Policies and Product Strategy." *Harvard Business Review,* March–April, pp. 113–120.

TWISS, B. C. [1980].   *Managing Technology Innovation,* 2nd ed. Longman, New York.

VOSS, C. A. [1986].   *Managing New Manufacturing Technologies.* Monograph No. 1, Operations Management Association, September.

WHEELWRIGHT, S. C., and R. H. HAYES [1985].   "Competing Through Manufacturing." *Harvard Business Review,* January–February, pp. 99–108.

WHITE, G. R., and M.B.W. GRAHAM [1978].   "How to Spot a Technological Winner." *Harvard Business Review,* March–April, pp. 146–152.

Chapter Six

MANAGING PRODUCTIVITY AND QUALITY IN THE TECHNOLOGICAL AGE

*Quality comes from people caring and comes
from people sharing. The customer shall always
be No. 1.*

A Nissan Slogan

INTRODUCTION

Undoubtedly, high productivity and quality are keys to success for any firm.
In fact, the decline in competitiveness of North American firms has been largely
attributed to their poor productivity and quality performance vis-à-vis the competition. In many respects, companies have been "... operating to some degree
on a philosophy of planned obsolescence. In that sort of world, quality takes
a back seat."[1] The American Society for Quality Control estimates that "making sure that things are done right," and "fixing things that are done wrong,"
consumes between 15 and 30 cents of every sales dollar in most American
manufacturing companies and about 35 cents of every dollar in the typical service
organization (see Mundt [1986]). The comparable Japanese figures for producing
roughly the same quality is 5 cents and 10 cents!

For many firms, one alternative to improve productivity and quality
seems to be the adoption of the new technology. It is customary to assume that
the company is operating as effectively as possible with the current technology,
so the way to improve the situation is to upgrade the technology. But it is ill
advised to regard the new technology as the solution to productivity and quality
problems. In fact, there is ample evidence to suggest that simple commitment
of the workforce is fundamental to any productivity and quality improvement.
In essence, the new technology should be viewed not as a device to be used in
isolation, but as an integrative tool to be used along with other well-targeted
programs.

[1]Knowlton [1988], p. 40.

161

Although the tendency is sometimes to look at productivity, quality, and technology as separate topics, it is important to consider them together and understand the interrelationships among the three. This is because the need for productivity and quality gains steers technology, and as Britney emphasizes: "...technology drives and provides support for quality and productivity gains... they are not mutually exclusive."[2]

Wheelwright [1981] explains that many North American managers perceive productivity and quality as being diametrically opposed, whereas Japanese managers tend to view them as being symbiotic in nature. The Japanese attitude is justified: it has been shown that increased quality is often accompanied by increased productivity. And, this integrative vision of productivity and quality is certainly no longer limited to Japan. In fact, some North American firms, including Harley-Davidson Motor Company, New United Motor Manufacturing, IBM, and GM, have already accepted the notion (see Sepehri [1987]). Consider the following example:

> The Westinghouse Productivity and Quality Center gives the company a way to integrate its efforts at improving quality and increasing productivity. The center was formed in 1980 and stresses the important roles of both people and technology in increasing productivity and quality. Ralph Barre, director of corporate quality, states that "it's a misconception that quality and productivity are somehow at odds, that you have to sacrifice quality to increase productivity. Quality precedes productivity."[3]

With this point of view, we will look at what the terms productivity and quality mean, describe how they can be measured, and provide some insight into how they can be managed more effectively. We will also explain the potential impact of the new technology on the management of productivity and quality.

THE QUEST FOR PRODUTIVITY[4]

Defining Productivity

The term productivity automatically conjures up an inherent meaning for most people. Everyone wants productivity! Productivity is also a concept that is often misunderstood and misused. Many consider productivity to be a measure of production efficiency. In practice, however, productivity should be examined from both an efficiency (output) and effectiveness (outcome) point of view.

---

[2]Britney [1986], p. 92. See also Edosomwan [1987].

[3]Adapted from Ryan [1983], pp. 26–29.

[4]Some of the ideas in this section are based on the findings of an ongoing research project sponsored by the National Research Council of Canada in which the following are the participants: B. Fournier, D. Gillen, G. McDougall, and H. Noori.

With reference to efficiency, productivity deals with the relationship between resource application and production (lower unit costs and more profit). With regard to effectiveness, productivity is concerned with performance in terms of the end user (greater flexibility, and a higher number of product variations). We maintain that with the new technology, companies can simultaneously achieve both effectiveness and efficiency in their production process. Exhibit 6.1 presents these notions graphically. With the existing technology, reductions in per unit cost are feasible through increasing the quantity lot size—Cost Curve I. Investment in the new technology, on the other hand, results in: (1) a lowering of the cost function in its entirety—Cost Curve II (the efficiency impact), and (2) a further reduction in per unit cost due to the synergistic effects of the new technology which accrue to associated features, such as flexibility in producing a variety of products in small lot sizes quickly (the effectiveness impact). In essence, the new technology results in a *pure* change (point *a* to *b* in Exhibit 6.1), as well as a *synergistic* change (point *b* to *c*) in unit cost. While the possibility of improving both (productivity) effectiveness and efficiency remains, it is more difficult to document which of these two improvements (*a* to *b* or *b* to *c*) is more significant. Current studies suggest that at best the impact of the new technology on the magnitude of effectiveness and efficiency of the operation is contingent upon the prevailing status of the operation and the form and the complexity of the technology adopted.

Exhibit 6.1   The Impact of New Technology on the Effectiveness and Efficiency of the Production System

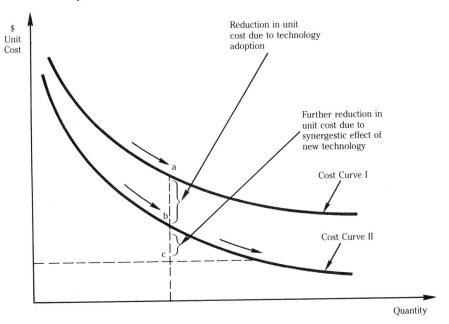

Note: Cost Curves I and II may not have the same slope.

Productivity, defined in terms of efficiency, is a ratio of outputs to inputs. More formally:

$$\text{productivity} = \frac{\text{output}}{\text{input}}.$$

That is, productivity gain is the rate of change in output with respect to input. Given this, it is easy to see that productivity can be improved by increasing output and/or decreasing input. In fact, as shown in Exhibit 6.2, there are nine possible ways to affect productivity through changes in the ratio of output to input, five of which can lead to productivity improvements.

Three general approaches have been used to view productivity: the macro approach, the micro approach, and the management approach. The marco approach is used by economists to measure the productivity of the whole economy or its sectors. The micro approach, on the other hand, is much more specific and deals with measuring productivity at individual work units. The management approach involves viewing, managing, and measuring the productivity of the organization/firm as a whole. It is this view of productivity that deals with effectiveness and that can be most useful to top managers when considering

Exhibit 6.2 Alternate Ways to Increase Productivity

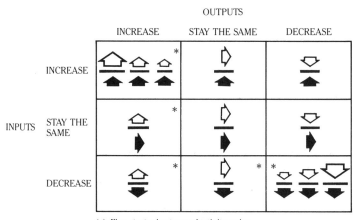

(∗): Five strategies to productivity gains.

Source: Britney et al. [1983], p. 39.

policy decisions. In this case, management should be able to answer five basic questions when dealing with any productivity improvement program. These are:

1. Do people know how to do their jobs?
2. Do lower levels of the organization know what upper levels expect?
3. Is the production equipment developed to its fullest potential?
4. Are people organized in the most effective way?
5. Do people want to do their jobs?

The questions at first glance seem deceptively simple and commonplace; they are not at all. The answers to them are fundamental to any management philosophy and strategy.[5]

Moreover, answering these questions will force managers to consider one further characteristic of productivity: hard versus soft productivity (see Thurow [1983]). By *hard* productivity, we mean more investment spending on R&D, and new technologically up-to-date plant and equipment. Soft productivity deals with issues such as employee motivation and managing resources (as opposed to simply pumping more resources into the system).[6]

The Importance of Productivity.   From management's perspective, improvements in productivity are synonymous with increasing profitability. Exhibit 6.3 illustrates this relationship. The profitability of a firm is determined by the difference between total revenues and total costs. Consequently, a firm can potentially increase its profitability by increasing the selling price of its products, or by purchasing inputs at a reduced cost. Both alternatives, however, might be to a large extent beyond the control of management. From a more practical point of view, profitability can be increased through changes in the input-output ratio of the productivity index, as shown in Exhibit 6.2. In this case, firms have a relatively greater amount of control over their internal operations. That is to say, improving the effectiveness and efficiency of operations is crucial to success in the marketplace and ultimately the bottom line—profit!

The Productivity Paradox

Understanding the factors affecting productivity growth at the firm level is perhaps as difficult as understanding those at the national level. The relationship between technology and productivity has been a matter of great debate over the years. For example, Buzacott [1985] has shown that with no technological change, the largest firm in an industry always has a cost advantage (and thus a productivity advantage) over its competitors unless it makes a gross mistake. The Japanese

---

[5]Kelly [1985], p. 25.
[6]Thurow [1983], pp. 13–14.

Exhibit 6.3 Productivity and How It Relates to Profitability

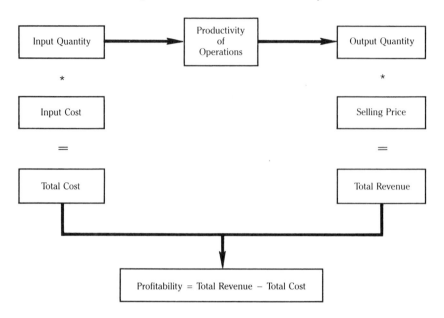

have invented the concept of TPM (total productivity maintenance), which is directed at equipment improvements (see Imai [1986]) to illustrate the importance of paying attention to the hardware side of operations.

Hayes and Clark [1985] have defined two groups of variable which influence productivity at the firm or individual operating unit level. They call them *structural factors* (the age of the equipment, the size and the location of the plant, and whether the workforce is unionized) and *managerial factors* (including equipment, materials control, and workforce policies).[7] They contend that management practices that increase the level of confusion in a plant are major contributors to productivity slowdowns. These practices include rapid and frequent changes in the manufacturing design and in the production rate, as well as adding new equipment (technology). This suggests that changes in product and process could be a major inhibitor of productivity growth.

On the other hand, Skinner [1985, 1986], argues that management's obsession with improving productivity has to a large extent contributed to the decline in competitiveness of North American firms. He states:

> Production experience regularly observes a "40-40-20" rule. Roughly 40 percent of any manufacturing-based competitive advantage derives from long term changes in manufacturing structure (decisions, for example, concerning the number, size, location, and capacity of facilities) and basic approaches in

---

[7]The structural factors are perceived to be out of the control of the plant's management, whereas the managerial factors are directly controlled by plant's management.

materials and workforce management. Another 40 percent comes from major changes in equipment and process technology. The final 20 percent—no more— rests on conventional approaches to productivity improvements.[8]

In other words, overemphasizing productivity growth could be harmful to the firm's long-range success and retention of its competitive edge. By focusing solely on productivity improvement from an efficiency point of view, management is choosing to pursue a low-cost strategy over other potentially superior strategies. The view of Hays and Clark and Skinner point to the notion of a productivity paradox that needs an explanation.

We mentioned earlier that traditional ways to improve productivity focus on the efficiency of operations; they often result in the incremental reduction of direct labor costs. This is not to say that the conventional productivity and cost-cutting approach is not an important objective for managers to pursue—it obviously is. However, a more powerful way to bolster competitive advantage is through changes in manufacturing structure and technology. As we pointed out in Chapter 3, the flexibility inherent in the new technology can provide a firm with additional ways to compete through rapid new product introductions, reliable delivery, short lead times, high-quality, custom-made products, and so on. But at this point a word of caution is in order. While the positive effect of the new technology on productivity improvement is theoretically inescapable, from the practical point of view management should expect (usually temporary) productivity declines with the introduction of the new technology. In this case, a proper response is to take steps to minimize the decline through proper planning and management of change (see Exhibit 6.4).

The center panel of the exhibit demonstrates the different paths productivity may take in the short term after a new technology introduction. Obviously, the ideal path from the firm's perspective is D. Which path is followed on a given project depends on the firm's experience with the technology and the presence of proper project planning, implementation, and control (discussed in Chapter 12).

The benefits of the new technology arise mainly out of the flexibility that it can provide and its ability to respond to the changing environment in which the firm competes. If managers blindly follow the objective of improving productivity, it is unlikely that the adoption of many new technologies will be economically justified. "The slow adoption of such manufacturing technologies as CAD/CAM, robotics, and flexible machining centers reflects managers' wise assumption that these investments would initially drive productivity down."[9] In many instances, the merit systems and evaluation standards (higher productivity ratios and higher profit margins) prohibit managers' acceptance of short-term losses for long-term gains. This approach has been referred to in economic literature as the agency theory.[10]

[8]Skinner [1986], p. 56.
[9]Skinner [1986], p. 57.

[10]The *agency theory* refers to the cases where the owner (or shareholder) is characterized as a principal and the manager as an agent who acts on the owner's behalf, but pursues his own interest. See Jensen and Smith [1985].

Exhihbit 6.4 Distribution of Productivity Increases Over Time

Source: Ebel and Ulrich [1987], p. 355.

Productivity Measurement

Conceptually, different measures of productivity growth are designed to reflect changes in the efficiency with which a firm uses different forms of inputs to produce a set of outputs. There are basically three types of productivity measurement techniques: single-factor (or partial) productivity, multifactor productivity, and total-factor productivity. Each expresses the efficiency of the use of one or more key plant resources.

Single-factor productivity (SFP) refers to a comparison of output to only one input:

$$\text{SFP} = \frac{\text{total output}}{\text{a single input}}$$

For example, the U.S. Bureau of Labor Statistics defines productivity as the ratio of national output per employee hour. Firms also use a number of SFP measures to evaluate their operations; a list of these is shown in Exhibit 6.5. An extension to SFP is multifactor productivity (MFP), which refers to the comparison of total output to more than one input (for example, labor and materials).

Many firms use only single-factor productivity measurements, especially

Exhibit 6.5 Examples of Single-Factor Productivity Measures Used by Firms

Labor Productivity:

> Units of output per labor-hour
> Value-added per labor-hour
> Dollar output per labor-hour
> Production value per labor-dollar
> Shipments per labor cost

Machine Productivity:

> Units of output per machine-hour
> Tons of output per machine-hour

Capital Productivity:

> Units of output per dollar input
> Dollar output per dollar input
> Inventory turnover ratio (dollar sales per dollar inventory)

Energy Productivity:

> Units of output per kilowatt-hour
> Units of output per energy cost
> Production value per barrel of fuel

Source: Reprinted by permission from *Applied Production and Operations Management,* 2nd Edition, by Evans, et al., copyright © 1987b West Publishing Company. All rights reserved.

with regard to labor hours. This approach might be misleading for at least two reasons. First, labor productivity can be enhanced without a corresponding improvement in the total productivity of the firm. Consider a simple example which higher quality (but more expensive) raw materials are purchased. Suppose that the higher quality of these materials leads to a reduction in the processing time required to transform the raw materials into finished goods. If this is the case, capital equipment and labor productivity would improve. However, this does not necessarily mean that the total productivity of the firm is also enhanced. That is, the equipment and labor productivity improvement may have been more than offset by a reduction in raw materials productivity due to the increase in the cost of the raw material input. This is due to the fact that the overall productivity of the firm is composed of a network of individual yet closely interrelated series of productivity measures. Therefore, the effect of a change in one input on all other inputs must be determined before the outcome on the productivity of the firm as a whole can be assessed. Second, a preoccupation with labor productivity limits other possible approaches for improving the overall productivity of the firm (for example, through increased capital or materials productivity). In the past, direct labor costs typically accounted for 40 to 50 percent of a firm's total costs. Hence, firms could realize substantial productivity increases by reducing these costs. Today, however, direct labor costs exceed 10 percent of sales in only a few industries (see Chapter 7). Therefore, even a dramatic improvement in the productivity of a firm's labor force may still not be enough to provide it with the competitive advantage it needs.

In practice, the most comprehensive way of measuring productivity is known as *total-factor productivity (TFP)*, or *total operational productivity (TOP)*. In this case, productivity reflects the use of the firm's total resources (including management skills, materials, and equipment and capital) to produce its products. That is:

$$\text{TFP} = \frac{\text{total output}}{\text{total inputs}} = \frac{\text{total output}}{(\text{labor} + \text{materials} + \text{capital} + \text{all other inputs})}$$

In North America, a number of companies have successfully implemented the TFP concept. For example, in 1976, General Foods adapted and installed a total factor productivity system known as the Productivity Index in response to a management question about the status of productivity in the plants. Today, the system is firmly in place and provides valuable information on the performance of each plant and division (see Brady [1985]).

We can conclude from this discussion that management must give priority to measuring and improving the overall productivity of the firm's operations vis-à-vis focusing on partial measures such as labor. In practice, however, many specific problems must be dealt with when calculating the TFP of a firm (valuing capital inputs; valuing products that have been introduced after the base year of comparison). But although these are important issues, they are beyond the scope of this chapter.[11]

The Objectives Matrix: An Approach to Measuring Productivity Gains through the New Technology. With the changes that are taking place in the global market[12] and the use of the new technology to address these needs, it is becoming increasingly important to look at the productivity measures that allow for both the effectiveness (outcome) and the efficiency (output) points of view. Ideally, one would like to implement measurements that offer explanations of *why productivity has changed as it has* as opposed to *what has changed.* In short, the methodology for productivity assessment must be capable of:

- Measuring the relative contributions of the sources of productivity changes.
- Quantitatively assessing the contribution of each factor in a benefit category.
- Providing a motivation as well as measure for productivity improvement.
- Providing a framework within which managers can collect data and evaluate divisional and firm performance on an ongoing basis.

[11]See Craig and Harris [1973], Hines [1976], and Sumanth [1984] for a discussion of ways to deal with these specific problems.

[12]These include shorter product life cycles, shorter delivery times, and a proliferation of products, to name a few. See Chapter 1 for more detail.

Riggs [1984] has developed a relatively simple method of assessing the productivity of an organization which he calls the *objectives matrix*. The objectives matrix can be used to assess the productivity gains made by a firm after it has implemented new technology. The main advantage of the matrix (from a new technology perspective) is that both efficiency and effectiveness of productivity considerations can be factored into the measurement process through decomposition or disaggregation of the total productivity factors.

While several studies have recently been devoted to the notion of production measures when the new technology is present (see, for example, Adler [1987]), we will use only this matrix to illustrate one rather vigorous way of appraising productivity in this context. An example showing how the objectives matrix can be used to assess productivity gains made through the new technology is presented in Exhibit 6.6. Along the top of the matrix, important productivity categories are listed.[13] Notice that these include both efficiency (machine utilization

Exhibit 6.6   The Objectives Matrix for Assessing the Productivity Gains Made through New Technology: A Hypothetical Example

Productivity Categories						
% Delivery Dates Met	*Labor Costs ($)*	*Average Lead Times (Days)*	*Work-in-Process Inventory ($)*	*% Scrap*	*Machine Utilization Rates (%)*	
90.1%	$458,000	22.3 days	$51,242	8.1%	78.8%	*Current Performance Level*
100	300,000	10	10,000	2	98	10	
98	320,000	12	20,000	3	97	9	
96	340,000	14	30,000	4	96	8	
94	360,000	16	40,000	5	95	7	S
92	380,000	18	50,000	6	93	6	C
90	400,000	20	60,000	7	90	5	O
88	420,000	22	70,000	8	85	4	R
86	440,000	24	80,000	9	80	3	E
84	460,000	26	90,000	10	75	2	S
82	480,000	28	100,000	11	70	1	
80	500,000	30	110,000	12	65	0	
5	2	4	5	4	3	Score
16	31	13	9	19	12	Weight
80	62	52	45	76	36	Value
				Total Value = 351		Index

Source: The idea of the matrix comes from Riggs [1984]. The numbers in the matrix are hypothetically assumed.

[13]Note that this list is for illustration purposes; it can be expanded to include a host of strategic, human, and technological components of the total productivity factors.

rates) and effectiveness (delivery dates met) productivity measures. Along the bottom of the matrix, weights are assigned to each of the variables listed at the top, according in order of importance as seen by management. In this example, labor costs are the most important factor (31 percent), and work-in-process inventory is the least important (9 percent). Obviously these numbers will change with different scenarios, but they should always add to 100. Realistically, the accuracy and value of using this matrix is limited by management's ability to assign weights that reflect the true values of the individual factors.

Along the right-hand column of the matrix are the numbers 0 to 10. The number 0 corresponds to the absolute worst level of conduct management will tolerate in each category, and is based on past performance. The number 3 corresponds to the average (current) level of conduct in each category, and the number 10 corresponds to the objective management hopes to achieve within a certain time frame (say, two years). The numbers in the body of the matrix conform to the numbers 0 to 10 for each category to be considered. For example, when looking at the category "% scrap," 12% scrap is the worst performance tolerable and thus matches the number 0, 9% scrap is the current level of performance and thus matches the number 3, and 2% scrap is a high (but attainable) objective management plans to achieve through new technology, and thus receives the number 10. Numbers between these three values simply reflect incremental performance levels.

To use the matrix, performance levels for each of the productivity categories are measured and recorded for an arbitrary time period (say every two months). These performance levels are then used to compute the productivity level for the time period being measured. As shown, the score for this period is 351, up from 300 (*Note:* all matrices begin with a score of 300). By using this matrix to compute the productivity index every two months, management can track the performance of the firm after implementing the new technology.

Where New Technology Can Be Most Effective

One of the most dramatic effects of the new technology on manufacturing is that it leads to end products composed of fewer and fewer components. We can already see this trend in a number of products, including automobiles, audio/video products, microcomputers, and watches. In the manufacture of sewing machines, for example, one microprocessor has replaced 350 mechanical parts. Similar changes have occurred in the manufacture of many electronic goods.

The implication of this is that we see a striking improvement in productivity through the price/performance ratio,[14] and as Kumpe and Bolwijn [1987] state, a shift in the distribution of added value from assembly of end products toward subassemblies and components: "This has radical consequences for the three production activities: final assembly, manufacture of subassemblies, and

---

[14]This ratio refers to the price of a given product relative to some important performance characteristics such as speed, size of memory, and tool-changing capability (for example, the price of a computer relative to its memory capacity).

component manufacture."[15] To assess the benefits of the new technology in improving productivity, we should look at these three activities more extensively.

Since the assembly of final products will take up so little time and add little value, productivity improvements in this area through large-scale utilization of the new technology may not be noticeable. This explains why the final assemblies in many Japanese companies are still based on conventional methods (see Bairstow [1986]). But subassemblies and component manufacturing play a key role in the added value and knowhow of the end product, so here the new technology can have a much more pronounced impact on productivity. Flexible automation can play an important role in designing or producing the high-quality components and parts demanded, with a very high price/performance ratio:

> In general (in the component area) there is a trend to be seen from high precision to ultra-high precision mechanics, from micron technologies to submicron technologies and from separable metal and plastic parts to integrated plastic/metal parts. Therefore, the manufacture of components will take place in large, high-tech factories with very high degree of automation.[16]

In short, enhancing productivity through new technology encompasses more than just improving production processes. It requires a diversified and integrated approach to management embracing many technical (manufacturing, production control, and manufacturing engineering) and nontechnical factors (personnel, distribution, and suppliers), all of which influence the overall productivity of the firm.

COMPETITIVENESS THROUGH QUALITY

In many respects, the decline in competitiveness of many North American firms has also been largely attributed to the inferior quality of the products they produce. In this section, we provide some insight into why a quality problem exists, make a number of recommendations as to how to achieve competitive quality levels, and explain how the new technology is making quality a more important issue than ever before. We have grouped the important quality issues into five general categories:

1. Understanding what quality is
2. Defining quality in terms of cost
3. Managing quality and investing in the prevention of quality costs
4. Performance as a goal
5. Employee participation and management commitment

---

[15]Kumpe and Bolwijn [1987], p. 49.
[16]Kumpe, and Bolwijn [1987], p. 49.

Understanding What Quality Is

Quality, much like productivity, has the same basic components: efficiency and effectiveness. A number of definitions, some of which are ambiguous, exist for the word *quality*. Garvin [1984], in an attempt to overcome some of the ambiguity and misunderstanding, has categorized five definitions of quality:

1. Transcendent Definition: Quality (like beauty) cannot be precisely defined; it is a universally recognized concept pertaining to excellence.
2. Product-Based Definition: Quality refers to the degree or quantity of some attribute contained within the product.
3. User-Based Definition: Quality refers to the degree to which a product satisfies customer wants.
4. Manufacturing-Based Definition: Quality means conformance to the required specifications.
5. Value-Based Definition: Quality refers to providing a product with acceptable quality at a reasonable price.

Exhibit 6.7 provides a list of references in which each of these five definitions of quality are used.

The crucial question then, is which, if any, of these definitions is more important or more representative. The answer is that all of them are valuable and necessary; they must be considered together to strengthen the competitive position of the firm. For example, it is up to marketing to determine what the firm's customers truly want (product-based, user-based, and value-based quality considerations); it is up to manufacturing to produce the required product to specification at the lowest possible cost (manufacturing-based, and value-based quality considerations); and it is up to upper management to foster a philosophy and set objectives to motivate staff and workers to achieve the highest standard of excellence at every task they perform (transcendent quality considerations). Furthermore, because some of these types of quality can conflict with one another, it is essential to have integration among the functional areas to avoid maximizing some at the unintended expense of others.

It becomes obvious, then, that quality is truly a composite concept. The significance of this is that managers should plan around the crucial dimensions of quality, some of which are admittedly nonquantifiable. These include: performance, features, maintainability, and serviceability. Doing this leads to the key competitive edge a firm needs to sell its products. Exhibit 6.8 highlights this point by showing how a customer might view the quality of an automobile based on eight dimensions (see Garvin [1984]).

There is evidence that, in many instances, these dimensional perspectives of quality might not be considered collectively when reporting on quality improvement programs. Consider the following example:

Exhibit 6.7 Five Ways of Looking at Quality Definitions

I. Transcendent Definition:

"Quality is neither mind nor matter, but a third entity independent of the two . . . even though Quality cannot be defined, you know what it is." (R. M. Pirsig, *Zen and the Art of Motorcycle Maintenance,* pp. 185–213).

". . . a condition of excellence implying fine quality as distinct from poor quality . . . Quality is achieving or reaching for the highest standard as against begin satisfied with the sloppy or fradulent." (B. W. Tuchman, "The Decline of Quality," *New York Times Magazine,* 2 November 1980, p. 38).

II. Product-Based Definition:

"Differences in quality amount to differences in the quantity of some desired ingredient or attribute." (L. Abbott, *Quality and Competition,* pp. 126–127).

"Quality refers to the amounts of the unpriced attributes contained in each unit of the priced attribute." (K. B. Leifler, "Ambiguous Changes in Product Quality," *American Economic Review,* December 1982, p. 956).

III. User-Based Definition:

"Quality Consists of the capacity to satisfy wants." (C. D. Edwards, "The Meaning of Quality," *Quality Progress,* October 1968, p. 37).

"Quality is the degree to which a specific product satisfies the wants of a specific consumer." (H. L. Gilmore, "Product Conformance Cost," *Quality Progress,* June 1974, p. 16).

"Quality is any aspect of a product, including the services included in the contract of sales, which influences the demand curve." (R. Dortman and P. O. Steiner, "Optimal Advertising and Optimal Quality," *American Economic Review,* December 1954, p. 831).

"In the final analysis of the marketplace, the quality of a product depends on how well it fits patterns of consumer preferences." (A. A. Keuhn and R. L. Day, "Strategy of Product Quality," *Harvard Business Review,* November–December 1954, p. 831).

"Quality consists of the extent to which a specimen [a product-brand-model-seller combination] possesses the service characteristics you desire." (E. S. Maynes, "The Concept and Measurement of Product Quality," in *Household Production and Consumption,* p. 542).

"Quality is fitness for use." (J. M. Juran, ed., *Quality Control Handbook,* p. 2–2).

IV. Manufacturing-Based Definition:

"Quality [means] conformance to requirements." (P. B. Crosby, *Quality Is Free,* p. 15).

"Quality is the degree to which a specific product conforms to a design or specification." (Gilmore, June 1974, p. 16).

V. Value-Based Definition:

"Quality is the degree of excellence at an acceptable price and the control of variability at an acceptable cost." (R. A. Broh, *Managing Quality for Higher Profits,* 1982, p. 3).

"Quality means best for certain customer conditions. These conditions are (a) the actual use and (b) the selling price of the product." (A. V. Feigenbaum, *Total Quality Control,* p. 1).

Source: Reprinted from "What Does 'Product Quality' Really Mean?" by D. A. Garvin, *Sloan Management Review.* (Fall 1984), p. 35, by permission of the publisher. Copyright © 1984 by the Sloan Management Review Association. All rights reserved.

Exhibit 6.8 An Example of How a Customer Might View the Quality of an Automobile Based on Eight Quality Dimensions

Quality Dimension	Customer Viewpoint
1. Performance	"I do a lot of highway driving—therefore I want quick acceleration combined with good gas mileage."
2. Features	"I like to relax when I drive—I want cruise control."
3. Reliability	"I go to work at 5:30 a.m. every morning in the winter—when I get in my car, I want it to start."
4. Conformance	"This car only gets 28 (not 33) miles to the gallon."
5. Durability	"I want a car that will last a lifetime."
6. Serviceability	"You don't have a parts warehouse in this city—forget it—I don't want to wait six weeks for my car to get fixed."
7. Esthetics	"I'd never buy a green car."
8. Perceived quality	"Chevy's new Nova must be a good car because my Dad's 1975 Nova was."

> When American automakers brag about improvements in customer satisfaction, they're actually talking about reducing customer complaints. That's because they measure customer satisfaction in terms of number of Things Gone Wrong—usually referred to as TGW. So when Ford, for example, claims that it has the "best quality of any car or truck designed and built in America" because its quality has improved 60 percent since 1980, what it is really saying is that its customer complaints have decreased 60 percent. Specifically, Ford's TGW has dropped from just over six to just under three complaints per vehicle. And although there is no question that Ford is perceived as the quality leader amongst American manufacturers, does its TGW survey really mean that Ford has the best quality?[17]

The question posed in this example deserves serious consideration. Quality means many things, and firms cannot unnecessarily limit the scope of their definition of quality if they hope to compete effectively.

The new technology can potentially enhance most of the dimensions of quality. For example, the flexibility inherent in the new technology allows firms to offer a wider range of features and esthetics with their products; the machining precision available with advanced manufacturing technologies enables tighter conformance to specifications; and the perceived quality of a firm's product may improve due to the positive image associated with the new technology. We will discuss the improvement of quality through the new technology in detail later in this chapter.

[17]McElroy [1987], p. 69.

Quality Costs and Quality Measurement

In order to facilitate an awareness of the importance of quality, it is essential to understand the costs involved in achieving (or more notably, not achieving) perfect quality. Quality costs are typically broken down into four categories:

1. Prevention Costs: These are costs incurred in an effort to minimize future quality costs and problems. Included in this category are the costs involved in quality planning and management, training, quality information systems, and process controls.
2. Appraisal Costs: These are the costs incurred to determine the quality level of a product, the bulk of which include inspection and testing costs.
3. Internal Failure Costs: These are the costs incurred when substandard quality products are produced but are discovered before being shipped to the customer. These costs include scrap, rework, repair, and retest costs.
4. External Failure Costs: These are the costs incurred after a defective product has been shipped to the customer, including the costs of answering complaints, returns, warranty charges, product liability charges, and most important, the future cost of lost business.

A number of important issues must be considered regarding the measurement of quality costs. To begin with, quality must be defined in terms of costs so that:

1. The true cost of quality becomes apparent to management.
2. Investments aimed at improving quality can be properly evaluated.
3. Quality programs do not conflict with other company programs and objectives focused primarily on reducing costs.
4. Problem-solvers will not automatically look for the cheapest solution to solve quality problems.

Many firms resist investing in quality improvement programs because of the costs involved. Management tends to dwell on these costs without realizing the savings that will be generated by implementing the program. In many cases, the potential cost savings of a quality program are not even known. By attempting to quantify all the costs and benefits, quality and cost will be viewed as being synonymous rather than oppositional in nature.

Having mentioned this, a word of caution is in order. Measuring the true cost of quality is very difficult. In practice, while many of the costs (for example, the labor and material components of rework and scrap) are quantifiable, others such as the poor image and loss of business associated with selling inferior products are difficult to quantify. This point becomes even more important considering the fact that market image is a long-term competitive tool which takes a great deal of time to alter. For example, "... analysts agree a car company needs three years or more to turn around a poor image."[18] Managers must be aware of the significance of intangible costs of quality such as market image when determining the true cost of quality. To enhance management's awareness of the costs of substandard quality, we present Exhibit 6.9, which provides a good sampling of the potential costs of low quality, and also gives appropriate classifications for each.

Exhibit 6.9   Quality Cost Classification Matrix

	Direct	Indirect

Quantifiable	Ineffective capacity utilization
	Scrap and rework
	Price discounts
	Training programs
	Returned products
	Complaints handling
	Lawsuits
	Value analyses and audits
	Resources expended testing
	   competitors' products
		Returning material to suppliers
		Idle time
		Downtime
		Inefficient system
		Resources expended to improve
		   firm's low quality image
		Insurance premiums
		Effects of faulty inputs

Nonquantifiable	Lower motivation Subcontracting Lost sales Lower product flexibility Poor product design Poor process design No information sharing Diverting resources to counteract lower quality	Poor choice of suppliers High inventory Lower prestige Organizational restructuring Planning/schedulinig changes Lower borrowing power Lower entry barriers

Source: Adapted from Kaeling, 1987 IIE Integrated Systems Conference. Copyright, Institute of Industrial Engineers.

Aiming for Perfection

As mentioned, intangible costs such as market image make up a large portion of the cost of quality. These intangible costs are so important and far-reaching that an argument can be made for pursuing quality improvement at any cost. Consider the Japanese attitude to quality:

> Their concept of "zero defects" is a good case in point. As one Japanese scholar phrased it, "If you do an economic analysis, you will usually find that it is advantageous to reduce your defect rate from 10 percent to 5 percent. If you repeat that analysis, it may or may not make sense to reduce it further to 1

[18]*Business Week* [1987], p. 138.

percent. The Japanese, however, will reduce it. Having accomplished this, they will attempt to reduce it to 0.01 percent. And then 0.1 percent. You might claim that this obsession is costly, that it makes no economic sense. They are heedless. They will not be satisfied with less than perfection."[19]

The Japanese pursuit of quality is not without reason. Consider a manufactured product requiring 70 operations. If each operation performs at 99 percent quality and efficiency, by the time the final product is complete, there is nothing left: $(.99)^{70} = 0.495!$

Exhibit 6.10 graphically compares the Japanese and North American approaches to quality. It seems that the long-term benefits of quality are far greater than most managers realize. With this in mind, the Japanese slogan which advocates "thinking quality in" rather than "measuring or inspecting it in" makes a lot of sense. To be successful, managers must establish the need for uncompromising quality standards as the dominant philosophy within their organizations.

Exhibit 6.10   The Japanese versus North American Quality Philosophy

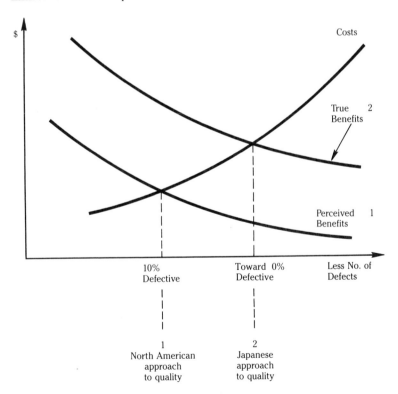

[19]Hayes [1981], p. 61.

Although the Japanese are known for their relentless pursuit of perfect quality at any cost, some North American firms are also striving for perfection at any cost. Consider the following example:

Frito-Lay, a subsidiary of Pepsi Co, sells well over $2 billion worth of potato chips and pretzels every year, owns market shares that run into the 60s and 70s in most of the country, and has margins that are the envy of the food industry. Why? A large reason for it is Frito's "99.5 percent service level." In practical terms, what does this mean? It means that Frito will do some things that in the short run clearly are uneconomic. It will spend several hundred dollars sending a truck to restock a store with a couple of $30 cartons of potato chips. You don't make money that way, it would seem. You can always make a case for saving money by cutting back a percentage or two. However, considering Frito's market share and margins, it's no wonder that Frito's management refuses to do so.[20]

The Japanese have also expressed the need to improve product quality continuously through a concept known as the quality loss function (QLF). Traditional statistical process control techniques, while very useful, may result in a lackadaisical attitude toward further quality improvements if process and/or part characteristics are already within specified tolerance levels. QLF, on the other hand, quantifies the cost savings associated with any incremental improvements in product characteristics, thereby encouraging continual quality improvements in order to reduce costs.

Quality Management and New Technology

In recent years, many Japanese companies and their East Asian counterparts have leaned toward using the notion of *quality management* to replace the concept of *quality control*.[21] The notion of quality control intends to meet a prespecified standard of quality (through inspections). Quality management, on the other hand, deals with much broader issues. It strives to improve quality levels by emphasizing problem elimination and quality improvement; inspection in this case serves only as an aid in detecting problems and signaling the need for improvement. The point is that more inspection does not necessarily lead to better quality; the emphasis should be upon defect prevention rather than defect detection (see Deming [1982]). In fact, one of the main signs of poor quality management is a large, impressive inspection operation! Studies have shown

---

[20]Adapted from Peters and Waterman [1982], pp. 164–165.

[21]One area of confusion has involved the terms quality assurance and quality control. According to the American Society for Quality Control (ASQC), *quality assurance* is ". . . all those planned or systematic actions necessary to provide adequate confidence that a product or service will satisfy given needs." *Quality control* is defined as ". . . the operational techniques and the activities which sustain a quality of product or service that will satisfy given needs" (see Freund [1987]).

a correlation between greater investment in prevention and lower total quality costs (Chauvel and Andre [1985]).

Preventing Quality Costs.   Once firms become aware of the various sources of quality costs (prevention, appraisal, internal failure, external failure), investment in the prevention of quality problems can significantly reduce the three other categories of quality expenditure, and thus reduce total quality costs. Exhibit 6.11 illustrates the connections among these cost components.

Exhibit 6.11   Preventing the Costs of Poor Quality

Prevention Costs	+	Appraisal Costs	+	Internal Failure Costs	+	External Failure Costs	=	Total Quality Costs
( )	+	( )	+	( )	+	( )	=	( )

The rationale for this is as follows: "It is estimated that from 60 to 90 percent of total quality costs are the result of internal and external failure problems...."[22] Furthermore, "...the typical factory invests a staggering 20 percent to 25 percent of its operating budget in finding and fixing mistakes...."[23] Supplementary to these costs are the bad reputation and poor image associated with selling a product of inferior quality. When consideration is given to all these facts, it is little wonder that investing in the prevention of quality makes good economic sense. The following example further highlights this point:

> Reed Tool Company is a U.S. based manufacturer of drilling tools for the oil and gas exploration and development industry. In September 1982, Reed management decided to launch a company-wide Product Quality Improvement Program to make the company's products the performance and quality leaders in the industry. By investing in preventative quality measures such as product design reviews, employee training, statistical process control procedures, and advanced process monitoring gauges, Reed was able to reduce total quality costs by 33 percent in two years. This was due to a dramatic drop in appraisal, internal and external failure costs. The results of this program included: (1) the percentage of parts requiring rework/repair was reduced by half, (2) the rate of parts being scrapped is one quarter of what it was in 1982, (3) drilling bit lives have been improved by over 20 percent, (4) field complaints dropped and customer expectations increased, and (5) domestic market share has increased by more than 20 percent.[24]

[22]Evans, Anderson, Sweeney, and Williams [1987], p. 47.
[23]*Business Week* [1987], p. 132.
[24]Adapted from Abill [1985], pp. 53–55.

Quality Improvement through New Technology. Many firms seem reluctant to replace old production equipment with newer technology until the old equipment becomes physically obsolete. Managers with this mindset are ignoring the dynamic nature of the new operations technology and its enormous potential for quality (and cost) improvements. Consider the following analogy:

> Home refrigerators now use far less energy. The electricity consumption rate of a new refrigerator is one-third of those of a decade ago. And yet, among the electric appliances found in the ordinary home , the refrigerator remains the largest electricity user. Any sensible housekeeper will immediately replace a 10-year-old model with the latest one after a glance at the electricity bill.
>
> You may postpone such a seemingly inevitable decision about refrigerators for one reason or another. But you cannot avoid the latest manufacturing equipment if you are an industrialist. Not only does the older equipment mean higher costs and lower product quality, it will prove totally unfit for the production of what customers more often than not start demanding.[25]

A number of technologies can be considered to improve quality and prevent future quality problems. These include investing in:

1. Computer-aided manufacturing technologies
2. Process monitoring and control technologies
3. Automated inspection systems
4. Quality information systems
5. Improved product and process design techniques

As we noted in Chapter 2, computer-aided manufacturing (CAM) technologies can lead to increased quality since, in addition to the fact that they are physically more accurate in their operations, they are not susceptible to making the careless mental errors that human operators would. This applies especially to jobs that require the constant repetition of simple tasks. With CAM technology, firms can significantly increase both the quality and productivity of their operations.

Process monitoring and control involves achieving quality through the measurement and control of the production process, rather than through the inspection of completed parts. In other words, the quality of the product is ensured by controlling the process that produces the product. This is facilitated by using methods such as *statistical process control (SPC)*. In its simplest form, SPC refers to the use of basic statistical concepts to monitor the process to ensure that a product consistently fits engineering specifications. At various stages of production runs, tests are made to check direct control of the quality of materials, parts, components, and assemblies throughout the production cycle.

---

[25]Karatsu [1988], p. 8.

Results are recorded and charted to show how the samples checked compared with specified tolerance.[26]

Today, computer process monitoring and control (CPM and CPC), described in Chapter 2, make the potential benefits of SPC even more powerful. Firms must explore the potential benefits this technology can provide in terms of preventing quality problems and providing high and consistent product quality. Consider General Electric's quality approach as an example:

> The compressor plant's computer system can monitor 1,000 different quality points and give instant feedback on how well each of the factory's components is running, including seven miles of material handling track.
>
> Because of the new control and information systems in place, employees do not simply correct mistakes after they are made. Instead, they anticipate and prevent time. When a machine shows the first signs of straying from acceptable tolerances, an alarm sounds, a controlman is alerted, and the problem is fixed—*before* any bad parts are produced.[27]

Automated inspection systems (described in Chapter 2) are also coming to the forefront in manufacturing quality control. Their attractiveness is due largely to the fact that they are about 97 percent accurate and effective in the inspection of products and the elimination of failures. Under optimal conditions, the human inspectors they replace are only about 78 percent accurate.[28] While this is only one aspect of a complete quality management program, it can amount to considerable cost savings and contribute significantly to higher-quality end products.

The advanced information technologies described in Chapter 2 can also provide a potential source for preventing quality problems. With this technology, management can receive timely and accurate quality information at minimal cost through software programs that automatically gather, summarize, and distribute relevant data. There are many examples of applications of computer simulation (Flowers and Cole [1987]), computer graphics (Gott [1987]), and expert systems (Gipe and Jasinski [1987]), being used to improve quality control and assurance.

Improved product and process design techniques can also reduce total quality costs. Genichi Taguchi, a Japanese quality specialist who is perhaps the most important quality expert to emerge since Deming and Juran, stresses that the design phase of a product's life cycle is the time when many future quality problems can be prevented. Taguchi's initial investigation confirmed that *experimentation* and *testing*, rather than creative brainstorming, accounted for the

---

[26]SPC was substantially ignored by North American firms, while Japanese firms were quicker to adopt this technique in the 1950s, brought over by Deming and later by Juran. Application of SPC is considered one of the key factors contributing to the high quality of their products. It is only recently that North American companies began to utilize this concept vigorously.

[27]Adapted from Emrich [1988], pp. 15–16.

[28]Lapidus [1986], pp. 10–11.

greatest expenditure of time and money in many manufacturing companies. He subsequently developed a procedure, known as the Taguchi method, to design experiments that would reduce weeks' worth of testing to hours or even minutes. In short, Taguchi has done for experimental design what Deming has done for SPC.

The basic concept behind Taguchi's methods is simple in theory: Design products to be "robust" enough to achieve high quality despite environmental fluctuations (for example, manufacturing process fluctuations and improper use of the product by the customer), and improve the manufacturing process through improved process design, rather than through expensive process control technologies.[29] Taguchi's stress on the design stage is understandable when one considers that Juran and other quality experts have asserted that no more than 20 percent of quality defects can actually be traced to the production line. The other 80 percent are locked in either at the design stage or by purchasing policies that value low price over the quality of purchased parts and materials (see Port [1987]). Yet, as with SPC, North American companies have been very slow in adapting Taguchi's concepts. In fact, it was only in 1983 that the American Supplier Institute (ASI), as a pioneer, began teaching the method. One striking difference in present applications of Taguchi methods in Japan and North America is that the Japanese use the methods primarily for optimizing product design, whereas the majority of American companies apply the methods in production/manufacturing process design. This difference is not accidental: ". . . Taguchi himself indicates product design is by far the most effectrive area in which to apply the technique."[30]

Closely related to product and process design techniques is the concept of quality function deployment (QFD). QFD is a planning tool for the firm to foresee through its marketing research the performance features the customer wants, and subsequently translate them into engineering parameters and values that must be met. Instead of guessing what the customer expects, QFD ensures that what the customer wants is actually manufactured the first time around.

In addition to improved quality through meeting the performance requirements of the customer, QFD can also lead to a significant reduction in the lead time required to design and manufacture new products. The potential for QFD, combined with CAD and CAPP, to reduce the lead time for new product introductions is phenomenal. The following example illustrates this point:

> In 1977 Toyota Autobody, a Toyota subsidiary which makes bodies for small vans, began to use QFD in its design process after four years of preparation through training and case study development. Only two years later, Toyota Autobody was able to document a reduction in start-up costs of 20 percent; by 1982 the reduction was 38 percent and by 1984 it was 61 percent, while the

---

[29]For a further description and explanation of Taguchi's philosophy and methods, see Kackar [1986] and Sullivan [1987].

[30]Ealey [1987], p. 23.

total time needed to engineer a new van was reduced by one-third. Now it is being used throughout the company and Toyota cites QFD as one of the prime reasons why it can produce an all-new car in three years.[31]

Finally, one must consider the need for improved product quality and reduced defect levels in incoming materials. With JIT, for example, if a firm receives defective supplies, its production schedule will be disrupted because it is designed to bring in exactly the needed amount of materials at exactly the time when production is to take place. JIT also implies that firms will have to rely less and less on incoming material inspection, since the constant inspection reduces the effectiveness of a just-in-time philosophy. Although firms may in some cases find it necessary to perform an inspection on incoming materials, in many instances they attempt to reduce the need by forcing suppliers to ensure the perfect quality of their supplies. In general, a JIT approach to production will require firms to develop a cooperative, long-term relationship with their suppliers so that quality can be emphasized. This is in contrast to the short-term, lowest bidder means of choosing suppliers that is currently employed by many North American firms. If firms find it necessary to perform incoming inspection, they should consider shifting to inspection methods such as constant growth inspection (CGI), which reduces the inspection workload for the small batch quantities typified by JIT.[32]

Management Commitment and Employee Participation

Leaving aside the question of technology adoption, one prerequisite for the achievement of competitive levels of quality is management commitment. Top management must strive to develop and maintain a philosophy and culture within the organization that emphasizes quality, and middle management must adopt this philosophy wholeheartedly. A program geared at improving quality will not work with the passive support of management, and this means that traditional control and evaluation methods may have to be modified to incorporate quality as a predominant philosophy. Without management commitment, employee participation in quality improvement programs will be negligible.

Employees can be both the cause of poor quality (through lack of motivation and/or training), and the source of many excellent improvement ideas. The key to minimizing the negative impact and maximizing the positive effect is to have the workers on the company's side. This commitment to quality is what we refer to as *employee participation.* It is also notable that this relationship is self-perpetuating. Once high quality levels have been achieved, employee morale should improve further. No one likes making bad parts or reworking the same

---

[31]McElroy [1987], p. 68.

[32]With the CGI method, a predetermined inspection level (say 10 percent) is aplied to *every* lot of production regardless of the lot sizes. For example, if the lot size is 400 units, then 40 units of each lot will be inspected. If the lot size changes, so will the sample size per lot. See Chung [1987] for a description of CGI.

part over and over, and thus morale improves with pride taken in producing high-quality products.

Two issues that have received considerable attention with regard to employee participation are the concepts of quality of work life (QWL) and quality circles (QC). *QWL* refers to how employees feel about every dimension of their work life, including economic benefits, working conditions, interpersonal relationships, and satisfaction with the meaning and scope of the job. Providing a high QWL for employees is a necessary step to ensure that workers are committed to the overall goals of the organization. *Quality circles* refers to the practice of bringing small groups of employees together for training and participative decision-making purposes. Proper training can lead to a significant reduction in quality problems, and participative decision-making can also be used to generate a significant number of quality improvement ideas. For example, "...quality circles at Toyota generated 25,000 suggestions last year, and 96 percent of them were adopted."[33] Many Japanese companies such as Toshiba, Hitachi, and NEC employ this philosophy to achieve constant incremental improvement in quality (see Wood [1987]).

To recapitulate: The goal of any competitive company, as far as product quality is concerned, is to produce a product or provide a service into which quality is designed, built, and maintained at the most economical cost. It is this comprehensive view which has led to the birth of the total quality concept (TQC). *TQC* means "...integrating the quality development, quality maintenance, and quality-improved efforts of various groups in an organization so as to enable marketing, engineering, production, and service at the most economical levels which allow for full customer satisfaction."[34] In short, TQC is software-oriented (as opposed to TPM) and is a movement centered on the improvement of managerial performance at all levels.

For successful implementation of TQC, a company must establish a quality system to serve as a structure for TQC. Supporting any quality system is based on the existence of a set of techniques such as SPC and the Taguchi Methods, which are applied to ensure effective utilization of the different components of TQC. In general, one can look at these relationships in terms of a multiechelon triangle (Feigenbaum [1983] refers to this structure as the technological triangle) which at its apex is TQC and at its lowest tier is the application of different quality techniques described in this chapter. Exhibit 6.12 displays this multiechelon triangle.

CONCLUDING OBSERVATIONS

Productivity and quality have recently become two widely discussed issues on North American business circles.

---

[33]Davis [1988], p. 590.
[34]Feigenbaum [1983], p. 234.

Exhibit 6.12   A Relationship between TQC, Quality System and Application of Various Quality Techniques

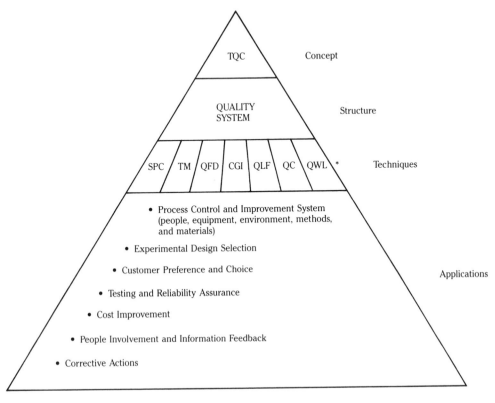

*Legends
SPC   = Statistical Process Control
TM   = Taguchi Methods
QFD   = Quality Function Development
CGI   = Constant Growth Inspection
QLF   = Quality Loss Function
QC   = Quality Circle
QWL   = Quality of Work Life

To measure productivity, management must be aware of the total productivity of the firm's operations, rather than judging performance solely on the productivity of the individual inputs. The new technology can be very effective in improving productivity at subassembly and component manufacturing activities, especially when the productivity matrix is used as a model. But although productivity is a crucial objective to strive for, it is not the only objective. Improving productivity is possible through various alternatives, and the choice of the best course of action must be made within the scope of the firm's strategic options. As was underscored in Chapter 5, an understanding of the relationship between the firm's business strategy, manufacturing strategy, and (new) technology strategy is crucial for the effective management and competitive success of the firm.

Quality we defined as an integrative concept comprised of a set of measures that gives us insight into the way an organization manages conformance to requirements/specifications and expectations. Investing in the prevention of quality costs is the best strategy for producing quality products without incurring unwanted and unnecessary expense. Investing in technology can also result in higher levels of quality. While there are many technologies and methods available for preventing quality problems, none of them will work up to their potential employees. Thus, management commitment and employee participation are regarded as crucial components of any quality improvement program.

RECOMMENDED READINGS

NACKAR, R. N. [1986]. "Taguchi's Quality Philosophy: Analysis and Commentary." *Quality Progress,* December, pp. 21–29.
SKINNER, W. [1986]. "The Productivity Paradox." *Harvard Business Review,* July–August, pp. 55–59.

DISCUSSION QUESTIONS

1. How much would you pay for a new technology which will guarantee that a defect-free product is produced every time? Explain.
2. Would you automatically adopt a technology that is guaranteed to increase the total factor productivity of your firm's operations? What else (if anything) would you consider? Explain.
3. Develop a productivity and quality framework which could be used by management to improve the operations of the firm.
4. There are two general ways of increasing productivity and quality within a firm—through technology (hardware and software) or through the improved performance of people. Which one do you feel has the greatest potential for improving the productivity and quality of a firm's operations?
5. How would you measure productivity and quality in service organizations?
6. Develop a model which illustrates how productivity, quality, and new technology are related.
7. How does a firm generate a cost/benefit analysis of a productivity and quality program, when quantifiable measurements are difficult to ascertain?
8. Honda's plant in the United States has fewer robots but is almost twice as productive as many auto plants in the country. Why is it important for North American firms to acquire the new technology to improve productivity?
9. Productivity should be examined from both an efficiency and an effectiveness point of view, where efficiency is concerned with the ratio of outputs to inputs, and effectiveness is concerned with the value of output to customers. For example, a company can build a high-quality, low-cost, 4-door, yellow, full-sized car (high efficiency), but no one may want this car (low effectiveness). Does new technology have a greater potential to improve the efficiency or effectiveness of a firm's operations? Explain.
10. Pick two products, and show how the eight dimensions of quality (see Exhibit 6.8) relate to each of the two products. Can the new technology help to improve any of these eight dimensions of quality? Which ones does the new technology have the greatest potential to improve?
11. A company implements a new computerized information system. Now, information such

as machine downtime and percent scrap produced is gathered, summarized, and distributed in real time. Have the productivity and/or quality of the firm's operations improved? Explain.

12. Much has been written and said about the low productivity and quality levels of North American firms when compared to Japanese companies. What do you feel are the major factors contributing to the North American productivity and quality "gap"? Is the reluctance to adopt the new technology the major contributing factor?

REFERENCES AND BIBLIOGRAPHY

ABELL, R. [1985]. "Revamped from Design to Application." *Quality Progress,* October, pp. 53–55.

ADLER, P. [1987]. "A Plant Productivity Measure for 'High-Tech' Manufacturing." *Interfaces,* Volume 17, No. 6, November–December, pp. 75–85.

BAIRSTOW, J. [1986]. "Automated Automaking." *High Technology,* Volume 6, No. 8, August, pp. 25–28.

BRADY, W. M. [1985]. "The Productivity Index: A Total Factor Measurement System That Works." In J. L. Hamlin (ed.), *Success Studies in Productivity Improvement.* Industrial Engineering and Management Press, Atlanta, Georgia, pp. 102–107.

BRITNEY, R. R., R. P. KUDAR, D. A. JOHNSON, J. M. LEGENTIL, and J. WALSH. Planning for Productivity Improvement: A Management Perspective." *Business Quarterly* (Winter 1983), p. 39.

BRITNEY, R. T. [1986]. "Improving Productivity and Quality." In H. Noori (ed.), *Proceedings: Technology Canada,* REMAT, Wilfrid Laurier University, May 21–22, pp. 90–95.

BULLOCK, R. J., and E. E. LAWLER [1984]. "Gainsharing: A Few Questions and Fewer Answers." *Human Resource Management,* Volume 23, No. 1, pp. 23–40.

Business Week [1987]. "The Push for Quality." June 8, pp. 130–143.

BUZACOTT, J. A. [1985]. "Productivity and Technological Change." *Interfaces,* Volume 15, No. 3, pp. 73–84.

CHAUVEL, A. M., and Y. A. ANDRE [1985]. "Quality Cost: Better Prevent Than Cure." *Quality Progress,* September, pp. 29–32.

CHUNG, CHEN-HUA [1987]. "Quality Control Sampling Plans Under Zero Inventories: An Alternative Method." *Production and Inventory Management,* Volume 28, No. 2, pp. 37–41.

CRAIG, C. E., and R. C. HARRIS [1973]. "Total Productivity Measurement at the Firm Level." *Sloan Management Review,* Volume 14, No. 3, pp. 13–28.

DAVIS, T. C. [1988]. "The Impact of the Factory of the Future on Society." In T. M. Kahill et al. (eds.), *Technology Management I, Proceedings of the First International Conference on Technology Management,* Miami, Florida, pp. 584–591.

DEMING, W. E. [1982]. "Quality, Productivity and Competitive Position." MIT Center for Advanced Engineering Study, Cambridge, Mass.

EALEY, L. [1987]. "Nippondenso: Hot Bed of Taguchi Methods." *Automotive Industries,* July, p. 23.

EBEL, K., and E. ULRICH [1987]. "Some Workplace Effects of CAD and CAM." *International Labor Review,* Volume 126, No. 3, May–June, pp. 351–370.

EDOSOMWAN, J. A. [1987]. *Integrating Productivity and Quality Management.* Marcel Dekker, Inc. New York.

EMRICH, M. [1988]. "Training Completes the Circle at GE." *Manufacturing Systems,* January, pp. 14–16.

EVANS, J. R., D. R. ANDERSON, D. J. SWEENEY, and T. A. WILLIAMS [1987]. *Applied Production and Operations Management,* 2nd ed. West Publishing Company, pp. 36–57.

FEIGENBAUM, A. V. [1983]. *Total Quality Control.* McGraw-Hill, New York.

FLOWERS, A. D., and J. R. COLE [1987]. "An Application of Computer Simulation to Quality Control in Manufacturing." In M. Sepehri (ed), *Quest for Quality.* Industrial Engineering and Management Press, Atlanta, Georgia, pp. 260–266.

FREUND, R. A. [1987]. "Definitions and Basic Quality Concepts." In M. Sepehri (ed.), *Quest for Quality.* Industrial Engineering and Management Press, pp. 27–33.

GARVIN, D. A. [1984]. "What Does 'Product Quality' Really Mean." *Sloan Mangagement Review,* Fall, pp. 25–43.

GIPE, J. P., and N. D. JASINSKI [1987]. "Expert Systems Applications in Quality Assurance." In M. Sepehri (ed.), *Quest for Quality.* Industrial Engineering and Management Press, pp. 272–276.

GOTT, V. W. [1987]. "Computer Graphics for Quality Assurance." In M. Sepehri (ed.), *Quest for Quality.* Industrial Engineering and Management Press, Atlanta, Georgia, pp. 267–271.

HAYES, R. H. [1981].   "Why Japanese Factories Work." *Harvard Business Review*, July–August, pp. 56–66.

HAYES, R. H., and K. B. CLARK [1985].   "Exploring the Sources of Productivity Differences at the Factory Level." In K. B. Clark, R. H. Hayes, and C. Lorenz (eds.), *The Uneasy Alliance: Managing the Productivity-Technology Dilemma*, Harvard Business School Press, pp. 151–188.

HINES, W. W. [1976].   "Guidelines for Implementing Productivity Measurement." *Industrial Engineering*, Volume 8, Number 6, pp. 40–43.

IMAI, M. [1986].   *KAIZEN: The Key to Japan's Competitive Success.* Random House Business Division, New York.

JENSEN, M. C., and C. W. SMITH [1985].   "Stockholders, Manager, and Creditor Interests: Applications of Agency Theory." In E. I. Altman and M. G. Subrahmanyam (eds.), *Recent Advances in Corporate Finance.* Richard D. Irwin, Homewood, Ill., pp. 93–131.

JURAN, J. M., and F. M. GRYNA, JR. [1980].   *Quality Planning and Analysis,* 2nd ed. McGraw-Hill, New York.

KACKAR, R. N. [1986].   "Taguchi's Quality Philosophy: Analysis and Commentary." *Quality Progress,* December, pp. 21–29.

KARATSU, H. [1988].   "Quality and New Technology." *The Japan Times Weekly Overseas Edition,* Saturday, January 23.

KELLY, C. M. [1985].   "Five Questions, and a Value, for Productivity." In J. Hamlin (ed.), *Success Stories in Productivity Improvement.* Industrial Engineering and Mangement Press, Atlanta, Georgia, pp. 24–29.

KNOWLTON, C. [1988].   "What America Makes Best." *Fortune,* pp. 40–54.

KOELLING, P. C., J. TENJERAS, and P. F. RIEL [1987].   "Total Quality Management." *Proceedings of IIE Integrated Conference,* Nashville, November 5–7, pp. 129–134.

KUMPE, T., and P. T. BOLWIJN [1987].   "Trends and Issues in Improving Productivity of Industrial Organizations Engaged in Medium to High-Volume Manufacturing of Discrete Products." In *Proceedings of World Productivity Forum,* International Industrial Engineering Conference, Washington, D.C., May 17–20, pp. 48–50.

LAPIDUS, S. N. [1986].   "Cost Justifying Vision." *Quality,* June, pp. 10–11.

McELROY, J. [1985].   "Experimental Design Hits Detroit." *Automotive Industries,* February, pp. 48–50.

McELROY, J. [1987].   "For Whom Are We Building Cars?" *Automotive Industries,* June, pp. 68–70.

MUNDT, B. M. [1986].   "Meeting the Quality/Productivity Challenge." *World,* Volume 5, pp. 16, 17.

PETERS, T. J., and R. H. WATERMAN, JR. [1982].   *In Search of Excellence.* Warner Books, New York, pp. 156–199.

PORT, O. [1987].   "The Push for Quality." *Business Week,* June, pp. 130–134.

RIGGS, J. L. [1984].   "The Objectives Matrix for Productivity Measurement." *Operations Management Review,* Summer, pp. 3–14.

RYAN, J. [1983].   "The Productivity/Quality Connection—Plugging in at Westinghouse Electric." *Quality Progress,* December, pp. 26–29.

SEPEHRI, M. [1987].   "Case Studies of Manufacturing Productivity Improvement." In *Proceedings of World Productivity Forum,* International Industrial Engineering Conference, Washington, D.C., May 17–20, pp. 35–40.

SKINNER, W. [1985].   "The Taming of Lions: How Manufacturing Leadership Evolved, 1780–1984." In K. B. Clark, R. H. Hayes, and C. Lorenz (eds.), *The Uneasy Alliance,* Harvard Business School Press, pp. 63–110.

SKINNER, W. [1986].   "The Productivity Paradox." *Harvard Business Review,* July–August, pp. 55–59.

SULLIVAN, L. P. [1987].   "The Power of Taguchi Methods." *Quality Progress,* June, pp. 76–79.

SUMANTH, D. J. [1985].   "A Review of Some Approaches to the Measurement of Total Productivity in a Company/Organization." In J. L. Hamlin, (ed.), *Success Stories in Productivity Improvement.* Industrial Engineering and Management Press, Atlanta, Georgia, pp. 40–49.

SUMANTH, D. J. [1984].   *Productivity Engineering and Management.* McGraw-Hill, New York.

THUROW, L. C. [1983].   "The 7½ Percent Solution." *The Princeton Papers,* September, pp. 13–14.

WHEELWRIGHT, S. C. [1981].   "Japan—Where Operations Really Are Strategic." *Harvard Business Review,* July–August, pp. 67–74.

WOOD, R. C. [1987].   "Assembly Lines Build Ideas." *High Technology Business,* December, p. 17.

Chapter Seven

ASSESSMENT, JUSTIFICATION, AND FINANCING THE NEW TECHNOLOGY

The management accounting systems used by railroads in the 1860s, in the Carnegie Steel Company in the 1880s, and in DuPont and General Motors earlier in this century served their owner-managers much better than most systems in existence today.

Thomas Johnson and Robert Kaplan

INTRODUCTION

The new technology is creating a strong need for many firms to assess the validity of their cost accounting and financial systems. Investing in technology is a strategic decision, and any commitment must be appraised within the context of the company's strategic plan. However, it is becoming apparent that traditional accounting and finance methodologies undermine the strategic potential of the new technology. Investments in the new technology are difficult to justify, owing to the lack of techniques to measure and quantify its benefits accurately.

In practical terms, firms are discovering that (1) the shift from labor to technology (and thus overheads) is making traditional cost management systems more of a hindrance than a help; (2) typical capital justification methods undervalue or fail to consider the most important benefits of new technology, and thus the technology is often not adopted; and (3) financing the acquisition of the new technology sometimes involves financial and legal considerations that are unique. In this chapter, we will discuss all three issues in detail.

ISSUES WITH THE TRADITIONAL COST MANAGEMENT SYSTEMS

Given the characteristics of the new technology, its assessment and justification requires criteria different from those traditionally used. That is, the rules companies typically apply for weighing such measures as return on investment to

192

support capital investments are out of place in a new technology environment. The inherent flexibility of the new technology results in a broader scope (as opposed to a well-specified and narrow range) of potential applications. This in turn allows the capabilities of the equipment to be extended (as opposed to being fixed and known) to future applications, making the costs and benefits of the technology more difficult to quantify. Yet "...91 percent of executives use conventional justification procedures as their major consideration in approving factory automation decisions."[1] On the other hand, some CEOs have admitted ignoring the conventional analysis completely and making multimillion-dollar investment decisions based on intuition. Clearly some problems with traditional methods do exist.

The purpose of this section is to identify the problems associated with traditional cost management systems, and to offer some advice as to how they can be improved to incorporate the realities of the new technology.

Cost Management Systems and New Technology

In many respects, outdated cost accounting systems may prohibit firms from pursuing the new technology, as exemplified by the following situation:

> The manager of engineering foresaw that investing in the creation of a CAM software program for machine calculations would enable manufacturing to make use of two of the company's numerically controlled machines which were sitting idle much of the time. The program would facilitate faster throughput and significantly fewer hours of direct labor input. However, both he and the manufacturing manager realized that such an innovation would throw out the 'magic' manufacturing ratio of 70 percent direct labor hours to 30 percent indirect. Even though direct labor and total costs could be reduced, the ratio would be distributed and the manufacturing manager would be called to account by the parent company. No wonder his first impulse was to leave well enough alone.[2]

This scenario is by no means a rare occurrence. Most traditional cost management systems use direct labor hours as the basis for allocating overhead expenses to product costs (see also Tatikonda [1988]). This was appropriate when direct labor costs made up a significant portion of the firm's total costs. However, automated manufacturing has shifted a large percentage of a firm's costs from direct labor to overhead. In fact, as mentioned in Chapter 6, direct labor costs currently account for only 10 to 15 percent of total product costs in many industries.[3] This propensity is likely to continue, and there are speculations that labor costs will eventually diminish to 1 to 10 percent of total cost of sales as

[1]O'Guin [1987], pp. 36–40.
[2]Adapted from Beatty [1987], p. 7.
[3]Overhead and materials account for roughly 35 percent and 50 percent, respectively.

manufacturers move toward the factory-of-the-future (see Bonsak [1986]). There are instances today where this has already happened. For example, IBM's direct labor cost is about 4 percent, and at Apple's Macintosh plant, it is 1 percent.[4] Exhibit 7.1 illustrates the trends in the contribution of both direct labor and overhead costs to overall manufacturing costs in the United States over a period of 120 years.

The shift from direct labor to nondirect costs (like overhead) can cause significant managerial problems for firms using outdated cost management systems, as the following illustrates:

> The Carmel Corporation...used a standard cost accounting system that allocated all nondirect costs on the basis of direct labor hours. The company had installed this procedure many years ago when direct labour accounted for more than 60 percent of total costs and machinery was both simple and inexpensive. Over the years, however, investment in sophisticated new machinery had greatly reduced the direct labor content of the company's products....

Exhibit 7.1 The Direct Labor and Overhead Components of Total Manufacturing Costs in the United States

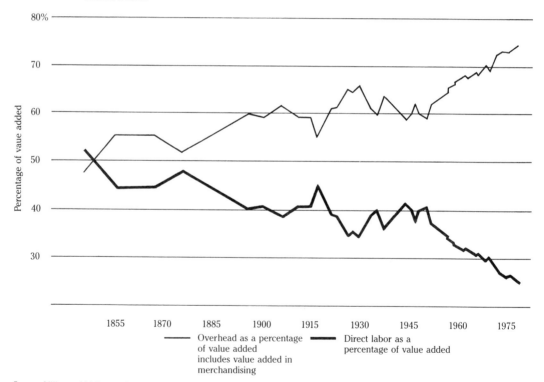

Source: Miller and Vollmann [1985], p. 143.

[4]Gould [1985], p. 57.

With direct labor (at an average wage of $12 per hour) plunging as a fraction of total costs, the accounting system was allocating the growing capital and overhead costs to a shrinking pool of direct labor hours.

The predictable result: a total cost per direct labor hour in excess of $60—and projections that it would soon rise to $80. Worse, efforts to offset these higher hourly rates by substituting capital and purchased materials for in-house production only compounded the problem. The accounting system was distracting management attention from the expansion of indirect costs.[5]

One of the most serious problems associated with the misallocation of overhead costs is in the pricing of products. Overpricing or underpricing could obviously have serious effects on the competitive strength of the company and its survival. Consider the following example:

> Rockwell International realized that its line of heavy-duty truck axles was selling erratically. One of its best selling axles had begun losing market share. To find out why, the division managers conducted a special study. They found that the practice of essentially allocating overhead in proportion to direct labor costs had created serious distortions. . . . The division had been "overcosting" its highest volume axle by roughly 20 percent, while underestimating the cost of other axles by as much as 40 percent. Because the company had priced its products in relation to their estimated costs, it had been overpricing the high-volume product. That lured competitors into the market.[6]

Exhibit 7.2 provides a numerical example highlighting how the use of direct labor hours to allocate overhead can result in faulty cost estimates for products and subsequently create pricing problems. The example also shows how the adoption of the new technology can make this problem even more severe. In short, the new technology will increase the level of overhead costs incurred by firms. In this case, companies should charge their overhead and indirect costs[7] directly to specific products, rather than allocating them arbitrarily on the basis of direct labor hours. Failing explicitly to account for overhead costs will be detrimental, as firms will be either reluctant or unable to incorporate the potential savings of the new technology into their justification process. This means that many technology proposals will be subject to rejection because the bulk of the benefits generated by the new technology are overhead savings and strategic gains, rather than direct labor savings.

Improving Present Cost Management Systems

In practice, companies should separate their cost management systems from their financial reporting mechanisms. While the latter concerns external justification,

[5]Kaplan [1984], p.96.

[6]Worthy [1987], p. 48.

[7]These costs include technology depreciation, research and development, product design, maintenance, utilities, scrap and rework, inventory, and marketing costs.

Exhibit 7.2   The Problem of Using Direct Labor Costs to Allocate Overhead: A Numerical Example

Let us assume a company produces two products. The company uses a traditional cost accounting system that applies overhead based on direct labor dollars. In our example, assume that Product A is technology-intensive (uses significant automated processes) and Product B is labor-intensive. The product cost for these two products is currently calculated as follows:

"TRUE"COSTS

	Product A	**Product B**
Labor	$ 50	$200
Material	300	300
Technology	200	50
Other Product Cost	375	375
Total Product Cost	$925	$925

Total Overhead for the two products equals

$$\frac{\text{Total cost less direct labor and material}}{\text{Total direct labor cost}}$$

$$\text{Total Overhead} = \frac{\$1,000}{\$250} = 400\%$$

The product cost of these two products is currently calculated by the traditional cost accounting system as follows:

	Product A	**Product B**
Direct Labor	$ 50	$ 200
Direct Material	300	300
Overhead	200*	800**
TotalProduct Cost	$550	$1,300

*($50 × 400%)   **($200 × 400%)

Product A is: $\dfrac{925-550}{925} = 40.5\%$ undercosted

Product B is: $\dfrac{1,300-925}{925} = 45.0\%$ overcosted

the former concerns mostly internal evaluation of the technology. Brimson and Berliner [1987] have proposed a number of important changes for improving current cost management systems. The following points are based primarily on their recommendations, along with those suggested by Kaplan [1984], Bonsack [1986], and Worthy [1987].

Exhibit 7.2   (continued)

The Product Manager for Product A is innovative and by investing in a new Numerical Control (NC) machine is able to reduce the direct labor content by $10 per unit. However, depreciation on the machine and higher software and maintenance support will increase the overhead costs by $7 per unit. The company will then realize a net savings of $3 per unit. Product B's cost will remain unchanged.

	Product A	**Product B**
Labor	$ 40	$200
Material	300	300
Technology	205	50
Other Product Cost	377	375
Total	$922	$925

The accounting system would calculate the new product cost as follows:

$$\text{Total Overhead} = \frac{\$1,007}{\$\ 240} = 420\%$$

The recalculated overhead rate is then applied to each product as before using direct labor dollars.

	Product A	**Product B**
Direct Labor	$ 40	$ 200
Direct Material	300	300
Overhead	168*	840**
Total Product Cost	$508	$1,340

*($40 × 420%)   **($200 × 420%)

It can be seen that the accounting system reported a $40 increase in the cost of Product B even though its cost was unaffected. If Product B was a marginally profitable product, the decision might be made to drop this product.

The primary reason for this distortion is that the overhead rate is inflated by technology cost. The inflated overhead cost is then allocated to the products using an erroneous direct labor base. In fact, the relationship between labor and technology is diametric rather than complementary.

Source: Adapted with minor changes from Brimson and Berliner, IIE Integrated Systems Conference [1987]. Copyright, Institute of Industrial Engineers.

Direct Charging of Technology Costs.   Companies should charge technology costs directly to products by using machine hours with separate cost centers for every homogeneous machine group. For example:

Rather than homogenizing the costs generated by its many fabrication departments, [Caterpillar] regards each piece of production machinery as an individual cost center. Each machine is like a small bucket that contains its share of overhead costs. At Caterpillar's heavy-equipment plant in Decatur, Illinois, the company breaks down costs into more than 1,300 overhead buckets. A machine that takes up a lot of floor space is allocated a larger portion of rent than a smaller machine. If the smaller machine is harder to maintain or uses a lot of electricity, it gets proportionately more of those costs. In most cases, Caterpillar assigns these buckets of overhead costs to specific products according to how much time each one spends passing through each machine.[8]

Life Cycle Reporting.   Companies should report the revenues and costs generated by a product throughout its life cycle, instead of on a periodic basis. This should also include preproduction costs (research, development, and design): "...studies have shown that between 70–90 percent of a product's cost is determined prior to the production stage."[9] Life cycle reporting is even more important if firms compete on product innovation by producing a constant stream of new products. In this situation, monthly or yearly profit reports may show new products to be generating high margins (relative to high-volume mature products), but if the product has a short life cycle, the full cost may not be recovered.

Cost-Based Pricing.   Companies must price products to ensure that fixed costs will be recovered. Although in the short term it may be beneficial for firms to price simply to recover variable costs, they obviously cannot remain profitable if they do not recuperate fixed investments as well. Pricing based on variable costs becomes even less appropriate in a new technology environment characterized by high fixed capital investments.

Identifying Non-Value-Added (Waste) Costs.   Traditionally, cost management systems have examined total product cost as the simple combination of labor, materials, and overhead. In a new technology environment, a somewhat more progressive approach would be to: (1) include consideration of the cost of the technology employed, and (2) divide each cost element into value-added and non-value-added components. While traditional cost management systems may account for some of these costs (such as absenteeism, obsolescence), the approach is by no means fully explicit or comprehensive.

If management explicitly tracks and reports all non-value-added costs as sugggested, the effort to control them will be eased. Take the following example:

> Consider the cost of a major integrated steel manufacturer that measured the cost of quality (a major source of non-value-added cost) at one finishing plant.

[8]Worthy [1987], p. 53.
[9]Brimson and Berliner [1987], p. 47.

The company had to make some assumptions and accept the fact that costs such as processing scrap would not be included. Yet, the costs that it was able to capture and directly associate to quality were over 10 percent of sales— higher than direct labor![10]

The explicit reporting of waste costs will also focus management attention on them, and motivate efforts to reduce or eliminate them. Finally, this approach allows the decision-maker to identify the true value of product cost components, and to use these data as the basis for justification efforts. Exhibit 7.3 illustrates the significance of using the concept of non-value-added costs.

Discerning the Cost of Significant Activities. Companies should adopt an activity cost system which traces the costs of a product all the way from the costs involved in purchasing the raw materials to those generated when the finished product is delivered to the customer.

Measuring Units Instead of Dollars. Naturally, a firm's profitability can vary as input prices change. In other words, if a firm is measuring inputs in dollars, temporary alterations in input prices can cause uncontrollable cost fluctuations. More important, input price variations can mask any productivity changes that may have occurred in the firm's operations. Firms must distinguish between quantity variances in dollars and in units. By measuring units of input instead of (or along with) dollar inputs, firms will be better able to identify an operation's problems and manage productivity more effectively.

Broadening the Cost Accounting Function. The cost accounting function should be expanded to incorporate more responsibility than it currently has. That is, "...the cost accounting function...[should] be broader in scope, providing both statistical and cost performance data."[11]

For a variety of apparently logical reasons, many internal decision-makers (both line managers and staff accountants) still insist on utilizing one multipurpose costing system. These logical reasons include minimizing duplication of effort, cost-benefit analysis, integration with the internal chart of accounts, simplicity, and rationalizing information systems. As Kaplan [1988] has noted, cost systems need to address three different functions:

- Inventory valuation for financial and tax statements (which requires allocating periodic production costs between cost of sales and ending inventories)
- Operational control, providing feedback to production and department managers on the resources consumed (labor, materials, energy, and overhead) during an operating period
- Individual product cost management

[10]Lammert and Ehrsam [1987], p. 36.
[11]Bonsack [1987], p. 32.

Exhibit 7.3   The Usefulness of Applying the Concept of Non-Value-Added Costs

Consider ABC Co. which has the following cost data on its Series 87 widgets, both pre- and post-technology adoption. In this case a flexible CNC machining center to repalce the conventional machinery.

	Pre-Adoption	Post-Adoption
Labor	$ 35.00	$ 26.00
Materials	87.50	68.50
Overhead	52.50	55.50
Total	$175.00	$150.00

ABC Co's current cost data reveals only the magnitude of the total, and the individual component unit cost reduction. There is little basis for further insight.

Now, consider a more enlightened ABC Co. which pursues a more progressive approach.

	Pre-Adoption			Post-Adoption		
	Value-Added	Non-Value-Added	Total	Value-Added	Non-Value-Added	Total
Labor	$ 30.00	$ 5.00	$ 35.00	$ 24.00	$ 2.00	$ 26.00
Materials	77.50	10.00	87.50	66.00	2.50	68.50
Overhead	40.00	12.50	52.50	38.00	5.00	43.00
Technology	–	–	–	11.50	1.00	12.50
Total	$147.50	$27.50	$175.00	$139.50	$10.50	$150.00

Let us examine the insights suggested by ABC's new data:

(a) Actual labor savings in the process are $6.00/per unit (not $9.00) perhaps due to the introduction of CNC machining centers. The other $3.00 probably came from reduced lateness, injury and absenteeism.

(b) Direct materials savings from the new technology, perhaps due to design improvements via CAD and CAE, have saved $11.50 per unit. The other $7.50 of savings perhaps came from reduced scrap, waste and rework.

(c) The overhead is split to account directly for technology contribution. For the nontechnology part of the overhead, the non-value-added is attributable to reduce expediting and supervision.

(d) The technology component in the post-adoption case is almost entirely value-added. Since the machine is efficient and can be used in the production of several different parts, there is little downtime or idle time. The $1.00 of non-value-added cost may come from occasional shutdowns for maintenance.

(e) Unit cost reductions are better understood, and so is the technology cost per unit required to achieve these reductions.

These different functions, which are predicated on different demands, give the accounting system a broad perspective. This will result in cost accounting becoming more integrated with the other functional areas such as production and quality control, purchasing, manufacturing, design, and marketing.

Two new approaches called *forward accounting* and *activity-based accounting* are gaining a lot of attention in practice. Under forward accounting, profit is considered as a function of value to a customer, not of financial accounting costs. In this case, the firm's accountants become actively involved early in the preproduction planning. Given that about 85 to 95 percent of a product's costs are determined prior to production, such an approach clearly has advantages. While admittedly less precise than traditional backward accounting, forward accounting creates a more proactive approach by asking the right questions about the product and evaluating its profit potential carefully before an expensive, time-consuming product introduction. Activity-based accounting also takes a cross-functional approach by tracing product costs through all resource-consuming activities (design, engineering, manufacture, sale, delivery, and service). By not considering manufacturing costs only, activity-based accounting focuses managers' attention on all underlying drivers of cost and profit across the entire value chain.

Achieving profitability and properly assigning cost requires two types of activity-based information. One type is nonfinancial information about sources of competitive value (quality, flexibility, and cost) in a company's operating activities. This provides information on how effectively operating activities deliver value to the customer. The second type of activity-based information, strategic cost information, enables managers to assess the long-term profitability of a company's current mix of products and activities. Strategic cost information can be helpful to assess if a company's activities are cost-effective in comparison to alternatives outside the company, and if the mix of products management has chosen to sell uses activities in the most profitable mode.

BARRIERS TO THE EVALUATION OF NEW TECHNOLOGY

Traditional capital justification techniques are viewed as a major reason for the relatively slow adoption rate of new technology by North American firms. In fact, one survey found that "...financial payback was classified as *very important* by 91 percent of the respondents," and 78 percent of another survey felt that "...most businesses in the United States will remain so tied to traditional investment criteria that they will be unable to realistically evaluate the potential of computer-aided manufacturing options."[12] Although a number of techniques are currently being utilized (for example, payback, net present value [NPV], internal rate of return [IRR], and return on investment [ROI]), they are all similar in that they tend to work best for projects showing easily quantifiable, short-term benefits.[13] In other words, typical investment methodologies ignore capital decay, and calculations tend to justify rather than to evaluate automation. This

---

[12]Utecht [1986], p. 87.

[13]For more informaiton, see Canada [1986] and Miltenburg [1986] for a critical review of the traditional methods.

results in erroneous attempts to weigh the benefits of the new technologies, which are usually characterized as being long-term, intangible, and often unknown or uncertain.

In short, traditional justification methods are better suited to meeting profitability criteria than to evaluating ways of reaching long-term strategic goals. Therefore, there is a need to establish priorities between the two. Consider the following comments:

> People say that American industry suffers because its managers pay too much attention to the short-term return on investment. Well, if you go at computer integrated manufacturing incrementally looking to get every penny back within a short and definite time scale, this competitive advantage will be lost to you.
>
> When we look back at the good things we've achieved along the way, it's no exaggeration to say that the most important improvements were totally unpredicted. We simply didn't know enough to see what could be achieved. How is it possible to predict what profit gains will result from improvements to come?[14]

While traditional justification methods can greatly underestimate the potential benefits of new technology, it is not our intention to deny their usefulness. In fact, some of these techniques can still be useful in evaluating component technologies such as NC machines or robotics. Nevertheless, it is essential to provide insight into the specific problems associated with using traditional methods to justify new technology, especially with regard to integrated technologies such as CAD/CAM, FMS, and CIM. The aim is to build a framework that will enable managers to make more informed and accurate decisions regarding the potential acquisition of new technology.

We start by explaining some of the specific problems associated with using traditional capital justification methods to evaluate potential new technology acquisitions. For discussion purposes, these problems will be grouped into two categories: (1) underestimating the costs, and (2) underestimating the benefits.

Underestimating the Costs

The first group of costs associated with new technology acquisition are those that are tangible and easily quantifiable. These include the purchase price of the equipment, associated software costs, site preparation and installation costs, maintenance costs, operating costs (energy), tooling costs, and training/ retraining or personnel costs. Although these costs are relatively easy to quantify, many firms either fail to consider or else underestimate some of them.

At the same time, other costs are much more difficult to foresee and/or quantify. These include benefits of the new technology that are overstated for various reasons. Based primarily on the work done by Gold [1983], the following issues must also be considered when evaluating new technology:

[14]Huber [1985], p. 51.

- As noted in Chapter 6, when a new technology is introduced, productivity often declines, at least until the technology becomes fully operational. There is a tendency to underestimate the time needed to achieve operational efficiency with the technology due to lack of consideration for such factors as debugging hardware and software, training operators, developing appropriate maintenance procedures, and ironing out scheduling and coordination difficulties.
- Related to the above point is the common assumption that the new technology will completely replace the old process upon installation. However, in many instances, both the old machinery and the new technology are used together until the new technology becomes fully operational. This makes it difficult to account accurately for all relevant cash flows.[15]
- There is a tendency to overestimate the average rate of use when calculating the benefits of the new technology, failing to incorporate the realities of fluctuating demand.
- The costs involved in adjusting support functions such as quality control, materials handling, production and maintenance scheduling, and product costing to match the needs and requirements of the new technology are often ignored or underestimated.
- It is difficult to estimate the costs involved (if any) of gaining labor acceptance of new technology. Firms must also realize that any significant savings generated by the technology will likely result in labor pressures to increase wage rates.
- It is often assumed (incorrectly) that cost reductions generated by the new technology will automatically be converted into profits. However, efforts to reduce the price of the product in order to capture a greater market share will most likely result in competitor price cuts, even if the competitors have not realized similar cost savings. Firms trying to keep their prices the same in order to generate larger margins will most likely be thwarted by competitor firms that have adopted similar technologies and subsequently reduce prices in order to increase their market shares.

Underestimating the Benefits

As has already been stressed, the underestimation of and/or failure to consider the full benefits of the new technology have resulted in the relatively slow adoption of the technology. Consider the following example:

> When the Yamazaki Machinery Company in Japan installed an $18 million flexible manufacturing system, the results were truly startling: a reduction in machines from 68 to 18, in employees from 215 to 12, in the floor space needed

---

[15]The *zero machine* concept can be used to alleviate this problem. Zero machine (ZM) is capable of producing all the required parts at no cost to the company. Both the current process and the proposed new technology are then compared to ZM. The main benefit of this approach is that all cash flows can be clearly identified during the transition from the old process to the new technology. See Primrose and Leonard [1985] for further discussion on this technique.

for production from 103,000 square feet to 30,000, and in average processing time from 35 days to 1.5. After two years, however, total savings came to only $6.9 million, $3.9 million of which had flowed from a one-time cut in inventory. Even if the system continued to produce labor savings of $1.5 million for 20 years the project's return would be less that 10 percent per year. Since many U.S. companies use hurdle rates of 15 percent or higher and payback periods of five years or less, they would find it hard to justify this investment in new technology—despite its enormous savings in number of employees, floor space, inventory, and throughput times.[16]

This example highlights the major reasons why traditional justification methods undervalue the potential benefits of the new technology: (1) They consider only benefits such as labor and inventory savings which can be easily quantified; and (2) they emphasize the need for short-term returns. Given these two points, we will focus our attention on the intangible benefits of new technology adoption and explain how some assumptions and procedures inherent in traditional justification techniques can undervalue the benefits. Before we do this, we need to discuss the tangible benefits available through the new technology.

Tangible (Monetary) Benefits.   Exhibit 7.4 summarizes the tangible (quantifiable) benefits of the new technology. Some of these benefits are already accounted for by firms using traditional justification techniques, and others could be included relatively easily.

One of the most common factors considered in the justification process is the potential savings in direct labor costs. It is a mistake for firms to focus their energy on or limit their analysis to direct labor alone, for several reasons. First, today only about one out of eight people in the factory is directly involved with manufacturing; the other seven are handling and processing information. Second, firms should not include labor savings without considering the potential labor problems that could be associated with layoffs. Last, it is very difficult to justify investments in the new technology on the basis of direct labor savings alone. This is primarily because: "...the monumental effort required to reduce this component by 20 percent will only yield [about] a 2 percent improvement in the cost of the product."[17]

In addition to potential labor savings, the increased flexibility, improved product quality, and reduced throughput times offered by the new technology can very often lead to significant reductions in work-in-process and finished goods inventory. When one considers that in an average North American manufacturing plant, for example, 80 percent of work-in-process inventory is not in process at all, but is in a queue waiting to move, it is clear that here is the true contribution of the new technology in reducing aggregate production costs. Consider the following example as an illustration:

[16]Kaplan [1986], p. 87.
[17]Hall [1987], p. 18.

Exhibit 7.4   A List of Tangible and Intangible Benefits of New Technology

Tangible/Operational (Easy to Quantify)	Intangible/Nonoperational (Difficult to Quantify)
Increased market share	Increased product uniformity
Increased sales volume	Increased ability to quickly enter new markets
Increased production volume	Increased goodwill generated through the new reputation the firm acquired
Successful development of new products	Synergy with other equipment
Reduced product development time	Better scheduling/workflow
Development of new markets	Increased flexibility leading to:
Fewer customer complaints	Increased strategic options
Reduced defect costs	Reduced risk of obsolescence
Reduced scrap costs	Improved product quality leading to improved market image
Shortening of delivery time	Ability to respond quickly to future technology advances
Direct labor savings	Offset technology adoption by competitors
Reduced work-in-process and finished-goods inventory levels	Increased employee morale
Reduced floor space requirements	Better customer service
Improved product quality leading to reduced inspection, rework, scrap, warranty, and service costs	Reduced training and supervision
Reduced tooling, utilities, maintenance, production control, fixturing, and materials costs	Increased utilization of manpower and equipment
	Reduced expediting
	Reduced materials handling
	More disciplined manufacturing process
	Increased safety

Another company reduced its inventories by more than 50 percent in five months, saving the company more than $12 million. These reductions freed up 30 percent more floorspace within the principal manufacturing plant, enabling the company to launch a new product line without buying additional production facilities.[18]

Cash inflows generated through reduced inventory levels can easily be factored into traditional justification methods. For example, a company with an annual cost of sales of $5 million and inventory turnover ratio of 5:1 would generate a one-time cash inflow of $500,000 with a 50 percent reduction in average inventory levels.[19] This savings would be even higher if reductions in floor space requirements, damaged inventory costs, and obsolescence, as well as the benefits of easier production scheduling and tracking, are considered.

Significant benefits also accrue through faster throughput. Consider the following example:

[18]Maskell [1987], p. 14.

[19]As a corollary, any annual sales growth also means additional savings (Kaplan [1986]). For instance, using the above example, if cost of sales increased annually by 10 percent (for example, to $5.5 million in year one and $6.05 million in year two), the cutback in average inventory would result in additional inventory savings of $50,000 in year one (($5.5M − $5M) * 1/5 * 50 percent) and $55,000 in year two (($6.05M − $5.5M) * 1/5 * 50 percent).

If the standard cycling time for a machine tool is 20 seconds, but its actual average cycle time is 21.6 seconds, then 8 percent more time is required for producing the same number of parts—cycle times of 8 to 15 percent below the average are fairly common. In general, each percent change in the production rate equals a 5 percent change in profits.

Let's assume an average small plant with 20 of the above machine tools is producing parts valued at $25 per hour. If the plant improves cycle time by 8 percent—not an unheard of goal—it can expect annual savings of almost $233,000 if it operates two eight-hour shifts per day, seven days a week.[20]

Using the new technology can also result in significant reductions in floor space requirements because of both fewer machines needed and less inventory space required. For example, in the Yamazaki Machinery Company example cited earlier, the floor space needed for production was reduced from 103,000 to 30,000 square feet. Current financial accounting systems may undervalue this space, especially if the building is greatly depreciated or was purchased at a much lower cost than it is currently worth. Firms should value savings in floor space at something close to the market value of the space, especially if the firm is able to make use of the space to facilitate a capacity expansion, or consolidate two or more separate operations under one roof and sell off the plant which is no longer needed at current market prices (Kaplan [1986]).

Improved product quality is another important benefit that the new technology can provide, and some of the savings generated by this can be measured. For example, reductions in inspection costs, reworked products, scrap, warranty, and service costs should all be quantified, since they can comprise up to 25 percent of the cost of a product. It was mentioned in Chapter 6 that automated quality inspection is 97 percent accurate, versus only 78 percent under optimal conditions for human inspection. In a $100 million per year manufacturing operation, this saves about $800,000 in direct costs alone, without even considering the costs of warranty repair and service, or customer dissatisfaction that can be linked to in-field failures due to faulty production and inspection (see Bader [1987]). Therefore, including cost savings generated by improved product quality can greatly increase the probability of a new technology being justified. Furthermore, enhancing product quality can also result in other intangible benefits, such as improved market image.

A number of other cost savings can also be quantified. They include reductions in tooling costs, utilities costs, maintenance costs, production control costs, fixture costs, and materials costs.[21] While some firms may find it difficult accurately to quantify some of these savings methods, a guesstimate of costs is certainly better than ignoring them.

[20]Adapted from Gould [1985], pp. 1–12.
[21]See Meyer [1982] and Klahorst [1983] for specific examples of how to quantify these and other benefits of the new technology.

Intangible (Nonmonetary) Benefits. With the increasing complexity of integrated technology such as FMS, CAD/CAM, and CIM, measuring the benefits of the new technology become more difficult and intangible. In fact, as we mentioned in Chapter 2, it is difficult to quantify many of the benefits achieved through CIM, since synergy is the major advantage. Exhibit 7.4 also shows some of the intangible benefits of new technology.

From a practical point of view, the shift from tangible to intangible benefits signifies a change in the basis for decision-making from numerical formulas to intuitive judgments. Furthermore, as was pointed out in Chapter 5, higher levels of automation have a greater (strategic) effect on the company, thereby implying that decision support should come from a broad rather than a narrow range of company personnel. This broad range of personnel should be drawn both horizontally (across different functions) and vertically (among different hierarchical levels). Exhibit 7.5 illustrates the implications that level of technological complexity has on the justification process.

Perhaps the most important intangible benefit of the new technology

Exhibit 7.5 The Justification Curve

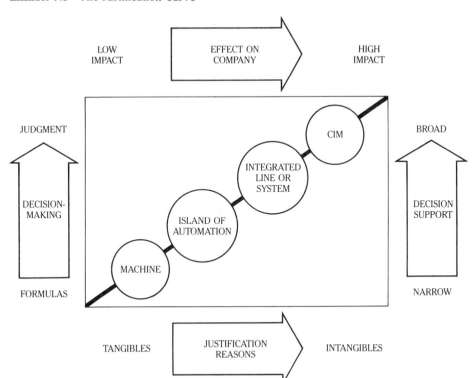

Source: Bernard [1986], Found in Meredith [1986a], p. 81.

is its inherrent flexibility. Briefly, the potential flexibility offered by new technology can enable firms to:

1. Produce a mix of parts economically in small batches and in random order.
2. Introduce new products quickly and easily into the production process.
3. Reroute production in the event of machine breakdowns.
4. Modify and produce customized products.
5. Service after-market sales for discontinued product models by producing replacement parts on the same equipment used to produce current models.

Naturally, the implication of incorporating and operationalizing the benefits of flexibility into the justification process is profound. That is, ". . .if flexibility is built in [to justification models], then it will be used. [For example] GE's flexible manufacturing center in Erie, PA was originally designed to make six different motor frames. Today, less than two years later, it has been expanded to handle 10 different motor frames.[22]

The new technology provides an environment conducive to quicker manufacturing designs, shorter throughput times, shorter lead times, and the ability to respond to customer orders quickly. Consider the following example:

> Boston Metal Products, a small Massachusetts manufacturer, was attempting to evaluate the benefits of a proposed $200,000 investment in robotics. "It was hard to scrape up enough evidence to convince us it was a reasonable risk, let alone a positive investment," says controller Greenberg. "It didn't even come close."
>
> The company's president decided to gamble on the purchase anyway. He hoped that the robotic equipment would inject new vigor into the company's manufacturing operations. In the three years that have followed his decision, the robotic equipment's prowess in welding has so speeded deliveries that the company's sales of steel shelving for supermarket refrigerators has increased four-fold and more than covered the costs of the investment.[23]

Subsequent benefits of new technology adoption come through improved production control and better scheduling. Integration of a plant's automated systems (through the advanced information technologies described in Chapter 2) allows accurate and current production data to be instantaneously and simultaneously available to multiple users. This results in a better understanding of the production process and an enhanced ability to meet production and delivery schedules.

Investing in newer technology can open up a number of options not previously considered. It can also provide companies with experience that will

---

[22]Baker [1984], p. 283.
[23]Unger [1987], p. 15.

enable them to respond more quickly to future advances in technology. Consider the following example:

> The companies that in the mid-1970s invested in automatic and electronically controlled machine tools were well positioned to exploit the microprocessor-based revolution in capabilities—much higher performance at much lower cost—than hit during the early 1980s. Because operators, maintenance personnel, and process engineers were already comfortable with electronic technology, it was relatively simple to retrofit existing machines with powerful microelectronics. Companies that had earlier deferred investment in electronically controlled machine tools fell behind.[24]

Closely related to this example is the point that firms failing to invest in new technology today, because of an inability to justify the investment, may find themselves hopelessly behind competitors that proactively sought new technology. Firms must always consider the scenario in which they do not automate but their competitors do. Furthermore, implemented correctly, the new technology can lead to increases in employee morale through both increased job responsibility and the elimination of unpleasant work. The earlier introduction of new technology may also lead to less resistance on future projects (and thus fewer implementation barriers).

Finally, we must stress the tremendous importance of attempting to quantify these intangibles and include them in the justification process. There are basically three reasons for this:

1. Leaving intangibles out is equivalent to assigning them an economic value of zero, and a value of zero is surely less accurate than an informed estimation by a qualified individual.
2. Since the actual size and value of the intangible benefits often exceed the tangible elements, ignoring intangibles is likely to result in an inability to justify many new technology investments, and thus slower adoption of the technologies needed to remain competitive.
3. If intangible benefits are not explicitly considered in the evaluation of the proposed investment, top management is less likely to insist that such goals be achieved, and so actual performance may be compromised.

Given these considerations, we will now describe how some of the assumptions and procedures inherent in the more traditional justification procedures reduce the chance of a new technology being economically justified, and then provide a model by which some of these problems may be overcome.

Assumptions and Procedures. Perhaps the most important technical assumption when using the traditional net present value (or discounted cash flow)

---

[24]Kaplan [1986], p. 92.

analysis is selection of the discount rate. An arbitrarily high discount rate (or short payback requirement) can considerably reduce the importance of many of the benefits that occur over a long time horizon. Kaplan [1986] explains that a number of firms use a discount rate which is much too high because they tend to use a nominal discount rate (which includes inflation) but project level cash flows (which fail to include inflation). The result is that future benefits are undervalued! Another study by the Ontario Task Force [1985] showed that in selected manufaturing industries, 78 percent of firms used the payback method in investment analysis, and that the average payback criterion used was 3.5 years. Certainly this is too short a period to account for all the benefits of most new technology investments.

Hill and Dimnik [1985] content that managers tend to increase the discount rate when evaluating new technology proposals. In a practical sense, however, it can be argued that the risks associated with the new technology do not warrant an increase but rather a decrease in the discount rate. This is so because the flexibility of the new technology actually makes it less likely to become obsolete in a comparable time horizon and thus increases its residual value. This point also applies to firms using a short payback requirement. Of course, this analogy is based on the assumption that the perils involved in the implementation of the new technology are no greater than the risks of other projects. As the technical bugs associated with the new technology are ironed out over time, this argument will carry even more weight.

In many instances, it is common to assume that market share will remain constant (that the status quo will be maintained) with no investment in the new technology (see Exhibit 7.6). This could very well be an unrealistic assumption, especially if competitors adopt technology which potentially will enable them to compete more effectively. Alternatively, a company that does not invest in the new technology may be able to maintain its market share by slashing prices, but this will also mean that status quo projections are wrong, since sales dollars and margins will be lower than estimated. In fact, a declining (as opposed to a stable) competitive position would probably be a more appropriate comparison basis.

Traditional justification procedures such as NPV or DCF also ignore the option that new technology can provide for investing in future profitable projects. "The higher the level of automation, the greater the potential for further automation."[25] Hill and Dimnik [1985] explain that the potential for future investment generated by a new technology acquisition should be included in the justification process (see Exhibit 7.7).

Furthermore, firms must be sure not to fall into the trap of investing only in small, incremental process improvements which have easily quantifiable benefits and positive NPVs. Although these smaller investments do show positive NPVs, they may prevent a firm from investing in a larger project which would generate a larger NPV than the sum of the smaller investments combined (Kaplan [1986]). Firms may find themselves caught in this trap because:

[25] Adler [1985], p. 8.

Exhibit 7.6   Comparing a New Technology Investment with the Status Quo

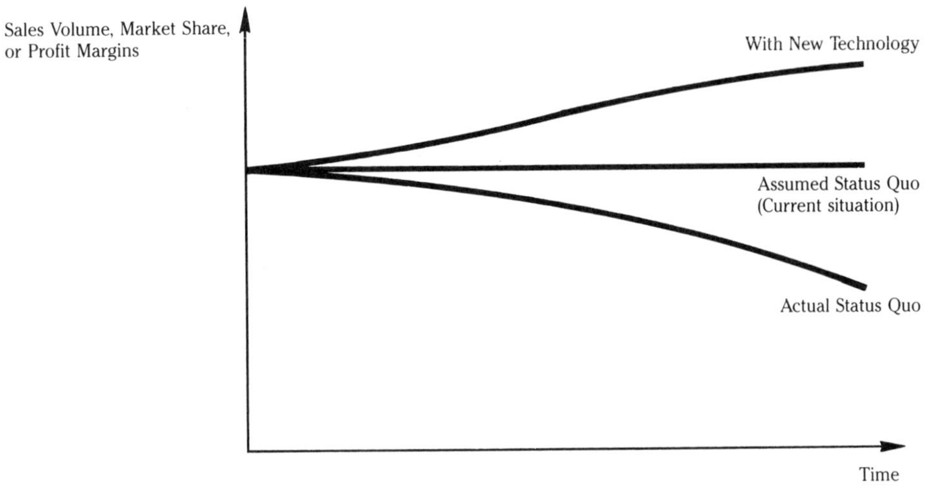

Sales Volume, Market Share,
or Profit Margins

With New Technology

Assumed Status Quo
(Current situation)

Actual Status Quo

Time

Message: Do not automatically assume that the status quo will remain constant if no investment in new technology is made. Chances are that it probably will not!

Also, do not assume that if the investment in new technology is made, the line will slope upwards, as these investments may be necessary just to maintain status-quo; therefore, this graph would give a "best-case" scenario.

The slope of the lin e s up (or down) from the current status-quo will depend on the success (or failure) with new technology implementation vis-a-vis the competitors.

1. Conventional theory says that any investment with a positive NPV should be pursued.
2. Many firms pass small investment proposals fairly easily but make it much more difficult to obtain the funds for large proposals. It is easy to quantify and justify small investments.
3. Large investments usually require a synthesis of information from across the company, making them easier to omit as potential alternatives.
4. Large investments such as the new technology may render useless incremental investments which have not yet been recovered.

As Kaplan [1986] argues, the emphasis should be on being vaguely right rather than precisely wrong. That is, rather than attempting to put a dollar tag on benefits that are difficult to quantify, management should reverse the process and estimate how large these benefits must be in order to justify the proposed investment, and then consider whether this criterion is met.

The Use of a Guideline for Justification Purposes

We have discussed many of the difficulties associated with justification of the new technology. Given all these caveats, we present a list of steps that firms should follow when attempting to justify investment in the new technology:

Exhibit 7.7   Evaluating Alternatives to Justifying New Technology

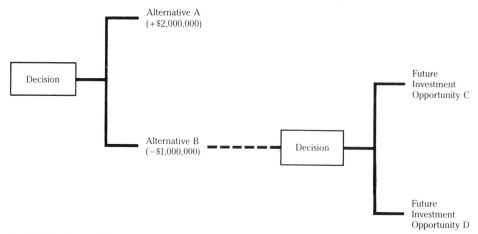

Consider the situation of the company evaluating the two investments diagrammed in the above figure. The Net Present Value (NPV) of alternative A is +$2 million, and the NPV of alternative B is −$1 million. Alternative A is an improvement at the current manual moulding operation. Alternative B is an investment in a robot and an automated plastic moulding operation. On the basis of NPV, alternative A would be selected, yet the basic alternatives do not tell the whole story. The company is a supplier to the automotive industry, and its major customer is General Motors (GM). GM and the rest of the auto industry are avoiding suppliers who do not meet their quality standards. Furthermore, GM has made it clear that there will be even more business for companies that use both GM-compatible computerized design systems, and robotics or other advanced process technologies. The company in our example has limited experience with new technology but recognizes that an investment in alternative B might lead to opportunities to invest in profitable projects in the future.

Precisely how and when such future options will be exercised depends entirely on future events. However, the array and attractiveness of future investment opportunities is critically dependent on today's investment in the new manufacturing technology. Since at this time C and D are only investment options, the discounted cash flow method cannot properly value them.

The real value of many strategic investments is their potential to exercise options on future investment opportunities. The accountant's traditional justification has focused on the NPV's of investments, while the engineer's "gut feelings" reflected the implicit options value associated with today's investments. Once the option value of an investment is recognized in the analysis, many high tech investment proposals that had previously been rejected could now be more readily justified.

Source: Adapted with changes from Hill and Dimnik [1985], pp. 93–94.

Step 1.   Determine how the new technology relates to the firm's long-term strategic goals and objectives, and ensure that the technology and the firm's strategy are aligned.

Step 2.   List all the costs and benefits (both tangible and intangible) associated with the new technology.

Step 3.   Quantify as many of the costs and benefits as possible.

Step 4.   Perform an NPV analysis of the project, using the costs and benefits quantified in Step 3. Carefully consider what discount rates and status quo assumptions should be used. Estimate the value of both incremental projects and the whole project.

Step 5.   If the NPV analysis is positive, accept the project. If the NPV analysis is negative, do not scrap the project. Top management must now decide whether the intangible benefits associated with the new technology warrant the acquisition. Move to Step 6.

Step 6.   Estimate the value of all the intangible (remaining) costs and benefits. Consider constructing a diagram such as the one in Exhibit 7.8 to demonstrate

Exhibit 7.8 The Cascading Effects of New Technology

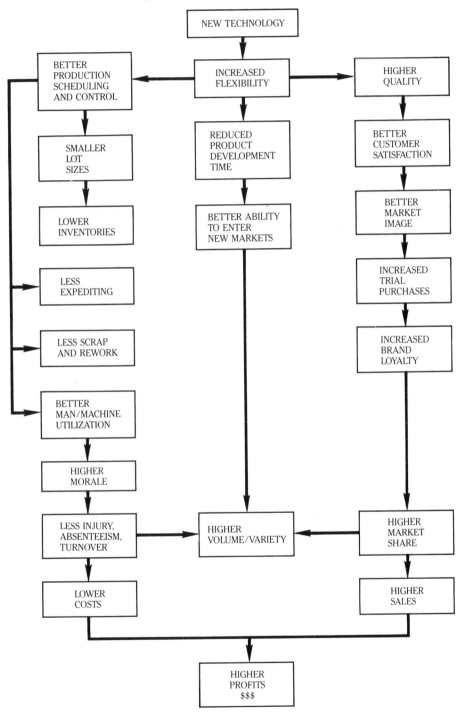

the flow-through effects of some of the intangible benefits. Do not ignore them! If hard numbers cannot be assigned to them, rank them in order of importance or estimate their values using probabilities or ranges.[26] Determine whether the intangible benefits outweigh the intangible costs, and by how much (chances are that the intangible benefits will be significantly more important). Questions such as "Can we afford not to adopt the technology?" and "Suppose we don't adopt the new technology?" and "Suppose we don't adopt this new technology but our competitor does?" must be addressed.

FINANCING THE NEW TECHNOLOGY

Once the justification hurdle has been overcome, the firm faces the task of appropriating sufficient funds to begin the project. The matter of financing a technology strategy and the issue of raising funds for technology development and/or acquisition are important managerial considerations. The Ontario Task Force [1985] noted that financing was, on average, the number two factor slowing the rate of new technology adoption.[27]

As we mentioned in Chapter 3, financing alternatives are fundamentally different for large versus small firms. However, in both cases the merits of the new technology must be sold to the lender. In the case of large companies, the lender is usually senior management or the board of directors; in the case of small firms, the lender is a source outside the firm—most likely a bank, a venture capitalist, or a government agency.

In general, small firms lack the ability to raise the funds required for a major new technology acquisition internally. Even when they do, small firms may find that it has a dramatic effect on their balance sheet. For example, when Zepf Technology, a small manufacturer in southwestern Ontario, purchased its first CNC machine, its debt:equity ratio jumped to 22:1. The usual consequence of this would be further difficulty in attracting outside financing, thus making the automation investment a "bet your company" scenario for many small firms.

Included in the category of small companies requiring outside financial funding are megagrowth technology companies (Collins [1985]). These firms typically have current (and projected) sales growth of 40 to 50 percent per year, and compete in a relatively new industry, market, and/or product. Financing is difficult due to the low capital and retained earnings levels in the company relative to sales. These firms never generate all the cash that they require internally, working capital is often a problem, and their growth can be stymied by a lack of financing.

[26]Note that while some of the intangible benefits of new technology may not be directly quantifiable, some of the benefits resulting from these intangibles may be easier to quantify. For example, it is practically impossible to quantify what higher morale will be worth. However, higher morale will usually translate into lower turnover and reduced absenteeism, thus reducing recruiting, training, and overtime costs, which can all be quantified.

[27]The number one reason given was poor economic conditions, which probably just exaggerate the inability to finance.

Sources of New Technology Financing

In general, new technology financing can be divided into three broad categories. First is what may be referred to as tax-motivating financing. One example of this is known as Scientific Research Tax Credit (SRTC). In this case, investors receive an immediate risk-free return on their investment and the company receives no-strings attached financing, provided it can come up with sufficient additional financing to carry out the project.

The second classification is based on limited partnerships with guaranteed features to achieve the same effect as the SRTC. The third broad category includes the traditional sources of financing, encompassing everything from bank debts to public share issues to venture capital. What all these instruments have in common is that the investors are interested in achieving a specific rate of return relative to levels of risk, and the investee is interested in obtaining the financing at the lowewt possible cost.

Banks and Term Lenders.   The bank is one potential financier of a new technology acquisition, although banks tend to be conservative lenders specializing in operating (rather than long-term capital) loans. They "...seldom [are] willing to allow loans to megagrowths to escalate at the same rate as current assets. Megagrowths must be ready to continually bring in outside equity to help support higher bank loans."[28] When banks do fund fixed assets, they want the assets to have a good resale value in case the company defaults. Firms attempting to secure bank financing stand a much better chance if the technology is general purpose enough to be used by other firms. In this respect, it is important that firms elaborate on the resale potential of the new technology, because many bank managers view the new technology as specialized equipment having minimal resale value. For example, one study noted that "...banks are quite weak at assessing the capabilities of new technologies, which could mean that many firms will be denied loans to modernize their facilities."[29]

Another potential source of new technology financing is term lenders that specialize in long-term financing. Included in this category are insurance companies, credit associations, trust companies, and venture and leasing companies. However, as with the bank, this financing source must be convinced of both the potential benefits of the technology and its resale value. For example:

> The Loans Account Officer of a term lender explained that his company has no problem in giving term loans secured by new technology. However, he said it is important to distinguish between multipurpose and specialized new technology because of the importance of the aftermarket for the equipment if the company defaulted on its loan. He further explained that companies had to sell themselves in order to be successful in obtaining financing. Any proposal

[28]Collins [1985], p. 44.
[29]Borins [1985], pp. 10–11.

submitted to his company had to be fully rationalized by the firm, and any benefits the new technology would bring should be specifically detailed.

Venture Capitalists.   Venture capitalists are dedicated professional firms that invest in companies by taking a strong equity position. These firms recognize the long-term nature of the potential payback from their investments, and they usually remain involved with the firms they invest in for relatively long periods of time. In practice, many firms wishing to adopt the new technology have been able to obtain financing through this means. For example, over 40 percent of 1984 venture capital dollars went into either computer hardware systems (CAD/CAM, CAE) or software services (AI) (Needham [1984]). To be successful in procuring funds, the firm must be able to demonstrate both the plausible benefits of the new technology and the strong potential for profit in its business.

Turf Financing.   Turf financing is described by Farwell [1985] as a new but a fairly well developed technique of creative financing, suitable mainly for companies developing their own technologies. It generally involves the sale of a bundle of rights to the technology being developed in lieu of equity or joint venture participation. The following exemplifies the benefits of pursuing this method of financing:

> Alza Corporation is a U.S. company involved in developing new methods of administering drugs, including transdermal (through the skin) technology. Alza recently combined turf financing with a limited partnership arrangement to own and finance development of new transdermal delivery techniques. A variety of U.S. investors purchased partnership interests for a total of $29.7 million. In addition, a European pharmaceutical company purchased an interest in the partnership to carry out the R&D project for a fee and holds an option to receive world-wide licenses to manufacture and market all products developed by the partnership. Alza also has a backup option to acquire all the partnership interests at various times and prices. Through this arrangement Alza has not only financed its next round of R&D projects off balance sheet but can also report a substantial revenue flow under the contract to carry out the R&D for the partnership.[30]

Some advantages of turf financing are:

- The investors are in for the long term because they hold an "entry philosophy" as opposed to an ownership one, and therefore may be a bit more patient for a return on investment.
- The young company has its hands full developing its own local market segment, and it will be a long time before its resources and knowhow are built up enough to go into other areas .

---

[30]Farwell [1985], p. 62.

- Endorsement of the technology by a large investor could be critical to rapid development of the new technology. If the new technology is strategically validated, local marketing efforts will be facilitated and there may be attraction of additional funds. The larger company may also turn out to be a valuable source of advice.

Government.   One final source of financing is the government. Although there are usually a variety of government programs available that can provide funds for a new technology acquisition, financing through this mode may not be as simple as it may appear. As one businessman has put it: "Don't rely on government programs for funding of a new technology project...look to other sources first and consider any money you receive from the government as gravy!" Government's role in new technology financing will be discussed further in Chapter 11.

Legal Aspects

Given the time, effort, and corporate resources expended in evaluating, justifying, financing, and implementing the new technology, a look at some of the legal issues which arise is appropriate at this point . While our intent is not a comprehensive review of the legal issues involved, we feel it is imperative that the topic be given some consideration. When investing in the new technology, a full range of corporate and commercial legal concerns in relation to new venture formation, financing, product liability, and general contractual matters should be dealt with. The various elements of intellectual property such as patents, industrial designs, trademarks, and copyrights;[31] provide tools for building a wall of protection around the investment.

   Contracts involving the new technology tend to be highly specialized. In a licensing agreement, for example, special attention and expertise must be brought to bear on key issues such as technology definition, future improvements, infringement by third parties, contingencies in the ongoing payment of royalties or other payments, and a host of secondary issues. Creating and defining property rights in the new technology are especially critical to contracts involving the transfer of technology. The licensing agreement or other contract must clearly define just what it is that is being licensed or transferred, and on what terms.

   Ownership issues often create major problems in new technology situations if they are not dealt with correctly and in detail at the outset. When a number of individuals or companies become involved in the development process, sorting out ownership claims after the technology is developed can be a nightmare. All too often, the parties find that they have made incorrect assumptions about owner-

---

[31]*Patents* protect new products, processes, machines, chemical compounds, and so on. *Industrial design registration* or *design patents* protect esthetic features of articles such as shapes and decorative patterns. *Trademark* law protects words, names, phrases, logos, distinctive packaging shapes and the like used in association with the sale of a product or the provision of a service. *Copyright* protects artistic, musical, and literary work, including computer software and engineering drawings.

ship of the technology, and that they all have different perceptions of who owns the relevant property rights.

Related to the financing of the new technology are the legal aspects of acquiring funds through such vehicles as joint ventures, R&D partnerships, and other technology transfer mechanisms (the transfer of knowledge for the manufacture of a product, application of a process, or rendering of a service). There are generally three categories of technology transfer:

Assignment: Sale or purchase of technology where the seller confers a right or interest in the technology to the buyer.

License: A license grants the right to do something not otherwise permitted by law. Turf financing is one example in this category, since the buyer gains a right to use, manufacture, or sell, whichever the case may be, the technology within geographic limits. It differs, however, in that the buyer attains some ownership in the company.

Joint venture: This has no precise definition except that it is an agreement between two or more parties to attain one or several objectives of mutual interest for mutual benefit.

Naturally, agreements can cover a wide variety of circumstances, but we will focus on the categories above in discussing the legal issues a company should consider when transferring its technology. The list below includes some of the legal questions to be answered:

1. Is the technology to be used exclusively by the buyer, or is some third party acquisition allowed?
2. What will be the form of payment—lump sum, royalty, currency or shares, options, etc.?
3. Who owns the right to any improvement to the technology if it is made by parties other than the seller?
4. How do we handle it if someone leaks trade secrets?
5. What are the mechanisms for resolving future disputes?
6. What is the process of terminating the association at the end of the contract?
7. What percentage of ownership, control, and day to day management control will be given up?
8. Is there a provision to include any other noncompetition clauses in the agreement?

CONCLUDING OBSERVATIONS

New technology is creating a need for restructuring the ways that companies assess, justify, and finance capital investments.

With regard to cost accounting systems, the new technology is accelerating the trend away from direct labor costs to overhead costs. This is the cause of some major misinterpretations, as traditional cost management systems allocate overhead to product costs on the basis of direct labor hours. This practice can lead to significant pricing, resource allocation, and capital justification problems. Solutions include focusing on the direct assignment of all relevant costs to particular products. In short, assessing the usefulness of the new technology can be a complex task. First, manufacturing must be an integral part of the strategic planning process. Second, traditional cost accounting systems have to be redefined to account for qualitative and intangible benefits of the new technology.

Additionally, conventional capital justification methods have the tendency significantly to undervalue the benefits of the new technology. Consequently, the technology is sometimes not adopted, when in fact it would be advantageous to do so. Specific problems with traditional justification methods include lack of consideration of the intangible (unquantifiable) benefits of the new technology, and procedures such as high discount rates and status quo assumptions that undermine its long-term potential. In reality, there are many benefits to the introduction of new technology; however, it is not feasible nor is it practical to try to accomplish to its business and consider the product life cycle stage of its products. Cost-benefit numbers may then be applied to the situation, based on internal and external environmental considerations.

Some unique financing and related legal issues face firms during the acquisition process. For large firms, top management must be convinced of the benefits of the new technology before internal financing can be secured. For small firms, traditional lenders may not be willing to finance a new technology acquisition, and so these firms may have to look to alternative sources of financing, such as venture capitalists and joint venture arrangements.

RECOMMENDED READINGS

KAPLAN, R. S. [1986]. "Must CIM be Justified by Faith Alone?" *Harvard Business Review*, March–April, pp. 87–95.
WORTHY, F. S. [1987]. "Accounting Bores You? Wake Up." *Fortune*, October 12, pp. 43–53.

DISCUSSION QUESTIONS

1. Develop a model which could assist managers in the new technology justification process.
2. It has been said time and time again that North American managers pay too much attention to short-term return on investment. This effectively becomes a barrier to the acquisition of the new technology. Why do North American managers have such a short-term focus when it comes to investment? Are there any ways that the problems with this short-term approach could be resolved? Could the factors pressuring managers to adopt this short-term approach ever likely to be changed? Explain.

3. In the context of financial justification, should the new technology be treated as a piece of machinery or as a part of strategy? Explain.
4. Recommend modifications that you feel are needed to conventional cost accounting systems. How would you go about operationalizing these recommendations? Are there any disadvantages to them?
5. What approach would you take if you were the president of a small company trying to get a loan from a bank for new technology?
6. How would you go about quantifying the intangible benefits of the new technology? Should you even try to quantify them?
7. What should be an acceptable non-value-added to value-added ratio?
8. You are making a presentation to the VP of finance for $1.5 million to purchase some new technology. What arguments will you include? What will the VP want to know?

REFERENCES AND BIBLIOGRAPHY

ADLER, P. S. [1985]. "Effective Implementation of Integrated CAD/CAM: A Model." Working Paper, Standford University, November.

BADER, M. [1987]. "The Machine Vision Maker—A Technology Impact Report Analyzing the Applications and Opportunities for Machine Vision in Electronics and Industry." Electronic Trends Publications.

BAKER, J. A. [1984]. "Winning Your Case for Automation." In Meredith [1986a], *Manufacturing Engineering.* July, pp. 282–283.

BEATTY, C. A. [1987]. "Organizational Barriers to the Implementation of CAD/CAM." National Center for Mangement Research and Development, Working Paper Series No. NC 87-17.

BEATTY, C. A. [1986]. "Productivity Issues in the Implementation of Computer Aided Design." Ph.D. Thesis, University of Western Ontario.

BENNET, R. E., and J. A. HENDRICKS [1987]. "Justifying the Acquisiton of Automated Equipment." *Management Accounting,* July, pp. 39–46.

BERNARD, P. [1986]. "Structured Project Methodology Provides Support for Informed Business Decisions." In Meredith [1986a]. *Industrial Engineering.* March, pp. 76–81.

BONSACK, R. A. [1986]. "Cost Accounting in the Factory of the Future." *CIM Review,* Spring, pp. 28–32.

BORINS, S. F. [1985]. "Interim Report on a Study of the Ontario Government's Technology Program." Faculty of Administrative Studies, York University.

BRIMSON, J. A., and C. BERLINER [1987]. "Cost Management System (CMS)." IIE Integrated Systems Conference Proceedings, November 5–7, pp. 43–49.

CANADA, J. R. [1986]. "Non-Traditional Methods for Evaluating CIM Opportunities Assigns Weights to Intangibles." *Industrial Engineering,* March, pp. 66–71.

COLLINS, J. I. [1985]. "Peculiarities of Financing Megagrowth Technology Companies." *The Dynamics of Technology: A Symposium,* November 27, pp. 39–44.

"Economic Justification—Strategy for Survival—Part III—Going Beyond the Basics" [1986]. *Modern Materials Handling,* October, pp. 68–71.

FARWELL, P. [1985]. "New Developments in Technology Financing." *The Dynamics of Technology: A Symposium,* November 28, pp. 57–72.

GOLD, B. [1983]. "Strengthening Managerial Approaches to Improving Technological Capabilities." *Strategic Management Journal,* Volume 4, pp. 209–220.

GOULD, L. [1985]. "Computers Run the Factory." *Electronics Week,* March, p. 57.

GOULD, L. [1985]. "Standalone Production Monitoring Offers Big Paybacks." *CIM Strategies,* Volume II, No. 8, August, pp. 1–12.

HALL, D. [1987]. "Managing Change." *Plant Management and Engineering,* August, pp. 18–19.

HILL, N., and T. DIMNIK [1985]. "Cost Justifying New Technologies." *Business Quarterly,* Winter, pp. 91–96.

HUBER, R. F. [1985]. "Justification: Barrier to Competitive Manufacturing." *Production,* September, pp. 46–51.

JOHNSON, T., and R. KAPLAN [1987]. "The Rise and Fall of Management Accounting." January, pp. 22–30.

KAPLAN, R. S. [1986]. "Must CIM Be Justified by Faith Alone?" *Harvard Business Review*, March–April. pp. 87–95.

KAPLAN, R. S. [1984]. "Yesterday's Accounting Undermines Production." *Harvard Business Review*, July–August, pp. 95–101.

KLAHORST, H. T. [1983]. "How to Justify Multimachine Systems." In Meredith [1986a]. *American Machinist*. September, pp. 149–152.

LAMMERT, T. B., and R. EHRSAM [1987]. "The Human Element: The Real Challenge in Modernizing Cost Systems." *Management Accounting*, July, pp. 32–37.

MEREDITH, J. R. [1986a]. *Justifying New Manufacturing Technology*. Industrial Engineering and Management Press, Atlanta, Georgia.

MEREDITH, J. R. [1986b]. "Strategic Planning for Factory Automation by the Championing Process." In Meredih [1986a], pp. 273–281.

MEREDITH, J. R., and N. C. SURESH [1986]. "Justification Techniques for Advanced Manufacturing Technologies." *International Journal of Production Research*, Volume 24, No. 5, pp. 1043–1057.

MEYER, R. J. [1982]. "A Cookbook Approach to Robotics and Automation Justification." In Meredith [1986a]. *Robots 6 Conference Proceedings*. pp. 119–148.

MILLER, J. G., and T. E. VOLLMANN [1985]. "The Hidden Factory." *Harvard Business Review*, September–October, pp. 142–150.

MASKELL, B. [1987]. "Just-In-Time—A Factory Evolution." *Manufacturing Systems*, October, pp. 14–20.

MILTENBURG, J. [1986]. "The Evaluation and Justification of Manufacturing Systems. In H. Noori (ed.), *Proceedings of Technology Canada Conference*, Wilfrid Laurier University Publication, pp. 201–230.

NEEDHAM, M. J. [1985]. "An Overview of the Venture Capital Market." *The Dynamics of Technology: A Symposium*, November 27, pp. 134–147.

O'GUIN, M. C. [1987]. "Information Age Calls for New Methods of Financial Analysis in Implementing Manufacturing Technologies." *Industrial Engineering*, Volume 19, No. 11, November, pp. 36–40.

PRIMROSE, P. L., and R. LEONARD [1985]. "The Use of a Conceptual Model to Evaluate Financially Flexible Manufacturing System Projects." *IMechE*, Volume 199, No. B1, pp. 15–21.

STAPLES, G. R. [1983]. "FMS—Convincing the Board." In Meredith [1986a], *Proceedings of the Second International Conference on FMS*. IFS (Publications) Ltd., pp. 287–293.

TATIKONDA, M. [1988]. "Just-In-Time and Modern Manufacturing Environments: Implications for Cost Accounting." *Production and Inventory Management Journal*, Volume 29, No. 1, pp. 1–5.

The Ontario Task Force on Employment and New Technology [1985]. "Employment and New Technology in Ontario's Manufacturing Sector: A Summary of Selected Industries."

THUROW, L. C. [1986]. "Books—A Positive Sum Strategy for Productivity." *Scientific American*, September, pp. 24–30.

UNGER, H. [1987]. "Revitalized Cost Accounting Could Boost Plant Automation." *Industrial Management*, February, pp. 14–16.

UTECHT, R. [1986]. "Need Help Justifying Automation? Here's a Plan That Makes Sense." *Production*, June, pp. 87–88.

WORTHY, F. S. [1987]. "Accounting Bores You? Wake Up." Fortune, October 12, pp. 43–53.

Chapter Eight

THE ORGANIZATIONAL IMPLICATIONS OF NEW TECHNOLOGY

222

The typical large business 20 years hence will have fewer than half the levels of management of its counterpart today, and no more than a third the managers.

Peter Drucker

INTRODUCTION

Changes in the internal and external business environment have, over the last 200 years, been the catalyst behind a dramatic organizational evolution. Organizations have, depending on the time period in which they operated, taken several forms. Exhibit 8.1 presents these trends. Clearly, change is imperative for survival.

Exhibit 8.1 Evolution of the Corporation

Date	Form	Description
1880	Owner-managed	Small companies, generally making one product for a regional market, are controlled by one person who performs many administrative tasks.
1850	Vertical	Companies grow larger and hire more managers, each to oversee a stage of the chain from raw material to finished product.
1900	Divisional	Large companies organize around a series of vertical chains of command to manage each product, or group of related products, that the company makes.
1950	Matrix	Large companies with vertical structures add a second, informal reporting chain that links managers with allied responsibilities or managers working together on temporary projects.
2000	Network	Small central organizations rely on other companies and suppliers to perform manufacturing, distribution, marketing, or other crucial business functions on a contract basis.

Source: Wilson and Dobrzynski [1986], pp. 64–71. Reprinted from March 3, 1988 issue of *Business Week* by special permission, copyright © 1988 by McGraw-Hill, Inc.

Exhibit 8.2 Towards The Organization of the Future

Drucker (1954)	Pascale & Athos (1981)	Peters & Waterman (1982)	NASA Symposium (1984)	Waterman (1987)
7 Key Result Areas	*7-S Model*	*8 Common Attributes*	*9 Themes*	*8 Renewal Factors*
Customer satisfaction	Structure	A Bias for action	Challenge for the competitive edge	Informed opportunism
Employee performance	Systems	Close to the customer	Make a management commitment to quality and productivity	Direction and empowerment
Innovation	Strategy	Autonomy and entrepreneurship	Mesh goals and responsibilities	Friendlldy facts, congenial controls
Management development	Style	Productivity through people	Make innovation rewarding	A different mirror
Internal productivity	Staff	Hands-on, value-driven	Build dedication, pride and team effort	Teamwork, trust, politics, and power
Social responsibility	Skills	Stick to the knitting	Unlock individual talent	Stability in motion
Operating budget	Shared values	Simple form, lean staff	Modernize for survival	Attitudes and attention
		Simultaneous loose-tight property	Maximize human capital	Causes and commitment
			Improve quality and productivity practices	

Source: This table is an extension of the original work by Sink and Koelling [1987], p. 282, IIE Integrated Systems Conference. Copyright Institute of Industrial Engineers.

Technological change alone creates the need for other types of metamorphosis, including the need to remodel organizational structures. Throughout the last 35 years, many attempts have been made to describe the thrusts and characteristics of the structures required by firms to prosper. Some of these are shown in Exhibit 8.2.

Drucker [1988] explains that we are entering an organizational era which is fundamentally different from the past, one which is characterized by "...the shift from the command-and-control organization...to the information based organization...."[1] These new forms of organizational structure involve fundamental reformations in managerial responsibilities and in communication and information flows, rather than simply minor adjustments to existing structural arrangements.

The new technology is one of the major forces underlying the organizational metamorphosis occurring today. In fact, we contend that changes in structure and organizational flows are both the inevitable consequences of and the prerequisites for the successful application of the new technology. Consider the following:

> Too much attention has been paid to technical development and not enough to the adjustments needed in organizations to accommodate the technology. This has produced a lack of fit between the demands made by the technology and the skills, attitudes, needs and values embodied in the social and technical structure of companies.[2]

DESCRIBING ORGANIZATIONAL STRUCTURES

A firm's organizational structure is part of its infrastructure. This is "...the network of nonphysical support systems that enable the technical structure to operate."[3] This is illustrated in Exhibit 8.3. Detailed organizational structure in companies varies, both in form and in substance. Even within companies in the same industry, it is common to find different structures. Therefore, in order to evaluate the effects of the new technology on organizational structure, it is necessary to choose an existing framework with which to compare. We will use the work done by Mintzberg [1979, 1981] as a basis for our discussion. The distinctive components of an organizational structure are illustrated in Exhibit 8.4. The basis for Mintzberg's thesis is that all organizations have most or all of these elements; however, the degree to which they are used or the extent to which they influence the actual operations of an organization dictates the form and shape of the organization.

[1]Drucker [1988], p. 53.
[2]Blumberg and Gerwin [1982].
[3]Meredith [1986], p. 68.

Exhibit 8.3 The Interrelationship between the Technical Structure and the Infrastructure

THE ORGANIZATION

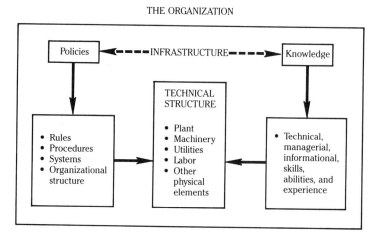

Types of Organizational Structures

The five basic types of organizational design are: (1) the simple structure, (2) the machine bureaucracy, (3) the professional bureaucracy, (4) the divisional form, and (5) the adhocracy. They are illustrated in Exhibit 8.5, and more elaboratively explained and compared in Exhibit 8.A1 in the Appendix. In each of these structures, different emphasis is given to each of the five basic components of a typical organization. While these organizational designs offer different characteristics and are suitable to diverse situations, two of them, the machine bureaucracy and the adhocracy, are directly related to the focus of this chapter.

The Machinie Bureaucracy. This form of organization relies on centralization of power and control. Hierarchy and chain of command are key. Decision-making is done at the top, communication lines are formal, and maintaining control is the key to the organization's success. Because of this, the technostructure is an important part of the organization. Their role in defining and standardizing everyone else's work is essential for smooth operation. The middle line is usually functionally oriented, and its power is limited, as it tends only to implement the strategies of the strategic apex within the standards imposed by the technostructure. The support staff is large, as machine bureaucracies tend to stabilize their internal environments by providing all support services in-house rather than purchasing them from outside. This form of organizational structure is common among large, mature, mass-production manufacturing companies.

The Adhocracy. The adhocracy is a nonstandardized organizational structure which relies on informal management interaction and communication.

Exhibit 8.4 The Five Basic Parts of a Typical Organizational Structure

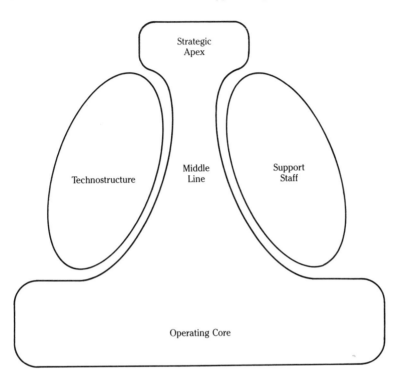

Level	Characteristics and Function
Strategic Apex	Head of the Organization—One person, a board of directors, the company's senior management or executive committee. It's primary role is one of decision making, and management and coordination of the organization's efforts.
Middle Line	The chain of managers (from senior managers to first-line supervisors) who work between the strategic apex and the workders. These managers have direct influence over the actual operations of a company.
Operating Core	The group of people who do the basic work of the organization (e.g. the unskilled laborers in an assembly plant).
Technostructure	The group of analysts in an organization who design systems concerned with the formal planning and control of work (e.g. engineering). Individuals making up the technostructure hold staff (as opposed to line) positions.
Support Staff	Individuals within the firm who provide indirect services to the company, including public relations, legal counsel, and janitorial services.

Source: Adapted for length from Mintzberg [1979], p. 20.

Exhibit 8.5 Five Types of Organizational Structures

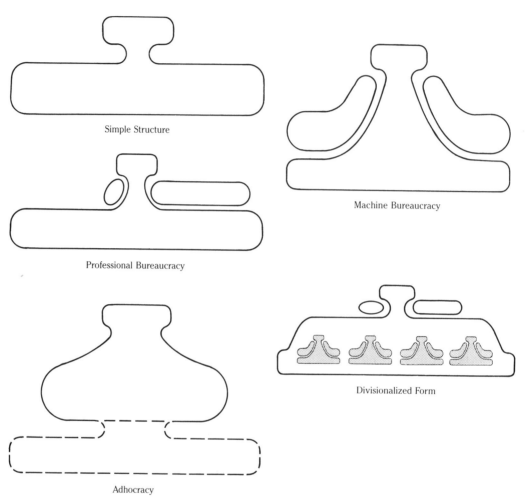

Simple Structure

Professional Bureaucracy

Machine Bureaucracy

Divisionalized Form

Adhocracy

Source: Mintzberg [1981], p. 106.

Complex problems are solved by project teams made up of individuals with different expertise. Power is based on expertise rather than on authority. Therefore, the key component of the structure tends to be either the support staff or the operating core or a combination of the two. The informal nature of the organization and the lack of controls required mean that the technostructure is limited, and the strategic apex is more concerned with the roles of coordinator and gatekeeper than strategic planner and controller. This form of organizational structure is appropriate for firms operating in a rapidly changing environment requiring high levels of innovation—for example, the microelectronics industry.

THE IMPACT OF NEW TECHNOLOGY
ON ORGANIZATIONAL STRUCTURE

Organizational structures can vary in a number of ways, such as whether they are mechanistic or organic in nature. Basically, mechanistic (or bureaucratic) structures are those which operate in a standardized, predetermined fashion, whereas organic structures are characterized by informal working relationships and lack of standardization. Exhibit 8.6 further details different attributes of mechanistic and organic structures.

In general, the new technology is expected to have a major impact on the structure of organizations. For example, changes in job design (which will be discussed in Chapter 9) often lead to large structural adjustments. The traditional organization layout based on functional specialization may no longer be appropriate due to the integration necessitated by the new technology (see, for example, McDougall and Noori [1986]).

Middle Management Extinction

Perhaps the most dramatic change in the structuring of future organizations will be a significant reduction in management levels and numbers of managers in large organizations. In fact, many organizations have already begun reducing the number of middle managers and white collar workers they employ, and studies have shown that many successful firms employ relatively small numbers of managers. For example:

> A (recent) survey...divided 41 large American companies into winners and losers based on long-term financial performance. It found that the winners had, on average, almost four fewer layers of management than the losers. The winners also had 500 fewer staff at headquarters for every $1 billion of turnover than the average for their industry. As a rule of thumb, the savings made by not employing these extra people was almost the same as the average net profit for those companies.[4]

Firms are finding that advanced information technology (AIT) is enabling them to eliminate several management layers (see, for example, Staffman [1988]). Middle managers are typically processors of information; AIT will make information processing much more efficient and thus eliminate the need for many of these people. For example:

> It seems likely that numerous middle management functions in supervision and control will disappear or will be taken over by the computer. While this will enhance the role of top management, at the same time, much decision-making

[4]*The Economist* [1988], p. 59.

Exhibit 8.6 Characteristics of Mechanistic and Organic Organizations

	Mechanistic Adaptation, or Muddlers	Organic Adaptation, or Foresight Notions
Objectives	Return on investments; stockholders' gains.	Market share; new product ratio multiple. Multiple objectives with emphasis on growth.
Strategy	Orientation towards wider domain. Agility resources development; effective use of management resources. High "stars" ratio. Meeting competition head-on. R&D emphasizing product improvement.	Long-term accumulation of management resources. High "dogs" ratio. Niche strategy. R&D emphasizing basic research and new product development.
Technology	Routine	Nonroutine
Organizational structure	Mechanistic (highly formalized, highly concentrated, highly standardized). Systematization of horizontal relations; strong power of control finance division. High degree of divisionalization. Sophisticated performance appraisal and clear linkage between performance and remuneration. Self-contained divisions with vertical control.	Organic (lowly formalized, lowly concentrated, lowly standardized). Strong power of production division. Low degree of divisionalization. Simple performance appraisal and weak linkage between performance appraisal and remuneration. Incompletely self-contained divisions with horizontal coordination network.
Organizational process	Decision-making emphasizing individual initiatives. Conflict resolution by confrontation. Output control.	Information-oriented leadership. Group-oriented consensual decision-making. Orientation to change, job rotation, and promotion from within.
Personal predisposition of managers	Specialist. High value commitment.	Generalist. Interpersonal relations skills. Initiative; innovative. Track-record-oriented.
Organizational improvement	Related to change in top management. Top down. Gradual improvement emphasizing primary functions.	High change. Reform emphasizing secondary functions.

Source: Rubinger [1986], p. 26.

will have to be delegated to lower hierarchical levels, constituting a job enrichment for skilled workers, engineers, technicians, designers and draughtsmen.
In fact, all levels will, in principle, have access to a common database. This
presupposes more communication among team members, but fewer hierarchical
levels in management.[5]

Furthermore, firms may find that in order to implement the new
technology, they may need to reduce the number of middle managers they
employ:

> The first step in accomplishing successful plant-floor implementation of new
> manufacturing approaches is the clearing out of all the middle managers and
> support-service layers that clog the wheels of change.[6]

In short, many of the benefits of new technology result from the increased ability
of firms to respond quickly to environmental pressures and market needs.
Excessive layers of middle management may slow a firm's ability to react and
respond quickly to change.

Organizational Alternatives

In the appendix to this chapter we present a literature review summarizing the
forecasted impact of the new technology on organizational structure. In general,
our findings indicate that the new technology ought to be accompanied by a
more organic structure. Otherwise, the rigid, mechanistic structures evident in
many traditional environments will increase response times to technological
change and forfeit the flexibility advantages offered by the new technology. This
is particularly true when applied to the question of technological leader-
ship/followership discussed in Chapter 5, as the following illustrates:

> An organic structure is most likely to have a culture that promotes innovation
> and originality. The mechanistic structure is less likely to have a culture that
> stresses innovation, and is more likely to promote the idea of being a strong
> and consistent follower within the given industry.[7]

In other words, the principle of hysteresis from physics (describing lags
in magnetic response) has been shown to operate in organizational structures

---

[5]Ebel and Ulrich [1987], p. 360.
[6]Peters [1988], p. 355.
[7]Bartels [1988], p. 562.

too.[8] Consequently, even the acquisition of appropriate technologies, implemented properly, can be thwarted in its contribution to strategic effectiveness if there is no appropriate shift in structure. Factors affecting hysteresis include inertia, tradition, vested power interests, lack of awareness of the new environmental demands (both internal and external environments), and lack of recognition of the new pressure points and opportunities presented by the new technology. Methods of overcoming some of these problems will be discussed in Chapter 9.

In practice, supporting a company's production activities requires organizational backing. Depending on the company's position in the product-process matrix, one can expect the organizational structure to take different forms. In one extreme, for companies that deal with high-volume production and specialized lines of products, one can expect the structure to be clustered around the product. This is also called product organization, in which "...essentially all resources—both personnel and equipment—are dedicated to a product line."[9] The opposite of the product organization is when companies engage in high-variety, low-volume production and arrange their operations around process or function areas in which "...all technical skills for a process exist in one area ."[10] The product and process organizations offer two distinctive organizational designs, one based on a centralized, homogeneous structure and the other built around a decentralized, heterogeneous arrangement.

The decentralized structure offers the firm a structure suited to the process of innovation. Since information flows rapidly into the organization, there is greater overall sensitivity to different parts of the firm's environment. This type of structure also allows for more lateral communication within the firm. Ideas formulate more rapidly, as do solutions to existing problems. John Akers, Chairman of IBM, comments on the advantage of decentralization: "The benefit will be that our management team will spend less time at corporate headquarters and more time with customers."[11] This structure, however, has its own limitations when it comes time for the firm to implement new ideas. Since the firm is so loosely structured, any attempts at a unified action will encounter difficulties, and this could result in an ineffective or inappropriate implementation of the technology.

[8]In this context, the following analogy can be made:

Hysteresis Analogy

Applied to Magnetic Field	Applied to Organization
Torroid/ferromagnetic core	Technology/organization
Toroid induced magnetic field	Technology induced benefits
Core magnetic field	Benefits due to organizational adjustment
Total magnetic field	Total system benefits

[9]Thurwachter [1986], p. 77.
[10]Thurwachter [1986], p. 77.
[11]McCarroll [1988], p. 49.

The counterpart to the decentralized structure, unfortunately, offers exactly the opposite results to the firm. The centralized or homogeneous structure, due to its unifying nature, is better designed for the implementation of the new technology. Decision-makers in the company have wider authority to implement a desirable innovation—yet they have a smaller pool of innovations from which to choose. For the firm which is interested in implementing a new technology, the centralized structure would seem to be most appropriate. But choosing a structure solely to fit the present situation is obviously not a wise strategic decision. What will happen to the firm a few years down the line when the present innovation becomes the old way of doing things? The challenge is to devise an organizational structure to match the flexibility and the complexity of new technology, a structure that meshes all the necessary technical and nontechnical elements and blends the functional expertise as needed, a flexible structure that accommodates the dynamics of flexible technology. The following are some organizational structures used by successful companies.

The Entrepreneurial Organization.   An examination of the structures of the most technologically successful companies shows that they are distinctively different. That is, they provide an environment for personal growth and innovation. The entrepreneurial organization is a hot discussion topic in corporate circles today. The problem, of course, is how an entrepreneurial environment can be established in the classic corporate structrure. The answer is that a truly effective entrepreneurial environment requires a corporate pattern based on simplicity in structure and the creation of small but autonomous divisions.

Johnson and Johnson and Magna International are two companies built around such a philosophy. Magna, the largest Canadian auto parts company with sales of close to $1 billion, is made up of over 90 separate divisions split into seven operating groups. Each division is run by a general manager, an entrepreneur who has the complete authority and responsibility for the operation of that unit. The unit may start with only two or three people and eventually grow to the 100 or so limit imposed by the structure. This ceiling is imposed for the simple reason that ". . . workers do not want to be treated as numbers"![12]

As with most structures, entrepreneurial organizations also have drawbacks. Some of the drawbacks related specifically to the new technology are described below.

1. Difficulty in justifying large automation expenditures by separate divisions.
2. Difficulty in formulating and implementing a corporate-wide technology strategy.
3. The divisions, being essentially autonomous, may encounter some of the same problems as small firms (for example, lack of in-house technical expertise).
4. Communication and sharing of information may be retarded as divisions compete against each other.

[12]Benninger [1986], p. 303.

The Matrix Structure. The matrix organization concept is certainly not new. In a structure based on a matrix philosophy, functional specialists report to both a functional manager and to a product, business unit, geographic, or project manager. In other words, the firm's organizational structure is laid out in the shape of a matrix, with functional specialists reporting to two bosses. Exhibit 8.7 shows the matrix organization based on an example from the auto industry.

We noted earlier that changes in the marketplace are typically frequent and uncertain. This provides a favorable opportunity for the implementation of the matrix organization, since one of its primary advantages "...is the ability to facilitate rapid management response to changing environment."[13]

Davis and Lawrence [1977] describe three conditions which favor the application of matrix structures. The first is external pressure for a "dual focus." This may arise when organizations undertake...complex tasks...essential to survival [and when the customers]...may require both a focus on their unique... product requirements, and on specialized complex technical issues."[14]

Exhibit 8.7 The Integration of Tasks in the Matrix Organization

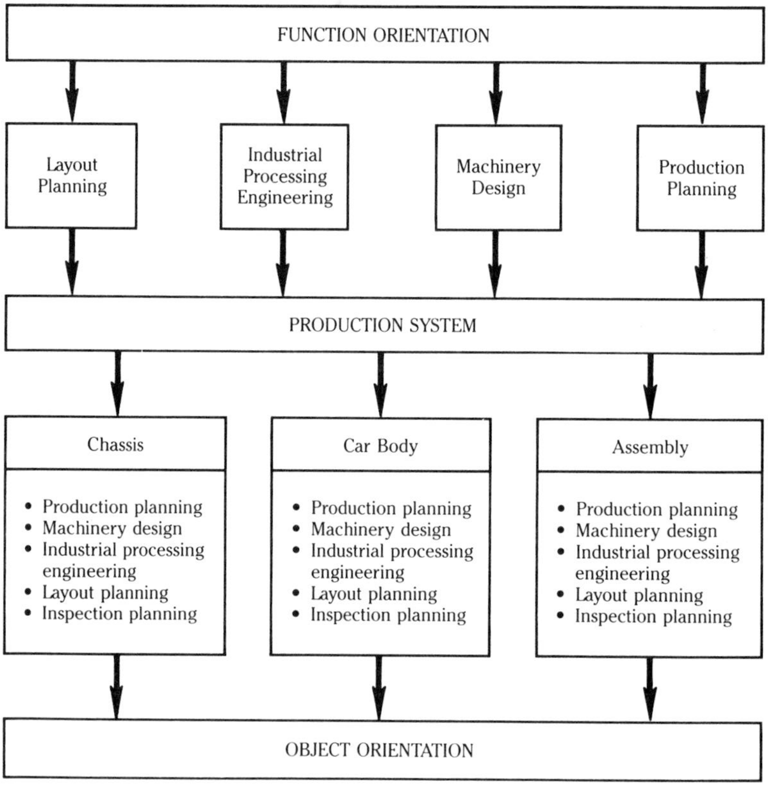

Source: Bullinger et al. [1985], p. LI

[13]Mar et al. [1985], p. 384.
[14]Mar et al. [1985], p. 385.

The second prerequisite compels the organization to have a high information processing capacity to share necessary information among different departments and to cope better with market uncertainties. The third condition is the urgency to share the technical, capital, and human resources of the organization. The following exemplifies this point:

> TRW recently established a computerized technology index that lists key personnel and their technological capabilities. This index tells company engineers and researchers what technological resources are available within TRW, and important in a company of 86,000 employees—where to find the experts.[15]

The matrix organization is potentially capable of providing the dual focus, information processing capacity, and integration needed in a new technology environment. Indeed, some companies, such as Proctor and Gamble, have successfully utilized this structure. However, Baetz and Beamish [1987] identify a number of potential disadvantages with matrix organizations:

1. They are very complex to manage.
2. It is hard to maintain a balance between the two lines of authority.
3. They require so much shared authority that disproportionate amounts of time may be spent on communication.
4. They make it difficult to move quickly and decisively because clearance is needed from so many other people.
5. They promote organizational bureaucracy, which restricts creative entrepreneurship.

In sum, it seems that if they are not implemented successfully, matrix organizations may in fact magnify some of the problems this form was created to solve (for example, it may increase the time needed to respond to a changing environment).

The Ad-hoc Organization.   In Chapter 4, we noted that the innovation process can be facilitated by having individuals work in project teams, with each being responsible for one of the six critical tasks. "Sophisticated innovation requires a very different structural configuration, one that is able to fuse experts drawn from different disciplines into smoothly functioning ad-hoc project teams."[16] The structural configuration that Mintzberg advocates to foster innovation is the *adhocracy* (based on the word popularized by Toffler [1970]).

Although the adhocracy provides the structure (or lack of structure) that is needed to promote innovation, it may also inhibit the implementation of inno-

---

[15]Senia [1987], p. 37.
[16]Mintzberg [1979], p. 432.

vations; this is the same problem that was discussed earlier with respect to decentralization. Consider the following:

> ...organizations that are characterized as loosely structured, organic, decentralized, complex or heterogeneous, tend to be more sensitive to the existence of innovations in their environment and to generate more innovations at a faster pace.
>
> [However]...organizations, that are "mechanistic," tightly-structured, centralized, highly formalized, not highly differentiated and homogeneous...seem better designed to accomplish the sometimes herculean task of implementation.[17]

Others would argue that an informal structure, while facilitating innovation, tends to undermine control as well.

An essential prerequisite to making an informal structure such as the adhocracy work is the existence of a set of shared values and a common culture. Gresov [1984] argues that a firm with a complex organizational structure (such as the adhocracy) can be strong at both innovation and implementation if a homogeneous culture exists. His point is that a strong, homogeneous culture will drive people to implement those innovations that can benefit the firm. He offers two interesting comments:

1. If culture homogeneity binds organizational members together, it is possible that many of the communication problems inherent in the phenomenon of structural heterogeneity can be overcome.
2. Cultural heterogeneity, where it exists in an organization, can alleviate the bureaucratic rigidities inherent in the highly centralized and formalized organization.

Although the implementation of adhocracy seems straightforward, it is far easier said than done. First of all, an adhocracy requires the right type of people—that is, those who react favorably to (or who are at least tolerant of) the ambiguity inherent in this type of structure. This is not easy, as many individuals prefer "...a life of stability and well-defined relationships," and "...even dedicated members of adhocracies periodically exhibit the same low tolerance for ambiguity."[18] Second, the creation of a strong, homogeneous organizational culture is a difficult task which requires a lot of time and a great deal of effort.

---

[17]Gresov [1984], p. 64.
[18]Mintzberg [1979], p. 461.

THE COMPATIBLE ORGANIZATION: BLENDING
THE MACHINE BUREAUCRACY AND ADHOCRACY
TO MATCH THE FLEXIBLE TECHNOLOGY

While Mintzberg's adhocracy appears to be the organizational structure most suited to the requirements of the new technology, it still has significant drawbacks. This leaves managers with the dilemma of choosing between a loosely structured organization (in order to foster innovation) and a tightly structured organization (in order to facilitate implementation and control). However, in practice, successful firms have been able to combine the two; Peters and Waterman [1982] refer to these firms as exhibiting simultaneous "loose-tight" properties. "Organizations that live by the loose-tight principle are on the one hand rigidly controlled, yet at the same time allow (indeed, insist on) autonomy, entrepreneurship, and innovation...."[19]

To benefit from flexible technology and to exploit the potential of economies of integration (discussed in Chapter 5), we propose the compatible structure or a flexible manufacturing management system (FMMS).[20] This is an organizational structure which encompasses many features of both process and product designs. An FMMS is the organizational design that best suits the requirements of the factory-of-the-future. It allows for the provision of cross-fertilization and a knowledge development process. In this case, the company's resources are organized to allow for maximum flexibility in producing either specialized or nonstandard products. An FMMS "... encourages cost effective design by focusing the organization along a common boundary of engineering and production activities."[21] The compatible structure allows for a more active partnership between the employees and the company, and promotes the integration of people into the technical system. Further, an FMMS inspires a flatter organization and direct partnership of management. In short, an FMMS is a school of thought which encompasses the entire organization at a corporate, strategic level. An FMMS is a looser organization than exists under the matrix structure. It encourages teaming across disciplines, and facilitates environmental scanning or environmental tracing (see Porter et al., pp. 162–173); it is a fast response organization. Consider the following example:

> Cooperation between Matsushita's design teams and employees on the shop floor eliminated more than three-quarters of the product's cost while dramatically improving its quality. In the process, the company turned a niche product into the man-market success story of the 1980s.[22]

[19]Peters and Waterman [1982], p. 318.
[20]Savage [1989] refers to this as fifth-generation management (FGM).
[21]Thurwachter [1986], p. 79.
[22]Wood [1987], p. 17.

The FMMS also overcomes several of the drawbacks of an entrepreneurial organization. It maintains a looseness to facilitate innovation, yet still maintains control of the corporate technology strategy. It emphasizes intergroup sharing of technical information, which may speed the rate and process of innovation within the firm.

The compatible structure can best be described as a simultaneous organization which is a hybrid of machine bureaucracy and adhocracy. It maintains the characteristics of both mechanistic and organic structures and aims at the best course of action in a most effective and efficient way. Exhibit 8.8 presents the concept of the FMMS, which necessitates the presence of both specialized

Exhibit 8.8   The Compatible Organization: A Hybrid of the Mechanistic and the Organic Structures

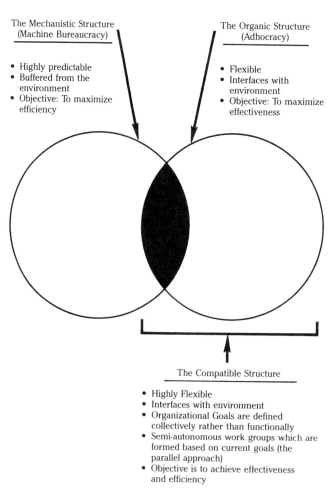

The Mechanistic Structure
(Machine Bureaucracy)

- Highly predictable
- Buffered from the environment
- Objective: To maximize efficiency

The Organic Structure
(Adhocracy)

- Flexible
- Interfaces with environment
- Objective: To maximize effectiveness

The Compatible Structure

- Highly Flexible
- Interfaces with environment
- Organizational Goals are defined collectively rather than functionally
- Semi-autonomous work groups which are formed based on current goals (the parallel approach)
- Objective is to achieve effectiveness and efficiency

departments (to deal with specific subjects such as design and process planning) as well as integration of certain tasks in a product-oriented manner.[23]

A Framework for the Compatible Structure

The true form of the compatible structure varies and is centered around four major questions under two types of environments. The first is the external environment, which includes the market, the economy, government, unions, and culture. The second is the sociotechnical environment that immediately surrounds the operating systems. The FMMS is designed based on the required interaction between the selected technology and the sociotechnical environment. In general, organizations must maintain a goodness of fit between themselves and their environment in order to survive. Today, maintaining that fit is a difficult job. The environment tends to be highy unstable due to the ever-increasing speed of technological change and the fragmentation of the mass market into segments that seek different goals.

The FMMS is based on four general questions. The first and most obvious question to ask is, Why should the company consider introducing the new technology? This question deals with environmental pressures including competitive pressures. Dominant factors to be considered (see Chapter 3) are economic indices such as production and labor costs; labor availability and employee unwillingness to work in certain hazardous or unpleasant environments; need for production flexibility in the face of declining lead times; employee morale and employment issues; and the cost and availability of alternative production technology. The why question is typically asked first, but the other three questions need to be considered simultaneously when contemplating the introduction of the new technology.

The second question to ask is: When should new technology be introduced? The key to this question is an analysis of the organization's need for and readiness to accept new technology, including specific consideration of technical, production, managerial, and social readiness. Dominant factors to be considered are managerial and employee acceptance of the new technology, likely economies of scale such as improved technical processes for high-volume production, cost and benefit analysis, the industry cost structure,the positioning of competitors on the production lerarning curve, and culture-dominant coalitions in the organization.

The third question to ask is: Where should new technology be introduced? Several studies have addressed this question, but they are all based on specific experiences with technology introduction from which it is difficult to

---

[23]Generally, the technological imperative and antitechnological imperative represent the two extreme views of the relationship between organizational structure and technology—see Noori [1987, p. 189]. A compromise view implies that technology and the prevailing social systems jointly and simultaneously determine structure. The key focus in this view is on adaptability and obtaining the best fit possible between the various functional elements of the organization.

generalize. In the main, however, the key to this question is an analysis of the technological feasibility and point of great impact of the proposed new technology. Dominant factors to be considered are departmental differences in readiness and enthusiasm, available technologies, product life cycle differences, and geographic and locality differences. Thus, it might be feasible to introduce the new technology on a partial basis in the more receptive areas of an assembly operation.

The fourth question to be asked is related to process: How should the new technology be introduced? The process of implementing technology underlies the where and when questions, for they cannot be answered without considering the way in which major changes, such as new forms of technology, will be introduced. The focal point here is the integration of technology, people, and organization. In general, the dominant factors to be considered are social and technical interfaces with workers and management, union participation in the implementation process, and the effects of the new technology on employment levels.

Exhibit 8.9 shows the relationship among the various components discussed above. In short, the compatible structure, or FMMS, is characterized by the following:

- Integration of functional areas and expertise
- Integration of people into the technical system
- Organization of resources along a common boundary of engineering and production activities
- Promotion of active partnership between the employees and the company
- Inspiration for a flatter organization and direct partnership of management
- Inspiration for a loose organizational structure and teaming across disciplines
- Streamlining of the operating cores and facilitating the environmental scanning and decision-making process
- Elimination of the redundancy at the middle line level and creation of new roles at the technostructure and support staff levels

CONCLUDING OBSERVATIONS

Before they can capitalize on the benefits of new technology, firms will have to consider the corresponding organizational issues. The new technology can be used by firms to compete in changing and uncertain environments. However, their efforts will be stymied if the organization in which they operate cannot respond quickly and effectively to these changes. In this chapter, we attempted to determine which type of organizational structure is best suited to the needs of a complex, changing environment characterized by the new technology. The basic conclusion was that in order to realize the full benefits of the new technology, an organization must be able to respond quickly to environmental forces. If an organization is too rigid and mechanistic, the strategic potential available through the flexibility of the new technology will be compromised.

Exhibit 8.9 The Making of the Compatible Organization

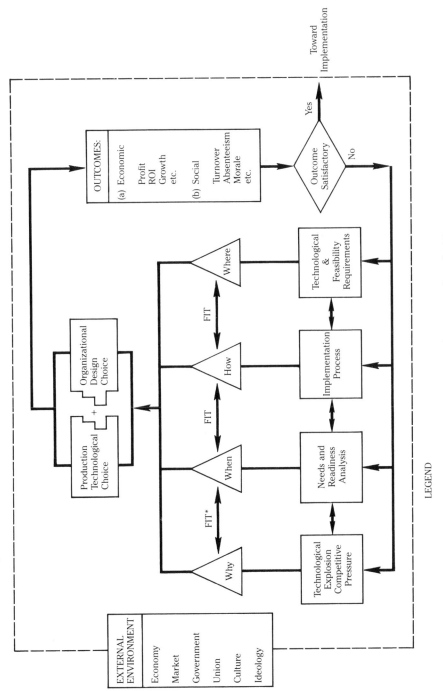

LEGEND

*FIT: Goodness of fit between pairs of components in each of the four categories of questions.

Source: Noori [1987], p. 192.

At the same time, companies must ensure that the organization is not too loose—that is, firms must maintain enough homogeneity to be able to implement innovations effectively. This implies that firms should create organizational structures which are organic enough to foster innovations, and at the same time contain enough mechanistic features to implement innovations successfully. With this tradeoff in mind, we introduced the compatible structure or flexible manufacturing management system (FMMS).

The compatible structure combines the organic characteristics of Mintzberg's adhocracy with the structure and standardization of the machine bureaucracy. The FMMS is the organizational design best suited to the requirements of the factory-of-the-future. It is a fast response organization with a structure based on simplicity of form, which allows for the flexibility to reorganize frequently and fluidly. Finally, the FMMS can make better use of temporary forms such as task forces and make employees less dependent on the particular organizational boundaries by which they are constrained.

RECOMMENDED READINGS

BARTELS, L. [1988].   "Use of Organizational Development Techniques in the Adoption and Implementation of Technology." In T. M. Khalil et al. (eds.), *Technology Management I.* Proceedings of the First International Conference on Technology Management, pp. 560–571.

DRUCKER, P. F. [1988].   "The Coming of the New Organization." *Harvard Business Review,* January–February, pp. 45–53.

DISCUSSION QUESTIONS

1. Do you feel that the new technology will reduce (or eliminate) the need for middle managers, and if so, what implications does this have? Will there be more generalists or specialists in future organizations?

2. a. It can be aruged that structure inhibits innovation. It can also be argued that structure facilitates implementation. Given this dilemma, recommend an organizational structure that can support successful innovation and implementation.

   b. How can a firm achieve the proper balance between performing day-to-day functional duties and participating in entrepreneurial activities?

3. Can a firm have too many entrepreneurs?

4. One can argue that effective implementation of the new technology requires the proper organizational structure. Will firms be forced to change their organizational structure before they can successively implement the new technology?

5. How will the new technology affect the various functional groups in an organization (manufacturing, marketing, purchasing and materials management, R&D, finance, accounting)?

6. Will the role and duties of marketing increase or decrease in a new technology environment?

7. Does technology determine structure, or does structure determine technology? Which of the following (if any) accurately depicts the relationship that should exist between strategy, structure, and new technology?

   Strategy → New Technology → Structure
   Structure → Strategy → New Technology
   Strategy → Structure → New Technology

Can you recommend a more desirable relationship than any of the three illustrated above?

8. Given the five types of organizational structures illustrated in Exhibit 8.2, sketch a diagram of the organizational structure that will evolve in firms which have adopted large amounts of the new technology.

9. In this chapter we advocated the FMMS (or compatible structure) as the structure best suited for technological innovation and the implementation of the new technology. Do you agree or disagree? Is this structure a feasible one? Are there any risks to pursuing this form of organizational structure? Is FMMS always the best structure to pursue? Explain.

10. McDonald's is sometimes cited as an example of a company that uses a combination of structure and culture to innovate and implement effectively. Do you agree? Comment.

REFERENCES AND BIBLIOGRAPHY

ALDRICH, H. E. [1972]. "Technology and Organizational Structure: A Reexamination of the Findings of the Aston Group." *Administrative Science Quarterly*, Volume 17, March, pp. 26–43.

ALEXANDER, C. P. [1985]. "Search for a Miracle Cure." *Time*, May 20, p. 36.

BAETZ, M. C., and P. W. BEAMISH [1987]. *Strategic Management: Canadian Cases.* Richard D. Irwin, Inc., Dorsey, Ill.

BARTELS, L. [1988]. "Use of Organizational Development Techniques in the Adoption and Implementation of Technology." In Tarek M. Khalil et al. (eds.), *Technology Management I.* Inderscience Ltd., Geneva, pp. 560–571.

BATES, F. L., and J. D. THOMPSON [1957]. "Technology, Organization and Administration." *Administrative Science Quarterly*, Volume 2, pp. 325–343.

BENNINGER, G. N. [1986]. "New Technology and the Entrepreneurial Organization." In H Noori (ed.), *Proceedings of Technology Canada Conference*, May 25–26, WLU, Waterloo, pp. 299–304.

BLUMBERG, M., and D. GERWIN [1982]. "Coping with Advanced Manufacturing Technology." *Proceedings of the Eighth Annual Conference.* European International Business Association, Fontainbleau, France, December.

BULLINGER, H., H. WARNECK, and H. LENTES [1985]. "Towards the Factory of the Future." In H. Bullinger and H. Warneck (eds.), *Toward the Factory of the Future.* Springer-Verlag, Berlin, pp. xxix–liv.

BURSTEIN, M. C., and M. JELINEK [1982]. "The Production Administrative Structure: A Paradigm for Strategic Fit." *Academy of Management Review*, Volume 2, pp. 242–252.

CHILD, J., and R. MANSFIELD [1972]. "Technology, Size and Organization Structure." *Sociology*, Volume 12, No. 3, pp. 211–223.

CORDELL, A. J. [1985]. *The Uneasy Eighties: The Transition to an Information Society.* Background Study 53, Science Council of Canada, March.

DAVIDSON, A. [1983]. "Opportunities in Technology: Redefining the Market." *Business Quarterly*, Fall, pp. 83–92.

DAVIS, L. E., and J. C. TAYLER [1975]. "Technology Effects on Job, Work, and Organizational Structure: A Contingency View." *The Quality of Working Life—Volume One—Problems, Prospects and the State of the Art.* The Free Press, New York, pp. 220–241.

DRUCKER, P. F. [1988]. "The Coming of the New Organization." *Harvard Business Review*, January–February, pp. 45–53.

EBEL, K., and E. ULRICH [1987]. "Some Workplace Effects of CAD and CAM." *International Labor Review*, Volume 126, No. 3, May–June, pp. 351–370.

FAGGIN, F. [1985]. "The Challenge of Bringing New Ideas to Market." *High Technology*, February, pp. 14–16.

FORD, J. D., and J. W. SLOCUM, JR. [1977]. "Size, Technology, Environment and the Structure of Organizations." *Academy of Management Review*, Volume 2, October, pp. 561–575.

FRY, L. W. [1982]. "Technology-Structure Research: Three Critical Issues." *Academy of Management Journal*, Volume 25, No. 3., pp. 532–551.

GERWIN, D. [1979]. "Relationships between Structure and Technology at the Organizational and Job Levels." *Journal Management Studies*, Volume 10, pp. 70–79.

GILLESPIE, D. F., and D. S. MILLER [1977]. "Technology and the Study of Organizations: An Overview and Appraisal." *Academy of Management Review*, Volume 2, pp. 7–16.

GRESOV, C. [1984]. "Designing Organizations to Innovate and Implement: Using Two Dilemmas to Create a Solution." *Columbia Journal of World Business*, Winter, pp. 63–67.

GRIMES, A. J., and S. M. KLEIN [1973]. "The Technological Imperative: The Relative Impact of Task Unit, Model Technology, and Hierarchy on Structure." *Academy of Management Journal*, Volume 16, No. 4, December, pp. 583–597.

HARVEY, E. [1968]. "Technology and the Structure of Organizations." *American Sociological Reviews*, Volume 33, No. 2, April, pp. 247–259.

HICKSON, D. J., D. S. PUGH, and C. R. HININGS [1969]. "An Empirical Taxonomy of Structures of Work Organization." *Administrative Science Quarterly*, Volume 14, pp. 115–126.

HICKSON, D. J., D. S. PUGH, and D. C. PHEYSEY [1972]. "Operations Technology and Organization Structure: An Empirical Reappraisal." *Administrative Science Quarterly*, Volume 14, No. 3., pp. 378–397.

HREBINIAK, L. G. [1974]. "Job Technology, Supervision, and Work-Group Structure." *Administrative Science Quarterly*, Volume 19, pp. 395–410.

JASINSKI, F. J. [1959]. "Adapting Organization to New Technology." *Harvard Business Review*, January–February, pp. 79–86.

JELINEK, M. [1981]. "Technology, Organizations and Contingency." *Organizations by Design: Theory and Practice.* Georgetown, Ontario, pp. 214–229.

KHANDWALLA, P. N. [1974]. "Mass Output Orientation of Operations Technology and Organizational Structure." *Administrative Science Quarterly*, Volume 19, March, pp. 74–97.

LEE, S. M., F. LUTHANS, and D. L. OLSEON [1982]. "A Management Science Approach to Contingency Models of Organizational Structure." *Academy of Management Journal*, Volume 25, No. 3, pp. 553–566.

LILLEY, W. [1984]. "Leading-Edge Disasters." *Canadian Business*, December, pp. 36–42.

MAHONEY, T. A., and P. J. FROST [1974]. "The Role of Technology in Models of Organizational Effectiveness." *Organizational Behavior and Human Resources*, Volume II, pp. 122–138.

MAR, B., W. T. NEWELL, and B. O. SAXBERG [1985]. "Project Management and Matrix Organizations: The Key to High Technology Management?" In B. W. Mar, W. T. Newell, and B. O. Saxberg (eds.), *Managing High Technology: An Interdisciplinary Perspective.* North-Holland, pp. 381–386.

MARTINO, J. P. [1980]. "Technological Forecasting—An Overview. *Management Science*, Volume 26, No. 1, pp. 28–33.

McCARROLL, T. [1988]. "Can this Elephant Dance?" *Time*, February 8, p. 49.

McDOUGALL, G., and H. NOORI [1986]. "Manufacturing-Marketing Strategic Interface: The Impact of Flexible Manufacturing Systems." In A. Kusiak (ed.), *Modelling and Design of Flexible Manufacturing Systems.* Elsevier, New York, pp. 189–205.

MEREDITH, J. [1986]. "Automation Strategy Must Acknowledge Organization's Infrastructure." *Industrial Engineering*, May, pp. 68–73.

MIAOULIS, G., and P. J. LA PLACA [1982]. "A Systems Approach for Developing High Technology Products." *Industrial Marketing Management II.* New York, pp. 253–262.

MINTZBERG, H. [1981]. "Organization Design: Fashion or Fit?" *Harvard Business Review*, January–February, pp. 104–115.

MINTZBERG, H. [1979]. *The Structuring of Organizations.* Prentice Hall, Englewood Cliffs, N.J.

MOHR, L. B. [1971]. "Organizational Technology and Organizational Structure." *Administrative Science Quarterly*, Volume 16, pp. 444–459.

NEW, R. J., and D. D. SINGER [1985]. "Understanding Why People Reject New Ideas Helps IE's Convert Resistance into Acceptance." *Industrial Engineering*, May, pp. 51–54.

NOORI, H. [1987]. "Production Policy and the Acquisition of New Technology." *Engineering Management International*, Volume 4, pp. 187–196.

PERROW, C. [1967]. "A Framework for the Comparative Analysis of Organizations." *American Sociological Review*, Volume 32, No. 3, April, pp. 194–208.

PETERS, T. J. [1988]. *Thriving on Chaos.* Alfred A. Knopf, New York.

PETERS, T. J., and R. H. WATERMAN, JR. [1982]. *In Search of Excellence.* Warner Books, New York.

PORTER, L. A., F. A. ROSSINI, S. R. CARPENTER, and A. T. ROPER [1982]. *A Guide for Technology Assessment and Impact Analysis.* Elsevier, New York.

PUGH, D. S., D. J. HICKSON, C. R. HININGS, and C. TURNER [1968]. "Dimensions of Organization Structure." *Administrative Science Quarterly*, Volume 13, pp. 65–105.

PUGH, D. S., D. J. HICKSON, C. R. HININGS, and C. TURNER [1969]. "The Contest of Organization Structures." *Administrative Science Quarterly*, Volume 14, pp. 91–114.

RIEMANN, B. C. [1980]. "Organization Structure and Technology in Manufacturing: System Versus Work Flow Level Perspectives." *Academy of Management Journal*, Volume 23, No. 1, pp. 61–77.

RUBINGOR, B. [1986]. "Competing Through Technology: The Success Factors." In J. Dermer (ed.), *Competitiveness Through Technology.* Lexington Books, Lexington, Mass., ,pp. 25–28.

RUMELT, R. P. [1981]. "New Technology and Organization." *Organizational Change*, October, pp. 245–266.

SAVAGE, C. M. [1989]. "CIM Management of Future: FGM." *Manufacturing Engineering*, January, pp 59–63.

SENIA, A. [1987]. "Companies Turned Old Ideas Into Profit." *High Technology Business*, December, pp. 36–39.

SCOTT, W. R. [1975]. "Organizational Structure." *Annual Review of Sociology*, Volume 1, pp. 1–20.

SINK, D. S., and C. P. KOELLING [1987]. "Organization of the Future Research and Development: A Case Study." *IIE Integrated Systems Conference Proceedings*, November 5–7.

SPOONER, P., and M. JOHNSON [1984]. "Technology—How Well Does It Fit in Your Office." *Chief Executive*, October, pp. 42–49.

STANFIELD, G. G. [1976]. "Technology and Organization Structure as Theoretical Categories." *Administrative Science Quarterly*, September, pp. 489–493.

STOFFMAN, D. [1988]. "Less Is More." *Report on Business Magazine*, June, pp. 90–99.

The Economist [1988]. "Middle Managers Face Extinction." January 23, p. 59.

TOFFLER, A. [1979]. *Future Shock*. Bantam Books, New York.

THURWACHTER, W. A. [1986]. "Simplified Integrated Manufacturing (SIM): A Byword for Operational Strategy." *Industrial Engineering*, November, pp. 74–81.

UDY, S. H. [1965]. "The Comparative Analysis of Organizations." *Handbook of Organizations*. Rand McNally, Chicago, pp. 678–709.

WALKER, C. R. [1982]. "Men, Machines and Organizations: A Reappraisal." *Modern Technology and Civilization*, Toronto, pp. 136–151.

WHITMORE, K. R. [1987]. "Industrial Engineers—The Link to Productivity Improvement." A Keynote Talk, IIE Integrated Systems Conference, Nashville, November 5–7.

WILSON, W., and J. H. DOBRZYNSKI [1986]. "And Now, the Post-Industrial Corporation." *Business Week*, March, pp. 64–71.

WIRTZ, W. W. [1964]. "Management Decisions to Automate." *Manpower/Automation Research Monograph*, U.S. Department of Labor, No. 3.

WOOD, R. C. [1987]. "Assembly Lines Build Ideas." *High Technology Business*, December, p. 17.

ZAJDEL, T. D. [1983a]. "A New Era for Management." *Business Week*, April 25, pp. 50–53.

ZAJDEL, T. D. [1983b]. "The Thinking of Middle Management." *Business Week*, April 25, pp. 54–64.

ZAJDEL, T. D. [1983c]. "How Computers Make the Manager's Job." *Business Week*, April 25, pp. 68–80.

ZAJDEL, T. D. [1984]. "Middle Managers Feel Automation Axe." *Computerworld*, March, p. 19.

APPENDIX: THE RELATIONSHIP BETWEEN STRUCTURE AND TECHNOLOGY

At the beginning of this chapter, we briefly mentioned five basic organizational structures as described by Mintzberg [1979, 1981]. To demonstrate the relationships between structure and technology, we have taken the organizational characteristics shown in Exhibit 8.A1 and summarized the respective effects of technology adoption as reported in the literature. The results are illustrated in Exhibit 8.A2.

Based on the impact analyses shown in Exhibit 8.A2, we now duplicate Exhibit 8.A1 showing the effects of the new technology on the five basic organization structures. This is done by removing various dimensions of the structures which are not synergistic with the challenging requirements of new technology adoption. The result is displayed in Exhibit 8.A3. The most significant impacts of new technology are on the simple structure, the machine and professional bureaucracies, and the divisionalized form. This indicates that none of these four structures appear to be able to handle the organizational requirements the new

Exhibit 8.A1 The Primary Characteristics of Five Types of Organizational Structures

	Simple Structure	Machine Bureaucracy	Professional Bureaucracy	Divisionalized Form	Adhocracy
Key Coordinating Mechanism:	Direct supervision	Standardization of work	Standardization of skills	Standardization of outputs	Mutual adjustment
Key Part of Organization	Strategic apex	Technostructure	Operating core	Middle line	Support staff (with operating core in operating adhocracy)
Structural Elements:					
Specialization of jobs	Little specialization	Much horizontal and vertical specialization	Much horizontal specialization	Some horizontal and vertical specialization (between divisions and HQ)	Much horizontal specialization
Training and indoctrination	Little training and indoctrination	Little training and indoctrination	Much training and indoctrination	Some training and indoctrination (of division managers)	Much training
Formalization of behavior, bureaucratic/organic	Little formalization, organic	Much formalization, bureaucratic	Little formalization, bureaucratic	Much formalization (within divisions), bureaucratic	Little formalization, organic
Grouping	Usually functional	Usually functional	Functional and market	Market	Functional and market
Unit size	Wide	Wide at bottom, narrow elsewhere	Wide at bottom, narrow elsewhere	Wide (at top)	Narrow throughout
Planning and control systems	Little planning and control	Action planning.	Little planning and control	Much performance control	Limited action planning (especially in adminis-tration adhocracy)
Liaison devices	Few liaison devices	Few liaison devices	Liaison devices in administration	Few liaison devices	Many liaison devices throughout
Decentralization	Centralization	Limited horizontal decentralization	Horizontal and vertical decentralization	Limited vertical decentralization	Selective decentralization

Exhibit 8.A1 (continued)

	Simple Structure	Machine Bureaucracy	Professional Bureaucracy	Divisionalized Form	Adhocracy
Functioning:					
Strategic apex	All administrative work	Fine tuning, coordination of functions, conflict resolution	External liaison, conflict resolution	Strategic portfolio, performance control	External liaison, conflict resolution, work balancing project monitoring
Operating core	Informal work with little discretion	Routine, formalized work with little discretion	Skilled, standardized work with much individual autonomy	Tendency to formalize due to divisionalization	Truncated (in administrative adhocracy) or merged with administrative to do informal project work (in operating adhocracy)
Middle line	Insignificant	Elaborated and differentiated; conflict resolution, staff liaison, support of vertical flows	Controlled by professionals: much mutual adjustment	Formulation of division strategy, managing operations	Excessive but blurred with staff; involved in project work
Technostructure	None	Elaborated to formalize work	Little	Elaborated at HQ for performance control	Small and blurred within middle in project work
Support staff	Small	Often elaborated to reduce uncertainty	Elaborated to support professionals; machine bureaucracy structure	Split between HQ and divisions	Highly elaborate (in administrative adhocracy) but blurred within middle in project work
Flow of authority	Significant from top	Significant throughout	Insignificant (except in support staff)	Significant throughout	Insignificant
Flow of regulated system	Insignificant	Significant throughout	Insignificant (except in support staff)	Significant throughout	Insignificant
Flow of informal communication	Significant	Discouraged	Significant in administration	Some between HQ and divisions	Significant throughout

247

Exhibit 8.A1 (continued)

	Simple Structure	Machine Bureaucracy	Professional Bureaucracy	Divisionalized Form	Adhocracy
Work constellations	None	Insignificant, especially at lower levels	Some in administration	Insignificant	Significant throughout (especially in administrative adhocracy)
Flow of decision-making	Top down	Top down	Bottom up	Differentiated between HQ and divisions	Mixed, all levels
Situational Elements:					
Age and size	Typically young and small (first stage)	Typically old and large (second stage)	Varies	Typically old and very large (third stage)	Typically young (operating adhocracy)
Technical system	Simple, not regulating	Regulating but not automated, not very sophisticated	Not regulating or sophisticated	Division, otherwise typically like mechine bureaucracy	Very sophisticated often automated (administrative adhocracy); regulating or sophisticated (operating adhocracy)
Environment	Simple and dynamic; sometimes hostile	Simple and stable	Complex and stable	Relatively simple and stable; diversified markets (especially products and services)	Complex and dynamic sometimes disparate (in administrative adhocracy)
Power	Chief executive control; often owner-managed; not fashionable	Technocratic and external control; not fashionable	Professional operator control; fashionable	Middle-line control; fashionable (especially in industry)	Expert control; very fashionable

Exhibit 8.A1 (continued) Elements of the Configurations

Elements of Structure

Job Specialization refers to the number of tasks in a given job and the worker's control over these tasks. A job is horizontally specialized to the extent that it encompasses few narrowly defined tasks, vertically specialized to the extent that the worker lacks control of the tasks he or she performs. Unskilled jobs are typically highly specialized in both dimensions, while skilled or professional jobs are typically specialized horizontally but not vertically. Job enrichment refers to the enlargement of jobs in both the vertical and horizontal dimensions.

Behavior formalization refers to the standardization of work processes by imposition of operating instructions, job descriptions, rules, regulations, and the like. Structures that rely on standardization for coordination are generally referred to as bureaucratic, those that do not as organic.

Training and indoctrination refer to the use of formal instructional programs to establish and standardize in people the requisite skills, knowledge, and norms to do particular jobs. Training is a key design parameter in all work we call professional. Training and formalization are basically substitutes for achieving the standardization (in effect, the bureaucratization) of behavior. In the one, the standards are internalized in formal training as skills or norms; in the other, they are imposed on the job as rules.

Unit grouping refers to the optional bases by which positions are grouped together into units and these units into higher-order units. Grouping encourages coordination by putting different jobs under common supervision, by requiring them to share common resources and achieve common measures of performance, and by facilitating mutual adjustment among them. The various bases for grouping—by work process, product, client, area, and so forth—can be reduced to two fundamentals; the function performed or the market served.

Unit size refers to the number of positions (or units) contained in a single unit. The equivalent term "span of control" is not used here because sometimes units are kept small despite an absence of close supervisory control, for example, when experts coordinate extensively by mutual adjustment, as in an engineering team in a space agency, they will form into small teams. In this case, unit size is small and span of control is low despite a relative absence of direct supervision. In contrast, when work is highly standardized (because of either formalization or training), unit size can be very large because there is little need for direct supervision. One foreman can supervize dozens of assemblers because they work according to very tight instructions.

Planning and control systems are used to standardize outputs. They may be divided into two types—action planning systems, which specify the results of specific actions before they are taken (for example, that holes should be drilled with diameters of three centimeters), and performance control systems, which specify the results of whole ranges of actions after the fact (for example, that sales of a division should grow by 10 percent in a given year).

Liaison devices refer to a whole set of mechanisms used to encourage mutual adjustment within and among units. They range from liaison positions (such as the purchasing engineer who stands between purchasing and engineering); through task forces, standing committees that bring together members of many departments, and integrating managers (such as brand managers), and finally to fully developed matrix structures.

Vertical decentralization describes the extent to which decision making is delegated to managers down the middle line, while horizontal decentralization describes the extent to which nonmangers (that is, people in the operating core, technostructure, and support staff) control decision processes. Moreover, decentralization may be selective, concerning only specific kinds of decisions, or parallel, concerning many kinds of decisions altogether. Five types of decentralization may be found: vertical and horizontal centralization, where all power rests at the strategic apex; limited horizontal decentralization (selective), where the strategic apex shares some power with the technostructure that standardizes everybody else's work; limited vertical decentralization (parallel), where managers of market-based units are delegated the power to control most of the decisions concerning their line units; vertical and horizontal decentralization, where most of the power rests in the operating core at the bottom of the structure; and selective vertical and horizontal decentralization, where the power over different decisions is dispersed widely in the organization—among managers, staff experts, and operators who work in groups at various levels in the hierarchy.

Exhibit 8.A1 (continued) Elements of the Configurations

Elements of Situation

The age and size of the organization affect particularly the extent to which its behavior is formalized and its administrative structure (technostructure and middle line) elaborated. As they age and grow, organizations appear to go through distinct structural transitions, much as inserts metamorphose—for example, from simple organic to elaborated bureaucratic structure, from functional grouping to market-based grouping.

The technical system of the organization influences especially the operating core of those staff units most clearly associated with it. When the technical system of the organization regulates the work of the operating core—as it typically does in mass production—it has the effect of bureaucratizing the organization by virtue of the standards it imposes on lower-level workers. Alternately, when the technical system succeeds in automating the operating work (as in much process production), it reduces the need for external rules and regulations; the necessary rules are automatically incorporated into the machines, enabling the structure to be organic. And when the technical system is complex, as is often the case in process production, the organization must create a significant professional support staff to deal with it and then must decentralize selectively to that staff many of the decisions concerned with the technical system.

The environment of the organization can vary in its degree of complexity, in how static or dynamic it is, in the diversity of its markets, and in the hostility it contains for the organization. The more complex the environment, the more difficulty central management has in comprehending it and the greater the need for decentralization. The more dynamic the environment, the greater the difficulty in standardizing work, outputs, or skills and so the less bureaucratic the structure. These relationships suggest four kinds of structures: two in stable environments (one simple, the other complex) leading, respectively, to a centralized and a decentralized bureaucracy; and two in dynamic environments (again, one simple, the other complex) leading, respectively, to a centralized and a decentralized organic structure. Market diversity, as noted earlier, encourages the organization to set up market-based divisions (instead of functional departments) to deal with each, while extreme hostility in the environment drives the organization to centralize power temporarily—no matter what its normal structure—to fight off the threat.

The power factors of the organization include external control, personal power needs, and fashion. The more an organization is controlled externally, the more centralized and bureaucratic it tends to become. This can be explained by the fact that the two most effective means to control an organization from the outside are to hold its most powerful decision maker, the chief executive officer, responsible for its actions and to impose clearly defined standards on it (performance targets or rules and regulations).

Moreover, because the externally controlled organization must be especially careful about its actions—often having to justify these to outsiders—it tends to formalize much of its behavior and insist that its chief executive authorize key decisions. A second factor, individual power needs (especially by the chief executive) tend to generate excessively centralized structures. And fashion has been shown to be a factor in organization design, the structure of the day often being favored even by organizations for which it is inappropriate.

Source: Adapted from Mintzberg [1979, 1981].

Exhibit 8.A2   The Impact of the New Technology on the Organizational Characteristics: A Brief Review of Literature

Parameter	Effect	Bibliography
Structural Elements:		
Specialization of jobs	Highly specialized	Child and Mansfield [1972] Davis and Taylor [1975] Harvey [1968]
Training and indoctrination	Much training required	Davis and Taylor [1975] Lilley [1984] New and Singer [1985]
Formalization of behavior, bureaucratic/organic	Varies	Khandwalla [1974] Mahoney and Frost [1974] Pugh et al. [1968]
Grouping	Functional and market	Faggin [1985] Lilley [1984]
Unit size	Narrow	Pugh et al. [1986] Scott [1975]
Planning and control systems	Planning is required	Bates and Thompson [1957] Davidson [1983] Lilley [1984] Miaoulis and La Placa [1982] Wirtz [1964] Zajdel [1984] Zajdel [1983b]
Liaison devices	N/A	
Decentralization	Can be either central or decentral	Khandwalla [1974] Perrow [1967]
Functioning:		
Strategic apex	Better decision-making capabilities Easier access to operating core Faster decision-making	Hrebiniak [1974] Khandwalla [1974] Riemann [1980] Spooner and Johnson [1984] Walker [1982]
Operating core	More specialization in work function Fewer people required Increased skill level required	Grimes and Klein [1973] Hrebiniak [1974]
Middle line	Biggest effect on this component Could become nonessential Requires steepest learning curve Must become more technically qualified	Child [1984] Davis and Taylor [1975] Zajdel [1983a] Zajdel [1983b]
Technostructure	Economies of scope versus economies of scale can now be addressed Less emphasis is now required on formal routine	Hrebiniak [1974] Jasinski [1959] Zajdel [1983c]

Exhibit 8.A2 (continued)

Parameter	Effect	Bibliography
Support staff	More and better tools available	Child [1984] Riemann [1980] Spooner and Johnson [1984] Udy [1965]
Flow of authority	N/A	
Flow of regulated system	N/A	
Flow of informal communication	Better at strategic apex Less at operating core and middle management	Child [1984] Miaoulis and La Placa [1982] New and Singer [1985] Walker [1982]
Work constellations	N/A	
Flow of decision-making	Unchanged flow but better More group decisions and input	Davis and Taylor [1975] Gillespie and Miller [1977] Zajdel [1984]
Situational Elements:		
Age and size	Varies but typically small	Pugh et al. [1969] Scott [1975]
Technical system	Sophisticated Automated Not regulating Allows for flexibility	Davidson [1983] Gerwin [1979] Rumelt [1981]
Environment	Complex and changing Increasing variety of products Quick development of new products Increasing fluctuation in product demands Shortening of product life cycle	Bates and Thompson [1957] Burnstein and Jelinek [1982] Davidson [1983] Ford and Slocum [1977] Jelinek [1981] Lee et al. [1982] Rumelt [1981]
Power	Expert control Easier access for strategic apex	Spooner and Johnson [1984] Zajdel [1984] Zajdel [1983b]

technology demands. Therefore, firms wishing to achieve the full benefits of the new technology are going to have to pursue alternative organizational structures such as Mintzberg's adhocracy. In this chapter, we discussed possible alternative structures and their various characteristics. We concluded that the compatible structure (a blend of the machine bureaucracy and the adhocracy) can be used by firms to achieve the maximum benefits available through the new technology.

Exhibit 8.A3 The Five Types of Organizational Structure Revisited: The Impact of New Technology

	Simple Structure	Machine Bureaucracy	Professional Bureaucracy	Divisionalized Form	Adhocracy
Key Coordinating Mechanism:	Direct supervision	Standardization of work	Standardization of skills	Standardization of outputs	Mutual adjustment
Key Part of Organization	Strategic apex	Technostructure	Operating core	Middle line	Support staff (with operating core in operating adhocracy)
Structural Elements:					
Specialization of jobs	*	Much horizontal and vertical specialization	Much horizontal specialization	*	Much horizontal specialization
Training and indoctrination	*	*	Much training and indoctrination	Some training and indoctrination (of Division Managers)	Much training
Formalization of behavior, bureaucratic/organic	Little formalization, organic	Much formalization, bureaucratic	Little formalization, bureaucratic	Much formalization (within divisions), bureaucratic	Little formalization—organic
Grouping	*	*	Functional and market	*	Functional and market
Unit size	*	*	*	*	Narrow throughout
Planning and control systems	*	Action planning	*	Much performance control	*
Liaison devices	Few liaison devices	Few liaison devices	Liaison devices in administration	Few liaison devices	Many liaison devices throughout
Decentralization	Centralization	Limited horizontal decentralization	Horizontal and vertical decentralization	Limited vertical decentralization	Selective decentralization
Functioning:					
Strategic apex	All administrative work	Fine tuning, coordination of functions, conflict resolution	External liaison, conflict resolution	Strategic portfolio, performance control	External liaison, conflict resolution, work balancing, project monitoring

Exhibit 8.A3 (continued)

	Simple Structure	Machine Bureaucracy	Professional Bureaucracy	Divisionalized Form	Adhocracy
Operating core	*	*	Skilled, standardized work with much individual autonomy	*	Truncated (in administrative adhocracy) or merged with administrative to do informal project work (in operating adhocracy)
Middle line	Insignificant	*	Controlled by professionals: much mutual adjustment	Formulation of division strategy, managing operations	Excessive but blurred with staff; involved in project work
Technostructure	None	*	Little	*	Small and blurred within middle in project work
Support staff	*	Often elaborated to reduce uncertainty	Elaborated to support professionals; machine bureaucracy structure	Split between HQ and divisions	Highly elaborate (in administrative adhocracy) but blurred within middle in project work.
Flow of authority	Significant from top	Significant throughout	Insignificant (except in support staff)	Significant throughout	Insignificant
Flow of regulated system	Insignificant	Significant throughout	Insignificant (except in support staff)	Significant throughout	Insignificant
Flow of informal communication	*	Discouraged	Significant in administration	Some between HQ and divisions	*
Work constellations	None	Insignificant, especially at lower levels	Some in administration	Insignificant	Significant throughout (especially in administrative adhocracy)
Flow of decision-making	Top down	Top down	Bottom up	Differentiated between HQ and divisions	Mixed, all levels

254

Exhibit 8.A3 (continued)

	Simple Structure	Machine Bureaucracy	Professional Bureaucracy	Divisionalized Form	Adhocracy
Situational Elements:					
Age and size	Typically young and small (first stage)	*	Varies	*	Typically young (operating adhocracy)
Technical system	*	*	*	*	Very sophisticated often automated (administrative adhocracy); regulating or sophisticated (operating adhocracy)
Environment	Dynamic Hostile	*	Complex	Especially products and services)	Complex and dynamic sometimes disparate (in administrative adhocracy)
Power	*	*	Professional operator control; fashionable	Middle-line control; fashionable (especially in industry)	Expert control; very fashionable

Note: * refers to the respective dimensions of the structure which are not synergistic with the requirements of new technology adoption.

Automated storage and retrieval systems and automated guided vehicles offer the flexibility and computer control compatibility that will be needed in the factory of the future.

Photo #1 *Source: Industrial Engineering*, July 1987, "Ergonomic Improvements Boost AS/RS Performance By Easing Physical Burden on Vital Human Element," by W. S. Winship and B. Mustafa Pulat, p. 39.

Photo #2 *Source: Industrial Engineering*, January 1986, "CIM and the Flexible Automated Factory of the Future," by Mikell P. Groover and John C. Wiginton, p. 74.

FMS in Action: FMS Corporation, Ordnance Division (Aiken, SC), flexible manufacturing system built by Cincinnati Milacron.

Photo #3 *Source: Manufacturing Engineering*, March 1987, "FMS: Too Much, Too Soon," p. 35.

FMS in Action: FMS with four machining centers in background, carts at left and to right of post, automatic work changer in foreground.

Photo #4 *Source: Industrial Engineering*, April 1988, "Installation of Flexible Manufacturing System Teaches Management Lessons in Integration, Labor, Cost, Benefits," by Jack Meredith, p. 20.

Chapter Nine

MANAGING CHANGE: INTEGRATING PEOPLE AND TECHNOLOGY

We need flexible, resourceful, resilient people
who can tolerate a lot of surprise and ambiguity.

Eric Trist

INTRODUCTION

In Chapter 7, we focused on the problem of justifying the new technology using traditional financial methods. We explained that these conventional techniques are to a large extent responsible for the relatively slow adoption of the new technology because they greatly underestimate its intangible benefits. However, even if firms are successful at justifying the new technology, they have won only half the battle in their efforts to benefit from it. Firms must also implement the new technology and integrate it successfully into the existing system in order to fully realize its benefits. The focus of this chapter is therefore on this very issue: the implementation and integration of the new technology.

This chapter focuses specifically on the managerial, human, and non-technical considerations involved in the implementation and integration of the new technology. It is these issues (rather than the technical concerns, which will be discussed in Chapter 12), that consistently appear in the literature as being the areas of greatest concern for firms implementing the new technology:

> The so-called high-tech age requires new levels of technical skills. But to cope with the changes evident in this high-tech world, the technical professionals have to be "high-touch" people, adept at communicating new concepts and at interacting with other individuals in all areas of an organization.
>
> Newspapers and technical publications keep reminding us that "everyone" has to become technically oriented. Still, our research indicates that the high-tech boom makes the development of people skills even more important.[1]

[1]Rosenbaum [1987], p. 107.

PREIMPLEMENTATION CONCERNS

Naturally, the successful adoption of the new technology requires the commitment and support of management. When justifying the technology, it is (top) management that in many cases must decide whether the intangible, strategic benefits of the technology warrant its adoption, even though the justification numbers do not show the desired return on investment. Similarly, it is management commitment that, to a large extent, influences the potential success of new technology implementation.

Goal Congruence

Management commitment, available financing, and technical expertise are sufficient to technically augment the adoption of the new technology. However, they will not guarantee strategic optimization, which is equally important. To elaborate, the decision to apply the new technology to the manufacturing process cannot be made in a vacuum. The needs of the system depend on the company's business goals, and the success of the chosen system depends on its ability to meet these needs. Corporate goals, and the manufacturing goals they define, must always be a fundamental consideration in any new technology application.

Project Champion and Project Sponsor

One of the six critical functions described in Chapter 4 as a prerequisite for successful innovation is the project champion. Experience has shown that the successful implementation of the new technology requires the presence of a project champion (Gerwin [1982], Meredith [1986b]). This usually means a senior manager at a fairly high level within the organization (typically a vice-president) who is willing to take the risks involved in adopting the technology, and who is dedicated and capable of selling the idea to others within the firm.

  The project champion role encompasses the overwhelming commitment that is required to push the project forward. In fact, in some cases the champion must be willing to risk his or her own position with the company in order to sell the idea to the rest of the organization. Unfortunately, as we noted in Chapter 7, short-term payback requirements can make this risk a reality for some managaers, as the following example shows:

> A manager of engineering in one Ontario manufacturer convinced senior management to invest in a CAD system and projected a 200 percent productivity improvement, meaning that the equipment would show a payback of two years. Two years after installation, this complex system was showing only a marginal productivity gain in terms of faster drawings by the operators. The manager was fired.[2]

[2]Beatty [1987b], p. 11.

Even with the wholehearted commitment of the champion, the project may still stall if he or she is not capable of securing the resources needed to complete various parts of the project—hence the need for a sponsor who can assure the required resources to move the project forward quickly and easily. In a practical sense, the alliance of the project champion and sponsor is crucial for the successful implementation of the new technology.

Planning for Action

Understanding the current situation is essential before attempting to implement the new technology. Prior to any decisive action, it is necessary for managers to ensure that the current operation is run effectively and efficiently to prevent the possibility of automating mistakes and to allow for a smooth transition to the new process and infrastructure.

Planning for the implementation of the new technology should be thorough and should encompass a relatively long time horizon to assure the stability of the new system.[3] The following example highlights the detrimental effects of poor or hasty planning:

> Some companies trained their employees up to six months before system installation and found that the operators forgot most of what they had learned while waiting for it to arrive. Others did not take the time and effort to customize their system and to build a parts library and therefore could not realize much of a productivity improvement. Top management at several other companies "forced" a system onto a department and pressed for quick returns, with the result that confusion and distrust set in at lower levels. Finally at some companies, middle managers enamored by CAD/CAM pressed for the "best" systems with all the latest bells and whistles, and then found that they had overbought and could not justify some of the equipment purchased.[4]

In short, the complex process of introducing a new technology necessitates a practical plan which focuses on employees' needs and deals with issues of concern to them. Key steps in this process are:

- Identify the target group.
- Locate and analyze the resistance to change.
- Assess actual ability to change.
- Assess capacity and resources to change.
- Assess perceived priority of change.

After the nature of the change is analyzed, the next phase involves specific planning. The principal procedures in this phase include:

[3]In practice, up to several years might be needed for the implementation of integrated systems.
[4]Beatty [1987b], pp. 25–26.

- Identify the division(s), section(s), and individuals involved in the change.
- Specify the extent of changes.
- Develop a change plan which embraces timing, communication methods, involvements of individuals, and responsibilities of individuals.

Generic project plans (see Exhibit 9.1) can be used to address the major considerations outlined above. However, as noted in Chapter 8, the infrastructure characteristics needed to support the technology must also be carefully considered.

Exhibit 9.1   The Project Plan Elements

1. Overview—A short summary of the objectives and scope of the project. Includes goals, managerial structure and milestones.
2. Objectives—Detailed statements of the goals, including profit and competitive aims as well as technical goals.
3. General Approach—Includes both managerial and technical approach, including any deviations from standard procedures. Technical approach relates the project to available technologies.
4. Contractual Aspects—Description of all reporting requirements, customer-supplied resources, liaison arrangements, advisory committees, project review and cancellation procedures, proprietary requirements, use of subcontractors, and the technical deliverables and their specifications and delivery schedule.
5. Schedules—Task schedules, with responsible signoffs, and milestone events.
6. Resources—Two parts: budgetary, consisting of capital and expense requirements by task, and cost monitoring and control procedures.
7. Personnel—Expected personnel requirements, including special skills, training required, recruiting problems expected, legal or policy restrictions, security clearances, and so forth. The needs are indexed to the project schedule.
8. Evaluation Procedures—The methods for monitoring, collecting, storing, and evaluating the project's progress.
9. Potential Problems—A description of the things that have a significant possibility of negatively affecting the project, such as weather, subcontractor default, technical requirements, and resource limitations.

Source: Meredith, *Industrial Engineering* magazine, May 1986. Copyright Institute of Industrial Engineers.

NONTECHNICAL FACTORS AFFECTING IMPLEMENTATION

There is growing recognition of two features of technological implementation (see Fournier [1986]), namely:

1. In most cases, technology is not deterministic; management should account for the uncertainties inherent in the process.
2. Many of the negative effects result from managers decisions for which other alternatives were available.

As indicated in Chapter 8, attention to the firm's support system is essential for successful adoption of the new technology. A key aspect of this support system is a well-balanced approach to the mix of people and machine, and the degree of human intervention. Consider the following example:

> After Quasar took over Motorola's failing plant, it was able to turn it into a success in the same product market using the same facility, equipment, and people. Clearly, what changed were the systems and procedures used to run the plant, not the technical elements.[5]

In many ways, the new technology is bringing with it the necessity for new workforce management practices. Walton [1985] compares traditional workforce strategies based on control with those structured around commitment (see Exhibit 9.2). A commitment approach to managing the work force is needed to implement the new technology successfully. "To realize the full potential of automation, leading-edge companies are integrating workers and technology in 'sociotechnical' systems that revolutionize the way work is organizaed and managed."[6] In the following section, we discuss important components of this approach. None of these appear stupendously innovative, but taken together, they make a big difference. We begin by stressing the role of culture in organizational structure.

Organizational Culture

Organizational culture refers to the set of beliefs and values that are shared by people within the organization. Organizational culture is often referred to as the soft side of a firm's organizational structure. It is to a large extent determined by communication systems, training, and labor-management relations.

Organizational culture can be instrumental in facilitating the implementation of technology. For example, if a company is to adopt new process monitoring and quality control technology successfully, it must first insure that everyone within the organization views quality as a number one priority. Furthermore, employees must also share a set of common values if a goal such as "the best quality" is to work. The following example describes an organizational culture set to support implementation of the new technology:

> Before beginning its U.S. operation in 1980, Nissan developed a set of commitments or goals. The very first goal they established was to build the highest quality vehicle sold in North America. Once that goal was set, Nissan decided to set out those common values that they knew everyone shared. Everyone in the company participated in the preparation of a one page statement which begins by saying that at Nissan, people are our most valued resources. At Nissan, an organizational culture has been fostered which gets people involved and has them committed to their work. Furthermore, all of the company's employees

[5]Adopted from Meredith [1986a], p. 68.
[6]Hoerr et al. [1986], p. 70.

Exhibit 9.2 Workforce Strategies

	Control	Transitional	Commitment
Job design principles	Individual attention limited to performing individual job	Scope of individual responsibility extended to upgrading system performance, via participation problem-solving groups in QWL, EI, and quality circle	Individual responsibility extended to upgrading system performance
	Job design deskills and fragments work and separates doing and thinking	No change in traditional job design or accountability	Job design enhances content of work, emphasizes whole task, and combines doing and thinking
	Accountability focused on individual		Frequent use of teams as basic accountable unit
	Fixed job definition		Flexible definition of duties, contingent on changing conditions
Performance expectations	Measured standards define minimum performance. Stability seen as desirable		Emphasis placed on higher, "stretch objectives," which tend to be dynamic and oriented to the marketplace
Management organization: structure, systems, and style	Structure tends to be layered, with top-down controls	No basic changes in approaches to structure, control, or authority	Flat organization structure with mutual influence systems
	Coordination and control rely on rules and procedures		Coordination and control based on shared goals, values, and traditions
	More emphasis on prerogatives and positional authority		Management emphasis on problem-solving and relevant information and expertise
	Status symbols distributed to reinforce hierarchy	A few visible symbols change	Minimum status differentials to deemphasize inherent hierarchy

264

Exhibit 9.2 (continued)

	Control	Transitional	Commitment
Compensation policies	Variable pay where feasible to provide individual incentive Individual pay geared to job evaluation In downturn, cuts concentrated on hourly payroll	Typically no basic changes in compensation concepts Equality of sacrifice among employee groups	Variable rewards to create equity and to reinforce group achievements; gain Individual pay linked to skills and mastery Equality of sacrifice
Employment assurances	Employees regarded as variable costs	Assurances that participation will not result in loss of job Extra effort to avoid layoffs	Assurances that participation will not result in loss of job High commitment to avoid or assist in reemployment Priority for training and retaining existing workforce
Employee voice policies	Employee input allowed on relatively narrow agenda. Attendant risks emphasized. Methods include open-door policy, attitude surveys, grievance procedures, and collective bargaining in some organizations.	Addition of limited, ad hoc consultation mechanisms; no change in corporate governance	Employee participation encouraged on wide range of issues; attendant benefits emphasized; new concepts of corporate governance
	Business information distributed on strictly defined "need to know" basis	Additional sharing of information	Business data shared widely
Labor-management relations	Adversarial labor relations: emphasis on interest conflict	Thawing of adversarial attitudes: joint sponsorship of QWL or EI; emphasis on common fate	Mutuality in labor relations; joint planning and problem-solving on expanded agenda Unions, management, and workers redefine their respective roles

Source: Reprinted by permission of the *Harvard Business Review.* An exhibit from "From Control to Commitment in the Workplaace" by Richard E. Walton (M/A 1985). Copyright © 1985 by the President and Fellows of Harvard College. All rights reserved.

find it even easier to adopt this philosophy knowing that they share a well-defined set of values with the other people that they work with.[7]

Establishing a common sense of what the company is all about is the first principle of what is called *participative management.* Nissan's participative management system involves most of the precepts of workforce management needed to implement the new technology effectively.

Labor-Management Relations

There is a difference in the flexibility offered by labor versus capital input utilization. Labor is much easier to divest in times of economic decline, or in a cyclical business. Machines, on the other hand, cannot be laid off. Similarly, the incremental cost relationship between the two resource inputs is ever changing.

Experience has shown that the potential success of a new technology implementation can be enhanced if labor-management relations are cooperative rather than adversarial in nature. In some cases, competitive pressures may force companies to implement the new technology in the face of adversarial labor-management relations. In these situations, management must resort to nonparticipative methods of technological change (these will be discussed later). However, if at all possible, management should strive to improve the relationship before attempting to implement the new technology. Improvements can be made through means such as open communication systems, employee participation programs, and positive employment continuity policies. In a new technology environment, management and unions will have to cooperate to find solutions to sensitive issues such as layoff policies and job classification categories. (Issues in industrial relations will be discussed further in Chapter 10.)

Communication Systems. Management ultimately decides on a proper strategy and course of action. This being the case, the responsibility to communicate plans for a technology introduction lies squarely on management's shoulders. Communication systems are an important means of securing employee commitment to the new technology implementation and creating the desired culture. Effective communication systems are characterized by open, two-way communication channels that allow for the sharing of a wide range of information.

To establish successful open communication, management should consider three, sometimes overlapping, objectives. These are:

1. Employees must understand and appreciate the company's competitive position, and more specifically, perceive and appreciate the need for the new technology.
2. Employees must recognize the objectives, capabilities, and limitations of the new technology as early as possible.

[7]Adapted from Runyon [1987].

3. Employees must become involved and participate early in the new technology adoption process.

Naturally, open communication implies that business information should be shared widely throughout the company, rather than being distributed solely on a need-to-know basis. The following exemplifies this point:

> At Perkins Engines Limited, the cornerstone of the company's communication process is the Team Brief—a monthly update of the current company business situation for employees by their immediate supervisor. The briefing includes facts on how the business performed in the previous month with regard to quality, output, and delivery, as well as an honest assessment of the market outlook for the three months ahead, and what is being done to secure improved sales. The brief is also a two-way process and constitutes a key vehicle for channeling employee views upward. From this realistic awareness of what Perkins has to deal with, employees are better able to understand the need to invest in the new technology to improve productivity and quality, and they are more willing to cooperate in making it happen with the knowledge that this is the way to secure and protect their own jobs.[8]

Management must communicate the competitive situation of the firm and the resulting need for the new technology. Experience has shown that employees must understand that in some cases the new technology, while affecting the level of employment, is a prerequisite for the continuity of the plant and the business as a whole.

Once employees are cognizant of the company's competitive position and the need to adopt the new technology, they should also be informed of the specific rationale, capabilities, and limitations of the technology being considered. That is, "...open discussion between management and employees about the uncertainties involved and the general direction to be taken will go far towards reducing anxieties."[9] For example:

> When Perkins decided to introduce a new robot assembly machine for cylinder heads, all of the operators who would be affected by the facility received a detailed briefing of the plan up to 18 months before the actual physical adoption of the new technology.[10]

Strong two-way communication motivates workers to provide valuable input to the appropriate selection and effective implementation of the new technology. It is the line workers who know best how the current process operates, where its inefficiencies are, and perhaps where it needs upgrading. Furthermore,

[8]Adapted from Towers [1986], pp. 14–15.
[9]Ashburn [1986], p. 100.
[10]Towers [1986], p. 15.

incorporating employee suggestions into the implementation process will help to promote a sense of ownership and commitment to the project among employees, thus minimizing resistance in later project phases. If employees participate in the successful implementation of a new technology, they will tend to be much more responsive to technological change in the future.

Employment Continuity and Employee Well-Being. Perhaps the most important issue of concern among workers is the potential reduction in the labor required in a new technology environment. To promote an atmosphere of cooperation, management must do its utmost to minimize the negative effects of any job reductions associated with the new technology adoption. In short, employees must appreciate management's intention in providing support for and considering their concerns. One option that has been suggested is for companies to offer employees an early retirement package as a nonthreatening way of reducing the size of the workforce. Other policies that have been utilized successfully to help minimize the negative effects of employment reductions due to the introduction of new technology include the following:[11]

1. Promoting and training solely from within the company
2. Retaining seniority rights in interplant transfers and providing moving allowances
3. Assigning employees for a 90-day trial at another plant with the opportunity to return to the original plant if no new niche is found
4. Offering full pay and benefits during retraining if employees were laid off because of technological change
5. Bringing subcontracted work into the plant
6. Understaffing strategically to reduce the likelihood of layoffs during business downturns
7. Slowing plant startup to reduce the likelihood of layoffs when a new plant reaches steady state

Finally, management must be committed to the general well-being of its employees. This practice should be incorporated into the firm's culture and its everyday functioning, and should not be restricted solely to those situations and areas which require a major change. If management shows a genuine concern for employees during routine operations, it will be much easier to gain their commitment in times of change. For example, at Nissan, an extensive fitness center and comprehensive health improvement plan contribute to employees' commitment to the company (Runyon [1987]).

Job Classification Categories. Several case studies have demonstrated that the new technology initiates a requirement for new relationships (worker

---

[11]Ashburn [1986], p. 99.

plus programmer versus worker plus foreman) and new ways of interacting (communicating cognitive notions rather than making decisions based on visual evaluations). The effectiveness of these new relationships will be largely determined by the methods used to classify jobs and the procedures established for ongoing relationships.

The broadening of job scope with the new technology leads to (or requires) a decrease in job classification categories: "A decrease in the number of job classifications was found at nearly every existing site that introduced new technology, and fewer classifications were seen at every greenfield site that could be compared with an existing, similar plant with conventional technology."[12] This reduction in job classifications and increased flexibility in work assignment requires the cooperation of the union before it can become a reality. Again, positive employee-management relations are a prerequisite for effective implementation of the new technology.

It should be noted that the widening scope of jobs with the new technology is not restricted to unskilled labor. The overlap between jobs that have traditionally been distinct spreads all the way from unskilled labor to maintenance, quality control, programming, design, and scheduling. Furthermore, it crosses the traditional line separating management and worker: "As manufacturing becomes integrated, the boundaries that have traditionally distinguished management and workforce functions will become more difficult to maintain."[13] This is another issue that must be resolved between management and unions.

Training and Selection Policies

Increased training and more stringent selection policies are necessary prerequisites for broadening the scope of the tasks and the autonomy associated with various jobs. Statistics show that in Japan, training is, on the average, about 30 times more than what it is in North America. However, there are some notable exceptions:

> General Motors highly automated front-axle plant located in Saginaw, Michigan, provdes an excellent example of the increased emphasis being placed on training and selection policies. The plant runs entirely by robots for part of each working day. It is operated by 38 hourly employees, all members of the United Auto Workers, who survived a stringent selection process. They have all been schooled in electronic, mechanical, and problem-solving skills and have more than a year of training before the plant began making axles.[14]

Overall, most training in North America has thus far been ". . . informal and of relatively short duration . . . where the new technologies changed high-level

[12]Ashburn [1986], p. 104.
[13]Ashburn [1986], p. 112.
[14]Adapted from Hoerr, Pollock, and Whiteside [1986], p. 73.

skills, companies seem to have opted for hiring new employees rather than retraining current ones."[15]

Due to the rapid change in technology, companies must establish continuous programs for their current employees:[16] "One compaany calculated that the occupational 'half-life' (the time in which one-half of a worker's knowledge and skills becomes obsolete) has declined from a range of seven to 14 years to three to five years."[17] Selection methods must also attempt to screen for employees who have the aptitude and desire to continuously upgrade and change skills.

Cost is usually cited as a major prohibitive factor for training blue-collar workers. Companies are often reluctant to invest large sums of money and resources[18] to train employees if they may be recruited by the competition. Other companies, however, in the interest of good labor-management relations and a positive corporate culture, do not hesitate to accept the expense of retraining their present workforce:

> Tektronix is an Oregon-based manufacturer of electronic equipment. As it tried to shift its traditional assembly-line workforce to a flexible manufacturing system four years ago, the company discovered that 20 percent of its production workers lacked rudimentary skills needed for the transition. Tektronix is solving its problem by contracting with nearby Portland Community College to run a remedial on-site program in basic math and English for its many non-English-speaking assemblers.[19]

In short, in the automation era, workers need lots of training to get started, and still more to stay employed.

Supervisor Training.   In concentrating on the training of line workers, firms sometimes overlook the importance of training supervisors. Foremen or supervisors may feel that their power and authority has been usurped if they do not receive any training. For example:

> When a pulp mill introduced a new computerized control room, vendor representatives trained the operators and their assistants. No similar effort was made with the foremen, who thought (with some justification) that they had lost control over the mill's operation. Some of the operators relinquished their novel power by tactfully educating their foreman, but others felt that they had earned the right to more autonomy because the foreman's knowledge was obsolete.[20]

[15]Economic Council of Canada [1987], p. 16.

[16]A recent study carried out by Bartel and Lichtenberg [1987] demonstrated a direct linkage between workers' education and training, and the newness of the technology being used.

[17]Walton and Susman [1987], p. 103.

[18]For example, it costs employers almost $100,000 to train a single tool and die maker (Roher [1988]).

[19]Richman [1988], p. 52.

[20]Leonard-Barton and Kraus [1985], p. 108.

One effective way to avoid such a situation is to train the supervisors as the experts on the new technology, and then have them train the workers. In some situations, job design changes may alter the relationship between workers and supervisors and thus change the focus of the supervisor training issue. In any event, implementers of the new technology must consider how supervisors will be trained and what role these supervisors will play in the training of workers.

Performance Appraisal and Compensation Policies

Walton [1985] outlines the difference between traditional (control) compensation policies and those which foster worker commitment (these were shown earlier in Exhibit 9.2). The increase in skill variety and the team approach to job design will make it much more difficult for management to judge, and thus reward, individual performance. Measured standards for work output will no longer be appropriate as the basis for employee evaluations and pay scales. Examples indicate that companies are dealing with this issue by (1) placing hourly workers on salary, (2) introducing profit sharing, gainsharing, and group incentive plans, and/or (3) developing pay-for-knowledge systems. The following is an example of the latter:

> One plant introducing new technology is in the process of replacing its standard job classification system with a pay-for-knowledge system. Fifty "work modules" have been developed, and employees are expected to learn them over a nine to 15 month period. Some of the modules are in the machining or assembly lines; others are in the tooling areas and material stores. Workers decide, with advice, what modules they will learn, and they develop plans for getting the training and experience they will need. The plant's long-term plan is to organize a much larger set of modules into levels of increasing pay and responsibility. The whole set will take several years to master.[21]

Perhaps an even more important consideration regarding employee compensation policies and their impact on long-term employee commitment is the issue of layoffs and pay cuts in the event of a business downturn (or as the result of a new technology adoption). Employee commitment can be more strongly secured if employees understand the negative effects of a business downturn. Cutting hourly wages and/or laying off hourly workers while maintaining (or increasing) management wages will undoubtedly have an adverse effect on employee commitment, even if higher management salaries are needed to attract talent. Management must not underestimate the relationship between commitment and equity in compensation policies.

---

[21]Walton and Susman [1987], p. 100.

MANAGING TECHNOLOGICAL CHANGE

People are affected in different ways by change. A change as significant as the one resulting from the implementation of the new technology can have a very consequential impact on the people within the organization. Therefore, technological change must be managed carefully and thoughtfully. In this section, we will address various strategies that can be used to implement a technological change.

Resistance to Change

With a firm, resistance to change can be considered at two levels: employees and management.

Employee Resistance.   New technology will affect people psychologically through alterations of job design and social interaction, as well as by the possibility of layoffs. This added pressure could be alarming to employees and could stimulate resistance to change. At the individual level, the new technology will affect people psychologically through alterations of job design and social interaction. The implications could be positive or negative, as summarized in Exhibit 9.3. The psychological changes may involve perceptions as well as realities, apprehensions, and uncertainty; and uncertainty is a source of anxiety, a major factor in job stress. These factors, as mentioned earlier, necessitate increased levels of participation and communication during the implementation process.

Proper job design should address employee fears and uncertainties. As Fournier [1986] notes, technological threats to workers include: deskilling, polarization, time pressures, uncertainties, being tied to the machine, isolation, loss of social interaction, job transfer, boredom, new accountability (including electronic surveillance), safety, mental hazards, and new demands in the form of a shift from physical manipulation skills based on visual and tactile inspection to conceptual, complex perceptual and communication skills. Consider the following case in point describing one company that did not fully realize how the implementation of the new technology would have a negative impact on job design:

> One company implemented a series of robots (called the Robogate system) which performed unpleasant welding operations. However, most of the 100-odd workers who remained on the new system disliked it because they were now tied to the line and could not work at their own pace. Furthermore, because the welding operation was now directly part of the assembly operation, there was trememdous pressure on the maintenance staff to keep Robogate up and running (or else the whole assembly process would shut down). In fact, welding-repair supervisors had an annual turnover rate of 150 percent in the first several years of operation.[22]

[22]Adapted from Shaiken [1985], pp. 22–23.

Exhibit 9.3 Effects of Technological Change on Psycho-Social Characteristics of Employees

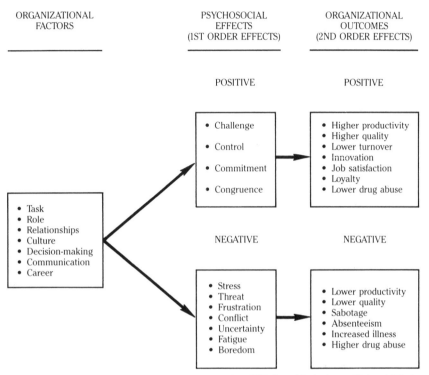

Source: Younge, *Industrial Engineering* magazine, November 1987. Copyright Institute of Industrial Engineers.

Research has shown that there is a link between personality types and approaches to change. Extrapolation of the data suggest that workers who are compliant, dependent, and risk-averse will have difficulty in circumstances where the nature of technological change is revolutionary. Conversely, while such workers may have an easier time with evolutionary change, slow change is likely to be frustrating to workers who are more aggressive, autonomous, adventurous, and change-seeking. The personalities of workers may have significant effects on their desire and ability to absorb or resist technological changes. Recruitment, selection, and training methods can be used by management to ensure that worker personality types match the technological needs of the company.

Middle Management Resistance. As we discussed in Chapter 8, new technology adoption suggests a flatter organization, which inevitably leads to a decreasing number of middle managers and supervisors. Thus, managers may also resist the implementation of the new technology. Companies must address this issue and ensure that middle managers have been attracted to the proposed changes before implementation is to start. Otherwise, the organization is faced with what is described as "frozen middle."

Leonard-Barton and Kraus [1985] use the term "hedgers" to describe managers who refuse to take a stand (either for or against) the adoption of the new technology. These managers are risk-averse and will not commit one way or the other to the technology until they receive signals telling them which way to go. Implementation of the new technology can be successful by ensuring that hedgers are on the company side before the process begins. This can best be done by signalling to hedgers that the company as a whole is embracing the change. Policy notices from top management, a strong operational interest in some objective the technology is to provide (such as quality), and changing performance measurement criteria can all be used to signal the hedgers that the company is fully behind the new technology adoption and that they too should support the technology.

Popp [1988] has identified eight personality types typically encountered in organizations. We have classified the eight into two groups: those who help to promote change, and those who inhibit change (see Exhibit 9.4). Again, recruitment and selection policies can be used to bring in personality types which are desirable, and various organizational change strategies, which will be discussesd shortly, can be used to convert inhibitors into promoters.

Exhibit 9.4 Organizational Personality Types

Promoters	Inhibitors
Participants—people who recognize their responsibility to the success of the project and the profitability of the company.	Spectators—people content with the scenic route and unimpressed with "newfangled" ways.
Movers—people who remove obstacles when they "bump" into them.	Protectors—people who are concerned with their kingdoms and the anticipated loss thereof.
Shakers—people who recognize an opportunity and will make it happen.	Doubters—people who are unsure of the adaptation of the new system to their "unique" company.
	Worriers—people who are afraid of the hardware and ignorant of the software.
	Switchers—people who delegate their own responsibilities.

Source: The terms used are adapted from Popp [1988], p. 46.

Strategies for Change

Our discussion of the implementation of the new technology has centered around the principles of communication, participation, and trust. However, it is possible that adversarial labor-management relations and employee resistance may make a strategy based on these principles inappropriate. This is especially true if management is faced with significant pressures (competition, customer requests to automate) to implement the new technology as quickly as possible. From a practical point of view, different situations demand a specific approach which may not work as effectively in other circumstances. In general, however, nonparticipative methods of implementing the new technology are very risky, and should be utilized only if it is deemed impossible to pursue employee education, communication, and participation. Exhibit 9.5 provides a comprehensive framework describing the sources of pressure for change, the sources of resistance to change, and how to deal with them to implement the new technology successfully. Exhibit 9.6 elaborates on some of the vehicles available to deal with resistance in the implementation process.

Pascale and Athos [1981] partially explain the differing levels of performance between North American and Japanese industry through the 7–S model. They posit that North American industry is similar to Japan on the hardball S's—strategy, structure, and systems. However, on the softball S's (skills, style, staff, and superinordinate goals), there exists a wide disparity between North American and Japanese management techniques. In general, the Japanese philosophy is geared toward process-oriented thinking, while in North America, the empahsis is on the result-oriented approach. More specifically, process-

Exhibit 9.5 Implementing Technological Change within Organizations

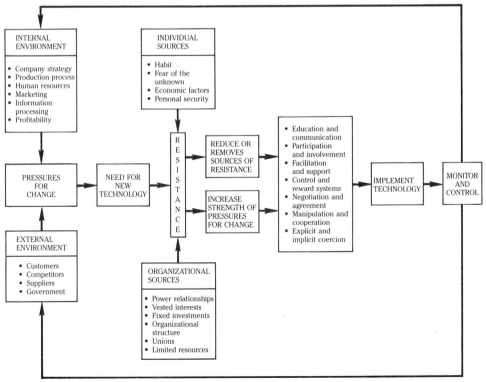

See Exhibit 9.6 for an elaboration on these methods for dealing with resistance.

Exhibit 9.6 Methods for Dealing with Resistance to Change

Approach	Commonly Used in Situations	Advantages	Drawbacks
Education + Communication	Where there is a lack of information or inaccurate information and analysis.	Once persuaded, people will often help with the implementation of the change.	Can be very time-consuming if lots of people are involved.
Participation + Involvement	Where the initiators do not have all the information they need to design the change, and where others have considerable power to resist.	People who participate will be committed to implementing change, and any relevant information they have will be integrated into the change plan.	Can be very time-consuming if participators design an inappropriate change.
Facilitation + Support	Where people are resisting because of adjustment problems.	No other approach works as well with adjustment problems.	Can be time-consuming, expensive, and still fail.
Negotiation + Agreement	Where someone or some group will clearly lose out in a change, and where that group has considerable power to resist.	Sometimes it is a relatively easy way to avoid major resistance.	Can be too expensive in many cases if it alerts others to negotiate for compliance.
Manipulation + Co-optation	Where other tactics will not work, or are too expensive.	It can be a relatively quick and inexpensive solution to resistance problems.	Can lead to future problems if people feel manipulated.
Explicit + Implicit Coercion	Where speed is essential, and the change initiators possess considerable power.	It is speedy, and can overcome any kind of resistance.	Can be risky if it leaves people mad at the initiators.

Source: Reprinted by permission of the *Harvard Business Review.* An exhibit from "Choosing Strategies for Change" by John P. Kotter and Leonard A. Schlesinger (March/April 1979). Copyright © 1979 by the President and Fellows of Harvard College. All rights reserved.

oriented (PO) thinking calls for a longer-term outlook, while result-oriented (RO) thinking is directed at short-term outcomes. In the context of our discussion, RO is "...a legacy of the mass-production society and...the PO criteria are gaining momentum in the post-industrial, high-tech, high-touch society."[23] A PO manager, on the other hand, is people-oriented and emphasizes nontechnical factors such as communication, training, team approach, and morale building. In short, adopting management practices based on softball S's requires a fundamental shift in management style from one based on legitimate power and control to one based on trust and commitment.

A Proper Management Style. Bibeault [1982] lists a variety of causes of implementation failure originating with managers. These include:

Incompetence	Lack of management depth
Narrow vision	Institutionalized contentment
Short-term control	Low tolerance for criticism
No big picture	Lack of attention to detail
Omission errors	Lack of information base
Ignorance of external environment	Lack of information control

Another important reason for new technology implementation failures is the fact that many managers simply do not understand important aspects of the technology that is being adopted.

Ironically, one of the major objectives of technological change is flexibility. However, many of the decisions management makes, particularly in the job design and social systems areas, undermine the long-term flexibility objective by emphasizing short-term goals such as the minimization of labor input costs. Furthermore, as Gerwin [1982] explains, firms must do whatever they can to ensure that the flexibility of CAM (or the new technology in general) does not make it indispensable to the production process. If firms design products that can be produced solely on CAM equipment, they will find themselves surprisingly inflexible if their equipment breaks down or if they have to subcontract work.

A proper management style pays paramount attention to the flexibility objective and has the following characteristics:[24]

1. More clarity and communication of goals.
2. Reduction of uncertainty where possible, but necessary resistance to enshrinement of "one best way" through rigidity and inflexibility.
3. Reward systems that encourage flexibility and innovation.
4. An increased emphasis on a problem-solving orientation.

[23]Imai [1986], p. 18.
[24]Fournier [1986], pp. 421–422.

5. Commitment to a developmental view of human resources.
6. Climate of trust and openness.
7. An emphasis on team playing to maximize total organizational effectiveness.

A successful introduction of the new technology requires the integration of both top-down (design) and bottom-up (analytical) management approaches. In the implementation of the new technology, managers can have significant influence in terms of retraining commitment to current workforces, identification of appropriate manpower pools, and the role of the union and job security.

The goal of any implementation should be to bring the new system on line smoothly, to minimize any period of underrealization of the benefits of the new technology, and to maximize the rewards. Exhibit 9.7 shows graphically

Exhibit 9.7   The Goal of Implementation Management

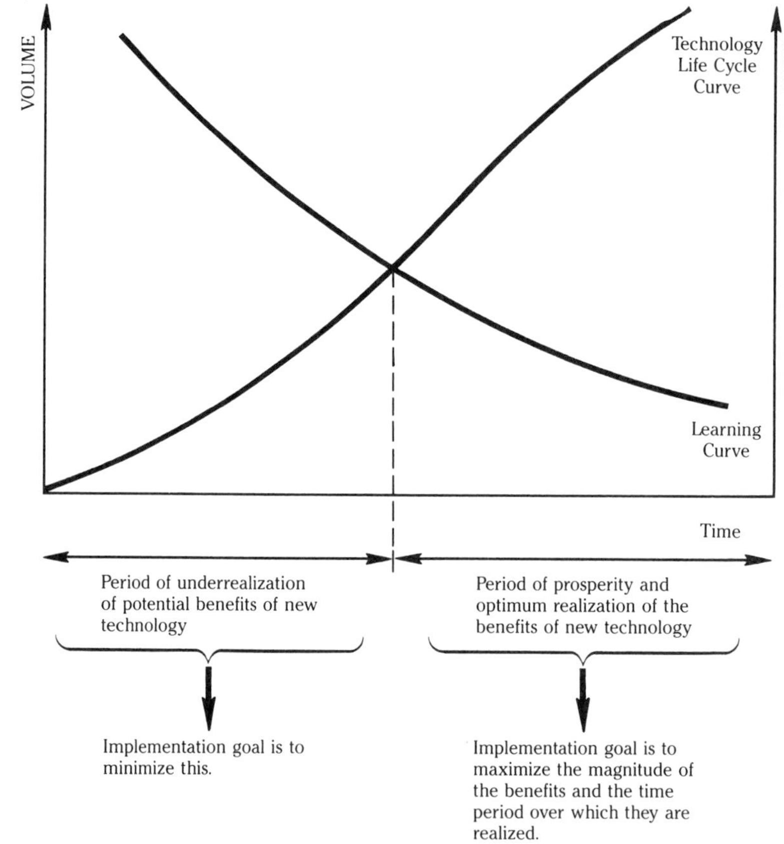

NOTE: Proper implementation management will accelerate the pace of learning (increase the slope of the learning curve), and accelerate the realization of technology benefits (increase the slope of the technology life cycle curve). Therefore the two curves will intersect earlier, and diverge faster after intersection. Thus both the implementation goals noted above will be simultaneously realized.

and explains clearly how proper change and implementation can fulfill all three goals.

Skill Level and Task Allocation

In Chapter 3 we discussed the notion of product complexity and noted that the multiplicative effect of changes in the complexity of products suggests that: (a) the number of microdecisions is increasing, and (b) the percentage of such decisions by machines (and not by humans) is expanding. A study recently carried out at GM's truck plant confirmed this point:

> The most startling result is that the total number of decisions (related to vehicle body welding operations) more than doubled, while number of machine decisions increased almost tenfold. . .and the number of human decisions declined by two-thirds.[25]

With the adoption of the new technology, management must choose whether to upgrade or downgrade the skill level of employees (Walton and Susman [1987]). This problem is complicated by the fact that not all employees perceive similar jobs in the same way. Downgrading assumes that middle managers will deal with all serious problems, leaving the workers to perform only simple tasks. Therefore, they have a lower skill level, are paid less, are easier to monitor and control, and ultimately are easier to replace as well. The risks and costs of downgrading include the following:

1. Costs more to pay middle managers.
2. Low skilled workers may not recognize a problem causing serious repercussions down the line.
3. The connection is cut between those who should recognize the problem and those who solve it.
4. Undermines labor-management relations.
5. Downgraded workers may not care as much.

Upgrading is the process of giving more operating and maintenance responsibility to workers. In practice, the new technology has inspired many companies to replace rigid, narrow jobs with broader ones to motivate workers and to enhance the flexibility of their operations (Walton and Susman [1987]). From a worker's perspective, the jobs and training associated with the new technology are generally perceived to be more attractive, and the skills acquired more marketable, than the jobs they replace (Ashburn [1986]). The following example speaks to the advantage of upgrading skill levels:

---

[25]Ayres [1986], p. 20.

The new technology installed at Frost, Inc. might, in some installations, require only a "button pusher" to operate. However, Frost has taken a different approach. The operators of the technology (called machine cell supervisors) can do everything from programming to maintenance and repair. Eventually, they will be skilled enough to trouble-shoot the printed circuit boards in the machines.[26]

Hackman and Oldham [1976] define five upgrading principles that contribute to employee motivation:

1. Skill variety—doing different activities, using a variety of skills
2. Task identity—completing a whole task rather than fragmenting the job
3. Task significance—understanding the importance of the job to the organization
4. Autonomy—freedom and discretion in how the work is done
5. Feedback—current and specific information about performance

Again, several case studies have demonstrated that companies successful in implementing the new technology tend to incorporate some or all of these principles. Perhaps the most obvious change has to do with the expansion of skill variety and task identity in new technology jobs. For example, workers might now perform a wide range of tasks, including:[27]

1. Routine machine maintenance and service: greasing chucks, oiling machines, maintaining coolant conditions, and performing housekeeping tasks
2. Increased responsibility for quality: in-process inspection and statistical process control, with emphasis on prevention of discrepancies instead of detection after the fact
3. Simple trouble-shooting and debugging
4. Simple machine programming
5. Tool grinding and repair
6. Inreased decision-making on scheduling and machine utilization

Obviously, these changes require a shift in management attitude. That is, workers must now be seen as having the aptitude and desire to contribute more fully than was previously expected. Furthermore, the culture of the organization must encourage employees to contribute, learn, and develop as individuals.

The Operator Midwife Approach. In practice, companies have taken different approaches to this job allocation issue. According to Wall [1986], the majority of firms, conscious of the extent of their investment in the new technology, have taken the safe way out. They have placed responsibility for utilization of the technology in the hands of specialists such as programmers

---

[26]Adapted from Witt [1985], pp. 90–91.
[27]Ashburn [1986], p. 106.

and tool-setters to the ". . . extent that these specialists function as an integral part of the production process."[28] Here the operator's most important role is to act as a warning system for the specialist. Put simply, the operator supervises production and calls for expert help whenever the technology deviates from normal performance. This is roughly equivalent to operator downgrading. Specialists deal with all the problems that arise, and thus effectively control system performance. Wall calls this the *operator monitor* approach.

A few organizations have taken a different approach. They have placed much more responsibility in the hands of operators, who are trained in various aspects of operations and support. This approach more closely approximates operator upgrading. In this case, the specialists deal with more unusual problems which fall outside the competence of the operators to rectify. Specialists are fewer in number, and a greater proportion of their time is spent on development and problem-solving work. Wall [1986] calls this the *operator midwife* approach. In this case, ". . . the operator's job is one of managing the technology . . . under normal circumstances, and calling for specialist advice when pathologies arise."[29] Exhibit 9.8 highlights the differences between the two approaches.

Exhibit 9.8   Main Features of Monitor and Midwife Approaches

	Operator Monitor Approach	Operator Midwife Approach
Logic	Expensive technology needs managing and controlling by different specialists (who support several machines).	Expensive technology needs dedicated expert generalist to solve problems at source.
Emphasis	Division of labor, centralized control through specialists.	Localized responsibility and expertise, devolved control with support specialists.
Roles	Machine-setters	No machine-setters
	Tool-setters	No tool-setters
	More programmers (write, prove-out and edit programs).	Fewer programmers (writing only).
	More engineers (electrical, electronic, mechanical, and so forth)	Fewer engineers (no routine maintenance).
	Operators who: mind macihnes and call for help when required.	Operators who: set machine, tool-set, prove out tapes, do edits, write simple programs and do routine maintenance.
Costs	Higher indirect labor costs and lower operator satisfaction and motivation, problems of coordination.	Higher direct labor costs, higher operator recruitment and training costs, less well controlled disciplines.
Benefits	Lower direct labor costs, lower operator training and recruitment costs, tight disciplines.	Lower indirect labor costs, higher operator motivation and satisfaction.

Source: Wall [1986], p. 315.

[28]Wall [1986], p. 311.
[29]Wall [1986], p. 312.

There are many reasons for the emergence of these alternative approaches. To some extent, they reflect differences in management styles and philosophies, skill levels among operators, and demarcation lines among existing groups of employees. Research done by Wall [1986] has shown that "... with systems which require frequent intervention, the operator midwife approach leads to better utilization. With systems requiring infrequent interventions the operator monitor approach is at least as effective."[30]

Team Approaches. A team approach to work design can be a practical means of training employees at a variety of tasks. It can also be used to increase the skill variety, task identity, task significance, and autonomy of a job, and hence increase the commitment of workers to their jobs. Last, it seems that in many cases, organizing and performing complete jobs in teams is the most productive way of getting a job done. For example:

> In the early 1980s, Shenandoah Life Insurance Co....installed a $2 million system to computerize processing and claims operations at its Roanoke (Va.) headquarters. But the results were disappointing. It still took 27 working days—and handling by 32 clerks in three departments—to process a typical application for a policy conversion.
>
> Shenandoah's problem stemmed from its bureaucratic maze, not from defects in the technology. Only by radically reorganizing its work system could it reap the benefits of automation. The company grouped the clerks in "semiautonomous" teams of five to seven members. Each team now performs all the functions that once were spread over three departments. Team members learned new skills, bringing them greater job satisfaction—and better pay. As a result, the typical case-handling time dropped to two days, and service complaints were practically eliminated. By 1986, Shenandoah was processing 50 percent more applications and queries with 10 percent fewer employees than it did in 1980.[31]

Dispatching and Integrating the Technology

Another important question deals with the timing of the introduction of new technology. Based on the competitive advantage of the company, new technology can be adopted quickly or slowly; although the terms quickly and slowly are difficult to define in absolute terms. There are competitive benefits and risks associated with each of these strategic options. Exhibit 9.9 illustrates the benefits and the risks of slow and quick adoption.

Clearly, the decision whether to adopt slowly (piecemeal or staged approach) or quickly (big bang approach) is tied to overall corporate and industry

[30]Wall [1986], p. 317.
[31]Hoerr et al. [1986], p. 70.

Exhibit 9.9   The Benefits and the Risks of Slow and Quick Adoption

Characteristics	Adoption Strategy	
	Slow (Staged)	*Quick (Big Bang)*
Benefits	Employees have more time to adapt, which may lead to greater acceptance.	Gain competitive advantage.
	Can get on further down the learning curve.	One compatible system throughout the organization—finance, marketing, and so forth, as well as manufacturing.
	Lower up-front capital requirements.	More commitment.
	The technology has a change to be tested and proven by competitors.	Derive full benefits from life cycle of technology when investing in the leading edge.
	Suppliers can provide the technology at lower prices and higher service levels.	
	Time is available for the strategic assessment of large-scale new technology.	Employees may learn together under pressure.
Risks	Loss of competitive advantage.	Bugs may crop up in new systems.
	Double spending on old and new technology.	Less time for adoption of the technology.
	Less commitment when not betting the shop.	Suppliers may not adapt quickly enough—for example, they may not be able to meet JIT needs.
	May never catch up with technology—always one generation behind.	Leading edge technology may become obsolete sooner.
	Islands of automation may be incompatible.	Much heavier up-front capital commitment.
		Starting high up the learning curve—company pays for the learning curve for the entire industry.
		May have to halt operations while implementing the technology.

norms and strategies. It is also dependent upon the particular firm's experience with the technology (a firm with no experience may be forced to adopt the technology slowly), and the extent of operator training, the resistance of personnel, and the simple economics of the alternate methods.

Related to the timing question is the issue of integration and combination of tasks within the operating components. Depending on the extensiveness of the task involved, the following aspects may be dominant (see Tompkins [1984]):

- Manufacturing Equipment: The task is to combine different manufacturing processes into appropriate and responsive machining centers.
- Material Handling Equipment: The objective is to design uniform interfaces among different handling components such as between AGVS and AS/RS (see Chapter 2).
- Computer Control System: The aim is to develop a network of some kind (such as MAP as discussed in Chapter 2) to allow for integration of computer control equipment.

The integration of manufacturing equipment, material handling equipment, and the computer control system in confined areas is referred to as islands of automation or island solutions. The challenge is to integrate and link these islands; this is the notion behind the factory-of-the-future concept and CIM. One approach to a successful implementation and integration of technology reported extensively in the literature deals with the notion of simplification. Thurwatcher [1986] calls this SIM, simplified integrated manufacturing: "As a byword for an operational strategy (for the 1980s), SIM provides a more appropriate emphasis on where the true benefit of integration lies."[32] Consider the following:

> When machine tool maker Yamazaki Mazak set about automating its Minokamo plant, one of the first steps was to lay out every part and every tool used in the current process on two huge tables. Plant engineers were told to walk through this vast array of hardware and justify why each item was needed. Result: the number of tools were reduced from 672 to 46, all but six of which had multiple users.[33]

In short, for implementation to be successful, it is necessary to deal with the degree and extent of integration well in advance and have employees involved from the beginning.

Ideas for Action

Many studies have discussed the key success factors for implementing new technologies. For years, theorists have promoted the need for a fit between an organization's social systems and its technical systems—this notion is referred to as sociotechnical systems.[34] In short, the sociotechnical approach has strong theoretical merit.

To better comprehend the issue involved in implementation, we can summarize the stages required in the implementation process in a matrix similar to Exhibit 9.10. In this matrix, it is important to note that the implementation steps, predelivery, delivery and installation, full use, and postevaluation, correspond to basic managerial tasks from planning to analysis and involve a variety of issues from structure to strategy.

Research has shown that successful companies usually adopt a proactive approach to implementing technology. This involves recognizing training needs and employees' concerns well in advance and formulating an appropriate course

---

[32]Thurwatcher [1986], p. 74.

[33]Brody [1986], p. 20.

[34]Classical studies by Woodward [1958], Burns and Stalker [1961], and Thompson [1967] among others have all indicated the importance of the sociotechnical fit for successful implementation of technology.

Exhibit 9.10   An Analogy Between Implementation Steps and Basic Structure ⟷ Strategy Issues

Implementation Steps	Primary Issues			
	Structural	*Technical*	*Behavioral*	*Strategic*
Predelivery	*			
Delivery & Installation		*		
Full Use			*	
Postevaluation				*

of action. This proactive approach can help to increase the benefits of automation by allowing the firm to gain valuable experience and knowledge in the management of the new technology. It is very important that the managers realize the effects of the new technology on functional areas and consider adopting a *systems integration* view. This means consideration should be given to a collective way of accounting for all the resources available to fulfill the company's objectives.

Shunk and Filley [1986] suggest some prerequisites for the successful introduction of systems integration into a firm's corporate culture. These include:

1. Recognizing that a vision is needed—a longer-term vision!
2. Start small and be subtle—don't change things overnight!
3. Recognize that people, not technologies, are the key to success.
4. Make systems integration an interdisciplinary team effort.

The literature emphasizes the need for the implementation manager to conduct a pilot operation before introducing an innovation in a firm. The reason for this is twofold. First, the pilot operation will serve as an experiment, as well as proving technical feasibility to top management. Second, the pilot operation will serve as a credible demonstration model for other units in the company.

It should be noted that more than one person can assume responsibility in more than one function. The most important fact to note, however, is that one of these individuals *must* have the organizational power to mobilize the necessary resources in order to make implementation a success. Other key areas which must be addressed by management in order to ensure successful implementation of the new technology are summarized in Exhibit 9.11. A critical factor for successful implementation of the new technology is for management to consider explicitly the human element in the production process. Incorporation of these human factors in system design and implementation will not eliminate all operational difficulties, but it will certainly reduce them substantially.

Exhibit 9.11 Key Areas of Concern for the Successful Implementation of the New Technology

- Anticipating opposition to the innovation (that is, loss of control and/or unclear benefits for the workers) and devising plans to deal with it. The firm must keep in mind that the more visible the costs of an innovation, the greater the importance of making potential benefits and rewards apparent.
- Making sure that upper management is technically oriented to the point that they know the system and can confidently explain it to someone else. This also includes a thorough understanding of the costs and benefits (tangible and intangible) involved. Having upper management that is not technically oriented can be a critical factor in the failure of a technical system. This stresses the need for retraining and education. That is, firms should not rely solely on the knowledge and technical expertise of vendors when implementing new technology.
- Likewise, technical managers must be able to communicate well with the other people in the organization. If these people do not have the ability to explain, communicate, and convince, the probability of a successful implementation will be quite small.
- Where would the technology be located? In isolation at a greenfield site or within the old site and closely linked with other processes? Finance is the most common constraint which affects this choice. A greenfield site can be beneficial as the firm is introducing new working practices with new labor. However, linking the innovation with the other processes in the firm offers a promising benefit— integration. Apart from the financial situation of the firm, the choice is up to the company.
- How should the technology be installed? Management is faced with the staged versus big bang approach dilemma. Although the big bang approach offers the benefit of instant readiness, the staged approach appears to be more popular. Many firms prefer using this approach due to the size of the project and the constraint on resources (both financial and people). An added benefit of the staged approach is that it allows for the learning process to occur.
- Introducing the workforce to the new technology early in the process is of great importance in successful implementation. In practice, some companies have considered it essential to have members of the workforce present at every meeting on the subject, and on the project team itself.

CONCLUDING OBSERVATIONS

This chapter focused specifically on the managerial, human, and nontechnical considerations involved in the implementation and integration of the new technology. Weir [1984] notes that there can be confusion between *what a company needs to do* and *what it is capable of doing* to accomplish implementation. There are also complications regarding *what it perceives its needs to be* and *what it wants to do*. The less overlap among these four, the greater the problems will be.

At a minimum, companies contemplating technological change need to be sure of the following:

1. That the project has the support of top management
2. That the organizational culture and labor-management relations of the firm are conducive to implementation. This involves the creation of a commitment to the change from everyone in the company

3. That a conscious decision regarding job designs has been made, including consideration of skill levels, job classification categories, and possible team approaches

4. That the training needs of the firm, including supervisor training, have been fully addressed

5. That the possibility of employee resistance (and middle management resistance) to the change has been considered and strategies to overcome this resistance have been developed

6. That a decision on the method of implementation (slow versus quick) has been made and that the implications of this decision are fully understood

7. That the implementation decision is not treated solely as a capital equipment purchase affecting only manufacturing, but as a business decision that would have a fundamental impact on the nature of the entire firm

RECOMMENDED READINGS

ASHBURN, A. [1986]. "People and Automation." *American Machinist and Automated Manufacturing,* June, pp. 97–112.
LEONARD-BARTON, D., and W. A. KRAUS [1985]. "Implementing New Technology. *Harvard Business Review,* November–December, pp. 102–110.

DISCUSSION QUESTIONS

1. One rather radical idea for fostering cooperation between management and labor is to give workers the right to veto any technological change. That is, make management responsible for convincing workers that it is in their interest to adopt new technology. Comment.

2. Should firms ever attempt to implement the new technology into an organization characterized by a poor organizational culture and adversarial labor-management relations? Could a firm be successful implementing the new technology in this environment? If so, how? Explain fully.

3. Develop a model which would help managers to plan for the implementation of the new technology.

4. Is participative management always the best approach to use when implementing the new technology?

5. Participative management practices include informing employees about the company's strategy, its plans to adopt technology, and so forth. How much do employees really have to know? Is there any danger of telling them too much?

6. Your company has 25 CNC machines. You can operate these machines with the same costs in one of two ways:

   Alternative 1: Hire three programmers to do all the programming for the machines and 25 button pushers to operate the machines.

   Alternative 2: Train all employees to program their own machines.

   Which approach would you choose? Why? Suppose it costs more for Alternative 1 than Alternative 2? Suppose it costs less?

7. How does a company deal with middle management cutbacks when adopting the new technology? Does it address this issue in the same manner as it addresses hourly workforce cutbacks?

REFERENCE AND BIBLIOGRAPHY

AYRES, R. [1986]. "Computer-Integrated Manufacturing and the Next Industrial Revolution." In J. Dermer, (ed.), *Competitiveness Through Technology*, Lexington Books, Lexington, Mass., pp. 11, 24.

ASHBURN, A. [1986]. "People and Automation." *American Machinist and Automated Manufacturing*, June, pp. 97–112.

BARTEL, A. P., and F. R. LICHTENBERG [1987]. "The Comparative Advantages of Educated Workers in Implementing New Technology." *The Review of Economics and Statistics*, Volume LXIX, No. 1, Feburary, pp. 1–11.

BEATTY, C. A. [1987]. *The Implementation of Technological Change*. The Industrial Relations Center, Queens University at Kingston.

BEATTY, C. A. [1987b]. "Organizational Barriers to the Implementation of CAD/CAM." National Center for Management Research and Development. The University of Western Ontario, Working Paper Series No. NC 87–17, August.

BIBEAULT, D. B. [1982]. *Corporate Turnaround*. McGraw-Hill, New York.

BRODY, H. [1986]. "Good Is Never Enough." *High Technology*, August, pp. 20–21.

BURNS, T., and G. M. STALKER [1961]. *The Management of Innovation*. Tavistock Press, London.

Economic Council of Canada [1987]. *Making Technology Work: Innovation and Jobs in Canada*. Minister of Supply and Services Canada.

FOURNIER, B. [1986]. "Non-Technical Factors Affecting the Effectiveness of Implementing Change. In H. Noori (ed.), *The Proceedings of Technology Canada Conference, REMAT*. WLU, Waterloo, May 21–22, pp. 311–323.

GERWIN, D. [1982]. "Do's and Don'ts of Computerized Manufacturing." *Harvard Business Review*, March–April, pp. 107–116.

HACKMAN, J. R., and G. R. OLDHAM [1976]. "Motivation Through the Design of Work: Test of a Theory." *Organizational Behavior and Human Performance*. Chicago, The Academy Press.

HOERR, J., M. A. POLLOCK, and D. E. WHITESIDE [1986]. "Management Discovers the Human Side of Automation." *Business Week*, September 29, pp. 70–75.

IMAI, M. [1986]. *Kaizen: The Key to Japan's Competitive Success*. Random House Business Division, New York.

KOTTER, J. P., and L. A. SCHLESINGER [1979]. "Choosing Strategies for Change." *Harvard Business Review*, March–April, pp. 106–114.

LEONARD-BARTON, D., and W. A. KRAUS [1985]. "Implementing New Technology." *Harvard Business Review*, November–December, pp. 102–110.

LIMPRECHT, J. A., and R. H. HAYES [1982]. "Germany's World Class Manufacturers." *Harvard Business Review*, November–December, pp. 137–145.

MEREDITH, J. [1986a]. "Automation Strategy Must Give Careful Attention to the Firm's Infrastructure." *Industrial Engineering*, May, pp. 68–73.

MEREDITH, J. [1986b]. "Strategic Planning for Factory Automation by the Championing Process." In J. Meredith (ed.), *Justifying New Manufacturing Technology*. Industrial Engineering and Management Press, pp. 273–281.

PASCALE, R. T., and A. G. ATHOS [1981]. *The Art of Japanese Management*. Warner Books, New York, p. 326.

POPP, R. J. [1988]. "The Development of Manufacturing Management Methods." *P&IM Review*, January, pp. 45–46.

RICHMAN, L. S. [1988]. "Tomorrow's Jobs: Plentiful, But . . . ." *Fortune*, April 11, pp. 42–56.

ROHER, E. [1988]. "Singing the Blue-Collar Blues." *The Globe and Mail*, Monday, March 14, p. A7.

ROSENBAUM, B. L. [1987]. "You'll Have to Show 'Em How to Make it Work." *Research & Development*, May, pp. 104–107.

RUNYON, M. [1987]. President and C.E.O., Nissan Motor Manufacturing Co., Keynote Speech, IIE Integrated Systems Conference, Nashville, November 5–7.

SHAIKEN, H. [1985]. "The Automated Factory: The View From the Shop Floor." *Technology Review*, January, pp. 17–24.

SHUNK, D. L., and R. D. FILLEY [1986]. "A New Breed of Industrial Engineers Is Demanded." *Industrial Engineering*, May, 64–67.

TOMPKINS, J. A. [1984]. "Successful Facilities Planner Must Fulfill Role of Integrator in the Automated Environment." *Industrial Engineering*, September, pp. 54–58.

THOMPSON, J. D. [1967]. *Organizations in Action*. McGraw-Hill, New York.

TOWERS, J. [1986]. "Human Resource Development for Advanced Manufacturing Technology." *IMechE*, pp. 13, 16.

TRIST, E. [1981]. *The Evolution of Socio-Technical Systems: A Conceptual Framework and an Action Research Program*. Ontario Ministry of Labor, Ontario Quality of Life Center.

WALL, T. [1986]. "Advanced Manufacturing Technologies—The Case for the Operator Midwife." In H. Noori (ed.), *The Proceedings of Technology Canada Conference, REMAT*. WLU, Waterloo, May 21–22, pp. 311–323.

WALTON, R. E., and G. I. SUSMAN [1987]. "People Policies for the New Machines." *Harvard Business Review*, March–April, pp. 98–106.

WALTON, R. E. [1985]. "From Control to Commitment in the Workplace." *Harvard Business Review*, March–April, pp. 77–84.

WEIR, D. H. [1984]. "Organizational Stress and the Introduction of New Technology. In T. Lupton (ed.), *Proceedings of the 1st Internationbal Conference on Human Factors in Manufacturing*. London, April.

WITT, C. E. [1985]. "Don't Automate Your Factory—Automate the Entire Company." *Material Handling Engineering*. May, pp. 88–98.

WOODWARD, J. [1958]. *Management and Technology*. Her Majesty's Stationary Office, London.

Chapter Ten

LIVING WITH THE NEW TECHNOLOGY: THE SOCIAL ISSUES

Since work remains the most central and important institution in our society, any factor that has the potential to substantially alter patterns of employment is likely to be a subject of wide public interest.

Richard Brown

INTRODUCTION

In the first nine chapters of this book, we emphasized the implications of the new technology for North American firms. In other words, a managerial, firm-specific micro approach was taken to the new technology issues. In this chapter and the next, the focus will be shifted to a macro, public policy approach to the new technology. However, this does not imply that the two are mutually exclusive. For example, a number of macro factors have been identified as being instrumental in influencing the speed with which the new technology are adopted by industry. These factors are listed in Exhibit 10.1.

The new technology brings new industries, new jobs, and new ways of doing things. This could very well result in a shift of the power base of society. Hence, the social implications of the new technology are at least as significant as the economic effects.

> At the level of society there is the overall task of grappling with the immense social and political problems posed by the new technologies—the problems of unemployment, of training and retraining at the young and adult level, the problems of developing new leisure activities, the problems of providing the right climate for the encouragement of R&D and of innovation, and of combining wealth creation with a proper distribution of the fruits of the new technologies.[1]

[1]Edwards [1984], p. 290.

291

Exhibit 10.1   Macro Factors Which Will Influence the Speed with Which New Technologies Are Applied by Industry

Economic Factors:

Pressure arising from competing firms, especially those abroad.
Overall levels of demand.
Availability of funds, including the profitability of industry.
Availability of appropriately skilled manpower.
Movements in real wages, which will determine the extent to which machinery is more profitable to employ than people.
The need to make full use of existing equipment. A rapid scrapping of obsolete equipment may not be economic.
Costs of hardware, and even more important, the cost of software development.

Social and Political Factors:

Awareness of the potential of new technologies and a new desire to use them.
Resistance to technological change because of concern about job security or a reluctance to change working practices.
Government policy—in particular, the extent to which it provides sensible encouragement for new technologies.
Concern about adequate social controls over new technology

Source: Adapted from Edwards [1984], p. 294.

Before we delve into a discussion of the specific social implications of the new technology, one final point should be addressed. Much hypothesizing has been done about the potential social consequences of the new technology. Generally, two points of view exist—a pessimistic view which implies that the new technology is inherently bad, and an optimistic view which treats the new technology as being intrinsically good. These views are contrasted in Exhibit 10.2.

Exhibit 10.2   Alternative Views on the Potential Social Impacts of the New Technology

Optimistic View	Pessimistic View
• Technology has been changing throughout history—past technological advances have led to increased standards of living—there is no reason why this trend should not continue.	• Because of the speed of today's technological advances and the nature of new technology, it is fundamentally different than previous technological advances—therefore, the past cannot be used to predict the future.
• New technology will lead to increased productivity, resulting in higher wages and lower costs for goods. This in turn will increase demand, and thus, create more jobs.	• Increased demand and consumption will in no way match the increased productivity gains realized through new technology. Therefore, massive unemployment will occur.
• New technology will result in increased skills and higher wages for everyone.	• New technology will lead to a greater split between high-skilled/high-wage and low-skilled/low-wage jobs (that is, an erosion of the middle class).
• Everyone will benefit from the fruits of new technology.	• Only top decision-makers will benefit from the fruits of the new technology.

It is our belief that each of these notions is appropriate to some extent, and that the true social impacts of the new technology will probably include elements of both views. It is also our conviction that an understanding of (and a proactive approach to) the social impacts of the new technology will, on the whole, maximize its benefits and minimize its costs.

THE IMPACT OF THE NEW TECHNOLOGY ON EMPLOYMENT LEVELS

Overall Employment Levels

There is little consistency in forecasts about the impact of the new technology on overall employment levels. Wild projections of millions unemployed are countered by arguments that additional economic output will spiral into overall employment expansions due to the multiplier effect.

Many factors make it difficult to determine the true effects of the new technology on employment levels. Some of these factors include the following:

1. Assessments of the employment situation are clouded by the recessionary realities of the early 1980s.
2. Firms may find themselves in situations where they can either adopt the new technology and layoff some workforce, or choose not to adopt the new technology, become uncompetitive, and consequently be forced to layoff all their workforce.
3. A declining pool of new workers due to the passage of the baby boom generation may help to minimize the negative effects of the new technology displacement.
4. In some instances, firms may choose not to layoff employees, preferring instead to find new jobs for them or offer them early retirement packages in order to minimize labor-management conflict and strengthen employee commitment and morale.
5. The new technology may create new industries and occupations that are not yet foreseeable.
6. Other factors such as increased international competition, the general economic health of a country, and changed social norms and values (retire at 65; 35-hour work week) may also cloud the issue.

Overall the new technology will have a significant impact on employment, although it seems impossible accurately to predict the net effect on overall employment levels. Zeeman and Russel [1980] summarize this point of view:

> There will be some jobs lost, and some jobs gained, and many jobs dislocated: some within a city, some within the various regions of the country, and some within the freer North American common market we see imposed upon us within this century. But how many people will be permanently out of jobs due to chip

technology? There are so many factors involved in unemployment that forecasting is all but guesswork.[2]

At the same time, there seems to be a growing amount of evidence which
indicates that the new technology will not lead to a significant reduction in employment levels.[3] In the short term, unemployment may occur as workers shift from
jobs lost to jobs created by new technology. Although this shift in the workforce
does present important issues, most sources maintain that the difference between
aggregate jobs gained and lost through the new technology may not be altogether
substantial in the long run.

> In 1982, the worst year for business since the great depression, Northern Telecom
> had to hire 800 new scientists and engineers to maintain its rate of expansion
> in research and development in electronics and telecommunications technologies.
> The chairman of Northern Telecom noted that his company would be hiring
> additional people every month, until 1987.[4]

Shifting Employment Patterns

The forecasted effect of the new technology on employment levels within various
occupational groups is illustrated in Exhibit 10.3. In a poor-performance, low-
growth industry, there is a higher likelihood of job loss as the new technologies
are introduced (see Brown [1985]). Demographically, older workers who lack
the willingness or flexibility to retrain and women in clerical positions may be
the most affected. At an occupational level, the new technology will lead to significant reductions in the number of employees required for matching and clerical
tasks, but many other occupations will experience net employment increases
(Economic Council of Canada [1987]). For example, "...the decrease in the
number of traditional blue-collar jobs will be paralleled by a demand for engineers
as automation becomes more prevalent."[5] If this demand for engineering and
manufacturing related skills is to be responded to, corporations must not only
emphasize, but also reward and promote these technically oriented individuals.

At a macro level, there is a trend toward more employment opportunities
in the service (tertiary) sector. For example, in the United States approximately
16 million new jobs are forecasted for the service industry between 1986 and
2000, whereas jobs in goods producing occupations are expected to remain
relatively constant (see Richman [1988]). It is evident that a shift from manufacturing to service employment will result in serious social issues that must be
addressed, such as the need for retraining. While this is true, shifting employment

---

[2]Zeeman and Russel [1980], p. 9.
[3]See, for example, The Ontario Task Force on Employment and New Technology [1985], and
Brown [1985a].
[4]Cordell [1985], p. 61.
[5]Davis [1988], p. 586.

Exhibit 10.3 How Technology Change Will Affect Employment by 1995

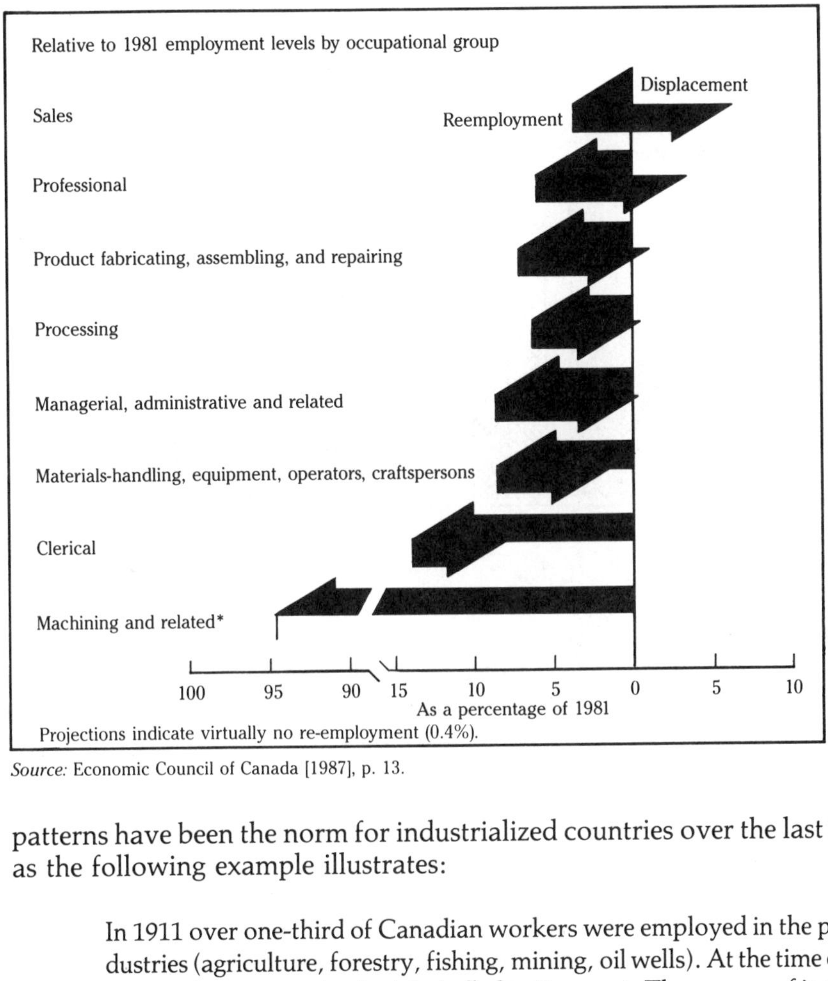

Relative to 1981 employment levels by occupational group

Sales

Professional

Product fabricating, assembling, and repairing

Processing

Managerial, administrative and related

Materials-handling, equipment, operators, craftspersons

Clerical

Machining and related*

Displacement

Reemployment

| 100 | 95 | 90 | 15 | 10 | 5 | 0 | 5 | 10 |

As a percentage of 1981

Projections indicate virtually no re-employment (0.4%).

Source: Economic Council of Canada [1987], p. 13.

patterns have been the norm for industrialized countries over the last 70 years, as the following example illustrates:

> In 1911 over one-third of Canadian workers were employed in the primary in-dustries (agriculture, forestry, fishing, mining, oil wells). At the time of the 1981 census, that proportion had dwindled to 7 percent. The process of industrializa-tion is reflected in the growth of employment in the secondary sector (manufac-turing and construction) between 1911 and 1951. Note, however, that while employment in the secondary sector has levelled off, the tertiary sector (which includes transportation, communications and utilities, trade, finance, insurance and real estate, community, business and personal services, and public admin-istration and defense) has rocketed from about one-third of the jobs in 1911 to two-thirds in 1981. The overall picture is one of massive shifts in the employ-ment structure in a period of 70 years.[6]

This situation is illustrated graphically in Exhibit 10.4.

[6]Newton [1985], p. 4.

Exhibit 10.4   Employment Patterns by Industry Sector (Canada)

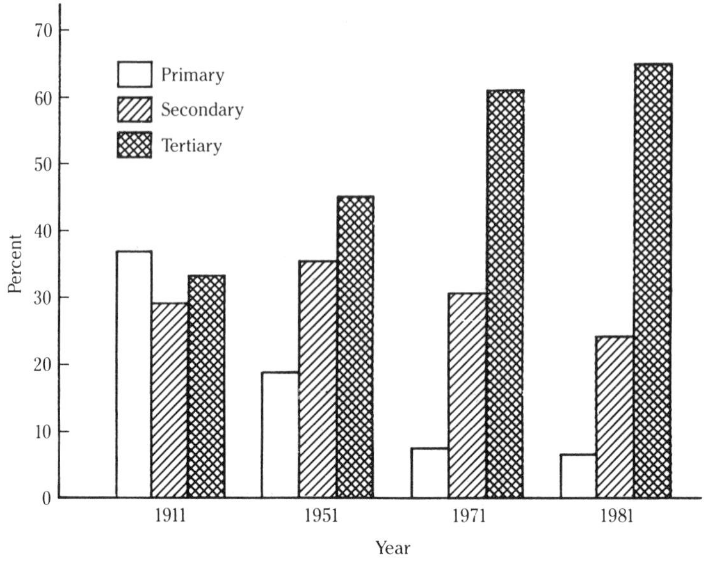

Source: Newton [1985], p. 5.

As is obvious, the displacement of workers from one sector of the economy has historically been matched by the expansion of another sector. Although there has been increasing productivity throughout this century, employment levels have continued to rise, mainly due to the expansion of service jobs and small entrepreneurial organizations (see Richman [1988]). Will this continue? No one has the answer, but history indicates that the transition to a new employment structure is possible, and probably inevitable:

> The fact remains that whereas previous technological change in pre- and postwar periods mostly had a labor saving effect, the new technology entering the market now saves both labor and capital. It also helps reduce the consumption of raw materials. In the past, job losses were partly offset by increased labor demand for the production of capital goods. That compensation effect may no longer work because the labor-saving machinery is now produced by labor-saving processes.[7]

Short-term Adjustment.   While the long-term impact of the new technology may be inconsequential, short-term unemployment may be unavoidable. To date, the new technology has been adopted at a relatively slow rate, and resulting layoffs have been minimal. As more companies become involved with

[7]Ebel and Ulrich [1987], p. 357.

the new technology, there will be a greater need for short-term adjustment. Consider the following example:

> As industrial robots and numerical control machines replace workers on the shop floor (especially in hazardous and undesirable jobs), the displaced employees must find other work. In many cases they will be retained by their employers, but their responsibilities will change. They may become welding machine operators instead of welders, or they might become involved with welding machine maintenance. There will be a general shift in the factor from manual to mental work.
>
> Other workers will not be so lucky. Many will simply lose their jobs. These workers will typically resort to unskilled service positions; as industries in their home towns reduce employment levels, they will become less likely to find jobs requiring skills commensurate with their ability.[8]

The ease of short-term adjustment and magnitude of short-term unemployment will be a function of five primary factors:

1. Management decisions on retraining versus hiring
2. Willingness and ability of displaced workers to acquire new skills
3. The speed of adoption of the new technology
4. The effectiveness of government programs designed to assist displaced workers
5. The degree of management-union cooperation

Short-term unemployment will to a large extent depend on management decisions which determine whether (a) current workers will be trained for the new positions, or (b) new employees with the appropriate skills will be hired. As noted in Chapter 9, the issue of retraining versus hiring new employees is an important one for management to address. The social implications must be factored into the decision process. The effectiveness of government programs geared to assisting displaced workers will also influence the ease of adjustment. Governments are going to have to cooperate with industry and labor to determine what forms of assistance are most appropriate. Government's role in the training and retraining of workers for the new technology will be discussed in Chapter 11.

Middle-class Erosion. A debate currently underway deals with the argument that the new technology will lead to a split between high-skill/high-pay and low-skill/low-pay jobs. The reasoning is that a large number of workers currently employed in the high-paying manufacturing sector will be reemployed only on a part-time basis or in the service sector where pay levels are much lower. Although there has been no evidence generated which points to definite middle-

---

[8]Davis [1988], p. 586.

class erosion, one study found that ". . . there are enough signs pointing to the possibility of middle-class erosion."[9]

Although the possibility of a reduced middle class is primarily a public policy issue, industry must also be conscious of it and its possible ramifications. That is, if an erosion of the middle class begins to occur, industry can almost be guaranteed that workers and unions will exert considerable pressure for higher wages or against technological change.

The Effect on Women. Changing lifestyles and social values have made employment a fixture and often a necessity in the lives of many women. However, the new technology could upset the recent social changes which have seen women incorporated into the labor force. Reports have indicated that it is women who will be the most affected by technological change, primarily because female-dominated clerical positions are likely to be reduced because of the new technology (see Cordell [1985], and "Toronto Star" [1985]). Special public policy considerations may have to be directed at the retraining and reemployment of women in the workforce.

TECHNOLOGICAL CHANGE AND INDUSTRIAL RELATIONS

As noted in Chapter 9, the new technology will have a significant impact on workers, and the effective implementation of the new technology will require fundamental changes in workforce management practices. This implies that the new technology will also necessitate adjustments in labor relations and union practices.

"Ideally the role of the labor movement is to ensure that as part of the process of change the values of concern to working people are preserved and enhanced."[10] Throughout the world, the impact of the new technology on these values is crystallizing in varying degrees into several issues in the union bargaining stance. Unions have identified a great number of issues concerning the impact of technological change on labor. They include:

1. Advanced notification of the new technology plans
2. Open access to information on the effects of the new technology
3. Participation in the technological decision-making process
4. Job security provisions and layoff policies
5. Organization of work and job design principles, including their impact on required skill levels and job classification categories
6. Occupational health and safety standards
7. The right to privacy (for example, the new technology cannot be used for the electronic surveillance of work performance)

[9]Economic Council of Canada [1987], p. 14.
[10]Mansfield [1983], p. 27.

8. Sharing the benefits of the new technology
9. Training and retraining practices
10. Wage levels (for example, maintenance of current salary levels for workers placed in lower rated jobs)

Unions in Norway, Sweden, and West Germany have been relatively successful in securing many of these points through collective bargaining agreements or legislation (Mansfield [1983]). In North America, in spite of some union success in obtaining provisions in collective bargaining agreements, a large percentage of unions have yet to secure these provisions. For example, one study revealed that the most common clause found in labor contracts with regard to the new technology is "advance notice prior to the introduction of tech change," but even this clause ". . . is not included in over 60 percent of the agreements examined."[11]

In short, the absence of technology clauses in collective bargaining agreements is potentially a serious problem for firms. If collective bargaining sessions address the inevitable issue of technological change, agreements with the unions and employees can be reached proactively, before the technology is adopted and problems arise. This will make it easier for firms to implement the technology when the adoption decision is made.

CHANGES IN THE PHILOSOPHY OF WORK

The new technology is having a fundamental impact on work philosophies and ethics. As is already evident, technology has the potential to increase the productivity of firms dramatically. This implies an increase in output per person. Traditionally, logic says that this productivity improvement will result in lower costs and/or higher wages, and hence people will be able to buy more. However, there are at least two major reasons why the argument may not hold in the future:

1. People may reach a consumption saturation point, preferring instead to work less and have increased leisure time.
2. Increased productivity through new technology may be offset by environmental and social needs.

Increased Leisure Time

The unemployment associated with the adoption of new technology is generally viewed as being a negative factor. However, one can approach the issue from a different point of view: "Man invented machines so man would not have to work and we have succeeded to the point of one and a half million unemployed. But instead of cheering about it, we're in despair. To me that is sheer, raging idiocy."[12]

[11]Economic Council of Canada [1987], p. 23.
[12]Cordell [1985], p. 43.

To address unemployment resulting from technology adoption, some would argue that what is needed is a shorter work week (reduced from 40 hours to 35, 30 or even 20 hours—see Von Weizsacker [1985]), longer vacation times, early retirement, and increased leisure for everyone. In that way, everyone could maintain their current standard of living while working less. In fact, the UAW has been pushing for reduced working hours as a means of creating new job opportunities. By negotiating for more paid time off, the total number of workers on the payroll will remain approximately constant or increase over time. The UAW hopes that four-day work weeks will become the standard in the auto industry by 1990 (Dodd [1981]). In fact, there is an interesting paradox here. The same new technology that many unions are fighting in the interest of job security is the technology that North America must employ to reach a level of international competitiveness and economic prosperity where shorter work weeks and longer vacations are possible! Therefore, the issue is not adoption of the new technology, but rather managing its introduction in an effective, socially conscious manner.

Many people also contend that many North Americans are reaching a consumption saturation point. In a way, they assert, people are reaching the point where they have enough money to buy what they want or need and would rather trade off increased income for increased leisure time. With this in mind, it should be noted that the transition to a leisure-based society will in all likelihood be difficult to achieve. As one expert puts it: "... the consumption of goods has become the chief means by which people define themselves and their lives."[13]

From a practical point of view, there are various barriers to the institutionalization of shorter work weeks or early retirement in our society. First of all, it is debatable whether or not most people, culturally or habitually, would want or be able to adjust to a lifestyle which traded work for increased leisure. Some may wish to work more in order to acquire more goods and services, and others simply may not know what to do with increased free time. Studies have shown that a relatively large percentage of people die in the first year after retirement, implying that they have not been able to cope with leisure time. This raises the need for educating people on how to spend leisure time constructively.

While the debate on the necessity of more leisure time continues, managers should be cognizant of how to address the issue of trading higher pay for increased leisure in the future. That is, firms should consider the possibility of implementing job structures that give individuals the flexibility to have various amounts of leisure time. In fact, the flextime approaches to scheduling work hours that have been institutionalized in many firms may be the beginning of a trend which will eventually see employees choosing how many hours they actually want to work. The following example provides evidence of this trend:

> A company with 40,000 employees had treated those employees pretty much the same for generations. It had to because that was the only way to keep track of them. With the computer to keep track, the employees can [now] be treated

[13]Shein [1988], p. 85.

differently, with a unique contract for each of the 40,000. Companies such as American Can and TRW are now offering a cafeteria of compensations. An employee can now decide to have a certain combination of salary, pensions, health benefits, insurance, flextime, job sharing, vacation arrangements, and job objectives.[14]

Environmental and Social Needs

It is important to think of the new technology as being society- and consumer-driven rather than solely profit-driven. North Americans are gradually becoming more and more aware of the need to address environmental and social issues. There is the strong possibility that the productivity gains made through the new technology, rather than being transformed into increased production of goods and services, will be used to address various environmental and social needs. For example, firms may be forced to pay higher prices for natural resources in order to promote conservation; they may have to allocate more resources for clean or cleaner technologies in order to meet stricter pollution emission standards. Consider the following:

> Mining productivity in the U.S. declined an absolute 30 percent over the last decade....About 20 percent of that decline can be traced to safety or environmentalism. If you have to fill up an open-pit mine as well as empty it, more hours of work will be required to produce each ton of copper.[15]

Companies may also face minimum wage requirements, and they may have to pay higher taxes in general as governments expand social programs. The ongoing debate suggests that in the future, we may see a shift in focus from an economic perspective based on output generation to one more concerned with resource (input) efficiency and sustainable development.

TECHNOLOGY ASSESSMENT AND ENVIRONMENTAL IMPACT ANALYSIS

Technology assessment (TA) and environment impact analysis (EIA) are two similar methods that can be used to assess the social implications of the new technology.[16] *Technology assessment* has been defined as:

> A class of policy studies which systematically examine the effects on society that may occur when a technology is introduced, extended, or modified. It emphasizes those consequences that are unintended, indirect, or delayed.[17]

---

[14]Adapted for length from Naisbitt, [1984], pp. 39–40.
[15]Thurow [1983], p. 14.
[16]For a detailed description of TA and EIA, see Porter et al. [1980].
[17]Coates [1976], p. 372.

Armstrong and Harman [1977] have identified five central elements of TA:

1. It is possible and indeed desirable to manage technology objectively toward goals that contribute to societal well-being.
2. The primary objective of TA is to make informed policy decisions through the provision of information on the potential advantages and disadvantages to various social groups of likely technological developments and alternatives.
3. TA is inherently and necessarily a multidisciplinary mode of analysis.
4. TA entails projecting into the future and subsequently addressing the uncertainties associated with these projections.
5. The term *technology*, when used in TA, includes both hard and soft technologies.

EIA in a large part started as a result of the United States National Environmental Policy Act (NEPA) [1969]). It is an analysis that is required whenever a major federal action will significantly affect the quality of the human environment. The assessment does not consider just environmental impacts (such as the quality of water), but also considers the human aspects, such as social systems, and economic costs.

TA/EIA can be performed on a larger number of problems, each of which will require a different approach. Three broad categories can be distinguished for assessments:

1. Project Assessments: Analyses of a particular, localized project, such as the building of a new warehouse run by robots.
2. Problem-oriented assessment: Focuses on a problem and is not limited to a regional focus. For example, the impact of the new technology on employment levels would fall into this category.
3. Technology-oriented assessment: Examines the effects of a new technology and the resulting impacts on society. A study of the effects of a new type of energy source would be an example of this type of assessment.

Porter et al. [1980] provides 10 components of a TA/EIA, as described in the following:

1. Problem Definition: This area defines the nature and the scope of the study. An important part of this area is the determination of the parties involved, the funds available for the study, and the eventual use of the assessment.
2. Technology Description: This component is a description of the technology under assessment.
3. Technology Forecast: Once the technology has been determined and described, a prediction is made of the nature of the technology in the future. It considers potential breakthroughs, substitution, and uncertainties.
4. Social Description: A description of the aspects of society (political, economic,

institutional) that are affected by the technology. It should consist of both qualitative and quantitative factors.

5. Social Forecast: This area is like technological forecasting, except that it is more difficult to do because of the increase in qualitative variables. It also depends on the technology forecast, since changes in technology may affect the societal factors.

6. Impact Identification: Impact identification is concerned with determining the relationship between the proposed technology and society. First-order impacts (these that are directly caused by the technology) and higher-order (those caused by the first order) impacts must be determined. A number of methods can be used to determine these impacts.

7. Impact Analysis: This component is very similar to the cost/benefit type of analysis. It should be qualitative and quantitative in nature, studying the probability of the impacts and the expected magnitude.

8. Impact Evaluation: This component ties the analysis together and considers various alternatives available to those responsible for the decision-making.

9. Policy Analysis: Policy analysis consists of implementation recommendations and subsequent consequences. It considers the consequences of implementing the technology, and in some cases who should be responsible for which part of the implementation. Depending on the requirements specified by the persons requesting the TA/EIA, this segment may or may not be very detailed.

10. Communication of Results: As with any type of study, this component is very important. The appropriate people must be informed of the results of the assessment.

Depending on the study, various components may be considered more important than others—but it is necessary to include all the activities in some form. They are not necessarily performed as sequential steps, but each component is adjusted as new information is received. Thus, multiple feedback loops exist.

Every assessment must be limited in terms of its scope (time frame, impact areas, purpose of report). This procedure is referred to as *bounding*, and is a very important part of the success of an assessment. Porter et al. [1980] suggest that bounding take place at the beginning of an assessment, and that a micro-assessment (of about a one-man month) be made to gain an idea of the technology and society factors involved to assist in the bounding procedure. A tradeoff between eliminating certain factors and depth of analysis of certain issues has to be made. It is recommended that the bounding limits remain flexible so that if information is gathered which suggests important areas to be analyzed, they can be included in the study.

Impact Identification: Scanning and Tracing Techniques

Porter et al. [1980] also describe two general techniques that can be used to identify the impact of the new technology on society: scanning and tracing. In its simplest form, *scanning* could consist of a comprehensive checklist which identifies all the potential impacts of the new technology. This checklist could be derived through literature reviews, surveys, and brainstorming. *Tracing* involves the use of relevance trees (or other more complicated tools) to represent the link between immediate (first-order) impacts and those that follow. Exhibit 10.5 illustrates how tracing can be used to identify the impacts of the new technology on employment levels. Probabilities or weights could be assigned to each of the branches on the tree to indicate the potential importance of each impact.

Exhibit 10.5 Tracing the Impact of New Technology on Employment

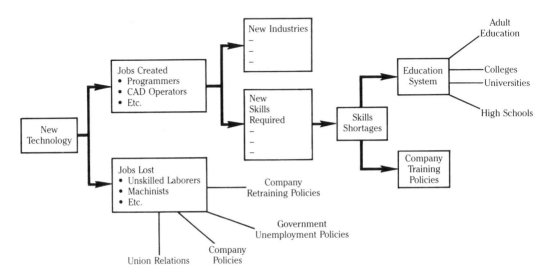

CONCLUDING OBSERVATIONS

The social implications of the new technology are becoming increasingly evident. In this chapter, discussion of these implications focused on three central themes:

1. The employment effects of the new technology
2. The implications of the new technology for industrial relations
3. The potential changes in the philosophy of work brought by the new technology

In general, we concluded that the new technology should not result in any significant net loss of jobs in the long run, but will most certainly create shifting employment patterns and short-term structural problems for particular segments of society. Industry, government, and labor must cooperate to come up with satisfactory solutions to these problems.

It appears that North American firms are lagging behind their European counterparts when it comes to including new technology issues in the collective bargaining process. This is an area of concern, as management and labor must eventually reach some agreement if firms are to adopt the new technology successfully. Firms ignoring the possibility of a new technology adoption will most likely encounter resistance and time delays if and when they do decide to acquire the new technology. A proactive rather than a reactive approach to this issue seems to be in the firm's best interests.

The new technology has the potential significantly to increase the productivity of North American industry. How these productivity gains are distributed could have a major effect on the philosophy of work in our society. Basically, there are three possible scenarios: (1) productivity gains could result in increased goods and services; (2) productivity gains could result in reduced working time and increased leisure time; or (3) productivity gains could be offset by various social pressures, such as tighter pollution standards and higher minimum wages. There are signs that any one (or a combination) of these three scenarios could become the norm in the future; much will depend on the desires of people.

The concepts of technology assessment and environmental impact analysis can be used to identify and address the social implications of the new technology.

RECOMMENDED READINGS

DAVIS, T. C. [1988]. "The Impact of the Factory of the Future on Society." In Tarek M. Kahlil et al. (eds.), *Technology Management I. Proceedings of the First International Conference on Technology Management*, pp. 584–591.

EBEL, K. H., and E. ULRICH [1987]. "Some Workplace Effects of CAD and CAM." *International Labor Review*, Volume 126, No. 3, May–June, pp. 351–370.

RICHMAN, L. S. [1988]. "Tomorrow's Jobs: Plentiful, But. . . ." *Fortune*, April 11, pp. 42–56.

DISCUSSION QUESTIONS

1. Do you feel that the adoption of the new technology by many firms will lead to an increase or decrease in overall employment levels? Explain fully.
2. As the new technology project manager of a large company, what steps would you take (with regard to workforce/social implications) if your company was considering the adoption of a new technology that would result in the elimination of 1,000 jobs?
3. The productivity gains associated with the new technology mean that in the future, fewer and fewer people will be required to produce more and more goods. This implies that the new technology has the potential to better society on the whole. However, how will this occur? Will people continue to work as much in order to receive more material goods? Will people work less and have the same amount of material goods with increased leisure time? Or will gains in productivity be offset by social and environmental pressures such as higher wages, tighter pollution standards, and increased costs for natural resources such as water?

4. Many people hypothesize that the new technology will cause a shift away from higher-paying manufacturing jobs to lower-paying service jobs. Will this occur, and if so, will it widen the gap between rich and poor?

5. Can the new technology be implemented successfully without positive union-management relations? If the answer to this question is no, what does this imply for many North American companies? Will union-management relations be forced to change to accommodate the new technology? What recommendations would you make to facilitate this change?

6. The Industrial Revolution had a significant impact on the social patterns of society. Similarly, the new technology revolution that is occurring today also has significant social implications. Do you feel that the new technology will have as significant an impact on society as the Industrial Revolution did? Compare and contrast the social implications of the new technology with the social effects of the Industrial Revolution.

7. a. Use scanning and/or tracing to identify the potential social impacts of the new technology.
   b. Use scanning and/or tracing to identify the potential impacts of the new technology within an organization.

8. Consider the following comments:
   Although a committed believer in the benefits of science and technology [Thomas] Jefferson rejected the idea of developing an American factory system on the ground that the emergence of an urban proletariat, which he then regarded as an inescapable consequence of the European factory system, would be too high a price to pay for any potential improvement in the American material standard of living. He regarded the existence of manufacturing cities and an industrial working class as incompatible with republican government and the happiness of the people. He argued that it was preferable, even if more costly in strictly economic terms, to ship raw materials to Europe and import manufacturerd goods. "The loss by the transportation of commodities across the Atlantic will be made up in happiness and permanence of government." In weighing political, moral, and aesthetic costs against economic benefits, he anticipated the viewpoint of the environmentalists and others of our time for whom the test of a technological innovation is its effect on the overall quality of life. (Marx [1987], p. 36)
   Regardless of whether you agree or disagree with Jefferson's viewpoint, his idea does seem to have some validity. Are there any noneconomic factors that should be considered when weighing the pros and cons of the new technology (from a social perspective)?

9. Kurt Vonnegut's 1952 novel *Player Piano* presents a harrowing picture of society. In this fictional world, all manufacturing facilities have been completely automated, leading to a serious division of social classes. One group is made up of the engineers and managers who run the automated plants, and the other consists of millions of displaced workers. Could this scenario become a reality in North America? Why or why not? What factors will influence the likelihood of this happening?

REFERENCES AND BIBLIOGRAPHY

ARMSTRONG, J. E., and W. W. HARMAN [1977]. *Strategies for Conducting Technology Assessments.* Stanford University, Department of Economic Systems, Stanford, California, December.

"Changing 45 Million Jobs" [1981]. *Business Week,* Special Report, August 3, pp. 62–67.

BROWN, R. [1985]. "Our Next Big Task Is the Development of Human Resources." *Toronto Star,* Monday, December 2, p. B9.

BROWN, R. [1986]. "The Findings of the Ontario Task Force on Employment and New Technology." In H. Noori, (ed.), *Proceedings of Technology Canada Conference,* REMAT. WLU Printing, pp. 409–416.

BRUNO, C. [1984]. "Labor Relations in the Age of Robotics." *Datamation,* March, pp. 179–182.

COATES, J. F. [1976]. "Technology Assessment—A Tool Kit." *Chemtech,* June, pp. 372–383.

CORDELL, A. J. [1985]. *The Uneasy Eighties: The Transition to an Information Society.* Background Study 53, Science Council of Canada, March.

DAVIS, T. C. [1988]. "The Impact of the Factory of the Future on Society." In Tarek M. Khalil et al. (eds.), *Technology Management*. Geneva, Inderscience Enterprises Ltd., pp. 584–591.

DINEEN, J. [1985]. "Will High Tech Mean Massive Layoffs." *Toronto Star*, April 28, p. B1.

DODD, J. [1981]. "Robots: The New 'Steel Collar' Workers." *Personnel Journal*, September, pp. 688–695.

EBEL, K. H., and E. ULRICH [1987]. "Some Workplace Effects of CAD and CAM." *International Labor Review*, Volume 126, No. 3, May–June, pp. 351–370.

Economic Council of Canada [1987]. *Making Technology Work: Innovation and Jobs in Canada*. Minister of Supply and Services, Canada.

EDWARDS, K. [1985]. "The Social and Industrial Implications of New Technology." *International Conference on Future Development in Technology: The Year 2000*, London, April 4–6, pp. 289–296.

FOULKES, F. K., and J. L. HIRSCH [1984]. "People Make Robots Work." *Harvard Business Review*, January–February, pp. 94–102.

HORSMAN, M. [1985]. "The Price We Pay in Jobs for High-Tech Know-How." *The Financial Post*, Computer Post: A Special Report, p. C13.

MANSFIELD, W. C. [1983]. "Technological Change and Trade Unions." *The Practicing Manager*, October, pp. 25–31.

MARX, L. [1987]. "Does Improved Technology Mean Progress?" *Technology Review*, January, pp. 33–41, 71.

NAISBITT, J. [1984]. *Megatrends*. Warner Books, New York, pp. 39–40.

NEWTON, K. [1985]. "Employment Effects of Technological Change: Some Implications for Education." Economic Council of Canada, May 27.

PORTER, A. L., F. ROSSINI, S. R. CARPENTER, and A. T. ROPER [1980]. *A Guidebook for Technology Assessment and Impact Analysis*. North-Holland.

RICHMAN, L. S. [1988]. "Tomorrow's Jobs: Plentiful, But . . ." *Fortune*, April 11, pp. 42–56.

SHEIN, B. [1988]. "Buy Me." *Report on Business Magazine*, April, pp. 78–85.

The Ontario Task Force on Employment and New Technology [1985]. Ontario Ministry of Labor Publications, Government of Ontario.

THUROW, L. C. [1983]. "The 7½ Percent Solution." *The Princeton Papers*, Northern Telecom Limited, Corporate Relations Department, pp. 13–14.

Toronto Star [1985]. "Technology Won't Cut Employment New Study Says." October 9, p. C4.

VON WEIZSACKER, E. V. [1985]. "Change in the Philosophy of Work." In H. J. Bullinger and H. J. Warneck (eds.), *Toward the Factory of the Future*. Springer-Verlag, Berlin, Heidelberg.

ZAND, D. E. [1981]. *Information, Organization and Power*. McGraw-Hill, New York, pp. 3–5.

ZEMAN, Z., and R. RUSSEL [1980]. "The New Waves of 'Technological Unemployment' Debates: An Overview." *Futures Canada*, Volume 4, No. 4, pp. 6–10.

THE GOVERNMENT AND THE NEW TECHNOLOGY

Businessmen are risk averse. Therefore, if the
invisible hand cannot drive the enterprise to
R&D, the visible hand must.
              Nashiro Amaya
              A Former Vice-Minister of Japan's MITI

INTRODUCTION

The implications arising from the adoption of the new technology can be discussed on four dimensions: (1) product-specific factors, (2) company-specific factors, (3) industry-specific factors, and (4) country-specific factors. Throughout Chapters 1 to 9, we reviewed the issues concerning the first three levels. In this chapter, as in Chapter 10, our thrust will be on the country-specific factors and the role of government in enhancing and promoting the development and the adoption of the new technology.

The potential roles government can play in promoting and facilitating technology adoption are quite diverse. These roles change from country to country, and from one administration to the next within a given country. It is not our intent here to critique current government policies or make specific recommendations for the future. We do, however, posit that government does have one crucial and ongoing contribution; that is, to foster a healthy economic climate, which itself promotes and facilitates new technology adoption. The particular tools and policies employed to do this will vary with the environmental context of which an administration operates.

The successful adoption and integration of the new technology requires a game plan for economic restructure at a national level (see Crane [1985]). A game plan would require (a) the establishment of an economic policy goal which generates good overall performance to encourage investment and innovation, and (b) an industrial strategy that brings the country into the age of technological competitiveness. A research study conducted in West Germany corroborates the need for goal-oriented behavior by citing a number of reasons why Japan and the United States appear to have an advantage in the technology areas. These reasons included the support offered to manufacturers and users of the new technology by the nation's economic policy and the employment of a large-scale viewpoint with respect to product development and assembly tasks.

Experience has shown that an economic game plan provides general direction and support to institutions as a nation attempts to shift its competitive role in the world economy. These revised efforts should ideally involve government, business, labor, and educational institutions and should mean a greater commitment to R&D in order to strengthen the country's contribution to new technological development and to enable faster incorporation of the new technology into processes and procedures.

Generally, a number of questions regarding the concept of economic policies or game plans have to be answered. Such policies imply the support of selected industries at the expense of others, presumably according to growth potential. Some of these related questions are:

1. Who is responsible for choosing which industries will be supported and which will not?
2. To what extent will government be involved in these decisions?
3. What mechanisms are in place to insure that the concerns of all affected stakeholders (government, business, labor) will be considered?
4. What will be the effects of such anticipated social disruptions as massive layoffs, an increased skill level in the labor force, and increased leisure time, to name a few? This is perhaps an appropriate application for the TA/EIA analyses discussed in Chapter 10.

Although there are no readily available set of solutions to these or similar questions, they do highlight government's responsibilities to not only consider the costs and benefits of proposed changes, but to also plan for them. In the following section we will discuss the role of government in expediting and directing technological advances.

GOVERNMENT'S ROLE: FACILITATING ADOPTION OF THE NEW TECHNOLOGY

There are three specific roles that a government can play in promoting new technology adoption, namely: (1) an assessor role, (2) an encouragement role, and (3) a participative role. There is general agreement that government should take an active part in fostering a national economic policy and in encouraging the adoption of the new technology, but that it should not be a direct, active participant in the process. The rationale for this statement is reinforced by the following example:

In recent years the U.S. government negotiated Voluntary-Restraint Agreements (VRAs) to give the automotive and steel industries time to revamp and adjust to increased foreign competitions. In both situations, government involvement did little to reverse the decline in U.S. market share. Automobile imports dropped to as low as 23 percent of the U.S. market at the height of the VRA in 1984, but have since rebounded to 29 percent. The failure of auto VRA rests with the auto companies. General Motors, for example, failed to use the four-year VRA to make its domestic automobile operations more competitive. Instead, GM invested in one Korean and two Japanese auto firms, abandoned plans to develop its own small car, formed a joint venture with Toyota, and purchased Hughes Aircraft and Electronic Data System. In other words, GM diversified out of the (domestic) auto industry.[1]

Given that the government has the means to assess the potential market, both domestically and internationally, and devise policies to promote the potential of the new technology, it is also possible that government play the role of an assessor. As an assessor, it is necessary for the government to develop an understanding of the importance of the new technology to different industrial sectors so that it can develop policies to enhance the adoption of the new technology.

Modeling the Industry-Government-University Interface

Industry, government, and university each have important roles to play in the development and utilization of the new technology. In different countries, there currently exist different levels of cooperation among these three players. For example, in the United States, industry and university have a relatively close alliance; in Canada, government and university are closely allied; and in Japan, strong cooperative ties exist between industry and government. This is illustrated in Exhibit 11.1. In the future, countries that are able to align the goals and objectives of industry, government, and university should find themselves enjoying a distinct competitive advantage.

Exhibit 11.1 Current Industry-Government-University Relations

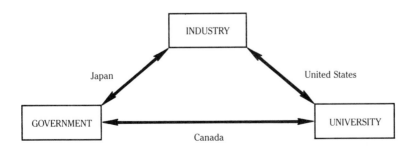

[1]Dallmeyer [1987], p. 50.

A number of specific methods can be used to enhance these relationships. For example, one study (Barnes and Peters [1987]) has identified eight forms of corporate-university collaboration: university-based interface institutes, joint ventures, contract research, research parks, university-based companies, cooperative education, continuing education, and personnel interchange programs. Aside from the differences between these forms of collaboration, a number of issues are common to all of them (and to industry-government-university relations in general). In order to facilitate discussion on these key issues, we will base this chapter on the model in Exhibit 11.2. University has two primary responsibilities: education and research. Similarly, industry has two major requirements from university, that is: (1) educated people who can perform in industry, and (2) access to research, inventions, and potential innovations. Government's role is to uphold the national interest by enhancing the exchange of people and information from university to industry (and vice versa), and by preserving important social objectives that may at times oppose the goals of private enterprise.

Research

Government Research.   Government research activities in different countries vary depending on particular policies and national capabilities. In general, most governments utilize each of the following approaches to some extent:

1. Operate their own research labs
2. Provide specific research aid to industries and firms
3. Aid universities in their research endeavors
4. Integrate the university-industry research relationship

In the United States, federal research labs house a large percentage of the country's talented researchers and sophisticated equipment. There are

Exhibit 11.2   Modeling the Interface: The Triangle of Cooperation

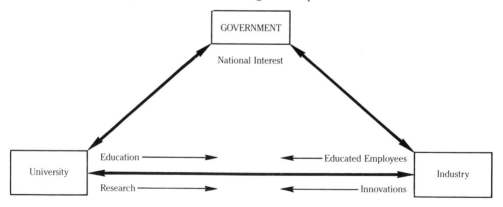

"... over 700 labs across the country spending more than $18 billion a year and employing one-sixth of the nation's research scientists and engineers."[2] Japan also has government laboratories, although a limited number compared to the United States. Usually, they focus their R&D in specific, well-targeted areas and put very little money in defense-related R&D expenditures. Rather, funding goes to projects with greater potential for private-sector commercialization (Barason [1986]).

At any rate, the focal points for national research vary significantly (see Exhibit 11.3). Japan, for instance, has an interest in long-term fissions. European countries (the EEC) are primarily concerned with the selection and support of high-tech projects. The United States has changed its focus several times over the last several decades, depending on the needs perceived:

Exhibit 11.3 Focal Points for National Innovation Efforts

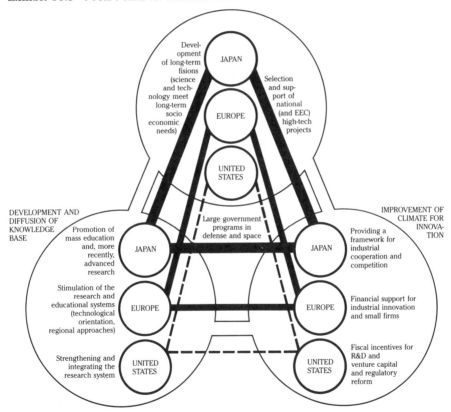

Note: The lines joining the three circles indicate the links and interactions among the three government policy areas. The dotted lines indicate weak indications, the solid lines stronger ones.

Source: Reprinted by permission of the publisher, from "Technological Change and Reindustrialization: In Search of a Policy Framework," in *Competitiveness Through Technology*, edited by Jerry Dermer. Lexington, Mass.: Lexington Books, D.C. Heath and Company, Copyright 1986, D. C. Heath and Company.

[2]Guteri [1987], p. 44.

In the fifties and sixties the emphasis was on military and space technology. In the seventies money went largely into health, environmental, and energy research. Today the concentration is on economic competitiveness, which in turn has focused attention on scientific research. Indeed, many people now regard competitiveness as a national security issue on par with military preparedness.[3]

However, statistics show that the United States still focuses its interests largely on defense and space (Rothwell [1986]). In fact, U.S. government expenditures on defense now accounts for 72 percent of its 1987 R&D spending, up from 51 percent in 1980 (Guteri [1987]). Clearly, the research focus selected by a government is a critical national issue, for it is the research of today that will determine economic direction and well-being in years to come.

University Research.   As well as operating federal research labs, governments are involved in research through collaboration with universities. For example, the governments of Canada and the United States are directly involved, though at different rates, in funding universities. At the same time, the extent of funding for university research is perhaps inadequate if we plan to maintain long-term competitive strength.

> A Silicon Valley Consulting firm concludes that the U.S. government's support of university microelectronics programs totalled only about $100 million for the years 1980–1987. To put that into perspective, the Department of Energy's program expense for just one unproven, highly speculative energy technique, magnetically constrained fusion, was $295 million in 1987 alone.[4]

Yet it is becoming apparent to policymakers that:

> If they fund research at a university the research gets done, and in addition, students are trained . . . and facilities are upgraded. Moreover, those students go to industry and help transition advanced research into concepts for industrial innovation. But, [if they] fund the same research at a national laboratory, [they] get research results but the research stays put.[5]

Schmitt [1984], to further emphasize the point, argues that unless national labs do a substantially better research job, the universities should get the funds. Universities, in comparison with government labs, are better able to disseminate the research results.

University-Industry Collaboration.   Finally, governments are involved in increasing the collaboration between universities and industries. University-

[3]Griffiths [1987], p. 64.
[4]Schmitt [1984], p. 9.
[5]Schmitt [1984], p. 9.

industry research relationships (UIRR) are today very important. Such relationships have been advocated by government task forces and federal grant agencies. The following is one specific example of government involvement in UIRR:

> One of the primary focuses of the Center for the Frontier Engineering Research (C-FER) at the University of Alberta in Edmonton is to help the petroleum industry develop technology for the tricky process of exploring for oil under the Beaufort Sea. It was set up in 1984, and has 40 private-sector members, primarily from the steel and petroleum industries. These companies pick up 55 percent of the $1.8 million operating budget. The government picks up the remainder.[6]

In spite of the current involvement of governments in fostering university and industry collaboration, some reservations do exist. For example, one argument which cautions against closer university-industry research ties is that a greater collaboration on research would result in a larger percentage of short-term applied research at the expense of long-term, fundamental (or basic) research. University research may become more and more geared toward specific industries and firms at the expense of others. University researchers may also find themselves in a conflict of interest position—they may be accused of using public information for private gain; they may infringe on private research and consulting practices; or they may find themselves neglecting university responsibilities in order to pursue industry-specific research. Finally, there is the issue of confidentiality:

> One of the most contentious issues that arises when university and industry seek to cooperate is the ownership and use of research results. From the point of view of the company that provides funding, R&D can give it a competitive advantage in the marketplace. It is thus in the company's interests to keep the results of the research secret. On the other hand, freedom of communiation is central to the university ethos. Researchers are also caught in the publish or perish syndrome. Their careers and those of their graduate students depend upon research publications.[7]

To overcome any potential problems associated with close university-industry relations, government involvement and intervention may be necessary. For example, government could commit a certain amount of funds to universities to be used solely for fundamental research purposes; applied research activities (as opposed to publications) could be factored into the university researcher's evaluation process; and time-delay agreements could be made which enable companies to maintain the confidentiality of their research results for a certain length of time (for example, six months to a year) and then allow the researcher to publish the information (Anderson [1987]). Since this is a management text, we offer Exhibit 11.4 as a guide to corporations attempting to foster or enhance relations with university research and education programs.

[6]Adapted from Gates [1988], p. 25.
[7]Anderson [1987], p. 12.

Exhibit 11.4 An Action Plan for the Alliance of Industry Needs and the University
Research Focus

1. Define the need for collaborative activity in terms of the corporate mission. (*Example:* Access to leading-edge processes that control costs are key to maintaining our competitive position).

2. Identify contact points by:

   Field of specialization
   Field of expertise
   Compatible universities

3. Allocate funds to support collaborative activity by examining corporate needs in terms of:

   The size of the corporation
   The number of employees
   Internal R&D capability

4. Develop corporate programs to decentralize and distribute the activity throughout the corporation. Appropriate mechanisms for collaboration include:

   Campus visits
   Part-time instructors
   Co-op education
   Graduate/undergraduate support
   Manpower transfer programs

5. Identify areas for more collaboration. Possibilities include:

   (a) Sponsor research through:

   Research contracts
   Affiliations with an institute
   Joint ventures

   (b) Improve the quality of education by:

   Funding a chair
   Donations of equipment
   Sharing facilities
   Designing credit courses to upgrade skills

Source: Maxwell and Currie [1984], p. 72.

Invention and Innovation

Governments in the industrialized countries have long been involved in implementing national innovation policies designed to stimulate economic prosperity and national well-being. The policies differ among countries, but essentially the alternatives available to governments are, to a large extent, similar (see Exhibit 11.5).

The specific use of the policy tools, however, is different. For example, currently, the policy emphasis in the United States and United Kingdom is on creation of a climate conducive to firm-based innovation. Japan and France utilize policies that reflect state intervention as a major part of a process of indicative planning (Rothwell [1986]).

Also different among countries are the strategic priorities and focal points

Exhibit 11.5   Classification of Government Policy Tools

Policy Tool	Examples
Public enterprise	Innovation by publicly-owned industries, setting up of new industries, pioneering use of new techniques by public corporations, participation in private enterprise.
Scientific and technical	Research laboratories, support for research associations, learned societies, professional associations, research grants.
Education	General education, universities, technical education, apprenticeship schemes, continuing and further education, retraining.
Information	Information networks and centers, libraries, advisory and consultancy services, data bases, liaison services.
Financial	Grants, loans, subsidies, financial sharing arrangements, provision of equipment, buildings, or services, loan guarantees, export credits.
Taxation	Company, personal, indirect and payroll taxation, tax allowances.
Legal and regulatory	Patents, environments and health regulations, inspectorates, monopoly regulations.
Political	Planning, regional policies, honors or awards for innovation, encouragement of mergers or joint consortia, public consultation.
Procurement	Central or local government purchases and contracts, public corporations, R&D contracts, prototype purchases.
Public services	Purchases, maintenance, supervision and innovation in health service, public building, construction, transport, telecommunications.
Commercial	Trade agreements, tariffs, currency regulations.
Overseas agent	Defense sales organizations.

Source: Reprinted by permission of the publisher, from "Technological Change and Reindustrialization: In Search of a Policy Framework," in *Competitiveness Through Technology,* edited by Jerry Dermer. Lexington, Mass.: Lexington Books, D. C. Heath and Company, Copyright 1986, D. C. Heath and Company.

for national innovation policies (refer to Exhibit 11.3). Of course, the government is the major participant in this decision. It outlines national policies at a macro level, with consideration given to macroeconomics, long-term strategic thinking within major national companies, as well as inherent limitations (financial, technological expertise, and so forth).

Government Involvement.   Given the growing impact of the new technology on the national economy, the role of government in defining and implementing an appropriate innovation policy is becoming increasingly important. An examination of past policies and their drawbacks will show how current and future policies must be modified to facilitate a more positive climate for innovation and economic growth. There are six primary problems to consider:[8]

[8]Rothwell [1986], pp. 104–106.

1. There has in the past been a lack of market knowhow among public policymakers.
2. Past subsidies have tended to assist mainly large firms, thus creating an imbalance.
3. Government has too often adopted a passive, rather than an active, stance toward information dissemination.
4. There has sometimes been a lack of interdepartmental coordination between the relevant organizations and agencies involved in the policy process.
5. There has been a tendency for innovation policies to be subjected to changes in political philosophy rather than to changing national or international economic needs or conditions.
6. There has been a general lack of practical knowledge or conceptualization of the process of industrial innovation by public policymakers.

Once the government sets a national policy, its role with regard to innovation and invention is, as with research, controversial but vital. Many opinions have been formulated with respect to government involvement, but there does seem to be a general agreement that "...government has a crucial role to play in creating favorable conditions for commercial innovation but not in actually producing those innovations."[10] Before expanding upon this consensus, it is necessary to separate innovation into two fields: (1) innovation in which the government is not a customer, and (2) innovation in which the government is a customer. Depending on the situation, governments can play varying roles.

In the situation where the government is not a customer, it should not get involved in the innovation process or the selection of developments. The government, more often than not, is unlikely to succeed as the shaper of innovation, but rather "...will end up being a third party—one that knows a great deal less about the technology than the developer and a great deal less about the market than the user."[11] The following example will illustrate this point:

> One bill before Congress (in 1984) called for a $30 million expenditure in such application areas as programmable automation, robotics, advanced sensors, and (CAD/CAM). But, a large number of companies are already addressing [these technologies]. General Electric, for one, is investing millions in each one of them and, in each case, [they're] faced with many tough competitors...In just one corner of AI for example—the field of solid modeling—GE's subsidiary Calma is up against at least a dozen capable competitors. In this dynamic, market-oriented situation it is simply not plausible that an administrator in Washington...can sit down and pick the winning solid modeling product better than the dozen firms slugging it out in the market.[12]

[9]See, for example, Schmitt [1984], Bartell [1984], and Rothwell [1985].
[10]Schmitt [1984], p. 6.
[11]Schmitt [1984], p. 6.
[12]Schmitt [1984], p. 6.

Such examples are not confined just to the United States. Japan has similar challenges. Historically, commercial innovation successes in Japan have not been driven by the Ministry of Internal Trade (MITI), but by Japanese industry itself.[13] For example:

> The industrial participants in the MITI-sponsored cooperative integrated circuits program went back to their own laboratories to develop the actual commercial 64K random access memory chips that have been so successful in the marketplace. OKI Electrics, the fastest growing Japanese producer of 64K chips . . . did not even participate in the program.[14]

In fact, ". . . the Japanese government have not been a significant force in commercial technology selection and development."[15] The same is true of Canada. Bartell [1984] stresses that:

> The fostering of innovation in Canada at the present time can best be accomplished by a limited and carefully defined role of government . . . The erection of large, bureaucratic organizations or the continual infusion of endless streams of funds, which distorts the operation of the marketplace and conceals or delays the appearance of failure, should be strongly discouraged.[16]

As an example where government help was not successful, he referred to the well-known case of Clairtone Sound Corporation. Here:

> . . . the firm received help from the government of Nova Scotia to build a large color television manufacturing plant. Unfortunately, a reduction in demand led to substantial unsold inventory and to increasing government investment in order to rescue the company. The intrusion of government decision-making created an arbitrarily large organization in relation to its market.[17]

To continue this discussion, Schmitt cites three reasons why government involvement does not usually foster a successful innovation process:

1. Successful innovation requires a close and intimate coupling between the developers of a technology and the businesses that will bring products based on that technology to market, and are themselves in touch with the market.
2. Innovation works best if this close coupling is in place during the entire innovation process.

---

[13]Baranson disagrees. See Baranson [1986].

[14]Schmitt [1984], p. 6.

[15]Schmitt [1984], p. 6.

[16]Bartell [1984], p. 90.

[17]Bartell [1984], p. 90.

3. Governments do not often create the markets for products; they are notoriously slow to react to shifts in the marketplace and they lack the crucial entrepreneurial opportunities early in their development.

Thus, government is often the third party. It is not involved in the intimate coupling and its involvement in the innovation process is typically cumbersome.

Roles Government Can Play. We mentioned the encouraging and assessing roles of government. These involve playing a vital part in creating the proper conditions and a supportive environment within which industries themselves can successfully select and develop commercial technology. This environment can be fostered by:

- Developing an information base for diagnosing and monitoring the technological competitiveness of various industries
- Increasing the financial attractiveness of innovation efforts by individual firms
- Reducing certain risks to the realization of expected innovation benefits
- Increasing the array of promising innovation opportunities
- Encouraging increases in basic research
- Allowing the entry of more scientists and engineering into neglected industrial sectors
- Ensuring that export control laws and regulations do not disrupt the interchange of scientific and technical information
- Permitting foreign scientists to remain
- Strengthening government capabilities for evaluating technological improvement needs and progress
- Supporting universities in their efforts to general research
- Supporting the training and retraining of employees

Successful Government Involvement. If the government is the customer for the innovation, then government selection and funding of innovation can be quite successful—both in generating better products for the government and in promoting technology that can sometimes be tapped for commercial uses. For example:

> The U.S. government has a clear need in the area of supercomputers—very high speed number crunchers, 100 to 1,000 times faster than today's fastest computers. It needs them for weapons research, weather forecasting, economic modeling . . . and many more uses. By meeting its needs in supercomputers, the government will also be sponsoring the development of a product that has many valuable civilian uses like improved oil exploration, better understanding of crack formation and propagation in alloys, and new techniques in computer-aided engineering.[18]

[18]Schmitt [1984], p. 7.

Therefore, if the government itself will benefit from the innovation, it is feasible for it to become involved in the process. If, however, government is not the customer of the invention, then it should not be directly involved in the process but should work to establish an economic climate and long-term research policy conducive to successful innovation at the industry level.

A further concern with respect to innovation and invention concerns the problems of transferring the research to the departments, firms, industries, and even countries that will benefit from the findings and ultimately use them.

Technology Transfer

In Chapter 4 we discussed the notion of intrafirm technology transfer—that is, the transfer of technology between different departments and divisions of the same firm. In this section, our focus is on the transfer of technology from government (and university) to industry, and from one country to another.

Federal Labs to Industry Transfers.   Government-produced technology has flowed out to industry for decades. However, compared to the vast amount of such technology available, the amount that has been spun off to private industry is only a trickle. Olken [1984] identified three reasons for the difficulties:

1. There is a failure of the national labs to write up technology developments they create. Therefore, because a great deal of technology created in government R&D programs is never written up, valuable developments are lost.
2. There is difficulty at national laboratories in making technology write-ups accessible to private industry. Often, because of security reasons, engineers in private industries are to a large extent, barred from using technology write-ups.
3. National laboratories have not organized information to permit spinofffs. Storage of records describing new technology is often chaotic and thus hard to utilize.

Further, Frosch [1984] suggests that the wrong attitude is used in transferring technology from the federal labs to industry. Rather than a business-oriented attitude (systematic management used to time scales, channels of command, and so forth), an engineering, scientific, and product-oriented attitude should be utilized. Research cannot be dealt with systematically; it is usually done by people who have odd modes of thought and who work in ways that are strange to business. Thus, research and its subsequent transfer is often stifled by bureaucracy and stringent business strategies and policies. The following example illustrates some of the problems inherent in transferring technology from the federal research labs to industry:

> In the United States, the DOE recently finished building the nation's first large-scale synchrotron at its Brookhaven National Laboratory in Upton, New York. But it is a general purpose synchrotron used by about 90 academic and cor-

porate research groups for a variety of projects. IBM Corp. is the only company using the synchrotron for X-ray lithography and its researchers have to wait in line to use. "The IBM people are pretty unhappy with the schedule," says William Marcuse, director of technology transfer at the lab. "They spend a lot of time twiddling their thumbs."[19]

In addition, there is also the concern of security. A large amount of U.S. government R&D is spent on defense. In fact a lion's share of the labs belong to two U.S. government departments: Defense and Energy. As a result, much of the research is classified, and "the need to keep classified (information) under wraps has impeded technology transfer in the DOE and the Defense Department."[20] The national defense mission is considered more important than the technology transfer mission.

Experience has made it clear that successful transfers require cooperative alliances and information exchanges between government and industry. As Dorf [1988] notes:

> The effective commercialization of new technologies is less of a relay race where players hand off a baton to the next player than it is a basketball game where players pass the ball back and forth as they advance towards the goal. Clearly, a team effort is required for most new technology development. This approach uses a team from engineering, research, marketing, manufacturing, sales, and finance to reach a joint consensus on features, performance and cost and then utilizes the team to accomplish all the necessary tasks. This approach is costly but fast, and in the long-term, economically efficient.[21]

In summary, it is apparent that of the massive amount of government-produced R&D, only a very small portion is transferred to private industry. Companies are discouraged from using the government labs as a resource, and any benefit derived from these labs is often nothing more than an afterthought (Guteri [1987]).

University to Industry Transfers.   As mentioned, university-industry collaboration is important, but the actual transfer of technology and research from the university to private industry, although often successful, is sometimes unnecessarily prohibited. To overcome the obstacle, Gordon [1986], suggests:

1. Technology transfer organizations should be established at all major universities.
2. University faculty, professional staff, private sector firms and government agencies should all be stakeholders in these enterprises.
3. University technology transfer organizations should be incorporated and have a business orientation and mission.

[19]Guteri [1987], p. 44.
[20]Guteri [1987], p. 45.

4. University technology transfer organizations should have the mandate to initiate technical development activities.

5. University technology transfer organizations should establilsh continuing linkages with private sector corporations that facilitate the transfer of a stream of new technologies.

To recapitulate, government has a key role to play in facilitating the collaboration between university and industry. Its role as a stakeholder, and its involvement as an assessor, is very important.

Transfers to Industrialized Nations. Technology transfer between industrialized nations involves large amounts of money. For instance, in 1982 the Organization for Economic Cooperation and Development (OECD) technology exports totaled $12 billion. "The United States has traditionally been the source of between 50 and 75 percent of technology in most importing countries."[22] However, "...there appears to be a trend that countries with comprehensive and broadly-based domestic technological capacity have reduced their level of direct reliance on imported technology."[23] For example:

> Japanese firms have consistently increased their own R&D efforts to use, improve, develop and perfect imported technology. Technology imports of firms performing R&D fell from 25 percent of the value of R&D expenditures in the early 1970s to 10 percent in 1982.[24]

The transfer of technology to other nations is a controversial issue. Consider the following:

> A just released report from the Office of Management and Budget says that military aerospace companies give away over half the value of their export sales to foreign countries in "offset deals." Concern has been rising in Congress for months that these deals threaten U.S. interests, and that commercial as well as military aircraft builders are creating foreign competitors in an industry that the U.S. still dominates... Congress is concerned that America's aviation companies are trading away jobs and technology to get foreign orders.[25]

Furthermore, there are also military and security anxieties:

> The United States research and development establishment is viewed by the Soviets as a mother lode of important and, very frequently, openly available

---

[21]Dorf [1988], p. 303.
[22]OECD [1986], p. 51.
[23]Rothwell [1986], p. 117.
[24]OECD [1984], p.
[25]Banks [1986], p. 36.

scientific and technical information. In fact, they tap into it so frequently that one must wonder if they regard U.S. research and development as their own national asset.[26]

For their country's own self-interest, many governments have attempted to control technology flow abroad. Most categorize technologies as classified and unclassified, with classified technology transfers being forbidden by the government through legislation and strict penalties.

Usually this controlled technology is military in nature. However, there are also government attempts to control much of the nonclassified technology that has dual use capabilities; that is, technology that has commercial applications but also, with limited modification, and significant military applications. An example of such dual use technology is integrated circuit manufacturing (Securities [1983]). The basic mechanism used by governments to control the dissemination of technology is export regulation. The goal is to facilitate maximum trade and maximum commercial development with friendly nations, while limiting exports to potential adversaries.

Transfers to Less Developed Countries.   Technology advances in the world have been uneven, and as a result, a technological gap has emerged between developed and less developed countries. An opportunity for technology transfer has arisen. Governments, either directly or indirectly, also play an important role in this situation. With respect to the recipient country, the government's direct roles involve:

1. Specifying national needs for the approval of the technology
2. Coericion of domestic industries to import the technology
3. Involvement in the direct importing of the technology
4. Participating in direct negotiations about the mechanics of importing the technology

The government also has indirect influences. It can provide special incentives so that certain technologies will be given a higher priority by the private sector that will take over the responsibility of importing. Furthermore, it can provide assistance to help make the imported technology successful (see Samli [1985]). The government of the transferring country also plays a key role. It has the authority to allow, approve, or reject joint ventures that can be instrumental in transferring the technology. Also, export regulations can be put in place to control the dissemination of technology.

Education, Training, and Retraining

As discussed in Chapter 10, the new technology will have an enormous impact on employment. When properly used, it can do much to enhance the quality

---

[26]Security [1983], p. 43.

of life, to supply consumers with better products and services, to upgrade work, to increase productivity, and to raise incomes. However, if workers are to reap their share of the benefits, they must be given the sort of training and education that will equip them to meet the challenges of the new technologies (Alfthan [1985]). If firms are to remain competitive, they must maintain a skilled workforce. Government and industry can both play an important part in educating, training, and retraining this workforce.

The Need for Education.   Because industry requires scientists, engineers, managers, and technicians, one can argue that businesses should be more involved and commit more financial resources to the university education system. This would strengthen the relationship between industry and university, and it would enable industry to train students to meet specific industry needs. However, concerns such as the monopolization of talented students by particular firms at the expense of others makes this approach questionable. Consequently, government tends to play the critical role in the education process.[27]

The new technology has led to the resurfacing of the educational concerns. There has been an increasing awareness of the fact that the scientific, engineering, and management issues that have resulted from the new technology must be incorporated into the university curriculum. At the same time, financial and human resource limitations constrain universities in their efforts to upgrade the level of technological education that they can offer. In any event, it is becoming clear that (a) the management of the new technology should receive more attention in university engineering, science, and business curricula, and (b) industry, government, and university will have to work closely together to ensure that this objective is met.[28]

The following example highlights one successful attempt at integrating the efforts of industry, government, and university to educate employees in the new technology:

> The Nova Scotia Institute of Technology has teamed up with Pratt & Whitney Canada, Inc. to provide employees with high automation technology skills.... Ottawa and the province provided $9.5 million to build the Automated Manufacturing Technology Center (AMTC) as an addition to the existing institute. AMTC trains its graduates in the principles of 'flexible manufacturing.' Of the 100 who have graduated since 1985, about 75 percent have been hired by Pratt & Whitney. And the plant will need more graduates over the next couple of years.[29]

While education is essential to bring properly qualified people into the labor force, to the extent that it does not address the problems of those currently

---

[27]Government funding can be used to ensure that the population of a country is as educated as possible, and that education is geared to benefitting both industry in particular and society in general.

[28]See, for example, Task Force on Management of Technology [1987].

[29]Harrison [1988], p. 26.

being affected by new technology adoption, it is incomplete. These concerns must then be met through training and retraining.

The Need for Training/Retraining.   As noted in Chapters 9 and 10, the new technology is expected to alter the occupational structure and change (or upgrade) the skills required in manufacturing. We are faced with increasing levels of illiteracy in the workforce while the complexity of the technologies involved demands higher skill levels. It is therefore apparent and indeed necessary for workers to be trained and/or retrained in these new skills. The following example highlights the importance of having skilled employees in the new technology environment:

> Numerically controlled (NC) machine tools were originally developed with the dual purpose of diminishing reliance on skilled machinists and augmenting technical capabilities. Early vendors' advertisements were very clear: with the new machines, after establishing the appropriate software to select and guide the cutting tools, "anyone can do the second piece."
>
> But in reality, in the three decades since the development of the NC machine tool, its adoption has not led to any general trend to the elimination of the skilled machinist. Surveys show repeatedly that not only are most NC machines operated by skilled operators, but new training requirements and higher levels of responsibility are the general rule.[30]

It appears that many firms are reluctant to retain employees whose skills have become obsolete, but rather prefer the easy option of replacing them by hiring workers with the necessary skills.[31] However, replacing workers is becoming a less desirable option today. Heightened social awareness of the employment effects of automation as well as union demands for job security provisions have forced firms to address the issues of training and development of current workers. In fact: "Workplace training and development is roughly equivalent in size to the entire elementary, secondary, and higher education systems combined."[32] Firms are beginning to see that employee training is in their own best interest:

> [APICS President, Gordon] Ellis contends that 80 percent of the problems in a plant are caused by management, and only 20 percent by workers. The fact is, workers run the shop floor, even though they aren't the cause of most problems; so why not give them the training tools to run it properly.[33]

---

[30]Alder [1986], p. 9.

[31]See Ortman [1984], Economic Council of Canada [1987].

[32]Gould [1987], p. 50.

[33]Cummings and Richardson [1987], p. 15.

In reality, government can often act as the impetus for firms to undertake this training and retraining.

Government Involvement in Training and Retraining.   Government involvement varies from country to country depending on the political and economic systems. One involvement that is fairly common, though, is the use of incentive for industries to train employees. Japanese firms, for example, progressively deduct from their taxable income additional or incremental training expenses incurred in the previous fiscal period. Singapore has established a Training Grants Scheme which provides grants to firms amounting to 30, 50, or 70 percent of the costs incurred in staff training, retraining and upgrading (Castley and Alfthan [1986]). Canada also utilizes incentives. For example, in 1985 the federal government switched the focus of its $2 billion employment budget from job creation to job training. This was after being confronted with "evidence that technological change [was] one of the important causes of Canada's high level of unemployment."[34] This new program ". . .envisages a cooperative effort under which government and employers will work together to provide training. . .and will share in the cost of the programs."[35] In short, such incentive programs are found all over the world, and most provide firms with the impetus to train and/or retrain employees.

Governments also offer their own retraining programs. Many federal retraining programs ". . .arose in part out of concern over the prospective impact of technological change upon the employability of experienced workers ."[36] In fact, such concerns are not new. In the United States in 1937, for instance, the Railroad Unemployment Insurance Act directed the Railroad Retirement Board to "encourage and assist in the adoption of practical methods of vocational training, retraining and vocational guidance; to promote the re-employment of unemployed employees."[37]

Finally, governments can coerce firms to train their employees. This is usually confined to industries where worker training is essential for their own well-being (the chemical industry). While governments can employ harsh action to get employers to take on more of a training role, it has been realized that ". . .although there must be a basic government legislation in order to show determination that training should take place, the system should be such that the law need only very rarely be invoked."[38]

It should be mentioned that governments are only one part of training/retraining programs. Employers must also become involved. They must appreciate that the changing technological environments affects their staff, and

[34]Anderson [1985], p. B2.
[35]Anderson [1985], p. B2.
[36]Hardin [1971], p. 3.
[37]Hardin [1971], p. 3.
[38]Castley and Alfhan [1986], p. 554.

should look upon the cost of training as an inherent part of running a business. In reality, the government can play a pivotal role, but not the only role.

Financial Support

Governments are also important sources of financial support for research and development, innovation and, ultimately, the development and adoption of new technologies. By financing certain technologies, while neglecting others, the government establishes and reestablishes innovation policies. Financing, then, is of the utmost importance.

Financial aid allows companies to start up, consolidate, and often expand. With respect to financing a particular new technology, it is becoming clear that "...getting assistance from [the] government is no different than having financial dealings with any other type of lending institution."[39] Firms should have a legitimate claim, a well-prepared case, and understand the rules of the game. However, as mentioned in Chapter 7, there are still some bureaucratic barriers which can prevent firms from obtaining quick financing. Government policies generally include tax measures, joint funding, or procurement policies that reduce private sector costs and risks. These policy tools are typically consistent from country to country, although the actual amount of aid usually differs.

Tax incentives are a key financial source. In Japan, for example:

> If a firm's research and development expenditure for a given year exceed the largest amount of annual R&D expenditure for any preceding year since 1966, 70 percent of the excess may be taken as a credit against the corporate income tax.[40]

In Canada, there are tax credit controversies. Rather than, as in the past, simply rubber stamping tax credits, Revenue Canada is now taking months or years to process claims for R&D tax credits (Carlisle [1988]). Over 85 percent of the claims eventually get approved, and the wait is often detrimental to a company's profit and loss statements and cash flows. For instance:

> Process Technology Ltd. slid from winning two Canada awards for Excellence in Innovation to filing for bankruptcy when Revenue Canada auditors held up tax credits worth $1.3 million for two years.[41]

This new approach to approving tax credits is the result of massive tax scams that revealed enormous loopholes in the now defunct Scientific Research Tax Credit program.[42]

---

[39]Collins [1986], p. 463.

[40]Baranson [1986], p. 155.

[41]Carlisle [1988], p. 6.

[42]In fact, the program resulted in a drain of $2.8 billion on the government treasury of which $925 million was wasted: $500 million in fradulent deals and the remaining in ill-conceived research projects.

COMPARING GOVERNMENT TECHNOLOGY SUPPORT POLICIES

There are vast differences among western industrialized countries (WIC) with respect to government policies (see Exhibit 11.6). Even more dramatic are the differences in the roles and scope of governments in newly industrialized countries (NIC). In general, a number of economy, industry, firm, and product-specific factors influence the effectiveness of the policy options available to governments. These factors include:

INDUSTRY-SPECIFIC FACTORS	FIRM-SPECIFIC FACTORS	PRODUCT-SPECIFIC FACTORS
Progressive/innovative	Multinational/domestic	Opportunity
Tariffs	Culture	Niche/growth
R&D/consortia	Short-/long-range	Product life cycle
Selective policy	planning	
Growth areas	Geography	
Financing		

Environmental factors, and specific policy tools, vary between countries. Even so, if new technology adoption is to be encouraged, all governments must set some goals and priorities, and then see to the implementation of consistent policies and incentives.

CONCLUDING OBSERVATIONS

The focus of this chapter has been the government's role in new technology, particularly with respect to four areas: research, invention and innovation, technology transfer, and education, training, and retraining.

Government can play varying roles in the research area. The most essential role, however, is to provide an impetus to and a focus for research, since the research being done today, to a large extent, influences the economic directions of the future.

Government involvement in the intervention and innovation process poses problems. Government is often a third party in the process, and thus its involvement is typically cumbersome. Nevertheless, government does have a vital role to play in creating an economic climate conducive to successful invention and innovation at the industry level.

The problems with technology transfer, and ways to overcome them, were discussed with respect to the five types of transfer:

- Federal labs to industry transfers
- University to industry transfers
- Transfers to industrialized countries
- Transfers to less developed countries
- Industry to industry transfers

Exhibit 11.6 Government Policy Comparisons

Policies	Western Industrialized Countries				
	USA	*Japan*	*West Germany*	*France*	*Sweden*
Industrial policy Trade policies Regulatory measures	Rely largely on market forces. Adversarial government relations.	Intervention to promote innovation. Sunrise industries support long-term.	Rely largely on market forces.	Highly supportive of high technology industries.	Rely largely on market forces.
Economic measures Capital measures Tax incentives Interest rates Growth	Tax incentives to promote capital investments. RDE generally budgetary deficits raise interest rates, appreciate currency, intensify foreign competition.	Funds to priority sectors. Bank leveraging and tax sheltered corporate reserves. Promote export—lead growth. Promote savings, low interest rates.	Mild and limited intervention.	Tax shelter capital funds in high-tech industries.	Mild and limited intervention.
R&D proocurement	Antitrust inhibits cooperative R&D efforts. Strong support of defense-related R&D policies neutral.	Jointly fund R&D of next generation technology. Credit for AMS leasing.	Limited support.	Highly supportive of AMS RD&E.	Limited support.

Source: Adapted from: Baranson [1986], p. 148 and reprinted by permission of the publisher, from "Technological Change and Reindustrialization: In Search of a Policy Framework," in *Competitiveness Through Technology*, edited by Jerry Dermer, Lexington, Mass.: Lexington Books, D.C. Heath and Company, Copyright 1986, D. C. Heath and Company.

Given the potential labor force displacement effects and the changing skills required by the new technology, a properly educated and trained workforce is essential. This is essentially an issue industry must face alone, but the government can also contribute. It can provide incentives to firms to train/retrain workers, establish government-run programs, or coerce firms to undertake the required training/retraining.

Finally, government has several policy-support vehicles available to encourage corporate investment in new technologies. Use of these vehicles differs across industrialized countries.

RECOMMENDED READINGS

DORF, R. C. [1988]. "Methods of Technology Transfer from Universities and Research Laboratories."
In Tarek M. Khalil et al. (eds.), *Technology Management I*, pp. 302–312.
GOULD, L. [1987]. "Balanced Workplace Retraining." Managing Automation, April, pp. 50–54.
MAXWELL, J., and S. CURIE [1984].   *Partnership for Growth.* Corporate-University Cooperation in
Canada.
"Technology and National Policy." *High Technology* (Special Report).
Technology Crossing Borders. [1984].   In Robert Stobaugh and Louis T. Wells, Jr., (eds.), *The Choice,
Transfer and Management of International Technology Flows.*

DISCUSSION QUESTIONS

1. Do you feel that funding for university research should come directly from industry and less from government? What are the implications of this approach? Explain fully.
2. Should government ever restrict the flow of nonmilitary technology to other countries? Explain.
3. As the government, how would you encourage firms to adopt advanced manufacturing technologies? What policies could/would you use?
4. Should government develop an industrial policy outlining which industries it will support and which it will not? How should winning/losing industries be determined?
5. As a company, how would you utilize the potential benefits that you could obtain from government for developing, financing, and training personnel for the new technology? Would you seek government assistance for the development and adoption of the new technology, even if the assistance is not a prerequisite (that is, you have sufficient internal resources to develop and acquire new technology)? Explain fully.
6. Should most government research be performed in universities or in government laboratories? Explain.
7. Should industry be forced by government to allocate more resources to training and retraining employees?

REFERENCES AND BIBLIOGRAPHY

ADLER, P. [1986]. "New Technologies, New Skills." *California Management Review,* Fall, pp. 9–12.
ALFTHAN, T. [1985]. "Developing Skills for Technological Change: Some Policy Issues." *International
Labor Review,* September–October, pp. 517–528.

ANDERSON, F. [1987]. *University-Industry Research Centers: An Interface Between University and Industry.* Science Council of Canada, Proceedings of a Workshop Held May 22-23, 1986.

ANDERSON, R. [1985]. "Ottawa's Move to Step Up Skill Training Makes Sense." *Globe and Mail,* July 3, p. B2.

BANKS, H. [1986]. "Fear of Dealing." *Forbes,* March 10, p. 36.

BARANSON, J. [1986]. "Government Policies in Support of Automated Manufacturing: Japan, the United States, and Western Europe." In J. Dermer (ed.), *Competitiveness Through Technology.* Lexington Books, Lexington, Mass.

BARNES, J. G., and G. R. PETERS [1987]. *The Teaching Company Scheme; A Study of Its Application in Canada.* Science Council of Canada, Discussion Paper, May.

BARTELL, M. [1984]. "Innovation and The Canadian Experience: A Perspective." *Columbia Journal of World Business,* Winter, pp. 88-91.

BODDY, D., and D. BUCHANAN [1985]. "New Technology with a Human Face." *Personnel Management,* April, pp. 28-31.

Canadian Advanced Technology Association [1986]. *The Report of the National Technology Policy Round-table.* Canadian High Technology Week, Toronto, September 23.

CARLISLE, T. [1988]. "A Jungle of Tax Credit Rules Confuses High-Tech Firms." *Financial Post,* February 2, p. 6.

CASTLEY, R., and T. ALFTHAN [1986]. "Training for Industrial Development; How Governments Can Help." *International Labor Review,* September-October, pp. 545-559.

CLARKE, T. E., and J. REAVLEY [1987]. *Educating Technological Innovators and Technical Entrepreneurs at Canadian Universities.* Science Council of Canada, Discussion Paper, May.

CRANE, D. [1985]. "High-Tech Can Help to Save Canada's Economy, *Toronto Star,* June 12.

CRELINSTEN, J. [1987]. *University Spin-Off Firms: Helping the Ivory Tower Go to Market.* Science Council of Canada, Proceedings of a Workshop held November 21-22, 1985.

CUMMINGS, C., and R. RICHARDSON [1987]. "Emphasis on Education." *Plant Management and Engineering,* February, pp. 15-17.

DALLMEYER, D. [1987]. "National Security and the Semiconductor Industry." *Technology Review,* November-December, pp. 47-55.

DORF, R. C. [1988]. "Models for Technology Transfer from Universities to Research Laboratories." In Tarek M. Khalil et al. (eds.), *Technology Management I, Proceedings of the First International Conference on Technology Management.* Inderscience Enterprises Ltd., Geneva, pp. 302-313.

DOWNER, G. H. [1986]. "The Role of the Universities in the Development of and Transfer of New Technology." In H. Noori (ed.), *Proceedings: Technology Canada, WLU, REMAT,* May 21-22, pp. 340-350.

Economic Council of Canada [1987]. *Making Technology Work: Innovation and Jobs in Canada.* Minister of Supply and Services Canada.

ENROS, P., and M. FARLEY [1986]. *University Offices for Technology Transfer: Toward the Service Industry.* Science Council of Canada, Discussion Paper, August.

ERDLICK, A., and A. ROPOPORT [1985]. "Conceptual and Measurement Problem . . . Technology Transfer." In A. Samli (ed.), *Technology Transfer.* Greenwood Press, Connecticut.

FROSCH, R. A. [1984]. "Linking R&D With Business . . . ." *Research Management,* Volume 28, No. 3, pp. 11-14.

FUDGE, C. [1986]. "Retraining for New Technologies: Six Success Stories." *Personnel Management,* February, pp. 42-45.

GATES, B. [1988]. "Corporations, Academics Forge Stronger Links—Brains Meet Marketing." *The Financial Post-Universities & Industry Special Report,* February 22, p. 25.

GOLDSTEIN, P. [1984]. "Firms Urged to Develop Employees." *The Globe and Mail,* October 17, p. B6.

GORDON, J. [1986]. "Commercializing University Inventions." In H. Noori (ed.), *Proceedings: Technology Canada Conference, WLU, REMAT.* May 21-22, p. 351-360.

GOULD, L. [1987]. "Balanced Workplace Retraining." *Managing Automation,* April, pp. 50-54.

GRIFFITHS, P. A. [1987]. "Research: A New Agenda." *High Technology,* August, p. 64.

GUTERI, F. [1987]. "Technology Transfer Isn't Working." *Business Month,* September, pp. 44-48.

HARDING, E., and M. BORUS [1971]. *The Economic Benefits and Costs of Retraining.* Lexington Books, Lexington, Mass.

HARRISON, M. [1988]. "Industry Gets Skilled Workers from Link-Ups." *The Financial Post—Universities & Industry Special Report,* February 22, p. 26.

MAXWELL, J., and S. CURRIE [1984]. *Partnership for Growth: Corporate-University Cooperation of Canada.* Corporate Higher Education Forum: Montreal, p. 72.

MONTGOMERY, C. [1981].   "Wasting Millions on Job Training Government Told." *Globe and Mail,* October 13, p. 16.

NEWTON, K. [1985].   "Impact of New Technology on Employment." *Canadian Business Review,* Winter, pp. 27–30.

OECD [1984].   *The Structure of International Flows of Technology.* Paris, November 13.

OECD [1986].   *STI Review,* Paris, Autumn.

OLKEN, H. [1984].   "Cooperation Between Private Industry and the National Laboratories." *Personnel Administrator,* June, p. 44.

ORTMAN, J. K. [1987].   *Economic Council of Canada.*

PRESTOWITZ, C. [1988].   "Japanese vs. Western Economies." *Technology Review,* May–June, pp. 27–36.

ROTHWELL, R. [1986].   "Technological Change and Reindustrialization: In Search of a Policy Framework." In J. Dermer (ed.), *Competitiveness Through Technology.* Lexington Books, Lexington, Mass., pp. 97–122.

RUJAN, A. [1985].   "New Technology and Jobs: The Counter Argument." *Personnel Management,* July, pp. 34–39.

SAMLI, A. [1985].   "Technology Transfer, The General Model/2." In A. Samli (ed.), *Technology Transfer.* Greenwood Press, Connecticut.

SCHMITT, R. [1984].   "An Industrial Perspective on National R&D Policy." *Research Management,* July–August, pp. 6–10.

Security Management [1983].   "Technology Transfer: What's Acceptable and Why." September, pp. 43–56.

Task Force on Management of Technology [1987].   *National Research Council.* National Academy Press.

Chapter Twelve

A DYNAMIC ANALYSIS OF ADOPTING THE NEW TECHNOLOGY

The most impressive feature, and the fact that makes Japanese manufacturing so effective, is how their manufacturing facilities are managed and the technology is applied. Japanese management is geared towards integrated manufacturing.

The CAD Council Task Force

INTRODUCTION

In preceding chapters, we have noted a number of prerequisites for success in planning and implementing the new technology. These include:

1. Coordinating business objectives and strategy with the goals of the project. That is, do not look solely for technical success.
2. Ensuring that senior management consistently supports the project.
3. Raising the employees' awareness of the potential and the impact of the new technology.
4. Detailing the initial plan to get realistic estimates and expectations.
5. Forming the project team well in advance, and getting a good assessment of the current technological capabilities of the company.
6. Having a realistic perception of the impact of the new technology and involving the end users in the planning phase.

The right approach to planning, acquiring, implementing, and integrating technology relies on a number of carefully executed steps, some of which can be carried out in parallel. Prior to exploring an appropriate action plan, we look at some of the important questions typically asked when adopting the new technology.

A REVIEW OF CRITICAL QUESTIONS: THE FIVE Ws AND THE ONE H

Before attempting to implement the new technology, it is crucial that a firm perform an environmental audit, giving explicit consideration to both internal and external factors. This is for the simple reason that if a company does not know where it is now, it is very difficult for it to get where it would like to be! Exhibit 12.1 presents a comprehensive list of the relevant environmental factors.

Exhibit 12.1   Environmental Considerations in Assessment of New Technology Implementations

Internal Considerations	External Considerations

Company Strategy
  Well defined?
  Will the acquisition of new technology aid the
    achievement of strategy?
	Customers
	  Concentration
	  Needs and requirements
	  Relations
	  Power, dependence

Production Process
  Flexibility
  Lead times
  Product quality
  Labor costs
  Material flow and handling
  Alternative production technologies available
	Competitors
	  Threat of new entrants
	  Relative use of new technology
	  Competitive advantage/disadvantage
	  Competitive environment
	  Substitutes

Human Resources
  Corporate culture
  Management attitudes
  Worker and union attitudes
	Supplier
	  Concentration
	  Power, dependence
	  Extent of automation
	  Relations

Finance
  Cost and benefit evaluation
  Information processing
  Capital budgeting, capital allocation
	Government
	  Aid, grants
	  Regulatory atmosphere
	  Tax incentives

Marketing
  Product strategy
  Number of products
  Distribution channels
  Pricing structure	

Information Processes
  Decentralization
  Centralization
  Integration	

To account properly for these factors, a number of questions should be asked before and during the acquisition process. In general, these queries can be classified under the following categories:

- Why should the new technology be adopted?
- What form of the new technology is needed?

- Whether to develop or acquire the new technology?
- When to acquire the new technology?
- Where should the new technology be installed?
- How should the new technology be introduced?

What follows is a detailed analysis of these questions. You may remember that four of these questions were also discussed in Chapter 9 (also see Noori [1987]).

Why Should the New Technology Be Adopted?

Some of the most relevant decisions and corresponding alternatives are included in the following:

DECISION CONSIDERATIONS		DECISION ALTERNATIVES
Increased technological availability	→	Seize opportunity; or retain existing processes.
Degree of new technology adoption by competition	→	Respond to competition/market demand; or maintain current processes.
Labor cost considerations	→	Reduce labor costs by seeking to improve existing workforce productivity; or substitute new technology applications and direct labor requirements.
Flexibility requirements	→	Introduce a complete flexible manufacturing system; or supplement existing process with new applications; or retain existing process.
Quality level	→	Utilize recent developments in new technology providing precision and consistency; or apply manual statistical quality control; or implement quality circles.
Degree of operating leverage	→	Increase application of new technology or decrease greater labor emphasis; or pursue existing policies.
Dependability	→	Achieve shorter lead times (resulting from increased efficiency of new technology applications); or change inventory policies; or reassess capacity constraint.
Total systems emphasis	→	Increase integration and interaction (among functional areas within the firm); or apply traditional organizational methods.
Information accessibility requirements	→	Bridge information gap (traditionally found between upper management and operations function) through automation of information systems; or address information requirements via existing organizational methods.
Engineering and design	→	Utilize CAD system, or implement traditional manual approach.

Economies of scale   →   Achieve similar benefits at lower volumes—with product diversity—by applications of new technology; or expand plant capacity with existing processes.

Distinctive competence   →   Utilize new technology to establish distinctive competence/retain such in face of environmental pressures; or pull strategic levels utilizing current process emphasis.

What Form of the New Technology Is Needed?

As Ayres [1988] states, if the technology decision process (for discrete-part manufacturing) can be broken up conceptually into distinct steps, the choice of technology will depend mainly on the following five major variables:

- Complexity of the product (the greater the complexity, in general, the greater the degree of automation required)
- Precision with which the product must be made (the greater the precision required, in general, the greater the degree of automation required)
- Batch or lot size (the larger the lot size, the less the degree of flexibility required in the manufacturing process and equipment)
- Diversity or the number of models in the family (the greater the diversity of models, the more flexibility is needed)
- Mass or linear dimension of the product (the more the dimensions of products, the more flexibility is needed)

Keeping these variables in mind, the question of the form of the new technology can best be answered through the integrative approach discussed in Chapter 4. For this to be successful, companies should have a good understanding of the market, the competition, and the emerging technologies. Given this, it appears appropriate to follow an interactive approach such as the one illustrated in Exhibit 12.2. The model is partially based on the work of Cooper [1983] and extends the relationship between changes in the product-explicit attributes (suitability, capability, and performance), and market responsiveness to include the impact of changes in the key, base, and generic technologies (see Chapter 5 for details). The exhibit suggests that the selection of technology in general and the key technology in particular should be done in connection with the product (implicit and explicit) attributes and market position of the firm.

Whether to Develop or Acquire the New Technology?

This question is directly linked to the previous question, and like the others should be dealt with strategically. To address this question, a matrix approach, such as the one shown in Exhibit 5.14, is appropriate.

Exhibit 12.2   An Interactive Approach to Determine the Required Technology

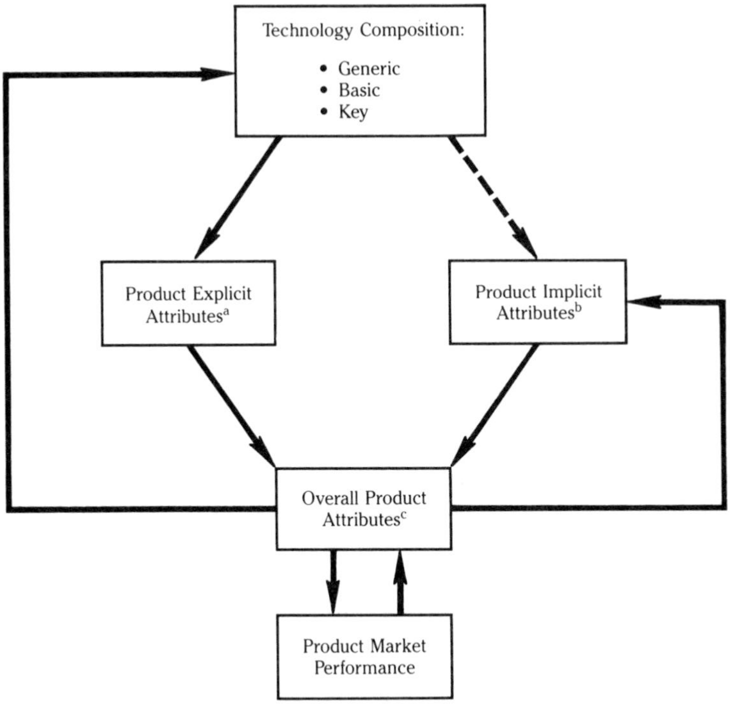

Note a: Explicit attributes include design, flexibility, suitability and cost—manufacturing's sphere of influence.

Note b: Implicit attributes consi sts of color, packaging, service availability, and warranty—marketing's sphere of influence.

Note c: Implicit attributes are less technological dependent in comparison with explicit attributes. However, implicit attributes of the product can fail due to a lack of attention to explicit attributes.

When to Acquire the New Technology?

Part of the related decisions and decision alternatives are these:

DECISION CONSIDERATIONS	DECISION ALTERNATIVES
Competitive pressure	→ Adopt reactive; or proactive strategy.
Social pressure/implications	→ Coordinates timing (so as to minimize negative social impacts/maximize positive social impacts); or base timing on internal factors to the firm only.
Product life cycle stage	→ Introduce new technology applications particular to specific products (which display adequate remaining sales potential); or allocate priorities based on other criteria.

Market considerations	→ Time new technology acquisitions in response to market demand; or independent of market demand.
Corporate culture	→ Base timing considerations on adherence to traditional corporate policies; or irrespective of past practices.
Managerial and technical preparedness	→ Introduce new technology applications at point in time when management and staff have developed capability; or do not postpone acquisition on other criteria (debt financing).
Cash flow considerations	→ Acquire new technology when incoming revenues can accommodate purchase; or base acquisitions on other criteria (debt financing).
New product introductions	→ Time new technology acquisitions in accordance with or irrespective of new product introductions.
Recency of the technological innovation	→ Acquire new technology applications immediately after market introduction; or postpone acquisition until developed further.

Several of these assessments involve areas within and outside the organization. A concise illustration of these internal and external considerations is provided in Exhibit 12.2.

Where Should the New Technology be Installedl?

Also prescribed in the following, is a set of decisions and alternatives that should be considered in this case.

DECISION CONSIDERATIONS	DECISION ALTERNATIVES
Plant and equipment condition	→ Introduce new technology as a means of replacing dated equipment and facilities; or introduce irrespective of existing condition.
Department/functional adaptability	→ Restrict the base of new technology introductions on suitability of process; or seek to alter given processes to broaden adaptability.
Impact ramifications	→ Focus new technology introductions on specific processes which have greatest potential for benefit; or adopt an encompassing approach.
Availability of labor	→ Introduce new technology specifically into areas lacking sufficient labor resource base; or adopt a policy of even dispersion coupled with retraining redistribution of displaced workers.

Growth implications   →   Incorporate new technology acquisitions into areas of anticipated growth; or utilize new technology applications to maintain consistent and broad support.

How Should the New Technology be Introduced?

Finally, the following are some relevant decision considerations and decision alternatives related to this question.

DECISION CONSIDERATIONS		DECISION ALTERNATIVES
Speed of introduction	→	Adopt gradual; or swift approach.
Employee/union participation	→	Involve employees in decision-making procedures; or conduct decisions independent of employee input.
Impact on employment levels	→	Consider whether immediate and long-term effects on employment play a considerable role; or insignificant role in implementation decisions.
Utilization of support services	→	Heavy reliance on government/consultant support services during implementation; or reliance on in-house expertise.
Pregeneration of concept acceptance	→	Initiate measures to encourage positive disposition among employees regarding new technology applications; or allow employee reactions to run their course.
Degree of prior orientation	→	Precede new technology implementation with training and orientation of personnel as well as process testing; or implement new technology and learn by doing.

DETAIL ANALYSIS: A BLUEPRINT

In this section we will be examining a framework and a set of actions for successfully planning, acquiring, and implementing the new technology. This blueprint takes into account the five key areas mentioned earlier. The steps described here do not necessarily have to be carried out in order, and some, in fact, can be considered in parallel. The points discussed in this section are covered in many parts of this book; this is an attempt to summarize some of the relevant issues within a decision-making framework.

The overall approach for technology adoption consists of five phases: (1) initiation and strategic planning phase, (2) feasibility study and justification phase, (3) system selection/development phase, (4) implementation phase, and (5) post implementation phase (see Exhibit 12.3).

Exhibit 12.3 The Five Basic Phases in Adopting New Technology

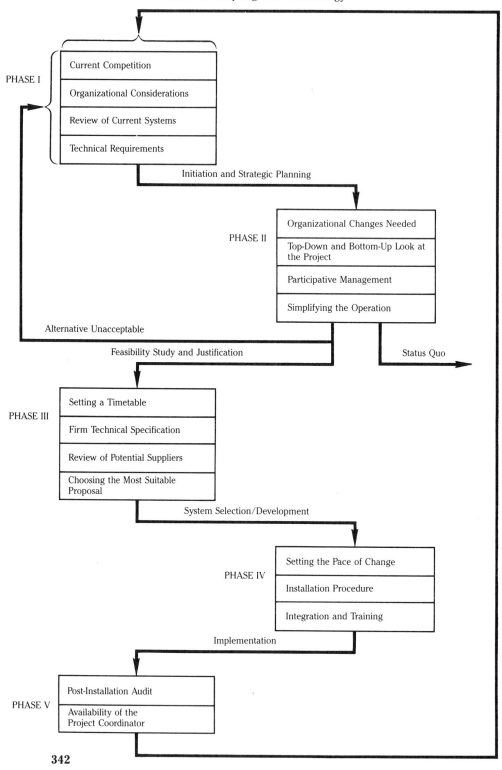

PHASE I

- Current Competition
- Organizational Considerations
- Review of Current Systems
- Technical Requirements

Initiation and Strategic Planning

PHASE II

- Organizational Changes Needed
- Top-Down and Bottom-Up Look at the Project
- Participative Management
- Simplifying the Operation

Alternative Unacceptable

Feasibility Study and Justification

Status Quo

PHASE III

- Setting a Timetable
- Firm Technical Specification
- Review of Potential Suppliers
- Choosing the Most Suitable Proposal

System Selection/Development

PHASE IV

- Setting the Pace of Change
- Installation Procedure
- Integration and Training

Implementation

PHASE V

- Post-Installation Audit
- Availability of the Project Coordinator

Initiation and Strategic Planning Phase

Objective: To identify those areas of the business where new technology will have the greatest impact and hence should be considered first.

Actions: A review of current marketing status and national/international competition.

An evaluation of all functional areas, including design, engineering, and manufacturing.

An examination of existing manufacturing systems and methods.

An identification of the company's technical requirements.

Results: Formulation of a management consensus on the priorities of the business. This should enable the company to measure its position vis-à-vis domestic and/or international competition. Subsequently, improvements may be carried out with no additional technology requisition.

Realization of the extent to which the current organizational structure and boundary lines inhibit the response perceived as necessary.

Commitment and support of senior management, establishment of the team, and emergence of the project champion or coordinator.

Decision whether a full feasibility study is necessary.

Feasibility Study and Justification Phase

Objective: To examine the characteristics of the available and potential technologies in terms of software/hardware.

Actions: An assessment of financial situation and justification plan.

A desire to carry out the review without cost constraints at first.

A review of organizational changes needed, and an evaluation of the technical and training aspects of the technology.

A top-down and bottom-up look at the project utilizing the experience of other businesses.

A participative management style and encouraging staff involvement. Selection of the project team.

An effort to simplify the process and the products whenever possible.

Examine proposed technology for consistency with existing infrastructure.

Evaluation of the potential sources of resistance to technological change within the organization.

Results: Formation of business plan to include new products, new buildings, and so forth.

Development of the necessary specifications.

Determination of where the equipment can be sited, with particular reference to integration requirement and environmental considerations.

Capturing the potential of the new technology and the creativiity of the technical staff.

Provision of backup facilities.

If deemed not feasible at present, firm has at least discerned what its technology goals should be.

System Selection/Development Phase

Objective: To develop a contract (or plan) which is unambiguous and to determine what exactly should be ordered (or done).

Actions: Setting a timetable.

Writing up a firm technical specification and defining the precise requirements.

Doing a review of potential suppliers and drawing up a list for detailed investigation.

Selection of a short list of suppliers who will be asked to quote.

Obtaining quotations and making a detailed logical evaluation.

Choosing the most suitable proposal, paying particular attention to the availability of a local supplier.

Results: Selection of the most strategically relevant technology and the most reliable supplier.

The Implementation Phase

Objective: To provide an environment for the smooth implementation of the technology, and to avoid negative transfers of learning and experience from one technology to another, which increase the error probability and reduce the productivity and reliability of the new system.

Actions: A definition for the pace of change contingent upon the training already done, employee resistance, and the simple economics of alternate methods.

Preparation of a detailed schedule for implementation, including key dates and performance measures.

Having all the installation procedures ready and clarifying detailed individual responsibilities.

Paying particular attention to the integration of the new technology into the rest of the system.

Prepartion of a detailed manual describing every step in the operation of the new system.

Have all parts of the new system checked and making judgments about its readiness.

Ensuring that all necessary training is completed.

Result: An optimally functional system.

Post Implementation Phase

Objective: To ensure the continuity of the operation and to begin preparing for the next cycle of change.

Actions: Availability of the project coordinator as a backstop for inquiries.

A detailed post-installation audit which closely monitors key result areas to uncover problems which a subjective evaluation would not.

Result: A continuous upgrading of the manufacturing and technology strategy and an easy transition to the forthcoming stage.

Exhibit 12.4 summarizes the logical steps in following these phases.

ONE FINAL REVIEW

A number of points must be considered in deciding whether to adopt new technology. In fact, "... the choice of the proper [technology] and manufacturing process becomes a multicriterion decision task, taking into account several characteristics of the product and the... process."[1] Some determinant factors discussed were as follows:

- The need to be abreast of the new technology. Is the technology pervasive in the industry and thus a key success factor for the company?
- Does the technology acquisition fit with the firm's corporate missions and policies?
- The impact upon factory cost and anaysis of the financial aspects of the technology adoption.
- Impact upon human resources and union involvement.
- Other issues such as the state of the economy (will it assist/hinder the success of the adoption), and customer reactions.
- Government support programs.
- Social and cultural impact.

Several case studies have identified the circumstances that affect the adoption decision. These can be categorized as follows:

1. *Risk*
   - Depends on the financial rather than the technological risk.
   - Depends upon the learning curve of the new technology.
   - Depends upon the number of other users of the new technology.
   - Depends on the extent of past experience with the technology.

[1]Ayres [1988], p. 33.

Exhibit 12.4 A Decision Flow Chart for Adopting New Technology

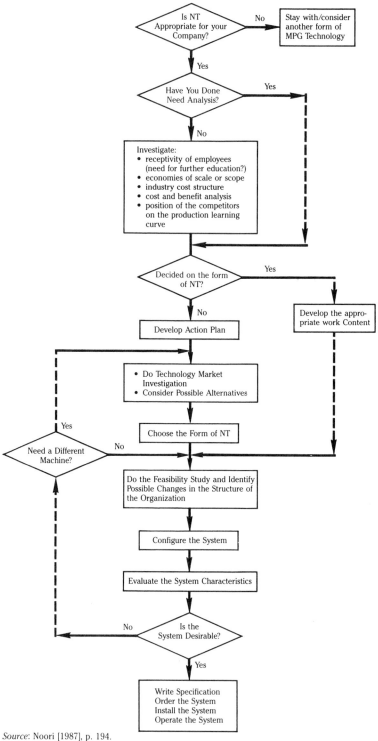

Source: Noori [1987], p. 194.

2. *Industry Market Structure*
   - Depends upon the mix of large and small firms.
   - The effect of this mix is open to interpretation and is in a large part related to the type of industry.
   - New firms often assist in diffusion since they have little bureaucracy and are not limited in their approach by past practices.

3. *Social Acceptability of the Technology*
   - Can have a major impact on the diffusion (for example, supersonic jets did not spread quickly due to the negative social impact of loud noise).

4. *Product*
   - Diffusion will depend upon the type of product and how quickly it fulfills the market needs.

5. *Public Policy*
   - Government plays a large role, since it can:
     —Stimulate research and development.
     —Adjust tax laws.
     —Alter patent laws.
     —Set standards that demand a certain technology (that is, building codes).
     —Control competition (monopoly laws).

From a practical point of view, to fully acknowledge the benefits of the new technology, three factors should be incorporated into the decision process.[2]

1. Implementing a more responsive and intelligent cost management system. That is, an accounting system which is based on profit maximization rather than solely on cost minimization procedures. For example, firms must measure not only the cost saving of quality improvement, but also the extra profit subsequently generated.

2. Blending strategic economic modeling with detailed system performance modeling. That is, any improvement resulting from technology adoption will have an equivalent economic value that must be recognized and appreciated. For example, what is the dollar value associated with a given improvement in throughput time or reduction of setup times?

3. Considering environmental and strategic uncertainties. That is, technology decisions are long-term decisions with many intrinsic uncertainties. For example, how long will the technology last before it becomes obsolete, and how will the competition respond?

---

[2]The discussion here is partially based on the presentation made by C. Fine at ORSA/TIMS Joint National Conference, Washington, April 25–27, 1988.

A SIMULATION EXERCISE:[3]
ELECTRONIC CRAFTSMEN LIMITED[4]

In November 1984, Electronic Craftsmen Limited (ECL) was experiencing production problems. The concerns related to an increasing backlog on order deliveries. Glen Bell, Vice President of operations, recognized the significance of these problems and feared their implications. Bell expressed these fears by saying "If delivery delays continue and if orders are turned down due to capability problems, I feel that we will lose business possibly to local firms or offshore sources." Bell knew something had to be done to solve the current capacity problems.

Company History

ECL is located in Waterloo, Ontario and is a subsidiary of a large Toronto-based company. ECL produces magnetic transformers and coils (see Exhibit 12.C1) and has an annual sales level between $3 and $4 million. ECL employs 13 people classified as staff and 75 nonunion people in production. The production workers generally have a low education level and require about one to two weeks training for satisfactory performance. Labor relations at ECL have always been good and the company encourages employees to upgrade skills and education.

Production Method

ECL had several production techniques in its assembly process. The size, type, and cost of the transformer dictated the particular method used. Seventy percent of the production volume involved either the stick or winding techniques. This proportion represents the small- to medium-sized transformers. The large transformers were produced using the unit or hand winding techniques. Bobbin winding, the most cost effective technique, is used for the smallest transformer coils and audio transformers. Currently, ECL employs a mix of fully- and semi-automated production methods in different areas.

Transformer Industry

From the early 1950s until the early 1970s, the transformer industry experienced rapid growth. ECL supplied transformers to large manufacturers such as Admiral and Electrohome as a component part for TVs and radios. Eighty-five percent of the OEM (Original Equipment Manufacturers) are located in the

---

[3]This exercise is intended to present the reader with an opportunity to apply the materials and concepts discussed throughout the text. An effective approach to analyzing this case is the application of the © NEWTECH *Expert Choice* software developed by the author. Contact Expert Choice, Inc. 4922 Ellsworth Ave., Pittsburgh, PA 15213, for more information.

[4]This is a shortened version of the case. This case in its complete form is available in *Readings and Cases in Management of New Technology*, By H. Noori and R. Radford, Prentice-Hall, Inc., 1990.

Exhibit 12.C1   ECL Complete Range of Products

ELECTRONIC
CRAFTSMEN
LIMITED

MAGNETIC COMPONENTS
FOR SWITCHING
POWER SUPPLIES

Transformers and Inductors engineered and manufactured to suit your particular applications.

Available for Flyback, Forward
and push pull configurations

- Insulation & Hipot to
  SELV Requirements
- Construction to MIL-T-27
- In house ferrite grinding to
  allow optimal use of various
  core sizes

Common
Mode
Inductors

Line
Inductors

Output
Filter
Chokes

High frequency
Current
Transformers

Main Convertor
Transformers

Drive
Transformers

Auxiliary Transformer

349

Guelph/Kitchener-Waterloo area. In the early 1970s, the good fortunes of the industry turned sour due to the introduction of silicon technology. Silicon technology made transformers less viable in a consumer market.

The trend toward offshore manufacturing for consumer products also had a negative impact on the transformer industry. Large domestic customers such as Admiral and Electrohome were either forced into bankruptcy or forced to buy from less expensive offshore suppliers.

ECL's Strategy

Given the downturn in the consumer transformer market, Glen Bell noticed the increasing strength of the telecommunication industry. With this focus, ECL decided to concentrate on securing contracts with Mitel, Motorola and Gandalf Technologies, which were leaders in the telecommunication magnetic industry and enjoyed a 25 percent annual growth in sales. This seemed to indicate that a market niche had been found and ECL was taking advantage of the situation.

However, the increasing success of ECL put strains on their production facility. The newer products required the bobbin and winding production techniques. In the past, the largest portion of the transformers were manufactured using the stock winding method. However, new techniques required more unit and bobbin winding. In an attempt to increase capacity, three unit and four bobbin machines were purchased at a cost of $6,000 and $10,000 each, respectively. Also, a partial night shift was implemented to further alleviate the backlog. This, however, was not successful due to absenteeism, shortage of skilled labor and quality problems.

Operations at ECL

The organization is structured around the following areas: Sales, Production, Engineering, Quality Control, and Administration/Finance (see Exhibit 12.C2). Each of these functional areas was positioned equally on the organizational chart. Quality control reports directly to the Vice President, who has the sole authority to overrule quality decisions. All engineering designs are built to meet ECL, UL and VDE specifications. Quality plays an important role in ECL's corporate strategy.

Custom-designed products and design innovation are key reasons for ECL's fine reputation. In a typical year there could be over 300 new designs, with over 1,000 designs being actively manufactured. Order quantities can vary from one to 50,000 pieces, although the typical job varied from 250 to 2,500 pieces. The wide range of products could cause potential problems in production since most materials were replenished only after the orders were confirmed.

Investigation of Automation

Glen Bell felt that the industry appeared to be automating in some areas although no machinery seemed appropriate for ECL. Also, the United States firms which

Exhibit 12.C2   Organizational Structure of ECL

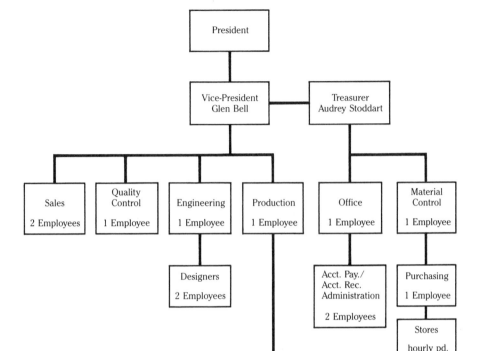

had automation were unwilling to share their knowledge. The new technology available was judged to be either hard automation (that is, specifically set up for one job) or where flexibility was required, was crudely piecemealed with some type of materials handling system. In the search for new technology, Bell discovered that there were a limited number of suppliers in Canada. Through one of ECL's suppliers, Bell became aware of European manufacturers capable of supplying suitable technology. After visiting Europe and attending a trade show, Bell located two possible vendors: Siemens and Amcoil.

Both vendors proposed a viable automation alternative. However, technical difficulties were expected by ECL due to the production differences in Canada. To rectify this problem, additional tooling would be required at a cost of between $3,000 and $6,000 U.S. Also, the purchase from a foreign vendor could result in future problems with implementation and maintenance. The geographic distance separating the two parties was considered a problem.

Exhibit 12.C3 Description of Operations Required for Winding and Audio Transformer Specification: Custom Audio Transformer 600:600 OHM (ECL) Part No. 2322–80109)

General Material: Bobbin 3/16 × 3/16:

Primary Wire:	#02–335 or #02–378
Secondary Wire:	36 SPN Bifilar
Insulating Tape:	41 SPN
Core:	3M #56
	186EL–8014

Comparison for Possible Construction Techniques and Times

Operations/Techniques	Present Technique	Time (seconds)	Modified Technique (Newly tooled bobbins)	Time (seconds)	Automated Technique	Time (seconds)
Coil Form Used	02–335 One Up		02–378 One Up		02–378 Six Up	6
Set-Up						
Primary						
Load bobbin	Place on arbor	10	Place on arbor	10	Place on arbor	
Anchor start	Wrap on pin	35	Wrap on pin	35	Machine anchor	
Insulate	Crossover	25	Not required	N/A	Not required	
Wind	145T Bifilar 36	60	145T Bifilar 36	60	Winds	
Anchor finish	Wrap on pin	35	Wrap on pin	35	Anchors	
Insulate	Tape winding	36	Tape winding	36	Insulate	
Unload bobbin	Unload bobbin	10	Unload bobbin	10	Unload bobbin	

Exhibit 12.C3 (continued)

Operations/Techniques		Present Technique	Time (seconds)	Modified Technique (Newly tooled bobbins)	Time (seconds)	Automated Technique	Time (seconds)
Coil Form Used		02–335 One Up		02–378 One Up		02–378 Six Up	
Set-Up							
Secondary	Load bobbin	Place on arbor	10	Place on arbor	10	Place on arbor	
	Anchor start	Wrap on pin	25	Wrap on pin	25	Machine anchor	
	Insulate	Crossover	25	Not required	N/A	Not required	
	Wind	725T #45SPN	60	725T #45SPN	60	Winds	7
	Anchor finish	Wrap on pin	25	Wrap on pin	25	Anchors	
	Insulate	Tape Winding	36	Tape Winding	36	Insulate	
	Unload bobbin	Unload bobbin	10	Unload bobbin	10	Not applicable	
Coil Assembly	Flux	Dip in flux	36	Dip in flux	36	Auto Dip	
	Solder	Dip in solder	72	Dip in solder	72	Auto solder	
	Unload	Not applicable		Not applicable		Unload	
Total Time per part			510 seconds		460 seconds		13 seconds
			8.5 minutes		7.67 minutes		0.21 minutes
Time/100 parts			14.2 hours		12.8 hours		0.36 hours

Exhibit 12.C4 Comparison Guide for Present Techniques Versus Automated Production System

Event/Operation	Situation 1—Part Has Never Been Manufactured Before—Tooling and Set-Up Cost Required			
	Present Production Techniques	Time/Cost	Automated Production System	Time/Cost

Order Taken for Part	—Check for arbor
	  If Yes
	  If No—Tooling
	—Check for bobbin
	  If Yes
	  If No—Tooling
		N/C
		$125–$200
		N/C
		$10,000
			—Check for winding arbor
			  If Yes
			  If No—Tooling
			—Check for bobbin
			  If Yes
			  If No—Tooling
				N/C
				$2,000–$5,000
				N/C
				$10,000

Part Released For Production	—Raw material brought to machine from stores
	—Single or double winding
	  Arbor located
		N/A
		
		5 minutes
			—Raw material brought to machine from stores
			—Multiple 24 set winding
			  Arbor 6 winding chucks, tape arbor soldering/fluxing arbor located. This is a complete set.
				N/A

Machine Set-Up or Program (Winding #1)	—Place arbor on machine
	—Program or set turns
	—Set winding pitch
	—Set winding length: 1 Up*
	                              2 Up*
	—Wind first off to check
	  Set up and adjust
		5 minutes
		2 minutes
		10 minutes
		5 minutes*
		7 minutes*
		5–10 minutes
			—Place 24 arbors on machine
			—Place in #1 winding chuck
			—"Teach In" program to wind
			
			—Place in tape arbor
			  Set and program
			—Place on solder flux arbor
			  Set and program
			—Place on next 5 winding chucks
			—Place wire on machine: 6 Up*
			                                    6×2 Up*
			—Function and adjust where necessary
				10 minutes
				5 minutes
				2–4 hours
				
				15–30 minutes
				
				15–30 minutes
				
				10 minutes
				15 minutes
				20 minutes
				30–60 minutes

	Estimated set up for first off	30–60 minutes	Estimate set up for first off	4–8 hours

Exhibit 12.C4 (continued)

Situation 1—Part Has Never Been Manufactured Before—Tooling and Set-Up Cost Required

Event/Operation	Present Production Techniques	Time/Cost	Automated Production System	Time/Cost
Production Wind	See Comparison Guide		See Comparison Guide	
Machine Set Up or Program (Winding #2)	—Program or set turns	2 minutes	—Remove 5 winding chucks for set up	10 minutes
	—Set winding pitch	10 minutes	—"Teach In" program for second winding	2–4 hours
	—Set winding length	10 minutes	(Note: Tape and soldering are set up from before)	
	—Place in second wire: 1 Up*	5 minutes*	—Place on 5 winding chucks	10 minutes
	2 Up*	7 minutes*	—Place wire on machine: 2 Up*	15 minutes*
	—Size & Tension		6×2 Up*	20 minutes*
	—Wind first off to check set up and adjust	5–10 minutes	—Function and adjust where necessary	30–60 minutes
Production Windings	Estimated set up for first off	15–45 minutes	Estimated set up for first off	3–6 hours
	See Comparison Chart		See Comparison Chart	

*Note: 1 up means winding one bobbin at a time.
2 up means winding two bobbins at a time.
6×2 up means winding 6 bobbins at a time with two separate windings.

Exhibit 12.C5 Comparison Guide for Present Techniques Versus Automated Production System

	Situation 2—Part Has Been Manufactured Before—Tooling and Set-Up Costs Have Been Accounted For			
Event/Operation	Present Production Techniques	Time/Cost	Automated Production System	Time/Cost
Part Released for Production	—Raw material brought to machine from stores	N/A	—Raw material brought to machine from stores	N/A
	—Single or double winding arbor located	5 minutes	—Multiple 24 set winding arbor 6 winding chucks, tape arbor soldering/flux arbor located. This is a complete set.	5 minutes
Machine Set-Up (Winding #1)	—Place arbor on machine	5 minutes	—Place 24 arbors on machine	10 minutes
	—Program or set turns	2 minutes	—Place 6 winding chucks on machine	15 minutes
	—Set winding pitch	10 minutes	—Place tape arbor on machine	5 minutes
	—Set winding length	10 minutes	—Place solder/flux arbor on machine	10 minutes
	—Place in wire & tension: 1 Up*	5 minutes	—Place in winding program disc and call up/load	5 minutes
	2 Up*	7 minutes	—Place wire on machine 6 Up*	15 minutes
			6×2 Up*	20 minutes
	—Wind first off to check set up and adjust	5–10 minutes	—Wind first off using step function and adjust where necessary	15–30 minutes
	Estimated set up for first off	30–60 minutes	Estimated set up for first off	60–120 minutes

356

Exhibit 12.C5 (continued)

Situation 2—Part Has Been Manufactured Before—Tooling and Set-Up Costs Have Been Accounted For

Event/Operation	Present Production Techniques	Time/Cost	Automated Production System	Time/Cost
Production Wind	See Comparison Guide		See Comparison Guide	
Machine Set-Up (Winding #2)	—Program or set turns	2 minutes	—Call up second winding	5minutes
	—Set winding pitch (continued)	10 minutes	—Program/load	
	—Set winding length	10 minutes	—Place wire on machine 6 Up*	15 minutes
	—Place in second wire 1 Up*	5 minutes	6×2 Up*	20 minutes
	—Size & tension 2 Up*	7 minutes	—Wind first off using step function	15–30 minutes
	—Wind first off to check set-up and adjust	5–10 minutes	and adjust where necessary	
	Estimated set up for first off	15–45 minutes	Estimated set up for first off	30–60 minutes
Production Wind	See Comparison Chart		See Comparison Chart	

Note: 1 up means winding one bobbin at a time.
2 up means winding two bobbins at a time.
6×2 means winding 6 bobbins at a time with two separate windings.

357

The next problem Bell identified was the high changeover costs that would be incurred to maximize system flexibility. These costs include a $10,000 to $15,000 one time fee for each different bobbin type. The technology would cost $325,000 for a Siemens machine and $365,000 for an Amcoil machine. Bank loans were available at 15 percent interest. However, in the past ECL self-financed projects and only required final approval from head office (see Exhibits 12.C3, 12.C4, and 12.C5).

Opportunity Arises

In November 1984, ECL was chosen as the sole supplier for a large customer who wanted to order two parts in large volumes. These volumes represented 10–13 times the average order quantity. However, the production facility was at near capacity, placing constraints on this opportunity. If the order was not accepted, Bell felt that the company would lose its market niche and its credibility. If the order was accepted, ECL would be required to outstrip existing capacity by not maintaining present customer orders. It was feared that new customers would be reluctant to purchase from ECL. The order was not considered a one shot deal.

Alternatives

1. Establish a second shift to increase short-term capacity.
2. Purchase additional winding machines at a cost of $8,000 each, with delivery in three to four months.
3. Possibility of the purchase of an automated winding machine, with a one to two year lead time.
4. The possibility of a merger or acquisition with a competitor. There were concerns of the perceived length of time of negotiations and the possibility of getting into a "can of worms."
5. Subcontract to other firms, but ECL did not want to give competitors any production knowledge that they might not already have.

Glen Bell outlined the benefits of adopting this technology:

- Increased flexibility.
- Bringing offshore business back to Canada.
- Reduce costs.
- Faster throughput in production of parts (parts can be produced in a fraction of the time that they are now produced).
- Expand market into other industries.
- Reduce turnaround times.
- Opportunity to benefit from economies of scope and scale.
- Could seriously jeopardize competitors' position.

Bell was faced with the following questions: How far (if at all) should ECL automate, allowing for the integration of existing techniques and processes into the operation? Which vendor should ECL adopt technology from? How can ECL justify the adoption of this new technology?

REFERENCES

AYRES, R. U. [1988]. "Complexity, Reliability, and Design: Manufacturing Implications." *Manufacturing Review*, Volume 1, No. 1, pp. 26–35.

COOPER, R. G. [1983]. "A Process Model For Industrial New Product Development." *IEEE Transactions on Engineering Management*, Volume EM–30, No. 1.

NOORI, H. [1987]. "Production Policy and the Acquisition of New Technology." *Engineering Management International*, Volume 4, pp. 187–196.

On Cartrac II, the final stage of the automated body shop at the GMAD-Orion and Wentzville plants, 18 pairs of robots apply final spot welds to give the unibody structural soundness. In all, nearly 5,000 separate welds make up eah body, 93 percent of them being applied automatically, compared to 18 percent on previous models of full-size luxury Cadillacs, Buicks and Oldsmobiles.

Photo #1 Courtesy of General Motors Corporation.

Photo #2 Courtesy of General Motors Corporation.

After welding is completed, underbody subassemblies for front-wheel-drive luxury cars move into this automatic probe checking station where 30 critical measurements are verified to assure sound, dimensionally-precise platforms upon which to build the rest of the vehicle. Data from the fixture are fed to a computer which prints out a copy for the employee in foreground. A board which flashes "go or no-go" lights for a quick visual verification can be seen on the panel at upper left. The GMAD plants in Orion Township, Mich. and Wentzville, Mo. each use more than 1,000 computers of every size to insure quality from beginning to end of the assembly line.

Some of the world's most sophisticated equipment is employed at GM's Orion and Wentzville plants to assure paint quality for the 1985 Cadillac, Buick and Oldsmobile front-wheel-drive luxury cars. Here, a body receives its final base coat/clear coat application as it emerges from the main color booth. In the booth, nine pair of tracking robots comprise GM's Numerically Controlled Painter, ensuring consistent paint thickness. The automated painter also eliminates the need for workers to perform a very demanding job in an undesirable environment.

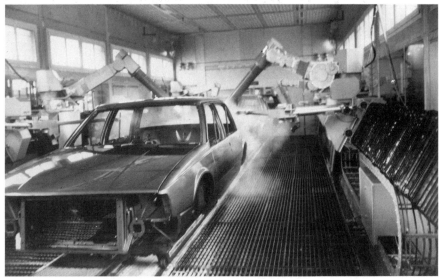

Photo #3 Courtesy of General Motors Corporation.

Four computer-controlled robots weld the underbody of full-size luxury cars at the GM-Orion assembly plant. These are among 138 robots used to weld bodies at the plant to achieve structural soundness as part of building a high-quality car.

Photo #4 Courtesy of General Motors Corporation.

361

Motorized robots with fork lifts help facilitate just-in-time inventory delivery at the GMAD-Orion Plant. The plant's Automated Guide Vehicle System (AGVS) uses 22 of these vehicles, which are directed through the 77-acre Orion plant by some 19,000 feet of wire buried in the floors. The AGVS machines are programmed through signals sent along the buried wire by two control computers, so they can load and unload parts automatically. Sensors automatically stop the vehicle if anything is in its path and start it up again when the way is clear.

Photo #5 Courtesy of General Motors Corporation.

Chapter Thirteen

FUTURE PROSPECTS

Barriers to communications of time, space or systems incompatibility are disappearing. The only limits left may be those of imagination.

Northern Telecom 1984 Annual Report

INTRODUCTION

It seems appropriate in this final chapter to reflect on the new technology as a phenomenon which will continue to have a significant impact on the production of goods and the composition of the labor force and thus will continue to preoccupy the industrialized nations for years to come.

Over the last two decades, the manufacturing sector has evolved into an undeniably complex operation. The factory-of-the-future concept is gaining acceptance and becoming a reality. It is true that when we look back, we see that each era of manufacturing contains unique technological characteristics, with its own focus and its own impact on manufacturing strategy. This progression is perhaps best summarized by Ebner and Vollmann [1988] and is presented in Exhibit 13.1.

CHALLENGES OF THE 1990s

The key to a successful operation in the 1990s is recognition of the world as a global market and the imperative for systems integration. Many of the changes in the marketplace cited in Chapter 3 will continue to have great impact on company operations. The manufacturing strategy will be based on an evaluation of organizational needs (structure and process), continuous measuring of company strengths (in design, manufacturing, marketing, finance, and human resources), and a persisting reinforcement of participative management style.

364

Exhibit 13.1   The Evolution of Manufacturing and a Look at the Future

	1960s	1970s	1980s	1990s
Competitive thrust	Cost	Market	Quality	Time

Manufacturing strategy	High volume
	Cost minimization
	Stabilize
	Product focus
		Functional integration
		Closed loop
			Process control
			Material velocity
			World class
			  manufacturing
			Overhead cost
				New product
				  introduction
				Responsiveness
				Manufacturing metrics
				New Organization
				  forms

Manufacturing systems	PICS NC	MRP MPS SFC CNC	MRP II JIT OPT DNC SPC, TQC CAD, CAM	CIM Supervisory systems Scenario generation Selective intervention Decentralization Simplification

Key: PICS = Production Inventory Control Systems
      MPS = Master Production Schedule
      SFC = Shop Floor Control
      OPT = Optimized Production Technology
      SPC = Statistical Process Control

Source: Ebner and Vollmann [1988], p. 319.

A Corporate Perspective

Waterman [1987] notes eight major themes that emerge as the most important characteristics of renewing companies/managers who intend to capitalize on the technological imperative. They are:

1. *Informed Opportunism:* Renewing companies comprehend uncertainty. They set direction, not detailed strategy. They treat information as their main competitive advantage and flexibility as their main strategic weapon.

2. *Direction and Empowerment:* Renewing companies treat everyone as a source of creative input. Their managers define the boundaries, and their people figure out the best way to do the job within those boundaries. Their management style is a combination of direction and empowerment. They give up tight control in order to gain control over what counts: results.

3. *Friendly Facts, Congenial Controls:* Renewing companies treat facts as friends and financial controls as liberating. They see information where others see only data.

4. *A Different Mirror:* Renewing companies have made curiosity an institutional attribute. They seek a different mirror, something to tell them that the world has changed and that, in the harsh light of the new reality, they are not as beautiful as they once were.

5. *Teamwork, Trust, Politics, and Power:* Renewing companies constantly use words such as *teamwork* and *trust.* They are relentless in fighting office politics and power contests, and in breaking down the we/they barriers that paralyze action.

6. *Stability in Motion:* Renewing companies know how to keep things moving. Sometimes they seem to change for its own sake.

7. *Attitudes and Attention:* Renewing companies realize that attention makes a difference, and so do attitudes and expectations. Action may start with words, but it has to be backed by symbolic behavior that makes those words come alive.

8. *Causes and Commitment:* Renewing companies run on causes—quality is the most prevalent cause. They also constantly review their course in light of the issues—the major problems and opportunities that shift with time.

The Lightless Factories

The decisive step toward the factory-of-the-future is linking the present islands of automation. This, to a large extent, depends on developments in the field of information technology (see Exhibit 13.2). As Bullinger et al. [1985] state, there are three general requirements for this:[1]

Exhibit 13.2 Integration of Islands of Information

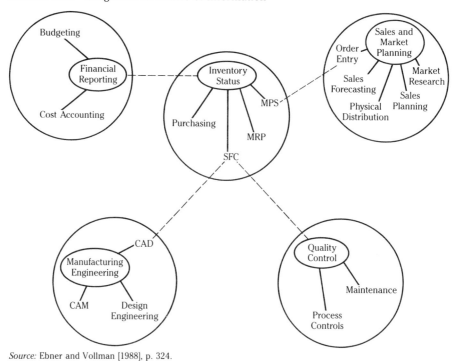

Source: Ebner and Vollman [1988], p. 324.

[1]Bullinger et al. [1985], pp. xxxiii–xxxiv.

- The information necessary for the work and the decision-making process will have to be selectively filtered out of the existing data and information flood and it will have to be available for decision-making in an improved condition.
- The concept of economy will have to be more in the foreground in the handling and processing of information in the future. Information will then turn from a cost factor to an income factor.
- The information problem will have to be understood as an all-embracing technical-organizational task.

Obviously, this integration[2] cannot be confined to the information area alone. On the contrary, "...it is necessary to integrate the computers already available today and those to be installed in the future into a hardware hierarchy."[3] The National Bureau of Standards (NBS), for example, is completing a project in this area named the Automated Manufacturing Research Facility (AMRF) which mainly investigates the computer hierarchy and interface points (see Jackson and Jones [1987]). Exhibit 13.3 shows the strucutre of this hierarchy.

Fifth-Generation Manufacturing Control: Putting Thought Processes into the Machine

The progression of the new technology is changing the nature of problems that have been preoccupying industrial engineers and operations research specialists. A number of classical research areas such as scheduling and lot sizing are being subjected to fundamental changes. What is certain is that the intellectual challenge of putting thought processes into machines is drawing top-notch theoretical talent to AI (artificial intelligence) research. In reality, the field of AI and ES (expert systems) is opening a window of opportunity for integration of manufacturing policy and corporate strategy (see, for example, Bitran and Papageorge [1988]).

WHAT THE FUTURE HOLDS

- Organizational innovation will continue. The new organization is outward-looking, future focused, idea driven, entrepreneurial, and change responsive.
- There will be faster rates of new technology adoption.
- Emphasis will be more and more on cooperation and hierarchy exchange. There will also be slower growth of overall employment and a change in patterns of industry and occupational employment growth.

[2]The issue of information integration can be approached from several dimensions (see Zygmont [1987]). One approach is to integrate inside to outside, between a manufacturer and its suppliers. Another approach calls for integration from beginning to end of a product's development and manufacturing cycles, from its design inception to its marketing. The last approach is based on integration from top to bottom in order to disseminate information for better control of manufacturing operations, as well as business management and planning.

[3]Bullinger et al. [1985], p. xxxvi.

Exhibit 13.3 The Five Level AMRF Control Architecture

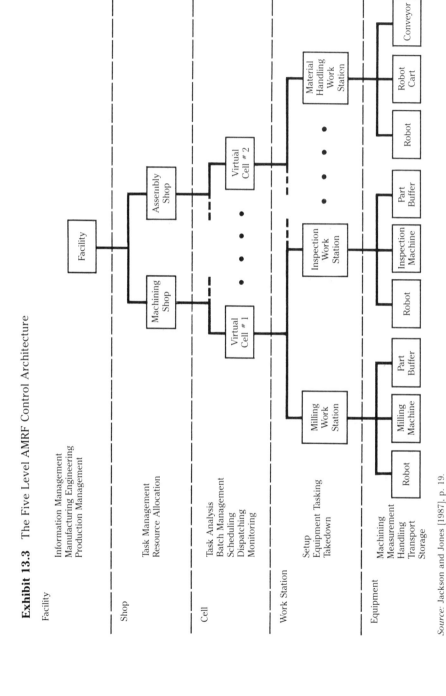

Facility

    Information Management
    Manufacturing Engineering
    Production Management

Shop

    Task Management
    Resource Allocation

Cell

    Task Analysis
    Batch Management
    Scheduling
    Dispatching
    Monitoring

Work Station

    Setup
    Equipment Tasking
    Takedown

Equipment

    Machining
    Measurement
    Handling
    Transport
    Storage

Source: Jackson and Jones [1987], p. 19.

- There will be a need for employees with both analytical capabilities and inter-personal skills.
- The softer side of technology will continue to receive more and more attention—the paperless operation will be a reality. The effort to reduce waste will continue.
- The impact of biotechnology on technical and industrial processes will be pronounced.
- Advanced materials will revolutionize the composition of products. They will be stronger, lighter, faster, and cheaper.
- Laser technology will be of growing importance in manufacturing.
- Full-scale computer-integrated manufacturing will be a reality.
- The advances in technology will promote the quest for new institutions, new forms of government participation, new ethical codes and social structures.

Consider this quotation as a guide to the future, and a final iteration of perhaps the central and most basic message of this text:

> *One does not need to gaze into a crystal ball looking for new technologies that do not yet exist. The building blocks of the future are scattered around us right now...our task is to sort them out and pull them together.*
>
> Duane Shull
> GE Fanuc North America

REFERENCES AND BIBLIOGRAPHY

BITRAN, G., and T. PAPAGEORGE [1988]. "Integration of Manufacturing Policy and Corporate Strategy with the Aid of Expert Systems." In M. Oliff (ed.), *Intelligent Manufacturing*, Proceedings from the First Internatnional Conference on Expert Systems. The Benjamin/Cummings Publishing Company, Inc., pp. 13–43.

BULLINGER, H., H. WARNECK, and H. LENTES [1985]. "Toward the Factory of the Future." In H. Bullinger and H. Warneck (eds.), *Toward the Factory of the Future.* Springer Verlag, Berlin, pp. xxix–liv.

EBNER, M., and T. E. VOLLMAN [1988]. "Manufacturing Systems for the 1990's." In M. Oliff (ed.), *Intelligent Manufacturing*, Proceedings from the First International Conference on Expert Systems. The Benjamin/Cummings Publishing Company, Inc., pp. 317–336.

JACKSON, R. F., and A. W. JONES [1987]. "An Architecture for Decision Making in the Factory of the Future." Interfaces, Volume 17, No. 6, November–December, pp. 15–28.

ZYGMONT, J. [1987]. "Manufacturers Move Toward Computer Integration." *High Technology*, February, pp. 28–31.

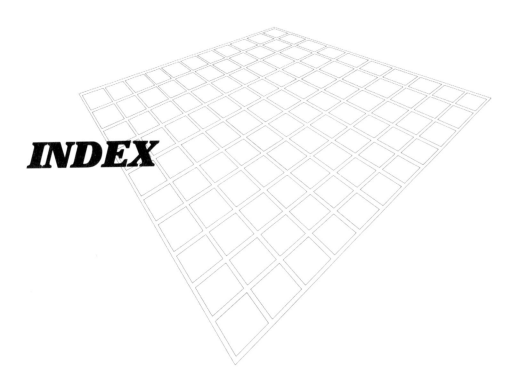

INDEX